Mining the Social Web

Matthew A. Russell

D1451751

O'REILLY®

Beijing · Cambridge · Farnham · Köln · Sebastopol · Tokyo

Mining the Social Web
by Matthew A. Russell

Copyright © 2011 Matthew Russell. All rights reserved.
Printed in the United States of America.

Published by O'Reilly Media, Inc., 1005 Gravenstein Highway North, Sebastopol, CA 95472.

O'Reilly books may be purchased for educational, business, or sales promotional use. Online editions are also available for most titles (*http://my.safaribooksonline.com*). For more information, contact our corporate/institutional sales department: (800) 998-9938 or *corporate@oreilly.com*.

Editor: Mike Loukides	**Indexer:** Ellen Troutman Zaig
Production Editor: Adam Zaremba	**Cover Designer:** Karen Montgomery
Copyeditor: Rachel Head	**Interior Designer:** David Futato
Proofreader: Marlowe Shaeffer	**Illustrator:** Robert Romano

January 2011:   First Edition.

Revision History for the First Edition:
      2011-01-13 First release
      2011-04-21 Second release
      2012-02-22 Third release
See *http://oreilly.com/catalog/errata.csp?isbn=9781449388348* for release details.

RepKover.
          This book uses RepKover™, a durable and flexible lay-flat binding.

ISBN: 978-1-449-38834-8

[LSI]

1329920028

Praise for *Mining the Social Web*

"*Mining the Social Web* is a must-read as data is distributed at a dizzying pace. A great primer for API jockeys, social media junkies, and data scientists alike, [Matthew] Russell deftly distills the prodigious opportunity in mining social media data."

—Nick Ducoff, CEO of Infochimps, Inc.

"This is an essential guide to tapping the new generation of online data sources. Russell has done a great job creating an accessible manual for anyone working with social information on the web, covering both how to access it and simple methods for extracting surprising insights from all that raw data."

—Pete Warden, Founder of OpenHeatMap.com

"*Mining the Social Web* is now my go-to book for any project that involves analyzing social data. It contains a multitude of useful examples and is highly recommended for any data mining project you're considering. Great for beginners and advanced readers alike."

—Abe Music, Principal, Zaffra

"This book is clearly a labor of love for the author. He has deftly woven together the use of classic text and graph mining libraries with current social media applications. Examples are concrete and concise while providing useful insights that facilitate future development and exploration by the reader. This text is a great primer for those just beginning their forays into extracting understanding from social networks, and also for advanced researchers needing access to the latest social media APIs."

—Chris Augeri, Senior Research Fellow, University of Nebraska

"This is a phenomenal book for anyone wanting to get started mining social data. It is well-researched and provides plenty of examples to get one going from the very first chapter. It is also very easy to follow and a real pleasure to read. This book is my first recommendation for anyone interested in the mining, analysis, and visualization of data from the social web."

—Jeffrey Humphries, PhD; Computer Scientist

"Few things will impact us the way automated understanding of human communication by software will in the coming years. This subject is broad and deep. It has been the subject of thousands of papers and hundreds of dissertations. What Matthew has pulled together is something that has really been missing: an applied introduction to a diverse and deep set of technologies and topics that make the knowledge buried in human communication inside the social web accessible. It is the work of a powerful technologist—someone who can equip capable programmers with new tools that are truly valuable.

Read this book. It will open up doors to where software is going in the next decade."

—Tim Estes, Founder and CEO, Digital Reasoning

"*Mining the Social Web* is a great resource on how to get the most out of the Twitter API."

—Raffi Krikorian, Platform Services group, Twitter

"Matthew covers an interesting and eclectic group of data sources, analysis techniques, data management tools, and visualizations that provide a thorough survey of the latest thinking on how to gain insight from the social web. His examples are vivid and serve as great starting points for further exploration. Matthew clearly cares that the reader understands the material; the book is chock full of timely, knowing, and truly helpful hints and advice. *Mining the Social Web* has me excited to dive further into this rich area of analysis."

—Roger Magoulas, Director of Market Research, O'Reilly Media

O'REILLY®

Strata
Making Data Work

Learn how to turn data into decisions.

From startups to the Fortune 500, smart companies are betting on data-driven insight, seizing the opportunities that are emerging from the convergence of four powerful trends:

- New methods of collecting, managing, and analyzing data

- Cloud computing that offers inexpensive storage and flexible, on-demand computing power for massive data sets

- Visualization techniques that turn complex data into images that tell a compelling story

- Tools that make the power of data available to anyone

Get control over big data and turn it into insight with O'Reilly's Strata offerings. Find the inspiration and information to create new products or revive existing ones, understand customer behavior, and get the data edge.

Visit oreilly.com/data to learn more.

To those seeking knowledge and wisdom:

Use wisdom and understanding to establish your home;
Let good sense fill the rooms with priceless treasures.
Wisdom brings strength, and knowledge gives power.
Battles are won by listening to advice and making a lot of plans.

May you find knowledge and wisdom.

Table of Contents

Preface

The Web is more a social creation than a technical one.
I designed it for a social effect—to help people work
together—and not as a technical toy. The ultimate goal
of the Web is to support and improve our weblike exis-
tence in the world. We clump into families, associations,
and companies. We develop trust across the miles and
distrust around the corner.

—Tim Berners-Lee, *Weaving the Web* (Harper)

Content Updates

February 22, 2012

- Thoroughly updated Chapter 7 from Buzz to Google+.
- Minor update to Chapter 9 to point readers to the community-supported Python Facebook SDK.
- Relatively minor updates to Chapter 1 to sort out common problems reported in errata, related to Twitter API changes and NetworkX.
- Closed out all errata for *Mining the Social Web* in the O'Reilly author portal, which involved a couple of minor updates to code listings and a few minor changes to Chapter 7.
- Updated all example code and checked it into GitHub.

To Read This Book?

If you have a basic programming background and are interested in insight surrounding the opportunities that arise from mining and analyzing data from the social web, you've come to the right place. We'll begin getting our hands dirty after just a few more pages of frontmatter. I'll be forthright, however, and say upfront that one of the chief complaints you're likely to have about this book is that all of the chapters are far too short.

Unfortunately, that's always the case when trying to capture a space that's evolving daily and is so rich and abundant with opportunities. That said, I'm a fan of the "80-20 rule" (*http://en.wikipedia.org/wiki/Pareto_principle*), and I sincerely believe that this book is a reasonable attempt at presenting the most interesting 20 percent of the space that you'd want to explore with 80 percent of your available time.

This book is short, but it does cover a lot of ground. Generally speaking, there's a little more breadth than depth, although where the situation lends itself and the subject matter is complex enough to warrant a more detailed discussion, there are a few deep dives into interesting mining and analysis techniques. The book was written so that you could have the option of either reading it from cover to cover to get a broad primer on working with social web data, or pick and choose chapters that are of particular interest to you. In other words, each chapter is designed to be bite-sized and fairly standalone, but special care was taken to introduce material in a particular order so that the book as a whole is an enjoyable read.

Social networking websites such as Facebook, Twitter, and LinkedIn have transitioned from fad to mainstream to global phenomena over the last few years. In the first quarter of 2010, the popular social networking site Facebook surpassed Google for the most page visits,[1] confirming a definite shift in how people are spending their time online. Asserting that this event indicates that the Web has now become more a social milieu than a tool for research and information might be somewhat indefensible; however, this data point undeniably indicates that social networking websites are satisfying some very basic human desires on a massive scale in ways that search engines were never designed to fulfill. Social networks really are changing the way we live our lives on and off the Web,[2] and they are enabling technology to bring out the best (and sometimes the worst) in us. The explosion of social networks is just one of the ways that the gap between the real world and cyberspace is continuing to narrow.

Generally speaking, each chapter of this book interlaces slivers of the social web along with data mining, analysis, and visualization techniques to answer the following kinds of questions:

- Who knows whom, and what friends do they have in common?
- How frequently are certain people communicating with one another?
- How symmetrical is the communication between people?
- Who are the quietest/chattiest people in a network?
- Who are the most influential/popular people in a network?
- What are people chatting about (and is it interesting)?

1. See the opening paragraph of Chapter 9.
2. Mark Zuckerberg, the creator of Facebook, was named Person of the Year for 2010 by Time magazine (*http://www.time.com/time/specials/packages/article/0,28804,2036683_2037183_2037185,00.html*)

The answers to these types of questions generally connect two or more people together and point back to a context indicating why the connection exists. The work involved in answering these kinds of questions is only the beginning of more complex analytic processes, but you have to start somewhere, and the low-hanging fruit is surprisingly easy to grasp, thanks to well-engineered social networking APIs and open source toolkits.

Loosely speaking, this book treats *the social web*[3] as a graph of people, activities, events, concepts, etc. Industry leaders such as Google and Facebook have begun to increasingly push graph-centric terminology rather than web-centric terminology as they simultaneously promote graph-based APIs. In fact, Tim Berners-Lee has suggested that perhaps he should have used the term Giant Global Graph (*http://dig.csail.mit.edu/breadcrumbs/node/215*) (GGG) instead of World Wide Web (WWW), because the terms "web" and "graph" can be so freely interchanged in the context of defining a topology for the Internet. Whether the fullness of Tim Berners-Lee's original vision will ever be realized remains to be seen, but the Web as we know it is getting richer and richer with social data all the time. When we look back years from now, it may well seem obvious that the second- and third-level effects created by an inherently social web were necessary enablers for the realization of a truly semantic web. The gap between the two seems to be closing.

Or Not to Read This Book?

Activities such as building your own natural language processor from scratch, venturing far beyond the typical usage of visualization libraries, and constructing just about anything state-of-the-art are not within the scope of this book. You'll be really disappointed if you purchase this book because you want to do one of those things. However, just because it's not realistic or our goal to capture the holy grail of text analytics or record matching in a mere few hundred pages doesn't mean that this book won't enable you to attain reasonable solutions to hard problems, apply those solutions to the social web as a domain, and have a lot of fun in the process. It also doesn't mean that taking a very active interest in these fascinating research areas wouldn't potentially be a great idea for you to consider. A short book like this one can't do much beyond whetting your appetite and giving you enough insight to go out and start making a difference somewhere with your newly found passion for data hacking.

Maybe it's obvious in this day and age, but another important item of note is that this book generally assumes that you're connected to the Internet. This wouldn't be a great book to take on vacation with you to a remote location, because it contains many references that have been hyperlinked, and all of the code examples are hyperlinked directly to GitHub (*http://github.com*), a very social Git (*http://git-scm.com*) repository

---

3. See *http://journal.planetwork.net/article.php?lab=reed0704* for another perspective on the social web that focuses on digital identities.

that will always reflect the most up-to-date example code available. The hope is that social coding will enhance collaboration between like-minded folks such as ourselves who want to work together to extend the examples and hack away at interesting problems. Hopefully, you'll fork, extend, and improve the source—and maybe even make some new friends along the way. Readily accessible sources of online information such as API docs are also liberally hyperlinked, and it is assumed that you'd rather look them up online than rely on inevitably stale copies in this printed book.

 The official GitHub repository that maintains the latest and greatest bug-fixed source code for this book is *http://github.com/ptwobrussell/ Mining-the-Social-Web*. The official Twitter account for this book is *@SocialWebMining* .

This book is also not recommended if you need a reference that gets you up to speed on distributed computing platforms such as sharded MySQL clusters or NoSQL (*http: //en.wikipedia.org/wiki/NoSQL*) technologies such as Hadoop or Cassandra. We do use some less-than-conventional storage technologies such as CouchDB (*http://couchdb .apache.org*) and Redis (*http://code.google.com/p/redis*), but always within the context of running on a single machine, and because they work well for the problem at hand. However, it really isn't that much of a stretch to port the examples into distributed technologies if you possess sufficient motivation and need the horizontal scalability. A strong recommendation is that you master the fundamentals and prove out your thesis in a slightly less complex environment first before migrating to an inherently more complex distributed system—and then be ready to make major adjustments to your algorithms to make them performant once data access is no longer local. A good option to investigate if you want to go this route is Dumbo (*http://github.com/klbostee/dumbo/ wiki/*). Stay tuned to this book's Twitter account (*@SocialWebMining*) for extended examples that involve Dumbo.

This book provides no advice whatsoever about the legal ramifications of what you may decide to do with the data that's made available to you from social networking sites, although it does sincerely attempt to comply with the letter and spirit of the terms governing the particular sites that are mentioned. It may seem unfortunate that many of the most popular social networking sites have licensing terms that prohibit the use of their data outside of their platforms, but at the moment, it's par for the course. Most social networking sites are like walled gardens, but from their standpoint (and the standpoint of their investors) a lot of the value these companies offer currently relies on controlling the platforms and protecting the privacy of their users; it's a tough balance to maintain and probably won't be all sorted out anytime soon.

A final and much lesser caveat is that this book slightly favors a *nix environment,[4] in that there are a select few visualizations that may give Windows users trouble. Whenever this is known to be a problem, however, advice is given on reasonable alternatives or workarounds, such as firing up a VirtualBox (*http://www.virtualbox.org*) to run the example in a Linux environment. Fortunately, this doesn't come up often, and the few times it does you can safely ignore those sections and move on without any substantive loss of reading enjoyment.

Tools and Prerequisites

The only real prerequisites for this book are that you need to be motivated enough to learn some Python and have the desire to get your hands (really) dirty with social data. None of the techniques or examples in this book require significant background knowledge of data analysis, high performance computing, distributed systems, machine learning, or anything else in particular. Some examples involve constructs you may not have used before, such as thread pools (*http://en.wikipedia.org/wiki/Thread_pool_pattern*), but don't fret—we're programming in Python. Python's intuitive syntax, amazing ecosystem of packages for data manipulation, and core data structures that are practically JSON (*http://www.json.org*) make it an excellent teaching tool that's powerful yet also very easy to get up and running. On other occasions we use some packages that do pretty advanced things, such as processing natural language, but we'll approach these from the standpoint of using the technology as an application programmer. Given the high likelihood that very similar bindings exist for other programming languages, it should be a fairly rote exercise to port the code examples should you so desire. (Hopefully, that's exactly the kind of thing that will happen on GitHub!) Beyond the previous explanation, this book makes no attempt to justify the selection of Python or apologize for using it, because it's a very suitable tool for the job. If you're new to programming or have never seen Python syntax, skimming ahead a few pages should hopefully be all the confirmation that you need. Excellent documentation is available online, and the official Python tutorial (*http://docs.python.org/tutorial/*) is a good place to start if you're looking for a solid introduction.

This book attempts to introduce a broad array of useful visualizations across a variety of visualization tools and toolkits, ranging from consumer staples like spreadsheets to industry staples like Graphviz (*http://www.graphviz.org*), to bleeding-edge HTML5 (*http://en.wikipedia.org/wiki/HTML5*) technologies such as Protovis (*http://vis.stanford .edu/protovis*). A reasonable attempt has been made to introduce a couple of new visualizations in each chapter, but in a way that follows naturally and makes sense. You'll need to be comfortable with the idea of building lightweight prototypes from these tools. That said, most of the visualizations in this book are little more than small

---

4. *nix* is a term used to refer to a Linux/Unix environment, which is basically synonymous with non-Windows at this point in time.

mutations on out-of-the-box examples or projects that minimally exercise the APIs, so as long as you're willing to learn, you should be in good shape.

Conventions Used in This Book

The following typographical conventions are used in this book:

Italic

> Indicates new terms, URLs, email addresses, filenames, and file extensions.

`Constant width`

> Indicates program listings, and is used within paragraphs to refer to program elements such as variable or function names, databases, data types, environment variables, statements, and keywords.

`Constant width bold`

> Shows commands or other text that should be typed literally by the user. Also occasionally used for emphasis in code listings.

`Constant width italic`

> Shows text that should be replaced with user-supplied values or values determined by context.

 This icon signifies a tip, suggestion, or general note.

 This icon indicates a warning or caution.

Using Code Examples

Most of the numbered examples in the following chapters are available for download at GitHub at *https://github.com/ptwobrussell/Mining-the-Social-Web*—the official code repository for this book. You are encouraged to monitor this repository for the latest bug-fixed code as well as extended examples by the author and the rest of the social coding community.

This book is here to help you get your job done. In general, you may use the code in this book in your programs and documentation. You do not need to contact us for permission unless you're reproducing a significant portion of the code. For example, writing a program that uses several chunks of code from this book does not require permission. Selling or distributing a CD-ROM of examples from O'Reilly books does require permission. Answering a question by citing this book and quoting example code does not require permission. Incorporating a significant amount of example code from this book into your product's documentation does require permission.

We appreciate, but do not require, attribution. An attribution usually includes the title, author, publisher, and ISBN. For example: "*Mining the Social Web* by Matthew A. Russell. Copyright 2011 Matthew Russell, 978-1-449-38834-8."

If you feel your use of code examples falls outside fair use or the permission given above, feel free to contact us at *permissions@oreilly.com*.

Safari® Books Online

 Safari Books Online is an on-demand digital library that lets you easily search over 7,500 technology and creative reference books and videos to find the answers you need quickly.

With a subscription, you can read any page and watch any video from our library online. Read books on your cell phone and mobile devices. Access new titles before they are available for print, and get exclusive access to manuscripts in development and post feedback for the authors. Copy and paste code samples, organize your favorites, download chapters, bookmark key sections, create notes, print out pages, and benefit from tons of other time-saving features.

O'Reilly Media has uploaded this book to the Safari Books Online service. To have full digital access to this book and others on similar topics from O'Reilly and other publishers, sign up for free at *http://my.safaribooksonline.com*.

How to Contact Us

Please address comments and questions concerning this book to the publisher:

O'Reilly Media, Inc.
1005 Gravenstein Highway North
Sebastopol, CA 95472
800-998-9938 (in the United States or Canada)
707-829-0515 (international or local)
707-829-0104 (fax)

We have a web page for this book, where we list errata, examples, and any additional information. You can access this page at:

http://oreilly.com/catalog/9781449388348/

Readers can request general help from the author and publisher through GetSatisfaction at:

http://getsatisfaction.com/oreilly

Readers may also file tickets for the sample code—as well as anything else in the book—through GitHub's issue tracker at:

   http://github.com/ptwobrussell/Mining-the-Social-Web/issues

To comment or ask technical questions about this book, send email to:

   bookquestions@oreilly.com

For more information about our books, conferences, Resource Centers, and the O'Reilly Network, see our website at:

   http://www.oreilly.com

Acknowledgments

To say the least, writing a technical book takes a *ridiculous* amount of sacrifice. On the home front, I gave up more time with my wife, Baseeret, and daughter, Lindsay Belle, than I'm proud to admit. Thanks most of all to both of you for loving me in spite of my ambitions to somehow take over the world one day. (It's just a phase, and I'm really trying to grow out of it—honest.)

I sincerely believe that the sum of your decisions gets you to where you are in life (especially professional life), but nobody could ever complete the journey alone, and it's an honor give credit where credit is due. I am truly blessed to have been in the company of some of the brightest people in the world while working on this book, including a technical editor as smart as Mike Loukides, a production staff as talented as the folks at O'Reilly, and an overwhelming battery of eager reviewers as amazing as everyone who helped me to complete this book. I especially want to thank Abe Music, Pete Warden, Tantek Celik, J. Chris Anderson, Salvatore Sanfilippo, Robert Newson, DJ Patil, Chimezie Ogbuji, Tim Golden, Brian Curtin, Raffi Krikorian, Jeff Hammerbacher, Nick Ducoff, and Cameron Marlowe for reviewing material or making particularly helpful comments that absolutely shaped its outcome for the best. I'd also like to thank Tim O'Reilly for graciously allowing me to put some of his Twitter and Google + data under the microscope in Chapters 4, 5, and 7; it definitely made those chapters much more interesting to read than they otherwise would have been. It would be impossible to recount all of the other folks who have directly or indirectly shaped my life or the outcome of this book.

Finally, thanks to you for giving this book a chance. If you're reading this, you're at least thinking about picking up a copy. If you do, you're probably going to find something wrong with it despite my best efforts; however, I really do believe that, in spite of the few inevitable glitches, you'll find it an enjoyable way to spend a few evenings/weekends and you'll manage to learn a few things somewhere along the line.

## CHAPTER 1

Introduction: Hacking on Twitter Data

Although we could get started with an extended discussion of specific social networking APIs, schemaless design, or many other things, let's instead dive right into some introductory examples that illustrate how simple it can be to collect and analyze some social web data. This chapter is a drive-by tutorial that aims to motivate you and get you thinking about some of the issues that the rest of the book revisits in greater detail. We'll start off by getting our development environment ready and then quickly move on to collecting and analyzing some Twitter data.

Installing Python Development Tools

The example code in this book is written in Python, so if you already have a recent version of Python and `easy_install` on your system, you obviously know your way around and should probably skip the remainder of this section. If you don't already have Python installed, the bad news is that you're probably not already a Python hacker. But don't worry, because you will be soon; Python has a way of doing that to people because it is easy to pick up and learn as you go along. Users of all platforms can find instructions for downloading and installing Python at *http://www.python.org/down load/*, but it is highly recommended that Windows users install ActivePython (*http://www.activestate.com/activepython*), which automatically adds Python to your path at the Windows Command Prompt (henceforth referred to as a "terminal") and comes with `easy_install`, which we'll discuss in just a moment. The examples in this book were authored in and tested against the latest Python 2.7 branch, but they should also work fine with other relatively up-to-date versions of Python. At the time this book was written, Python Version 2 is still the status quo in the Python community (*http://wiki .python.org/moin/Python2orPython3*), and it is recommended that you stick with it unless you are confident that all of the dependencies you'll need have been ported to Version 3, and you are willing to debug any idiosyncrasies involved in the switch.

Once Python is installed, you should be able to type `python` in a terminal to spawn an interpreter. Try following along with Example 1-1.

Example 1-1. Your very first Python interpreter session

```
>>> print "Hello World"
Hello World
>>> #this is a comment
...
>>> for i in range(0,10): # a loop
...     print i, # the comma suppresses line breaks
...
0 1 2 3 4 5 6 7 8 9
>>> numbers = [ i for i in range(0,10) ] # a list comprehension
>>> print numbers
[0, 1, 2, 3, 4, 5, 6, 7, 8, 9]
>>> if 10 in numbers: # conditional logic
...     print True
... else:
...     print False
...
False
```

One other tool you'll want to have on hand is `easy_install`,[1] which is similar to a package manager on Linux systems; it allows you to effortlessly install Python packages instead of downloading, building, and installing them from source. You can download the latest version of `easy_install` from *http://pypi.python.org/pypi/setuptools*, where there are specific instructions for each platform. Generally speaking, *nix users will want to `sudo easy_install` so that modules are written to Python's global installation directories. It is assumed that Windows users have taken the advice to use ActivePython, which automatically includes `easy_install` as part of its installation.

 Windows users might also benefit from reviewing the blog post "Installing easy_install...could be easier" (*http://blog.sadphaeton.com/ 2009/01/20/python-development-windows-part-2-installing-easyinstall could-be-easier.html*), which discusses some common problems related to compiling C code that you may encounter when running `easy_install`.

Once you have properly configured `easy_install`, you should be able to run the following command to install NetworkX—a package we'll use throughout the book for building and analyzing graphs—and observe similar output:

```
$ easy_install networkx
Searching for networkx
```

---

1. Although the examples in this book use the well-known `easy_install`, the Python community has slowly been gravitating toward `pip` (*http://pip.openplans.org/*) , another build tool you should be aware of and that generally "just works" with any package that can be `easy_install`'d. If you have git tooling already installed, `pip` is also handy for installing directly from GitHub repositories for packages that aren't available through PyPi (*http://pypi.python.org/pypi*) as illustrated in "Exploring the Graph API one connection at a time" on page 282.

```
...truncated output...

Finished processing dependencies for networkx
```

With NetworkX installed, you might think that you could just import it from the interpreter and get right to work, but occasionally some packages might surprise you. For example, suppose this were to happen:

```
>>> import networkx
Traceback (most recent call last):

... truncated output ...

ImportError: No module named numpy
```

Whenever an `ImportError` happens, it means there's a missing package. In this illustration, the module we installed, `networkx`, has an unsatisfied dependency called `numpy` (*http://numpy.scipy.org*), a highly optimized collection of tools for scientific computing. Usually, another invocation of `easy_install` fixes the problem, and this situation is no different. Just close your interpreter and install the dependency by typing `easy_install numpy` in the terminal:

```
$ easy_install numpy
Searching for numpy

...truncated output...

Finished processing dependencies for numpy
```

Now that `numpy` is installed, you should be able to open up a new interpreter, `import networkx`, and use it to build up graphs. Example 1-2 demonstrates.

Example 1-2. Using NetworkX to create a graph of nodes and edges

```
>>> import networkx
>>> g=networkx.Graph()
>>> g.add_edge(1,2)
>>> g.add_node("spam")
>>> print g.nodes()
[1, 2, 'spam']
>>> print g.edges()
[(1, 2)]
```

At this point, you have some of your core Python development tools installed and are ready to move on to some more interesting tasks. If most of the content in this section has been a learning experience for you, it would be worthwhile to review the official Python tutorial (*http://docs.python.org/tutorial/*) online before proceeding further.

Collecting and Manipulating Twitter Data

In the extremely unlikely event that you don't know much about Twitter yet, it's a real-time, highly social microblogging service that allows you to post short messages of 140 characters or less; these messages are called *tweets*. Unlike social networks like Facebook and LinkedIn, where a connection is bidirectional, Twitter has an asymmetric network infrastructure of "friends" and "followers." Assuming you have a Twitter account, your friends are the accounts that you are following and your followers are the accounts that are following you. While you can choose to follow all of the users who are following you, this generally doesn't happen because you only want your Home Timeline[2] to include tweets from accounts whose content you find interesting. Twitter is an important phenomenon from the standpoint of its incredibly high number of users, as well as its use as a marketing device and emerging use as a transport layer for third-party messaging services. It offers an extensive collection of APIs, and although you can use a lot of the APIs without registering, it's much more interesting to build up and mine your own network. Take a moment to review Twitter's liberal terms of service (*http://twitter.com/tos*), API documentation (*http://apiwiki.twitter.com*), and API rules (*http://twitter.com/apirules*), which allow you to do just about anything you could reasonably expect to do with Twitter data before doing any heavy-duty development. The rest of this book assumes that you have a Twitter account and enough friends/followers that you have data to mine.

 The official Twitter account for this book is *@SocialWebMining* .

Tinkering with Twitter's API

A minimal wrapper around Twitter's web API is available through a package called twitter (*http://github.com/sixohsix/twitter*) can be installed with easy_install per the norm:

```
$ easy_install twitter
Searching for twitter

...truncated output...

Finished processing dependencies for twitter
```

The package also includes a handy command-line utility and IRC bot, so after installing the module you should be able to simply type twitter in a shell to get a usage screen about how to use the command-line utility. However, we'll focus on working within the interactive Python interpreter. We'll work though some examples, but note that you can always skim the documentation by running pydoc from the terminal. *nix users can simply type pydoc twitter.Twitter to view the documentation on the Twitter class, while Windows users need to type python -mpydoc twitter.Twitter. If you find yourself reviewing the documentation for certain modules often, you can elect to pass the -w

2. *http://support.twitter.com/entries/164083-what-is-a-timeline*

option to pydoc and write out an HTML page that you can save and bookmark in your browser. It's also worth knowing that running pydoc on a module or class brings up the inline documentation in the same way that running the help() command in the interpreter would. Try typing help(twitter.Twitter) in the interpreter to see for yourself.

Without further ado, let's find out what people are talking about by inspecting the trends available to us through Twitter's trends API (*http://dev.twitter.com/doc/get/trends*). Let's fire up the interpreter and initiate a search. Try following along with Example 1-3, and use the help() function as needed to try to answer as many of your own questions as possible before proceeding.

Example 1-3. Retrieving Twitter trends

```
>>> import twitter
>>> twitter_api = twitter.Twitter(domain="api.twitter.com", api_version='1')
>>> WORLD_WOE_ID = 1 # The Yahoo! Where On Earth ID for the entire world
>>> world_trends = twitter_api.trends._(WORLD_WOE_ID) # get back a callable
>>> [ trend['name'] for trend in world_trends()[0]['trends'] ] # iterate through the trends
[u'#ZodiacFacts', u'#nowplaying', u'#ItsOverWhen', u'#Christoferdrew',
u'Justin Bieber', u'#WhatwouldItBeLike', u'#Sagittarius', u'SNL', u'#SurveySays',
u'#iDoit2']
```

Since you're probably wondering, the pattern for using the twitter module is simple and predictable: instantiate the Twitter class with a base URL and then invoke methods on the object that correspond to URL contexts. For example, twitter_api._trends(WORLD_WOE_ID) initiates an HTTP call to GET *http://api.twitter.com/trends/1.json*, which you could type into your web browser to get the same set of results. As further context for the previous interpreter session, this chapter was originally drafted on a Saturday night, so it's not a coincidence that the trend *SNL* (*Saturday Night Live*, a popular comedy show that airs in the United States) appears in the list. Now might be a good time to go ahead and bookmark the official Twitter API documentation (*http://dev.twitter.com/doc*) since you'll be referring to it quite frequently.

Given that *SNL* is trending, the next logical step might be to grab some search results about it by using the search API to search for tweets containing that text and then print them out in a readable way as a JSON (*http://json.org*) structure. Example 1-4 illustrates.

Example 1-4. Paging through Twitter search results

```
>>> twitter_search = twitter.Twitter(domain="search.twitter.com")
>>> search_results = []
>>> for page in range(1,6):
...         search_results.append(twitter_search.search(q="SNL", rpp=100, page=page))
```

The code fetches and stores five consecutive batches (pages) of results for a query (q) of SNL, with 100 results per page (rpp). It's again instructive to observe that the equivalent REST query[3] that we execute in the loop is of the form *http://search.twitter.com/search.json?&q=SNL&rpp=100&page=1*. The trivial mapping between the REST API and the twitter module makes it very simple to write Python code that interacts with

Twitter services. After executing the search, the `search_results` list contains five objects, each of which is a batch of 100 results. You can print out the results in a readable way for inspection by using the `json` package that comes built-in as of Python Version 2.6, as shown in Example 1-5.

Example 1-5. Pretty-printing Twitter data as JSON

```
>>> import json
>>> print json.dumps(search_results, sort_keys=True, indent=1)
[
 {
  "completed_in": 0.088122000000000006,
  "max_id": 11966285265,
  "next_page": "?page=2&max_id=11966285265&rpp=100&q=SNL",
  "page": 1,
  "query": "SNL",
  "refresh_url": "?since_id=11966285265&q=SNL",
  "results": [
   {
    "created_at": "Sun, 11 Apr 2010 01:34:52 +0000",
    "from_user": "bieber_luv2",
    "from_user_id": 106998169,
    "geo": null,
    "id": 11966285265,
    "iso_language_code": "en",
    "metadata": {
     "result_type": "recent"
    },
    "profile_image_url": "http://a1.twimg.com/profile_images/809471978/DSC00522...",
    "source": "&lt;a href=&quot;http://twitter.com/&quot;&gt;web&lt;/a&gt;",
    "text": " ...truncated... im nt gonna go to sleep happy unless i see @justin...",
    "to_user_id": null
   }
            ... output truncated - 99 more tweets ...

  ],
  "results_per_page": 100,
  "since_id": 0
 },

    ... output truncated - 4 more pages ...
]
```

 As of Nov 7, 2011, the `from_user_id` field in each search result *does* correspond to the tweet author's actual Twitter id, which was previously not the case. See Twitter API Issue #214 (*http://code.google.com/p/twitter-api/issues/detail?id=214#c73*) for details on the evolution and resolution of this issue.

---

3. If you're not familiar with REST, see the sidebar "RESTful Web Services" on page 49 in Chapter 7 for a brief explanation.

We'll wait until later in the book to pick apart many of the details in this query (see Chapter 5); the important observation at the moment is that the tweets are keyed by results in the response. We can distill the text of the 500 tweets into a list with the following approach. Example 1-6 illustrates a double list comprehension that's indented to illustrate the intuition behind it being nothing more than a nested loop.

Example 1-6. A simple list comprehension in Python

```
>>> tweets = [ r['text'] \
...     for result in search_results \
...         for r in result['results'] ]
```

List comprehensions are used frequently throughout this book. Although they can look quite confusing if written on a single line, printing them out as nested loops clarifies the meaning. The result of tweets in this particular case is equivalent to defining an empty list called tweets and invoking tweets.append(r['text']) in the same kind of nested loop as presented here. See the "Data Structures" section (*http://docs.python.org/ tutorial/datastructures.html*) in the official Python tutorial for more details. List comprehensions are particularly powerful because they usually yield substantial performance gains over nested lists and provide an intuitive (once you're familiar with them) yet terse syntax.

Frequency Analysis and Lexical Diversity

One of the most intuitive measurements that can be applied to unstructured text is a metric called *lexical diversity*. Put simply, this is an expression of the number of unique tokens in the text divided by the total number of tokens in the text, which are elementary yet important metrics in and of themselves. It could be computed as shown in Example 1-7.

Example 1-7. Calculating lexical diversity for tweets

```
>>> words = []
>>> for t in tweets:
...     words += [ w for w in t.split() ]
...
>>> len(words) # total words
7238
>>> len(set(words)) # unique words
1636
>>> 1.0*len(set(words))/len(words) # lexical diversity
0.22602928985907708
>>> 1.0*sum([ len(t.split()) for t in tweets ])/len(tweets) # avg words per tweet
14.476000000000001
```

Prior to Python 3.0, the division operator applies the floor function and returns an integer value (unless one of the operands is a floating-point value). Multiply either the numerator or the denominator by 1.0 to avoid truncation errors.

One way to interpret a lexical diversity of around 0.23 would be to say that about one out of every four words in the aggregated tweets is unique. Given that the average number of words in each tweet is around 14, that translates to just over 3 unique words per tweet. Without introducing any additional information, that could be interpreted as meaning that each tweet carries about 20 percent unique information. What would be interesting to know at this point is how "noisy" the tweets are with uncommon abbreviations users may have employed to stay within the 140 characters, as well as what the most frequent and infrequent terms used in the tweets are. A distribution of the words and their frequencies would be helpful. Although these are not difficult to compute, we'd be better off installing a tool that offers a built-in frequency distribution and many other tools for text analysis.

The Natural Language Toolkit (*http://www.nltk.org*) (NLTK) is a popular module we'll use throughout this book: it delivers a vast amount of tools for various kinds of text analytics, including the calculation of common metrics, information extraction, and natural language processing (NLP). Although NLTK isn't necessarily state-of-the-art as compared to ongoing efforts in the commercial space and academia, it nonetheless provides a solid and broad foundation—especially if this is your first experience trying to process natural language. If your project is sufficiently sophisticated that the quality or efficiency that NLTK provides isn't adequate for your needs, you have approximately three options, depending on the amount of time and money you are willing to put in: scour the open source space for a suitable alternative by running comparative experiments and benchmarks, churn through whitepapers and prototype your own toolkit, or license a commercial product. None of these options is cheap (assuming you believe that time is money) or easy.

NLTK can be installed per the norm with `easy_install`, but you'll need to restart the interpreter to take advantage of it. You can use the `cPickle` module to save ("pickle") your data before exiting your current working session, as shown in Example 1-8.

Example 1-8. Pickling your data

```
>>> f = open("myData.pickle", "wb")
>>> import cPickle
>>> cPickle.dump(words, f)
>>> f.close()
>>>
$ easy_install nltk
Searching for nltk

...truncated output...

Finished processing dependencies for nltk
```

 If you encounter an "ImportError: No module named yaml" problem when you try to `import nltk`, execute an `easy_install pyYaml`, which should clear it up.

After installing NLTK, you might want to take a moment to visit its official website (*http://www.nltk.org*), where you can review its documentation. This includes the full text of Steven Bird, Ewan Klein, and Edward Loper's *Natural Language Processing with Python* (O'Reilly), NLTK's authoritative reference.

What are people talking about right now?

Among the most compelling reasons for mining Twitter data is to try to answer the question of what people are talking about *right now*. One of the simplest techniques you could apply to answer this question is basic frequency analysis. NLTK simplifies this task by providing an API for frequency analysis, so let's save ourselves some work and let NLTK take care of those details. Example 1-9 demonstrates the findings from creating a frequency distribution and takes a look at the 50 most frequent and least frequent terms.

Example 1-9. Using NLTK to perform basic frequency analysis

```
>>> import nltk
>>> import cPickle
>>> words = cPickle.load(open("myData.pickle"))
>>> freq_dist = nltk.FreqDist(words)
>>> freq_dist.keys()[:50] # 50 most frequent tokens
[u'snl', u'on', u'rt', u'is', u'to', u'i', u'watch', u'justin', u'@justinbieber',
u'be', u'the', u'tonight', u'gonna', u'at', u'in', u'bieber', u'and', u'you',
u'watching', u'tina', u'for', u'a', u'wait', u'fey', u'of', u'@justinbieber:',
u'if', u'with', u'so', u"can't", u'who', u'great', u'it', u'going',
u'im', u':)', u'snl...', u'2nite...', u'are', u'cant', u'dress', u'rehearsal',
u'see', u'that', u'what', u'but', u'tonight!', u':d', u'2', u'will']

>>> freq_dist.keys()[-50:] # 50 least frequent tokens
[u'what?!', u'whens', u'where', u'while', u'white', u'whoever', u'whoooo!!!!',
u'whose', u'wiating', u'wii', u'wiig', u'win...', u'wink.', u'wknd.', u'wohh', u'won',
 u'wonder', u'wondering', u'wootwoot!', u'worked', u'worth', u'xo.', u'xx', u'ya',
u'ya&lt;3miranda', u'yay', u'yay!', u'ya\u2665', u'yea', u'yea.', u'yeaa', u'yeah!',
u'yeah.', u'yeahhh.', u'yes,', u'yes;)', u'yess', u'yess,', u'you!!!!!',
u"you'll", u'you+snl=', u'you,', u'youll', u'youtube??', u'youu&lt;3',
u'youuuuu', u'yum', u'yumyum', u'~', u'\xac\xac']
```

 Python 2.7 added a collections.Counter (*http://docs.python.org/library/ collections.html#collections.Counter*) class that facilitates counting operations. You might find it useful if you're in a situation where you can't easily install NLTK, or if you just want to experiment with the latest and greatest classes from Python's standard library.

A very quick skim of the results from Example 1-9 shows that a lot more useful information is carried in the frequent tokens than the infrequent tokens. Although some work would need to be done to get a machine to recognize as much, the frequent tokens refer to entities such as people, times, and activities, while the infrequent terms amount to mostly noise from which no meaningful conclusion could be drawn.

The first thing you might have noticed about the most frequent tokens is that "snl" is at the top of the list. Given that it is the basis of the original search query, this isn't surprising at all. Where it gets more interesting is when you skim the remaining tokens: there is apparently a lot of chatter about a fellow named Justin Bieber, as evidenced by the tokens @justinbieber, justin, and bieber. Anyone familiar with *SNL* would also know that the occurrences of the tokens "tina" and "fey" are no coincidence, given Tina Fey's longstanding affiliation with the show. Hopefully, it's not too difficult (as a human) to skim the tokens and form the conjecture that Justin Bieber is a popular guy, and that a lot of folks were very excited that he was going to be on the show on the Saturday evening the search query was executed.

At this point, you might be thinking, "So what? I could skim a few tweets and deduce as much." While that may be true, would you want to do it 24/7, or pay someone to do it for you around the clock? And what if you were working in a different domain that wasn't as amenable to skimming random samples of short message blurbs? The point is that frequency analysis is a very simple, yet very powerful tool that shouldn't be overlooked just because it's so obvious. On the contrary, it should be tried out first for precisely the reason that it's so obvious and simple. Thus, one preliminary takeaway here is that the application of a very simple technique can get you quite a long way toward answering the question, "What are people talking about right now?"

As a final observation, the presence of "rt" is also a very important clue as to the nature of the conversations going on. The token RT is a special symbol that is often prepended to a message to indicate that you are *retweeting* it on behalf of someone else. Given the high frequency of this token, it's reasonable to infer that there were a large amount of duplicate or near-duplicate tweets involving the subject matter at hand. In fact, this observation is the basis of our next analysis.

 The token RT can be prepended to a message to indicate that it is being relayed, or "retweeted" in Twitter parlance. For example, a tweet of "RT @SocialWebMining Justin Bieber is on SNL 2nite. w00t?!?" would indicate that the sender is retweeting information gained via the user @SocialWebMining (*http://twitter.com/SocialWebMining*). An equivalent form of the retweet would be "Justin Bieber is on SNL 2nite. w00t?!? Ummm...(via @SocialWebMining)".

Extracting relationships from the tweets

Because the social web is first and foremost about the linkages between people in the real world, one highly convenient format for storing social web data is a graph. Let's use NetworkX to build out a graph connecting Twitterers who have retweeted information. We'll include directionality in the graph to indicate the direction that information is flowing, so it's more precisely called a *digraph* (*http://en.wikipedia.org/wiki/Directed_graph*). Although the Twitter APIs do offer some capabilities for determining and analyzing statuses that have been retweeted, these APIs are not a great fit for our current use case because we'd have to make a lot of API calls back and forth to the server, which would be a waste of the API calls included in our quota.

 At the time this book was written, Twitter imposes a rate limit of 350 API calls per hour for authenticated requests; anonymous requests are limited to 150 per hour. You can read more about the specifics at *http://dev.twitter.com/pages/rate-limiting*. In Chapters 4 and 5, we'll discuss techniques for making the most of the rate limiting, as well as some other creative options for collecting data.

Besides, we can use the clues in the tweets themselves to reliably extract retweet information with a simple regular expression. By convention, Twitter usernames begin with an @ symbol and can only include letters, numbers, and underscores. Thus, given the conventions for retweeting, we only have to search for the following patterns:

- *RT* followed by a username
- *via* followed by a username

Although Chapter 5 introduces a module specifically designed to parse entities out of tweets, Example 1-10 demonstrates that you can use the re module to compile[4] a pattern and extract the originator of a tweet in a lightweight fashion, without any special libraries.

Example 1-10. Using regular expressions to find retweets

```
>>> import re
>>> rt_patterns = re.compile(r"(RT|via)((?:\b\W*@\w+)+)", re.IGNORECASE)
>>> example_tweets = ["RT @SocialWebMining Justin Bieber is on SNL 2nite. w00t?!?",
...     "Justin Bieber is on SNL 2nite. w00t?!? (via @SocialWebMining)"]
>>> for t in example_tweets:
...     rt_patterns.findall(t)
...
[('RT', ' @SocialWebMining')]
[('via', ' @SocialWebMining')]
```

In case it's not obvious, the call to findall returns a list of tuples in which each tuple contains either the matching text or an empty string for each group in the pattern; note that the regex does leave a leading space on the extracted entities, but that's easily fixed with a call to strip(), as demonstrated in Example 1-11. Since neither of the example tweets contains both of the groups enclosed in the parenthetical expressions, one string is empty in each of the tuples.

---

4. In the present context, compiling a regular expression means transforming it into bytecode so that it can be executed by a matching engine written in C.

Regular expressions are a basic programming concept whose explanation is outside the scope of this book. The re module documentation (*http://docs.python.org/library/re.html*) is a good place to start getting up to speed, and you can always consult Friedl's classic *Mastering Regular Expressions* (*http://oreilly.com/catalog/9780596528126/*) (O'Reilly) if you want to learn more than you'll probably ever need to know about them.

Given that the tweet data structure as returned by the API provides the username of the person tweeting and the newly found ability to extract the originator of a retweet, it's a simple matter to load this information into a NetworkX graph. Let's create a graph in which nodes represent usernames and a directed edge between two nodes signifies that there is a retweet relationship between the nodes. The edge itself will carry a payload of the tweet ID and tweet text itself.

Example 1-11 demonstrates the process of generating such a graph. The basic steps involved are generalizing a routine for extracting usernames in retweets, flattening out the pages of tweets into a flat list for easier processing in a loop, and finally, iterating over the tweets and adding edges to a graph. Although we'll generate an image of the graph later, it's worthwhile to note that you can gain a lot of insight by analyzing the characteristics of graphs without necessarily visualizing them.

Example 1-11. Building and analyzing a graph describing who retweeted whom

```
>>> import networkx as nx
>>> import re
>>> g = nx.DiGraph()
>>>
>>> all_tweets = [ tweet
...                    for page in search_results
...                        for tweet in page["results"] ]
>>>
>>> def get_rt_sources(tweet):
...     rt_patterns = re.compile(r"(RT|via)((?:\b\W*@\w+)+)", re.IGNORECASE)
...     return [ source.strip()
...                for tuple in rt_patterns.findall(tweet)
...                    for source in tuple
...                        if source not in ("RT", "via") ]
...
>>> for tweet in all_tweets:
...     rt_sources = get_rt_sources(tweet["text"])
...     if not rt_sources: continue
...     for rt_source in rt_sources:
...         g.add_edge(rt_source, tweet["from_user"], {"tweet_id" : tweet["id"]})
...
>>> g.number_of_nodes()
160
>>> g.number_of_edges()
125
>>> g.edges(data=True)[0]
(u'@ericastolte', u'bonitasworld', {'tweet_id': 11965974697L})
```

```
>>> len(nx.connected_components(g.to_undirected()))
37
>>> sorted(nx.degree(g).values())
[1, 1, 1, 1, 1, 1, 1, 1, 1, 1, 1, 1, 1, 1, 1, 1, 1, 1, 1, 1, 1, 1, 1, 1, 1, 1,
1, 1, 1, 1, 1, 1, 1, 1, 1, 1, 1, 1, 1, 1, 1, 1, 1, 1, 1, 1, 1, 1, 1, 1, 1, 1,
1, 1, 1, 1, 1, 1, 1, 1, 1, 1, 1, 1, 1, 1, 1, 1, 1, 1, 1, 1, 1, 1, 1, 1, 1, 1,
1, 1, 1, 1, 1, 1, 1, 1, 1, 1, 1, 1, 1, 1, 1, 1, 1, 1, 1, 1, 1, 1, 1, 1, 1, 1,
1, 1, 1, 1, 1, 1, 1, 1, 1, 1, 1, 1, 1, 1, 1, 1, 1, 2, 2, 2, 2, 2, 2, 2, 2, 2,
2, 2, 2, 2, 2, 2, 2, 3, 3, 3, 4, 4, 4, 5, 6, 6, 9, 37]
```

The built-in operations that NetworkX provides are a useful starting point to make
sense of the data, but it's important to keep in mind that we're only looking at a very
small slice of the overall conversation happening on Twitter about *SNL*—500 tweets
out of potentially tens of thousands (or more). For example, the number of nodes in
the graph tells us that out of 500 tweets, there were 160 users involved in retweet
relationships with one another, with 125 edges connecting those nodes. The ratio of
160/125 (approximately 1.28) is an important clue that tells us that the average degree (*http://en.wikipedia.org/wiki/Degree_(graph_theory)*) of a node is approximately
one—meaning that although some nodes are connected to more than one other node,
the average is approximately one connection per node.

The call to connected_components shows us that the graph consists of 37 subgraphs and
is not fully connected. The output of degree might seem a bit cryptic at first, but it
actually confirms insight we've already gleaned: think of it as a way to get the *gist* of
how well connected the nodes in the graph are without having to render an actual
graph. In this case, most of the values are 1, meaning all of those nodes have a degree
of 1 and are connected to only one other node in the graph. A few values are between
2 and 9, indicating that those nodes are connected to anywhere between 2 and 9 other
nodes. The extreme outlier is the node with a degree of 37. The gist of the graph is that
it's mostly composed of disjoint nodes, but there is one very highly connected node.
Figure 1-1 illustrates a distribution of degree as a column chart. The trendline shows
that the distribution closely follows a Power Law (*http://en.wikipedia.org/wiki/Power
_law*) and has a "heavy" or "long" tail. Although the characteristics of distributions
with long tails are by no means treated with rigor in this book, you'll find that lots of
distributions we'll encounter exhibit this property, and you're highly encouraged to
take the initiative to dig deeper if you feel the urge. A good starting point is Zipf's
law (*http://en.wikipedia.org/wiki/Zipf's_law*).

We'll spend a lot more time in this book using automatable heuristics to make sense
of the data; this chapter is intended simply as an introduction to rattle your brain and
get you thinking about ways that you could exploit data with the low-hanging fruit
that's available to you. Before we wrap up this chapter, however, let's visualize the
graph just to be sure that our intuition is leading us in the right direction.

Figure 1-1. A distribution illustrating the degree of each node in the graph, which reveals insight into the graph's connectedness

Visualizing Tweet Graphs

Graphviz is a staple in the visualization community. This section introduces one possible approach for visualizing graphs of tweet data: exporting them to the DOT language (*http://www.graphviz.org/doc/info/lang.html*), a simple text-based format that Graphviz consumes. Graphviz binaries for all platforms can be downloaded from its official website (*http://www.graphviz.org*), and the installation is straightforward regardless of platform. Once Graphviz is installed, *nix users should be able to `easy_install pygraphviz` per the norm to satisfy the PyGraphviz (*http://networkx.lanl .gov/pygraphviz/*) dependency NetworkX requires to emit DOT. Windows users will most likely experience difficulties installing PyGraphviz,[5] but this turns out to be of little consequence since it's trivial to tailor a few lines of code to generate the DOT language output that we need in this section.

Example 1-12 illustrates an approach that works for both platforms.

Example 1-12. Generating DOT language output is easy regardless of platform

```
OUT = "snl_search_results.dot"

try:
    nx.drawing.write_dot(g, OUT)
except ImportError, e:
```

---

5. See NetworkX Ticket #117 (*https://networkx.lanl.gov/trac/ticket/117*), which reveals that this has been a long-standing issue that somehow has not garnered the support to be overcome even after many years of frustration. The underlying issue has to do with the need to compile C code during the `easy_install` process. The ability to work around this issue fairly easily by generating DOT language output may be partly responsible for why it has remained unresolved for so long.

```
# Help for Windows users:
# Not a general-purpose method, but representative of
# the same output write_dot would provide for this graph
# if installed and easy to implement

dot = ['"%s" -> "%s" [tweet_id=%s]' % (n1, n2, g[n1][n2]['tweet_id']) \
    for n1, n2 in g.edges()]
f = open(OUT, 'w')
f.write('strict digraph {\n%s\n}' % (';\n'.join(dot),))
f.close()
```

The DOT output that is generated is of the form shown in Example 1-13.

Example 1-13. Example DOT language output

```
strict digraph {
"@ericastolte" -> "bonitasworld" [tweet_id=11965974697];
"@mpcoelho" -> "Lil_Amaral" [tweet_id=11965954427];
"@BieberBelle123" -> "BELIEBE4EVER" [tweet_id=11966261062];
"@BieberBelle123" -> "sabrina9451" [tweet_id=11966197327];
}
```

With DOT language output on hand, the next step is to convert it into an image. Graphviz itself provides a variety of layout algorithms to visualize the exported graph; circo, a tool used to render graphs in a circular-style layout, should work well given that the data suggested that the graph would exhibit the shape of an ego graph (*http:// networkx.lanl.gov/examples/drawing/ego_graph.html*) with a "hub and spoke"-style topology, with one central node being highly connected to many nodes having a degree of 1. On a *nix platform, the following command converts the *snl_search _results.dot* file exported from NetworkX into an *snl_search_results.dot.png* file that you can open in an image viewer (the result of the operation is displayed in Figure 1-2):

```
$ circo -Tpng -Osnl_search_results snl_search_results.dot
```

Windows users can use the GVedit application to render the file as shown in Figure 1-3. You can read more about the various Graphviz options in the online documentation (*http://www.graphviz.org/Documentation.php*). Visual inspection of the entire graphic file confirms that the characteristics of the graph align with our previous analysis, and we can visually confirm that the node with the highest degree is @justin bieber, the subject of so much discussion (and, in case you missed that episode of *SNL*, the guest host of the evening). Keep in mind that if we had harvested a lot more tweets, it is very likely that we would have seen many more interconnected subgraphs than are evidenced in the sampling of 500 tweets that we have been analyzing. Further analysis of the graph is left as a voluntary exercise for the reader, as the primary objective of this chapter was to get your development environment squared away and whet your appetite for more interesting topics.

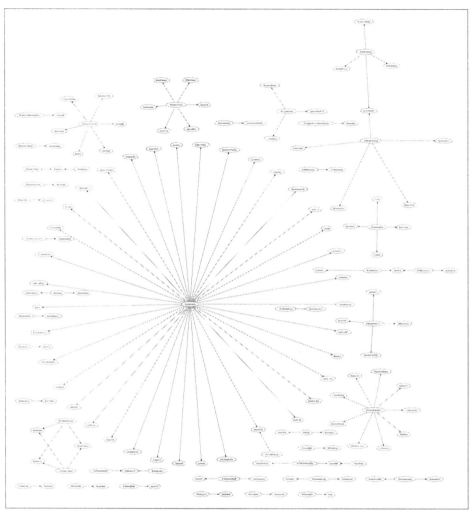

Figure 1-2. Our search results rendered in a circular layout with Graphviz

Graphviz appears elsewhere in this book, and if you consider yourself to be a data scientist (or are aspiring to be one), it is a tool that you'll want to master. That said, we'll also look at many other useful approaches to visualizing graphs. In the chapters to come, we'll cover additional outlets of social web data and techniques for analysis.

Synthesis: Visualizing Retweets with Protovis

A turn-key example script that synthesizes much of the content from this chapter and adds a visualization is how we'll wrap up this chapter. In addition to spitting some useful information out to the console, it accepts a search term as a command line parameter, fetches, parses, and pops up your web browser to visualize the data as an interactive HTML5-based graph. It is available through the official code repository for this book at *http://github.com/ptwobrussell/Mining-the-Social-Web/blob/master/python _code/introduction__retweet_visualization.py*. You are highly encouraged to try it out. We'll revisit Protovis (*http://vis.stanford.edu/protovis/*), the underlying visualization toolkit for this example, in several chapters later in the book. Figure 1-4 illustrates Protovis output from this script. The boilerplate in the sample script is just the beginning—much more can be done!

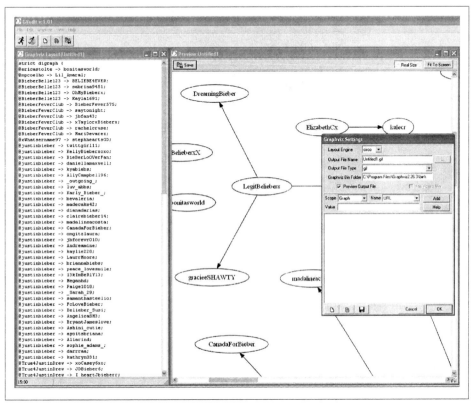

Figure 1-3. Windows users can use GVedit instead of interacting with Graphviz at the command prompt

Closing Remarks

This chapter got you up and running, and illustrated how easy it is to use Python's interactive interpreter to explore and visualize Twitter data. Before you move on to other chapters, it's important that you feel comfortable with your Python development environment, and it's highly recommended that you spend some time with the Twitter APIs and Graphviz. If you feel like going out on a tangent, you might want to check out canviz (*http://code.google.com/p/canviz/*), a project that aims to draw Graphviz graphs on a web browser `<canvas>` element. You might also want to investigate IPython (*http://ipython.scipy.org/moin/*), a "better" Python interpreter that offers tab completion, history tracking, and more. Most of the work we'll do in this book from here on out will involve runnable scripts, but it's important that you're as productive as possible when trying out new ideas, debugging, etc.

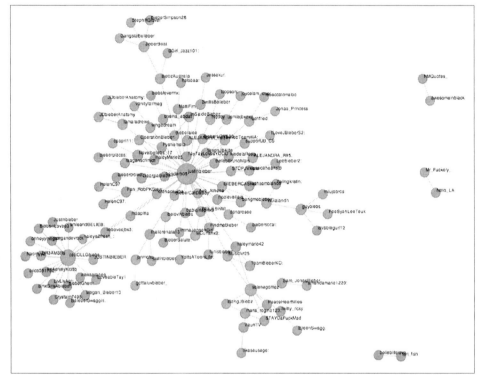

Figure 1-4. An interactive Protovis graph with a force-directed layout that visualizes retweet relationships for a "JustinBieber" query

## CHAPTER 2

Microformats: Semantic Markup and Common Sense Collide

In terms of the Web's ongoing evolution, microformats are an important step forward because they provide an effective mechanism for embedding "smarter data" into web pages and are easy for content authors to implement. Put succinctly, microformats (*http://www.microformats.org*) are simply conventions for unambiguously including structured data into web pages in an entirely value-added way. This chapter begins by briefly introducing the microformats landscape and then digs right into some examples involving specific uses of the XFN (XHTML Friends Network) (*http://gmpg.org/xfn/*), geo (*http://microformats.org/wiki/geo*), hRecipe (*http://microformats.org/wiki/hrecipe*), and hReview (*http://microformats.org/wiki/hReview*) microformats. In particular, we'll mine human relationships out of blogrolls, extract coordinates from web pages, parse out recipes from foodnetwork.com (*http://foodnetwork.com*), and analyze reviews on some of those recipes. The example code listings in this chapter aren't implemented with the intention of being "full spec parsers," but should be more than enough to get you on your way.

Although it might be somewhat of a stretch to call data decorated with microformats like geo or hRecipe "social data," it's still interesting and will inevitably play an increased role in social data mashups. At the time this book was written, nearly half of all web developers reported some use of microformats (*http://www.webdirections.org/sotw10/markup/*), the microformats.org community had just celebrated its fifth birthday (*http://microformats.org/2010/07/08/microformats-org-at-5-hcards-rich-snippets*), and Google reported that 94% of the time, microformats are involved in Rich Snippets (*http://microformats.org/2010/07/08/microformats-org-at-5-hcards-rich-snippets*). If Google has anything to say about it, we'll see significant growth in microformats; in fact, according to ReadWriteWeb, Google wants to see at least 50% of web pages contain some form of semantic markup and is encouraging "beneficial peer pressure" for companies to support such initiatives (*http://www.readwriteweb.com/archives/google_semantic_web_push_rich_snippets_usage_grow.php*). Any way you slice it, you'll be seeing more of microformats in the future if you're paying attention to the web space, so let's get to work.

XFN and Friends

Semantic web enthusiasts herald that technologies such as FOAF (*http://en.wikipedia .org/wiki/FOAF_(software)*) (Friend of a Friend—an ontology describing relations between people, their activities, etc.) may one day be the catalyst that drives robust decentralized social networks that could be construed as the antithesis of tightly controlled platforms like Facebook. And although so-called semantic web technologies such as FOAF don't seem to have quite yet reached the tipping point that would lead them into ubiquity, this isn't too surprising. If you know much about the short history of the Web, you'll recognize that innovation is rampant and that the highly decentralized nature in which the Web operates is not very conducive to overnight revolutions (see Chapter 10). Rather, change seems to happen continually, fluidly, and in a very evolutionary way. The way that microformats have evolved to fill the void of "intelligent data" on the Web is a particularly good example of bridging existing technology with up-and-coming standards that aren't quite there yet. In this particular case, it's a story of narrowing the gap between a fairly ambiguous web, primarily based on the human-readable HTML 4.01 (*http://www.w3.org/TR/REC-html40/*) standard, with a more semantic web in which information is much less ambiguous and friendlier to machine interpretation.

The beauty of microformats is that they provide a way to embed data that's related to social networking, calendaring, resumes, and shared bookmarks, and they are much more into existing HTML markup *right now*, in an entirely backward-compatible way. The overall ecosystem is quite diverse with some microformats, such as *geo*, being quite established while others are slowly gaining ground and achieving newfound popularity with search engines, social media sites, and blogging platforms. As this book was written, notable developments in the microformats community were underway, including an announcement from Google that they had begun supporting hRecipe as part of their Rich Snippets (*http://googlewebmastercentral.blogspot.com/2010/04/better-recipes-on -web-introducing.html*) initiative. Table 2-1 provides a synopsis of a few popular microformats and related initiatives you're likely to encounter if you look around on the Web. For more examples, see *http://microformats.org/wiki/examples-in-the-wild*.

Table 2-1. Some popular technologies for embedding structured data into web pages

Technology	Purpose	Popularity	Markup specification	Type
XFN	Representing human-readable relationships in hyperlinks	Widely used, especially by blogging platforms	Semantic HTML, XHTML	Microformat

Technology	Purpose	Popularity	Markup specification	Type
geo	Embedding geocoordinates for people and objects	Widely used, especially by sites such as MapQuest and Wikipedia	Semantic HTML, XHTML	Microformat
hCard	Identifying people, companies, and other contact info	Widely used	Semantic HTML, XHTML	Microformat
hCalendar	Embedding iCalendar data	Steadily gaining traction (*http://microformats .org/2010/04/28/google -adds-support-for-hca lendar-and-hrecipe-rich -snippets*)	Semantic HTML, XHTML	Microformat
hResume	Embedding resume and CV information	Widely used by sites such as LinkedIn[a]	Semantic HTML, XHTML	Microformat
hRecipe	Identifying recipes	Widely used by niche sites such as foodnet-work.com	Semantic HTML, XHTML	Microformat
Microdata	Embedding name/value pairs into web pages authored in HTML5	An emerging technology, but gaining traction (*http://google webmastercentral.blog spot.com/2010/03/micro data-support-for-rich -snippets.html*)	HTML5	W3C initiative
RDFa	Embedding unambiguous facts into XHTML pages according to specialized vocabularies created by subject-matter experts	Hit-or-miss depending on the particular vocabulary; vocabularies such as FOAF are steadily gaining ground while others are remaining obscure	XHTML[b]	W3C initiative
Open Graph protocol	Embedding profiles of real-world things into XHTML pages	Steadily gaining traction and has tremendous potential given the reach of the Facebook platform (*http://www.facebook .com/press/info.php?sta tistics*)	XHTML (RDFa-based)	Facebook platform initiative

[a] LinkedIn presents public resumes in hResume format (*http://steve.ganz.name/blog/2007/01/linkedin-launches-hresume.html*) for its more than 75 million worldwide users (*http://press.linkedin.com*).

[b] Embedding RDFa into semantic markup and HTML5 is an active effort at the time of this writing. See the W3C HTML+RDFa 1.1 Working Draft (*http://www.w3.org/TR/rdfa-in-html/*).

There are many other microformats that you're likely to encounter, but a good rule of thumb is to watch what the bigger fish in the pond—such as Google, Yahoo!, and Facebook—are doing. The more support a microformat gets from a player with significant leverage, the more likely it will be to succeed and become useful for data mining.

Semantic Markup?

Given that the purpose of microformats is to embed semantic knowledge into web pages, it makes sense that either XHTML or semantic HTML is required. But what exactly is the difference between semantic HTML or semantic markup versus XHTML? One way of looking at it is from the angle of separating content from presentation. Semantic HTML is markup that emphasizes the meaning of the information in the page via tags that are content-focused as opposed to presentation-focused. Unfortunately, HTML as originally defined and as it initially evolved did very little to promote semantic markup. XHTML, on the other hand, is *well-formed* XML and was developed in the late 1990s to solve the considerable problem of separating content from presentation that had arisen with HTML. The idea was that original content could be authored in XML with no focus whatsoever on presentation, but tools could transform the content into something that could easily be consumed and rendered by browsers. The target for the transformed content came to be known as XHTML. XHTML is nearly identical to HTML, except that it is still valid XML and, as such, requires that all elements be closed or self-closing, properly nested, and defined in lowercase.

In terms of design, it appeared that XHTML was exactly what the Web needed. There was a lot to gain and virtually nothing to lose from the proposition: *well-formed* XHTML content could be proven *valid* against an XML schema and enjoy all of the other perks of XML, such as custom attributes using namespaces (a device that semantic web technologies such as RDFa rely upon). The problem is that it just didn't catch on. Whether it was the fault of Internet Explorer, confusion amongst web developers about delivering the correct MIME types to browsers, the quality of the XML developer tools that were available, or the fact that it just wasn't reasonable to expect the entire Web to take a brief timeout to perform the conversion is a contentious discussion that we should probably avoid. The reality is that it just didn't happen as we might have expected. As a result, we now live in a world where semantic markup based on the HTML 4.01 standard that's over a decade old continues to thrive while XHTML-based technologies such as RDFa remain on the fringe. Most of the web development world is holding its breath and hoping that HTML5 will create a long-overdue convergence.

Exploring Social Connections with XFN

With a bit of context established for how microformats fit into the overall web space, let's now turn to some practical applications of XFN, which is by far the most popular microformat you're likely to encounter. As you already know, XFN is a means of identifying relationships to other people by including a few keywords in the rel attribute of an anchor tag. XFN is commonly used in blogs, and particularly in "blogroll" plug-ins such as those offered by WordPress.[1] Consider the following HTML content, shown in Example 2-1, that might be present in a blogroll.

Example 2-1. Example XFN markup

```
<div>
    <a href="http://example.org/matthew" rel="me">Matthew</a>
    <a href="http://example.com/users/jc" rel="friend met">J.C.</a>
    <a href="http://example.com/users/abe" rel="friend met co-worker">Abe</a>
    <a href="http://example.net/~baseeret" rel="spouse met">Baseeret</a>
    <a href="http://example.net/~lindsaybelle" rel="child met">Lindsay Belle</a>
</div>
```

From reading the content in the `rel` tags, it's hopefully pretty obvious what the relationships are between the various people. Namely, some guy named Matthew has a couple of friends, a spouse, and a child. He works with one of these friends and has met everyone in "real life" (which wouldn't be the case for a strictly online associate). Apart from using a well-defined vocabulary (*http://gmpg.org/xfn/1*), that's about all there is to XFN. The good news is that it's deceptively simple, yet incredibly powerful when employed at a large enough scale because it is deliberately authored structured information. Unless you run across some content that's just drastically out of date— as in two best friends becoming archenemies but just forgot to update their blogrolls accordingly—XFN gives you a very accurate indicator as to how two people are connected. Given that most blogging platforms support XFN, there's quite a bit of information that can be discovered. The bad news is that XFN doesn't really tell you anything beyond those basics, so you have to use other sources of information and techniques to discover anything beyond conclusions, such as, "Matthew and Baseeret are married and have a child named Lindsay Belle." But you have to start somewhere, right?

Let's whip up a simple script for harvesting XFN data similar to the service offered by rubhub (*http://rubhub.com/*), a social search engine that crawls and indexes a large number of websites using XFN. You might also want to check out one of the many online XFN tools (*http://gmpg.org/xfn/creator*) if you want to explore the full specification before moving on to the next section.

A Breadth-First Crawl of XFN Data

Let's get social by mining some XFN data and building out a social graph from it. Given that XFN can be embedded into any conceivable web page, the bad news is that we're about to do some web scraping. The good news, however, is that it's probably the most trivial web scraping you'll ever do, and the `BeautifulSoup` package absolutely minimizes the burden. The code in Example 2-2 uses Ajaxian (*http://ajaxian.com*), a popular blog about modern-day web development, as the basis of the graph. Do yourself a favor and `easy_install BeautifulSoup` before trying to run it.

---

1. See *http://codex.wordpress.org/Links_Add_New_SubPanel* for an example of one popular plug-in.

Example 2-2. Scraping XFN content from a web page (microformats__xfn_scrape.py)

```
# -*- coding: utf-8 -*-

import sys
import urllib2
import HTMLParser
from BeautifulSoup import BeautifulSoup

# Try http://ajaxian.com/
URL = sys.argv[1]

XFN_TAGS = set([
    'colleague',
    'sweetheart',
    'parent',
    'co-resident',
    'co-worker',
    'muse',
    'neighbor',
    'sibling',
    'kin',
    'child',
    'date',
    'spouse',
    'me',
    'acquaintance',
    'met',
    'crush',
    'contact',
    'friend',
    ])

try:
    page = urllib2.urlopen(URL)
except urllib2.URLError:
    print 'Failed to fetch ' + item

try:
    soup = BeautifulSoup(page)
except HTMLParser.HTMLParseError:
    print 'Failed to parse ' + item

anchorTags = soup.findAll('a')

for a in anchorTags:
    if a.has_key('rel'):
        if len(set(a['rel'].split()) & XFN_TAGS) > 0:
            tags = a['rel'].split()
            print a.contents[0], a['href'], tags
```

As of Version 3.1.x, BeautifulSoup switched to using HTMLParser (*http://docs.python.org/library/htmlparser.html*) instead of the SGMLParser (*http://docs.python.org/library/sgmllib.html*), and as a result, a common complaint is that BeautifulSoup seems a little less robust than in the 3.0.x release branch. The author of BeautifulSoup recommends a number of options (*http://www.crummy.com/software/BeautifulSoup/3.1-problems.html*), with the most obvious choice being to simply use the 3.0.x version if 3.1.x isn't robust enough for your needs. Alternatively, you can catch the `HTMLParseError`, as shown in Example 2-2, and discard the content.

Running the code against a URL that includes XFN information returns the name, type of relationship, and a URL for each of a person's friends. Sample output follows:

```
Dion Almaer http://www.almaer.com/blog/ [u'me']
Ben Galbraith http://weblogs.java.net/blog/javaben/ [u'co-worker']
Rey Bango http://reybango.com/ [u'friend']
Michael Mahemoff http://softwareas.com/ [u'friend']
Chris Cornutt http://blog.phpdeveloper.org/ [u'friend']
Rob Sanheim http://www.robsanheim.com/ [u'friend']
Dietrich Kappe http://blogs.pathf.com/agileajax/ [u'friend']
Chris Heilmann http://wait-till-i.com/ [u'friend']
Brad Neuberg http://codinginparadise.org/about/ [u'friend']
```

Assuming that the URL for each friend includes XFN or other useful information, it's straightforward enough to follow the links and build out more social graph information in a systematic way. That approach is exactly what the next code example does: it builds out a graph in a breadth-first manner, which is to say that it does something like what is described in Example 2-3 in pseudocode.

Example 2-3. Pseudocode for a breadth-first search

```
Create an empty graph
Create an empty queue to keep track of nodes that need to be processed

Add the starting point to the graph as the root node
Add the root node to a queue for processing

Repeat until some maximum depth is reached or the queue is empty:
  Remove a node from the queue
  For each of the node's neighbors:
    If the neighbor hasn't already been processed:
      Add it to the queue
      Add it to the graph
      Create an edge in the graph that connects the node and its neighbor
```

Note that this approach to building out a graph has the advantage of naturally creating edges between nodes in both directions, if such edges exist, without any additional bookkeeping required. This is useful for social situations since it naturally lends itself to identifying mutual friends without any additional logic. The refinement of the code from Example 2-2 presented in Example 2-4 takes a breadth-first approach to building up a NetworkX graph by following hyperlinks if they appear to have XFN data encoded in them. Running the example code for even the shallow depth of two can return quite a large graph, depending on the popularity of XFN within the niche community of friends at hand, as can be seen by generating an image file of the graph and inspecting it or running various graph metrics on it (see Figure 2-1).

 Windows users may want to review "Visualizing Tweet Graphs" on page 14 for an explanation of why the workaround for nx.drawing.write_dot is necessary in Example 2-4.

Example 2-4. Using a breadth-first search to crawl XFN links (microformats__xfn_crawl.py)

```
# -*- coding: utf-8 -*-

import sys
import os
import urllib2
from BeautifulSoup import BeautifulSoup
import HTMLParser
import networkx as nx

ROOT_URL = sys.argv[1]

if len(sys.argv) > 2:
    MAX_DEPTH = int(sys.argv[2])
else:
    MAX_DEPTH = 1

XFN_TAGS = set([
    'colleague',
    'sweetheart',
    'parent',
    'co-resident',
    'co-worker',
    'muse',
    'neighbor',
    'sibling',
    'kin',
    'child',
    'date',
    'spouse',
    'me',
    'acquaintance',
    'met',
    'crush',
    'contact',
    'friend',
    ])

OUT = "graph.dot"
```

```
depth = 0

g = nx.DiGraph()

next_queue = [ROOT_URL]

while depth < MAX_DEPTH:

    depth += 1
    (queue, next_queue) = (next_queue, [])

    for item in queue:
        try:
            page = urllib2.urlopen(item)
        except urllib2.URLError:
            print 'Failed to fetch ' + item
            continue

        try:
            soup = BeautifulSoup(page)
        except HTMLParser.HTMLParseError:
            print 'Failed to parse ' + item
            continue

        anchorTags = soup.findAll('a')

        if not g.has_node(item):
            g.add_node(item)

        for a in anchorTags:
            if a.has_key('rel'):
                if len(set(a['rel'].split()) & XFN_TAGS) > 0:
                    friend_url = a['href']
                    g.add_edge(item, friend_url)
                    g[item][friend_url]['label'] = a['rel'].encode('utf-8')
                    g.node[friend_url]['label'] = a.contents[0].encode('utf-8')

                    next_queue.append(friend_url)

        # Further analysis of the graph could be accomplished here

if not os.path.isdir('out'):
    os.mkdir('out')

try:
    nx.drawing.write_dot(g, os.path.join('out', OUT))
except ImportError, e:

    # Help for Windows users:
    # Not a general purpose method, but representative of
    # the same output write_dot would provide for this graph
    # if installed and easy to implement
```

```
dot = []
for (n1, n2) in g.edges():
    dot.append('"%s" [label="%s"]' % (n2, g.node[n2]['label']))
    dot.append('"%s" -> "%s" [label="%s"]' % (n1, n2, g[n1][n2]['label']))

f = open(os.path.join('out', OUT), 'w')
f.write('''strict digraph {
%s
}''' % (';\n'.join(dot), ))
f.close()

# *nix users could produce an image file with a good layout
# as follows from a terminal:
# $ circo -Tpng -Ograph graph.dot
# Windows users could use the same options with circo.exe
# or use the GVedit desktop application
```

 The use of the attribute `label` for the nodes and edges in the `DiGraph` isn't arbitrary. Attributes included in nodes and edges are serialized into the DOT language, and Graphviz tools recognize `label` as a special attribute (*http://www.graphviz.org/doc/info/attrs.html#d:label*).

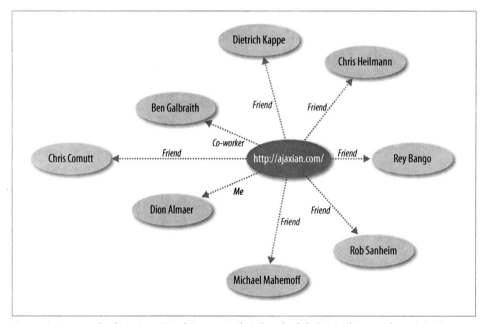

Figure 2-1. Digraph of Ajaxian XFN data—note that the edge label "Me" between http://ajaxian.com and Dion Almaer indicates that Dion owns the blog

Despite its simplicity, the graph is very interesting. It connects eight people, with a gentleman by the name of Dion Almaer being the common thread. Note, however, that crawling out one or more levels might introduce other nodes in the graph that are connected to everyone else. From the graph alone, it's unclear whether Dion might have a closer relationship with Ben Galbraith than the other folks because of the difference between "co-worker" and "friend" relationships, but we could nonetheless crawl Ben's XFN information, if he has provided any at the destination identified by his hyperlink, and search for other co-worker tags to build out a social network of who works with whom. See Chapter 6 for more on mining data as it relates to colleagues and coworkers.

Brief analysis of breadth-first techniques

We generally won't take quite this long of a pause to analyze the approach, but given that this example is the first *real* algorithm we've written, and that this isn't the last we'll see of it in this book, it's worthwhile to examine it more closely. In general, there are two criteria for examination that you should always consider for an algorithm: efficiency and effectiveness. Or, to put it another way: performance and quality.

Standard performance analysis of any algorithm generally involves examining its worst-case time and space complexity—in other words, the amount of time it would take the program to execute, and the amount of memory required for execution over a very large data set. The breadth-first approach we've taken is essentially a breadth-first search, except that we're not actually searching for anything in particular because there are no exit criteria beyond expanding the graph out either to a maximum depth or until we run out of nodes. If we were searching for something specific instead of just crawling links indefinitely, that would be considered an actual breadth-first search. In practice, however, almost all searches impose some kind of exit criteria because of the limitations of finite computing resources. Thus, a more common variation of a breadth-first search is called a *bounded breadth-first* search, which imposes a limit on the maximum depth of the search just as we do in this example.

For a breadth-first search (or breadth-first crawl), both the time and space complexity can be bounded in the worst case by b^d, where b is the branching factor of the graph and d is the depth. If you sketch out an example on paper and think about it, this analysis makes a lot of sense. If every node in a graph had five neighbors, and you only went out to a depth of one, you'd end up with six nodes in all: the root node and its five neighbors. If all five of those neighbors had five neighbors too, and you expanded out another level, you'd end up with 31 nodes in all: the root node, the root node's five neighbors, and five neighbors for each of the root node's neighbors. Such analysis may seem pedantic, but in the emerging era of *big data*, being able to perform at least a crude level of analysis based on what you know of the data set is more important than ever. Table 2-2 provides an overview of how b^d grows for a few sizes of b and d.

Table 2-2. Example branching factor calculations for graphs of varying depths

Branching factor	Nodes for depth = 1	Nodes for depth = 2	Nodes for depth = 3	Nodes for depth = 4	Nodes for depth = 5
2	3	7	15	31	63
3	4	13	40	121	364
4	5	21	85	341	1365
5	6	31	156	781	3906
6	7	43	259	1555	9331

While the previous comments pertain primarily to the theoretical bounds of the algorithm, one final consideration worth noting is the practical performance of the algorithm for a data set of a fixed size. Mild profiling of the code would reveal that it is primarily *I/O bound* from the standpoint that the vast majority of time is spent waiting for the urlopen method to return content to be processed. A later example, "Threading Together Conversations" on page 67, introduces and demonstrates the use of a *thread pool* to increase performance in exchange for a modicum of complexity.

A final consideration in analysis is the overall quality of the results. From the standpoint of quality analysis, basic visual inspection of the graph output reveals that there actually is a graph that connects people. Mission accomplished? Yes, but there's always room for improvement. One consideration is that slight variations in URLs result in multiple nodes potentially appearing in the graph for the same person. For example, if Matthew is referenced in one hyperlink with the URL *http://example.com/~matthew* but as *http://www.example.com/~matthew* in another URL, those two nodes will remain distinct in the graph even though they most likely point to the same resource on the Web. Fortunately, XFN defines a special rel="me" value that can be used for identity consolidation (*http://gmpg.org/xfn/and/#idconsolidation*). Google's Social Graph API (*http://code.google.com/apis/socialgraph/*) takes this very approach to connect a user's various profiles, and there exist many examples of services that use rel="me" to allow users to connect profiles across multiple external sites. Another (much lesser) issue in resolving URLs is the use or omission of a trailing slash at the end. Most well-designed sites will automatically redirect one to the other, so this detail is mostly a nonissue.

Fortunately, others have also recognized these kinds of problems and decided to do something about them. SocialGraph Node Mapper (*http://code.google.com/p/google -sgnodemapper/*) is an interesting open source project that standardizes URLs relative to trailing slashes, the presence of "www", etc., but it also recognizes that various social networking sites might expose different URLs that all link back to the same person. For example, *http://blog.example.com/matthew* and *http://status.example.com? user=matthew* might resolve to the same person for a given social networking site.

Geocoordinates: A Common Thread for Just About Anything

Omitting a discussion of microformats like geo and hRecipe as not being particularly useful for mining the social web would be a big mistake. Although it's certainly true that standalone geo data in no particular context isn't necessarily social, important but much less than obvious relationships often emerge from disparate data sets that are tied together with a common geographic context. Geo data is ubiquitous and plays a powerful part in too many social mashups to even name, because a particular point in space can be used as the glue to cluster people together. The divide between "real life" and life on the Web continues to close, and just about any kind of data becomes social the moment that it is tied to a particular individual in the real world. For example, there's an awful lot that you might be able to tell about a person based on where she lives, what kinds of food she prefers to cook at home, and even the specifics about ingredients in those recipes. This section works through some examples of finding, parsing, and visualizing geo and hRecipe data, since it'll likely be sooner rather than later that you'll think of something useful to do with it.

Wikipedia Articles + Google Maps = Road Trip?

One of the simplest and most widely used microformats that embeds geolocation information into web pages is appropriately called geo. The specification is inspired by a property with the same name from vCard (*http://www.ietf.org/rfc/rfc2426.txt*), which provides a means of specifying a location. There are two possible means of embedding a microformat with geo. The HTML snippet in Example 2-5 illustrates the two techniques for describing Franklin, the best small town in Tennessee.

Example 2-5. Sample geo markup

```
<!-- The multiple class approach -->
<span style="display: none" class="geo">
    <span class="latitude">36.166</span>
    <span class="longitude">-86.784</span>
</span>

<!-- When used as one class, the separator must be a semicolon -->
<span style="display: none" class="geo">36.166; -86.784</span>
```

As you can see, this microformat simply wraps latitude and longitude values in tags with corresponding class names, and packages them both inside a tag with a class of geo. A slew of popular sites—including Wikipedia, Yahoo! Local, and MapQuest Local, among many others—use geo and other microformats to expose structured data in their pages.

A common practice when using geo is to hide the information that's encoded from the user. There are two ways that you might do this with traditional CSS: style="display: none" and style="visibility: hidden". The former removes the element's placement on the page entirely so that the layout behaves as though it is not there at all. The latter hides the content but reserves the space it takes up on the page.

Example 2-6 illustrates a simple program that parses geo microformat data from a MapQuest Local page to show how you could extract coordinates from content implementing the geo microformat.

Example 2-6. Extracting geo data from MapQuest Local (microformats__mapquest_geo.py)

```
# -*- coding: utf-8 -*-

import sys
import urllib2
from BeautifulSoup import BeautifulSoup
import HTMLParser

# Pass in a URL such as http://local.mapquest.com/franklin-tn

url = sys.argv[1]

try:
    page = urllib2.urlopen(url)
except urllib2.URLError, e:
    print 'Failed to fetch ' + url
    raise e
    exit()

try:
    soup = BeautifulSoup(page)
except HTMLParser.HTMLParseError:
    print 'Failed to parse ' + url
    exit()

geoTag = soup.find(True, 'geo')

if geoTag and len(geoTag) > 1:
    lat = geoTag.find(True, 'latitude').string
    lon = geoTag.find(True, 'longitude').string
    print 'Location is at', lat, lon
elif geoTag and len(geoTag) == 1:
    (lat, lon) = geoTag.string.split(';')
    (lat, lon) = (lat.strip(), lon.strip())
    print 'Location is at', lat, lon
else:
    print 'No location found'
```

The implications of using microformats are subtle yet somewhat profound: while a human might be reading an article about a place like Franklin, TN and just intuitively know that a dot on a map on the page denotes the town's location, a robot would not be able to come to the same conclusion very easily without specialized logic that targets various pattern-matching possibilities. Such page scraping is a messy proposition, and typically just when you think you have all of the possibilities figured out, you find that you've missed one. Embedding proper semantics into the page that effectively tag unstructured data in a way that even our pal Robby the Robot (*http://en.wikipedia.org/ wiki/Robby_the_Robot*) could understand removes ambiguity and lowers the bar for crawlers and developers such as yourself. It's a win-win situation for the producer and the consumer, and hopefully the net effect is increased innovation for everyone.

Plotting geo data via microform.at and Google Maps

The moment you find a web page with interesting geo data embedded, the first thing you'll want to do is visualize it. For example, consider the "List of National Parks of the United States" (*http://en.wikipedia.org/wiki/List_of_U.S._national_parks*) Wikipedia article. It displays a nice tabular view of the national parks and marks them up with geo formatting, but wouldn't it be nice to quickly load the data into an interactive tool for visual inspection? Well, microform.at (*http://microform.at*) is a terrific little web service that extracts several types of microformats from a given URL and passes them back in a variety of useful formats. It exposes a variety of options for detecting and interacting with microformat data in web pages, as shown in Figure 2-2.

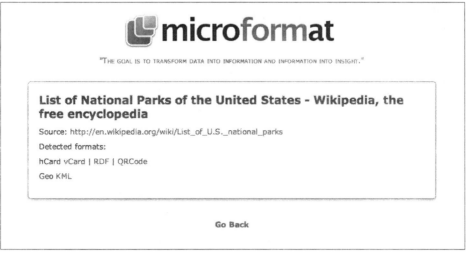

Figure 2-2. http://microform.at's results for the Wikipedia article entitled "List of National Parks of the United States"

If given the option, KML (*http://code.google.com/apis/kml/documentation/*) (Keyhole Markup Language) output is perhaps the easiest way to visualize geo data. You can either download Google Earth and load the KML file locally, or type a URL containing KML data directly into the Google Maps search bar to bring it up without any additional effort required. In the results displayed for microform.at, clicking on the "KML" link triggers a file download that you can use in Google Earth, but you can copy it to the clipboard via a right-click and pass that to Google Maps. Figure 2-3 displays the Google Maps visualization for *http://microform.at/?type=geo&url=http%3A%2F%2Fen.wikipe dia.org%2Fwiki%2FList_of_U.S._national_parks*—the KML results for the aforementioned Wikipedia article, which is just the base URL *http://microform.at* with `type` and `url` query string parameters.

Figure 2-3. Google Maps results that display all of the national parks in the United States when passed KML results from microform.at

The ability to start with a Wikipedia article containing semantic markup such as geo data and trivially visualize it is a powerful analytical capability because it delivers insight quickly for so little effort. Browser extensions such as the Firefox Operator add-on (*https://addons.mozilla.org/en-US/firefox/addon/4106/*) aim to minimize the effort even further. Only so much can be said in one chapter, but a neat way to spend an hour or so would be to mash up the national park data from this section with contact information from your LinkedIn professional network to discover how you might be able to have a little bit more fun on your next (possibly contrived) business trip. (See "Geographically Clustering Your Network" on page 193 for an example of how to harvest and analyze geo data by applying the k-means technique for finding clusters and computing centroids for those clusters.)

Slicing and Dicing Recipes (for the Health of It)

Since Google's Rich Snippets initiative took off, there's been an ever-increasing awareness of microformats, and many of the most popular foodie websites have made solid progress in exposing recipes and reviews with hRecipe and hReview. Consider the potential for a fictitious online dating service that crawls blogs and other social hubs, attempting to pair people together for dinner dates. One could reasonably expect that having access to enough geo and hRecipe information linked to specific people would make a profound difference in the "success rate" of first dates. People could be paired according to two criteria: how close they live to one another and what kinds of foods they eat. For example, you might expect a dinner date between two individuals who prefer to cook vegetarian meals with organic ingredients to go a lot better than a date between a BBQ-lover and a vegan. Dining preferences and whether specific types of allergens or organic ingredients are used could be useful clues to power the right business idea. While we won't be trying to launch a new online data service, we'll get the ball rolling in case you decide to take this idea and run with it.

The Food Network (*http://www.foodnetwork.com*) is one of many online sites that's really embracing microformat initiatives for the betterment of the entire Web, exposing recipe information in the hRecipe microformat and using the hReview microformat for reviews of the recipes.[2] This section demonstrates how search engines (or you) might parse out the structured data from recipes and reviews contained in Food Network web pages for indexing or analyzing. Although we won't do any analysis of the free text in the recipes or reviews, or permanently store the information extracted, later chapters will demonstrate how to do these things if you're interested. In particular, Chapter 3 introduces CouchDB, a great way to store *and share* data (and analysis) you extract from microformat-powered web content, and Chapter 7 introduces some fundamentals for natural language processing (NLP) that you can use to gain a deeper understanding

---

2. In mid 2010, The Food Network implemented hReview in much the same fashion as Yelp, which is introduced in the next section; however, as of early January 2011, Food Network's implementation changed to include only hreview-aggregate (*http://microformats.org/wiki/hreview-aggregate*).

of the content in the reviews. (Coincidentally, it turns out that a recipe even shows up in that chapter.)

An adaptation of Example 2-6 that parses out hRecipe-formatted data is shown in Example 2-7.

Example 2-7. Parsing hRecipe data for a Pad Thai recipe (microformats__foodnetwork_hrecipe.py)

```
# -*- coding: utf-8 -*-

import sys
import urllib2
import json
import HTMLParser
import BeautifulSoup

# Pass in a URL such as
# http://www.foodnetwork.com/recipes/alton-brown/pad-thai-recipe/index.html

url = sys.argv[1]

# Parse out some of the pertinent information for a recipe
# See http://microformats.org/wiki/hrecipe


def parse_hrecipe(url):
    try:
        page = urllib2.urlopen(url)
    except urllib2.URLError, e:
        print 'Failed to fetch ' + url
        raise e

    try:
        soup = BeautifulSoup.BeautifulSoup(page)
    except HTMLParser.HTMLParseError, e:
        print 'Failed to parse ' + url
        raise e

    hrecipe = soup.find(True, 'hrecipe')

    if hrecipe and len(hrecipe) > 1:
        fn = hrecipe.find(True, 'fn').string
        author = hrecipe.find(True, 'author').find(text=True)
        ingredients = [i.string
                            for i in hrecipe.findAll(True, 'ingredient')
                                if i.string is not None]

        instructions = []
        for i in hrecipe.find(True, 'instructions'):
            if type(i) == BeautifulSoup.Tag:
                s = ''.join(i.findAll(text=True)).strip()
            elif type(i) == BeautifulSoup.NavigableString:
                s = i.string.strip()
            else:
                continue
```

```
            if s != '':
                instructions += [s]

        return {
            'name': fn,
            'author': author,
            'ingredients': ingredients,
            'instructions': instructions,
            }
    else:
        return {}


recipe = parse_hrecipe(url)
print json.dumps(recipe, indent=4)
```

For a sample URL such as Alton Brown's acclaimed Pad Thai recipe, you should get the results shown in Example 2-8.

Example 2-8. Parsed results for the Pad Thai recipe from Example 2-7

```
{
    "instructions": [
        "Place the tamarind paste in the boiling water and set aside ...",
        "Combine the fish sauce, palm sugar, and rice wine vinegar in ...",
        "Place the rice stick noodles in a mixing bowl and cover with ...",
        "Press the tamarind paste through a fine mesh strainer and add ...",
        "Place a wok over high heat. Once hot, add 1 tablespoon of the ...",
        "If necessary, add some more peanut oil to the pan and heat until ..."
    ],
    "ingredients": [
        "1-ounce tamarind paste",
        "3/4 cup boiling water",
        "2 tablespoons fish sauce",
        "2 tablespoons palm sugar",
        "1 tablespoon rice wine vinegar",
        "4 ounces rice stick noodles",
        "6 ounces Marinated Tofu, recipe follows",
        "1 to 2 tablespoons peanut oil",
        "1 cup chopped scallions, divided",
        "2 teaspoons minced garlic",
        "2 whole eggs, beaten",
        "2 teaspoons salted cabbage",
        "1 tablespoon dried shrimp",
        "3 ounces bean sprouts, divided",
        "1/2 cup roasted salted peanuts, chopped, divided",
        "Freshly ground dried red chile peppers, to taste",
        "1 lime, cut into wedges"
    ],
    "name": "Pad Thai",
    "author": "Recipe courtesy Alton Brown, 2005"
}
```

Although it's not really a form of social analysis, it could be interesting to analyze variations of the same recipe and see whether there are any correlations between the appearance or lack of certain ingredients and ratings/reviews for the recipes. For example, you might try to pull down a few different Pad Thai recipes and determine which ingredients are common to all recipes and which are less common.

Collecting Restaurant Reviews

This section concludes our studies of microformats—and Thai food—by briefly introducing hReview. Yelp is a popular service that implements hReview so that the ratings customers have left for restaurants can be exposed. Example 2-9 demonstrates how to extract hReview information as implemented by Yelp. A sample URL you might try is in the sample code and represents a Thai restaurant you definitely don't want to miss if you ever have the opportunity to visit it.

Although the spec is pretty stable, hReview implementations seem to vary and include arbitrary deviations. In particular, Example 2-9 does not parse the **reviewer** as an hCard because Yelp's implementation did not include it as such.

Example 2-9. Parsing hReview data for a Pad Thai recipe (microformats__yelp_hreview.py)

```
# -*- coding: utf-8 -*-

import sys
import re
import urllib2
import json
import HTMLParser
from BeautifulSoup import BeautifulSoup

# Pass in a URL that contains hReview info such as
# http://www.yelp.com/biz/bangkok-golden-fort-washington-2

url = sys.argv[1]

# Parse out some of the pertinent information for a Yelp review
# Unfortunately, the quality of hReview implementations varies
# widely so your mileage may vary. This code is *not* a spec
# parser by any stretch. See http://microformats.org/wiki/hreview

def parse_hreviews(url):
    try:
        page = urllib2.urlopen(url)
    except urllib2.URLError, e:
        print 'Failed to fetch ' + url
        raise e

    try:
        soup = BeautifulSoup(page)
```

```
    except HTMLParser.HTMLParseError, e:
        print 'Failed to parse ' + url
        raise e

    hreviews = soup.findAll(True, 'hreview')

    all_hreviews = []
    for hreview in hreviews:
        if hreview and len(hreview) > 1:

            # As of 1 Jan 2010, Yelp does not implement reviewer as an hCard,
            # per the spec

            reviewer = hreview.find(True, 'reviewer').text

            dtreviewed = hreview.find(True, 'dtreviewed').text
            rating = hreview.find(True, 'rating').find(True, 'value-title')['title']
            description = hreview.find(True, 'description').text
            item = hreview.find(True, 'item').text

            all_hreviews.append({
                'reviewer': reviewer,
                'dtreviewed': dtreviewed,
                'rating': rating,
                'description': description,
                })
    return all_hreviews

reviews = parse_hreviews(url)

# Do something interesting like plot out reviews over time
# or mine the text in the descriptions...

print json.dumps(reviews, indent=4)
```

Truncated sample results for Example 2-9 are shown in Example 2-10. They include the reviewer, which is parsed out of the hCard microformatted nodes, as its own object.

Example 2-10. Sample hReview results corresponding to Example 2-9

```
[
    {
        "reviewer": "Nick L.",
        "description": "Probably the best Thai food in the metro area...",
        "dtreviewed": "4/27/2009",
        "rating": "5"
    },

    ...truncated...

]
```

Unfortunately, neither Yelp, nor the Food Network, nor anyone else provides specific enough information to tie reviewers together in very meaningful ways, but hopefully that will change soon, opening up additional possibilities for the social web. In the meantime, you might make the most with the data you have available and plot out the average rating for a restaurant over time to see if it has improved or declined. Another idea might be to mine the `description` fields in the text. See Chapters 7 and 8 for some fodder on how that might work.

 For brevity, the grunt work in massaging the JSON data into a single list of output and loading it into a spreadsheet isn't shown here, but a spreadsheet of the data is available for download if you're feeling especially lazy.

There's no limit to the innovation that can happen when you combine geeks and food data, as evidenced by the popularity of the recently published *Cooking for Geeks* (*http://www.cookingforgeeks.com*), also from O'Reilly. As the capabilities of food sites evolve to provide additional APIs, so will the innovations that we see in this space.

Summary

If you remember nothing else from this chapter, remember that microformats are a way of decorating markup to expose specific types of structured information such as recipes, contact information, and human relationships. Microformats have vast potential because they allow us to take existing content and make the data that's in it explicit and conformant to a predictable standard. Expect to see significant growth and interest in microformats over the months ahead. You'll also see amazing innovations based on HTML5's microdata (*http://www.w3.org/TR/html5/microdata.html*) as HTML5 gains market share. If you find yourself with copious free time, be sure to check out Google's Social Graph API (*http://code.google.com/apis/socialgraph/*). This is not to be confused with Facebook's RDFa-based (*http://en.wikipedia.org/wiki/RDFa*) Open Graph protocol (*http://developers.facebook.com/docs/opengraph*) or the related Graph API (*http://developers.facebook.com/docs/api*) that's covered in Chapter 9, which includes an index of XFN (*http://gmpg.org/xfn/*), FOAF (*http://www.foaf-project.org*), and other publicly declared connections.

## CHAPTER 3

Mailboxes: Oldies but Goodies

This chapter introduces some fundamental tools and techniques for analyzing your mail—a classic data staple of the Internet that despite all of the advances in social networking will still be around for ages to come—to answer questions such as:

- Who sends out the most mail?
- Is there a particular time of the day (or day of the week) when the sender is most likely to get a response to a question?
- Which people send the most messages among one another?
- What are the subjects of the liveliest discussion threads?

Although social media sites are racking up petabytes of near-real-time social data, there is still the significant drawback that, unlike email, social networking data is centrally managed by a service provider who gets to create the rules about exactly how you can access it and what you can and can't do with it.[1] Mail data, on the other hand, is largely decentralized and is scattered across the Web in the form of rich mailing list discussions about a litany of interesting topics. Although it's true that service providers such as Google and Yahoo! restrict your use of mailing list data if you retrieve it using their services, there are slightly less formidable ways to mine the content that have a higher probability of success: you can easily collect data yourself by subscribing to a list and waiting for the box to start filling up, ask the list owner to provide you with an archive, etc. Another interesting consideration is that unlike social media sites, enterprises generally have full control of their mailboxes and may want to perform aggregate analyses and identify certain kinds of trends.

As you might have guessed, it's not always easy (if possible at all) to find realistic social data sets for purposes of illustration, but fortunately, this chapter has some of the most realistic data imaginable: the public Enron data set (*http://www.cs.cmu.edu/~enron/*).

---

1. Quite understandably, nobody has had a good enough reason (yet) to be the first to defend against multimillion-dollar litigation cases to find out whether the terms of use imposed by some social media sites are even enforceable. Hence, the status quo (to date) has been to play by the rules and back down when approached about possible infringements.

mbox: The Quick and Dirty on Unix Mailboxes

In case you haven't come across an mbox file before, it's basically just a large text file of concatenated mail messages that are easily accessible by text-based tools. The beginning of each message is signaled by a special *From_* line formatted to the pattern `"From user@example.com Fri Dec 25 00:06:42 2009"`, where the date/time stamp is asctime (*http://opengroup.org/onlinepubs/007908775/xsh/asctime.html*), a standardized fixed-width representation of a timestamp.

 The mbox format is very common, and most mail clients provide an "export" or "save as" option to export data to this format regardless of the underlying implementation.

In an mbox file, the boundary between messages is determined by a *From_* line preceded (except for the first occurrence) by exactly two new lines. Example 3-1 is a small slice from a fictitious mbox containing two messages.

Example 3-1. A slice of a sample mbox file

```
From santa@northpole.example.org Fri Dec 25 00:06:42 2009
Message-ID: <16159836.1075855377439@mail.northpole.example.org>
References: <88364590.8837464573838@mail.northpole.example.org>
In-Reply-To: <194756537.0293874783209@mail.northpole.example.org>
Date: Fri, 25 Dec 2001 00:06:42 -0000 (GMT)
From: St. Nick <santa@northpole.example.org>
To: rudolph@northpole.example.org
Subject: RE: FWD: Tonight
Mime-Version: 1.0
Content-Type: text/plain; charset=us-ascii
Content-Transfer-Encoding: 7bit

Sounds good. See you at the usual location.

Thanks,
-S


  -----Original Message-----
From:   Rudolph
Sent:   Friday, December 25, 2009 12:04 AM
To: Claus, Santa
Subject:   FWD:  Tonight

Santa -

Running a bit late. Will come grab you shortly. Standby.

Rudy

Begin forwarded message:
```

```
> Last batch of toys was just loaded onto sleigh.
>
> Please proceed per the norm.
>
> Regards,
> Buddy
>
> --
> Buddy the Elf
> Chief Elf
> Workshop Operations
> North Pole
> buddy.the.elf@northpole.example.org

From buddy.the.elf@northpole.example.org Fri Dec 25 00:03:34 2009
Message-ID: <88364590.8837464573838@mail.northpole.example.org>
Date: Fri, 25 Dec 2001 00:03:34 -0000 (GMT)
From: Buddy <buddy.the.elf@northpole.example.org>
To: workshop@northpole.example.org
Subject: Tonight
Mime-Version: 1.0
Content-Type: text/plain; charset=us-ascii
Content-Transfer-Encoding: 7bit

Last batch of toys was just loaded onto sleigh.

Please proceed per the norm.

Regards,
Buddy


--
Buddy the Elf
Chief Elf
Workshop Operations
North Pole
buddy.the.elf@northpole.example.org
```

In Example 3-1 we see two messages, although there is evidence of at least one other message that might exist in the mbox. Chronologically, the first message is authored by a fellow named Buddy and was sent out to *workshop@northpole.example.org* to announce that the toys had just been loaded. The other message in the mbox is a reply from Santa to Rudolph. Not shown in the sample mbox is an intermediate message in which Rudolph forwarded Buddy's message to Santa with the note about how he is running late. Although we could infer these things by reading the text of the messages themselves, we also have important clues by way of the Message-ID, References, and In-Reply-To headers. These headers are pretty intuitive and provide the basis for algorithms that display threaded discussions and things of that nature. We'll look at a well-known algorithm that uses these fields to thread messages a bit later, but the gist is that each message has a unique message ID, contains a reference to the exact message that is being replied to in the case of it being a reply, and can reference multiple other messages in the reply chain, which are part of the larger discussion thread at hand.

Beyond using some Python modules to do the dirty work for us, we won't journey into discussions concerning the nuances of email messages such as multipart content, MIME (*http://en.wikipedia.org/wiki/ MIME*), 7-bit content transfer encoding, etc. You won't have to look very hard to find a number of excellent references that cover these topics in depth if you're interested in taking a closer look.

These headers are vitally important. Even with this simple example, you can already see how things can get messy when you're parsing the actual body of a message: Rudolph's client quoted forwarded content with > characters, while the mail client Santa used to reply apparently didn't quote anything, but instead included a human-readable message header. Trying to parse out the exact flow of a conversation from mailbox data can be a very tricky business, if not completely impossible, because of the ambiguity involved. Most mail clients have an option to display extended mail headers beyond the ones you normally see, if you're interested in a technique a little more accessible than digging into raw storage when you want to view this kind of information. Example 3-2 illustrates the message flow from Example 3-1, and Figure 3-1 shows sample headers as displayed by Apple Mail.

From:	Matthew Russell
Subject:	**Message to self**
Date:	September 28, 2010 9:31:01 PM CDT
To:	Matthew Russell
Return-Path:	<matthew@zaffra.com>
X-Spam-Checker-Version:	SpamAssassin 3.1.9 (2007-02-13) on mail2.webfaction.com
X-Spam-Level:	
X-Spam-Status:	No, score=-2.6 required=5.0 tests=BAYES_00 autolearn=ham version=3.1.9
Received:	from smtp.webfaction.com (mail6.webfaction.com [74.55.86.74]) by mail2.webfaction.com (8.13.1/8.13.3) with ESMTP id o8T2V254026699 for <matthew@zaffra.com>; Tue, 28 Sep 2010 21:31:02 -0500
Received:	from [192.168.1.67] (99-0-32-163.lightspeed.nsvltn.sbcglobal.net [99.0.32.163]) by smtp.webfaction.com (Postfix) with ESMTP id 9CE61324B7D for <matthew@zaffra.com>; Tue, 28 Sep 2010 21:31:02 -0500 (CDT)
Message-Id:	<D9A2277D-A6A1-4CD2-B891-C0A1E4C6C6CD@zaffra.com>
Content-Type:	text/plain; charset=US-ASCII; format=flowed
Content-Transfer-Encoding:	7bit
Mime-Version:	1.0 (Apple Message framework v936)
X-Mailer:	Apple Mail (2.936)

Hello Matthew!

Regards - Matthew

---
http://www.linkedin.com/in/ptwobrussell

Figure 3-1. Most mail clients allow you to view the extended headers through an options menu

Example 3-2. Message flow from Example 3-1

```
Fri, 25 Dec 2001 00:03:34 -0000 (GMT) - Buddy sends a message to the workshop
Friday, December 25, 2009 12:04 AM   - Rudolph forwards Buddy's message to Santa
                                       with an additional note
Fri, 25 Dec 2001 00:06:42 -0000 (GMT) - Santa replies to Rudolph
```

Lucky for us, there's a lot you can do without having to essentially reimplement a mail client. Besides, if all you wanted to do was browse the mailbox, you'd simply import it into a mail client and browse away, right? Although it's a rote exercise, it's worth taking a moment to explore whether your mail client has an option to import/export data in the mbox format so that you can use the tools in this chapter to slice and dice it.

Python offers some basic tools for parsing mbox data, and the script in Example 3-3 introduces a basic technique for converting mbox data to an array of JSON objects.

 Note that Example 3-3 includes the decode('utf-8', 'ignore') function in several places. When working with text-based data such as email or web pages, it's not at all uncommon to run into the infamous Unico deDecodeError because of funky character encodings, and it's not always obvious what's going on or how to fix the problem. The short answer is that you can run the decode function on any string value and pass it a second argument that specifies what to do in the event of a UnicodeDe codeError. The default value is 'strict', which results in the exception being raised, but you can use 'ignore' or 'replace' instead, depending on your needs.

Example 3-3. Converting an mbox to a more convenient JSON structure (mailboxes__jsonify_mbox.py)

```python
# -*- coding: utf-8 -*-

import sys
import mailbox
import email
import quopri
from BeautifulSoup import BeautifulSoup

try:
    import jsonlib2 as json  # much faster then Python 2.6.x's stdlib
except ImportError:
    import json

MBOX = sys.argv[1]

def cleanContent(msg):

    # Decode message from "quoted printable" format

    msg = quopri.decodestring(msg)
```

```
    # Strip out HTML tags, if any are present

    soup = BeautifulSoup(msg)
    return ''.join(soup.findAll(text=True))


def jsonifyMessage(msg):
    json_msg = {'parts': []}
    for (k, v) in msg.items():
        json_msg[k] = v.decode('utf-8', 'ignore')

    # The To, CC, and Bcc fields, if present, could have multiple items
    # Note that not all of these fields are necessarily defined

    for k in ['To', 'Cc', 'Bcc']:
        if not json_msg.get(k):
            continue
        json_msg[k] = json_msg[k].replace('\n', '').replace('\t', '').replace('\r'
                , '').replace(' ', '').decode('utf-8', 'ignore').split(',')

    try:
        for part in msg.walk():
            json_part = {}
            if part.get_content_maintype() == 'multipart':
                continue
            json_part['contentType'] = part.get_content_type()
            content = part.get_payload(decode=False).decode('utf-8', 'ignore')
            json_part['content'] = cleanContent(content)

            json_msg['parts'].append(json_part)
    except Exception, e:
        sys.stderr.write('Skipping message - error encountered (%s)' % (str(e), ))
    finally:
        return json_msg

# Note: opening in binary mode is recommended
mbox = mailbox.UnixMailbox(open(MBOX, 'rb'), email.message_from_file)
json_msgs = []
while 1:
    msg = mbox.next()
    if msg is None:
        break
    json_msgs.append(jsonifyMessage(msg))

print json.dumps(json_msgs, indent=4)
```

 As of Python 2.6.x, third-party C-based modules such as jsonlib2 (available via easy_install) are significantly faster than the standard library's module, but Python 2.7 ships with an update (*http://bugs .python.org/issue4136*) that's on par with modules such as jsonlib2. For the purposes of illustration, the difference between using the standard library versus jsonlib2 for reasonably large JSON structures (north of 100 MB) can be on the order of tens of seconds.

This short script does a pretty decent job of parsing out the most pertinent information from an email and builds out a portable JSON object. There's more that we could do, but it addresses some of the most common issues, including a primitive mechanism for decoding quoted-printable text and stripping out any HTML tags. The quopri module is used to handle the quoted-printable format, an encoding that is used to transfer 8-bit content over a 7-bit channel.[2] Abbreviated sample output from Example 3-3 follows in Example 3-4.

Example 3-4. Sample JSON output as produced by Example 3-3 from the sample mbox in Example 3-1

```
[
    {
        "From": "St. Nick <santa@northpole.example.org>",
        "Content-Transfer-Encoding": "7bit",
        "To": [
            "rudolph@northpole.example.org"
        ],
        "parts": [
            {
                "content": "Sounds good. See you at the usual location.\n\nThanks,...",
                "contentType": "text/plain"
            }
        ],
        "References": "<88364590.8837464573838@mail.northpole.example.org>",
        "Mime-Version": "1.0",
        "In-Reply-To": "<194756537.0293874783209@mail.northpole.example.org>",
        "Date": "Fri, 25 Dec 2001 00:06:42 -0000 (GMT)",
        "Message-ID": "<16159836.1075855377439@mail.northpole.example.org>",
        "Content-Type": "text/plain; charset=us-ascii",
        "Subject": "RE: FWD: Tonight"
    },
    {
        "From": "Buddy <buddy.the.elf@northpole.example.org>",
        "Content-Transfer-Encoding": "7bit",
        "To": [
            "workshop@northpole.example.org"
        ],
        "parts": [
            {
                "content": "Last batch of toys was just loaded onto sleigh. \n\n...",
                "contentType": "text/plain"
            }
        ],
        "Mime-Version": "1.0",
        "Date": "Fri, 25 Dec 2001 00:03:34 -0000 (GMT)",
        "Message-ID": "<88364590.8837464573838@mail.northpole.example.org>",
        "Content-Type": "text/plain; charset=us-ascii",
        "Subject": "Tonight"
    }
]
```

2. See *http://en.wikipedia.org/wiki/Quoted-printable* for an overview, or RFC 2045 (*http://tools.ietf.org/html/rfc2045*) if you are interested in the nuts and bolts.

With your newly found skills to parse mail data into an accessible format, the urge to start analyzing it is only natural. The remainder of this chapter will use the publicly available Enron mail data, available as mbox downloads. The *enron.mbox.gz* file is an mbox constructed from messages appearing in "inbox" folders from the original Enron corpus, while the *enron.mbox.json.gz* file is that same data converted to JSON with the script shown in Example 3-3. Although not shown as an example, you can download the script that performed the conversion of raw Enron data to the mbox format with the *mailboxes__convert_enron_inbox_to_mbox.py* script (*http://github.com/ptwobrus sell/Mining-the-Social-Web/blob/master/python_code/mailboxes__convert_enron_in box_to_mbox.py*). Note that if you search online, you'll find that the closest thing to the official Enron data available at *http://www.cs.cmu.edu/~enron/* is available in a non-standard format that's a little more suited to research and includes calendaring information, notes, etc. The script that was used to convert the portions of this data set explicitly marked as "Inbox data" into the mbox format is available at *http://github.com/ ptwobrussell/Mining-the-Social-Web/blob/master/python_code/mailboxes__convert_en ron_inbox_to_mbox.py*. The remainder of this chapter assumes that you are using the mbox data that is provided as downloads.

mbox + CouchDB = Relaxed Email Analysis

Using the right tool for the job can significantly streamline the effort involved in analyzing data. While the most obvious approach for analyzing the structured data might be to spend some extra time creating an a priori schema, importing data into it, modifying the schema because there's something we forgot about, and then repeating the process yet a few more times, this surely wouldn't be a very relaxing[3] thing to do. Given the very natural mapping between the document-centric nature of an email message and a JSON data structure, we'll import our mbox data into CouchDB (*http://couchdb .apache.org*), a document-oriented database that provides map/reduce capabilities that are quite nice for building up indexes on the data and performing an aggregate frequency analysis that answers questions such as, "How many messages were sent by so-and-so?" or "How many messages were sent out on such-and-such a date?"

 A full-blown discussion about CouchDB, where it fits into the overall data storage landscape, and many of its other unique capabilities outside the ones most germane to basic analysis is outside the scope of this book. However, it should be straightforward enough to follow along with this section even if you've never heard of CouchDB before.

---

3. CouchDB folks tend to overuse the word "relax," and this discussion follows suit in an effort to be as authentic as possible.

Another nice benefit of using CouchDB for the task of document analysis is that it provides an entirely REST-based interface (*http://en.wikipedia.org/wiki/Representational_State_Transfer*) that you can integrate into any web-based architecture, as well as trivial-to-use replication capabilities that are handy if you'd like to allow others to clone your databases (and analyses).

RESTful Web Services

REST (*http://en.wikipedia.org/wiki/Representational_State_Transfer*) (REpresentational State Transfer) is an architectural style that was canonized as a PhD dissertation by Roy Fielding (*http://www.ics.uci.edu/~taylor/documents/2002-REST-TOIT.pdf*), but you don't actually have to read the dissertation to get the gist of it. While entire books have been written about REST, understanding a few key principles should suffice for our purposes: clients and servers should engage in stateless communication, and URIs should describe resources that can be acted upon by standard HTTP verbs such as GET, PUT, POST, HEAD, and DELETE. For example, the hierarchical URL *http://example.com/blog* might describe a "blog" resource. A GET on that resource would fetch it, whereas a PUT on the context /blog/foo might create a new blog for user "foo." A DELETE on the context /blog/foo would delete the blog, and a POST /blog/foo might append a new blog post to foo's blog. The book *RESTful Web Services* (*http://oreilly.com/catalog/9780596529260*) (O'Reilly) is a great resource to have on hand if you'd like to take a more serious look at REST and want to see lots of practical examples for handling not-so-obvious situations.

The remainder of this section assumes that you're able to locate and install a CouchDB binary for your system, or compile and install it from source if that's the way you roll. You might want to check out CouchOne (*http://www.couchone.com*), a company staffed by the creator of and primary committers for CouchDB, which provides binary downloads for most platforms and also offers some free CouchDB hosting options that you might find useful. Cloudant (*https://cloudant.com*) is another online hosting option you might want to consider.

As you're getting warmed up, you might just think of CouchDB as a key-value store where keys are arbitrary identifiers and values are JSON-based documents of your own devising. Figure 3-2 illustrates a collection of documents, as well as individual document in the collection via Futon, CouchDB's web-based administrative interface. You can access Futon on your local installation at *http://localhost:5984/_utils/*.

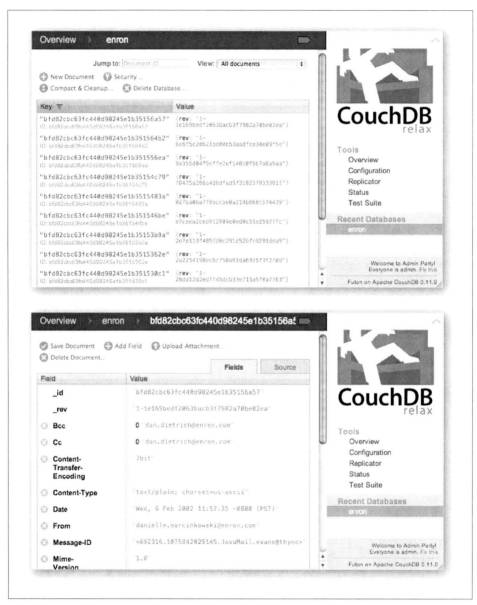

Figure 3-2. An aggregate view of the Enron database and one of its individual documents

Once CouchDB is installed, the other administrative task you'll need to perform is installing the Python client module couchdb via the usual easy_install couchdb approach. You can read more about couchdb via pydoc or online at *http://packages.python .org/CouchDB/*. With CouchDB and a Python client now installed, it's time to relax and lay down some code to ingest our JSONified mbox data—but do feel free to take a few minutes to play around in Futon if this is your first encounter with CouchDB. If playing things by ear doesn't make you feel very relaxed, you should take a brief time-out to skim the first few chapters of *CouchDB: The Definitive Guide* (O'Reilly), which is available online at *http://books.couchdb.org/relax*.

Bulk Loading Documents into CouchDB

Running the script from Example 3-3 on the uncompressed *enron.mbox* file and redirecting the output to a file yields a fairly large JSON structure (approaching 200 MB). The script provided in Example 3-5 demonstrates how to load the data as-is into CouchDB using `couchdb-python`, which you should have already installed via `easy_install couchdb`. (You have to admit that the code does look pretty relaxing compared to the alternative gobs that would be required to load a relational schema.) Note that it may take a couple of minutes for the script to complete if you are using typical consumer hardware such as a laptop computer.[4] At first, a couple of minutes might seem a bit slow, but when you consider that the JSON structure contains more than 40,000 objects that get written out as CouchDB documents, that's north of 300 document transactions per second, which is actually quite reasonable for performance on an ordinary laptop. Using a performance-monitoring utility such as `top` on a *nix system or the Task Manager on Windows should reveal that one core (*http://en.wiki pedia.org/wiki/Multi-core_processor*) of your CPU is being pegged out, which would indicate maximum throughput. During development, it's a good idea to work with a smaller set of documents than your full data set. You can easily slice out a dozen or so of the JSONified Enron messages to follow along with the examples in this chapter.

 Although Erlang, CouchDB's underlying programming language, is well known for being a language that supports high concurrency, this doesn't mean that CouchDB or any other application platform built using Erlang can necessarily keep all of the cores across all available CPUs running hot. For example, in CouchDB, write operations to a database are append-only operations that are serialized to the B-Tree on disk, and even large numbers of batch writes cannot easily be spread out across more than one core. In that regard, there is a one-to-one mapping between databases and cores for write operations. However, you could perform batch writes to multiple databases at the same time and maximize throughput across more than one core.

---

4. For the purposes of comparison, it takes about two minutes to execute Example 3-5 on a MacBook Pro 2.8GHz Core 2 Duo with CouchDB 0.11.0 installed using stock settings.

Example 3-5. A short script that demonstrates loading JSON data into CouchDB (mailboxes__load_json_mbox.py)

```
# -*- coding: utf-8 -*-

import sys
import os
import couchdb
try:
    import jsonlib2 as json
except ImportError:
    import json

JSON_MBOX = sys.argv[1]  # i.e. enron.mbox.json
DB = os.path.basename(JSON_MBOX).split('.')[0]

server = couchdb.Server('http://localhost:5984')
db = server.create(DB)
docs = json.loads(open(JSON_MBOX).read())
db.update(docs, all_or_nothing=True)
```

With the data loaded, it might be tempting to just sit back and relax for a while, but browsing through some of it with Futon begins to stir up some questions about the nature of who is communicating, how often, and when. Let's put CouchDB's map/reduce functionality to work so that we can answer some of these questions.

 If you're not all that up-to-speed on map/reduce (*http://en.wikipedia .org/wiki/MapReduce*), don't fret: learning more about it is part of what this section is all about.

In short, mapping functions take a collection of documents and *map* out a new key/value pair for each document, while reduction functions take a collection of documents and *reduce* them in some way. For example, computing the arithmetic sum of squares, $f(x) = x_1^2 + x_2^2 + ... + x_n^2$, could be expressed as a mapping function that squares each value, producing a one-to-one correspondence for each input value, while the reducer simply sums the output of the mappers and reduces it to a single value. This programming pattern lends itself well to trivially parallelizable problems but is certainly not a good (performant) fit for every problem. It should be clear that using CouchDB for a problem necessarily requires making some assumptions about the suitability of this computing paradigm for the task at hand.

Sensible Sorting

It may not be immediately obvious, but if you take a closer look at Figure 3-2, you'll see that the documents you just ingested into CouchDB are sorted by key. By default, the key is the special _id value that's automatically assigned by CouchDB itself, so sort order is pretty much meaningless at this point. In order to browse the data in Futon in a more sensible manner, as well as performing efficient range queries, we'll want to perform a mapping operation to create a view that sorts by something else. Sorting by date seems like a good idea and opens the door to certain kinds of time-series analysis, so let's start there and see what happens. But first, we'll need to make a small configuration change so that we can write our map/reduce functions to perform this task in Python.

CouchDB is especially intriguing in that it's written in Erlang, a language engineered to support super-high concurrency[5] and fault tolerance. The de facto out-of-the-box language you use to query and transform your data via map/reduce functions is JavaScript. Note that we could certainly opt to write map/reduce functions in JavaScript and realize some benefits from built-in JavaScript functions CouchDB offers—such as _sum, _count, and _stats. But the benefit gained from your development environment's syntax checking/highlighting may prove more useful and easier on the eyes than staring at JavaScript functions wrapped up as triple-quoted string values that exist inside of Python code. Besides, assuming you have couchdb installed, a small configuration tweak is all that it takes to specify a Python view server so that you can write your CouchDB code in Python. More precisely speaking, in CouchDB parlance, the map/reduce functions are said to be *view* functions that reside in a special document called a *design document* (*http://guide.couchdb.org/draft/design.html*).

Simply insert the following line (or a Windows compatible equivalent) into the appropriate section of CouchDB's *local.ini* configuration file, where the couchpy executable is a view server that will have been automatically installed along with the couchdb module. Don't forget to restart CouchDB after making the change:

```
[query_servers] python = /path/to/couchpy
```

 If you're having trouble locating your couchpy executable on a *nix environment, try using which couchpy in a terminal session to find its absolute path. For Windows folks, using the easy_install provided by ActivePython should place a *couchpy.exe* file in C:\PythonXY\Scripts. Watching the output when you easy_install couchdb reveals this information.

Unless you want to write gobs and gobs of code to parse inherently variable date strings into a standardized format, you'll also want to easy_install dateutil. This is a lifesaving package that standardizes most date formats, since you won't necessarily know what you're up against when it comes to date stamps from a messy email corpus. Example 3-6 demonstrates script mapping documents by their date/time stamps that you should be able to run on the sample data we imported after configuring your

---

5. Generally speaking, the characteristic of having "high concurrency" means that multiple operations can be run at the same time (concurrently) across multiple cores on a microprocessor, yielding maximum CPU throughput.

CouchDB for Python. Sample output is just a list of the documents matching the query and is omitted for brevity.

Example 3-6. A simple mapper that uses Python to map documents by their date/time stamps (mailboxes__map_json_mbox_by_date_time.py)

```python
# -*- coding: utf-8 -*-

import sys
import couchdb
from couchdb.design import ViewDefinition
try:
    import jsonlib2 as json
except ImportError:
    import json

DB = sys.argv[1]
START_DATE = sys.argv[2] #YYYY-MM-DD
END_DATE = sys.argv[3]   #YYYY-MM-DD

server = couchdb.Server('http://localhost:5984')
db = server[DB]

def dateTimeToDocMapper(doc):

    # Note that you need to include imports used by your mapper
    # inside the function definition

    from dateutil.parser import parse
    from datetime import datetime as dt
    if doc.get('Date'):
        # [year, month, day, hour, min, sec]
        _date = list(dt.timetuple(parse(doc['Date'])))[:-3])
        yield (_date, doc)

# Specify an index to back the query. Note that the index won't be
# created until the first time the query is run

view = ViewDefinition('index', 'by_date_time', dateTimeToDocMapper,
                      language='python')
view.sync(db)

# Now query, by slicing over items sorted by date

start = [int(i) for i in START_DATE.split("-")]
end = [int(i) for i in END_DATE.split("-")]
print 'Finding docs dated from %s-%s-%s to %s-%s-%s' % tuple(start + end)

docs = []
for row in db.view('index/by_date_time', startkey=start, endkey=end):
    docs.append(db.get(row.id))
print json.dumps(docs, indent=4)
```

The most fundamentally important thing to understand about the code is the role of the function dateTimeToDocMapper, a custom *generator*.[6] It accepts a document as a parameter and emits the same document; however, the document is keyed by a convenient date value that lends itself to being easily manipulated and sorted. Note that mapping functions in CouchDB are side-effect-free; regardless of what takes place in the mapping function or what the mapping function emits, the document passed in as a parameter remains unaltered. In CouchDB-speak, the dateTimeToDocMapper is a *view* named "by_date_time" that's part of a *design document* called "index." Taking a look at Futon, you can change the combo box value in the upper-right corner from "All documents" to "Design documents" and verify for yourself, as shown in Figure 3-3. You can also take a look at the pydoc for ViewDefinition for more of the same.

The first time you run the code, it should take somewhere on the order of five minutes to perform the mapping function and will keep one of your cores pegged out for most of that duration. About 80% of that time is dedicated to building the index, while the remaining time is taken up with performing the query. However, note that the index only needs to be established one time, so subsequent queries are relatively efficient, taking around 20 seconds to slice out and return approximately 2,200 documents for the date range specified, which is around 110 documents per second.

The key takeaway from this mapping function is that all of your documents are indexed by date, as can be verified in Futon by choosing the "by_date_time" index value in the "View" combo box in the upper-right corner of the screen, as shown in Figure 3-4. Although sorting documents by some criterion may not be the most interesting activity in the world, it's a necessary step in many aggregate analytic functions, such as counting the number of documents that meet a specific criterion across an entire corpus. The next section demonstrates some basic building blocks for such analysis.

Map/Reduce-Inspired Frequency Analysis

Tabulating frequencies is usually one of the first exploratory tasks you'll want to consider when faced with a new data set, because it can tell you so much with so little effort. This section investigates a couple of ways you can use CouchDB to build frequency-based indexes.

Frequency by date/time range

While our by_date_time index did a fine job of creating an index that sorts documents by date/time, it's not a useful index for counting the frequencies of documents transmitted by common boundaries such as the year, month, week, etc. While we could certainly write client code that would calculate frequencies from a call to db.view('index/by_date_time', startkey=start, endkey=end), it would be more efficient (and relaxing) to let CouchDB do this work for us. All that's needed is a trivial change to our

---

6. Loosely speaking, a generator is a function that returns an iterator. See *http://docs.python.org/tutorial/classes.html*.

mapping function and the introduction of a reducing function that's just as trivial. The mapping function will simply emit a value of 1 for each date/time stamp, and the reducer will count the number of keys that are equivalent. Example 3-7 illustrates this approach. Note that you'll need to `easy_install prettytable`, a package that produces nice tabular output, before running this example.

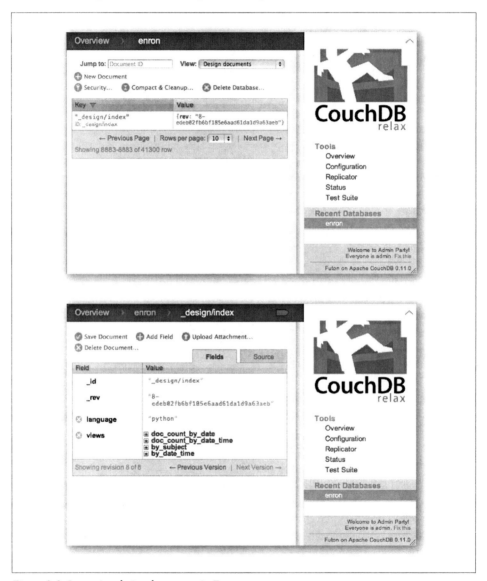

Figure 3-3. Inspecting design documents in Futon

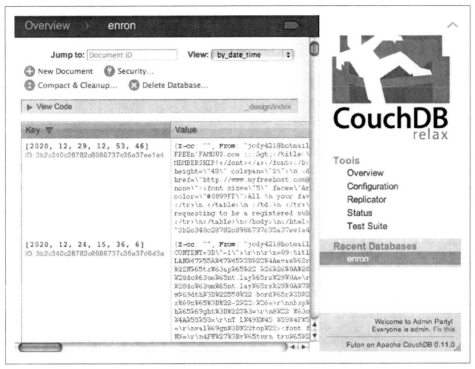

Figure 3-4. Documents are now sorted by date/time values

 It's incredibly important to understand that reducing functions only operate on values that map to the same key. A full-blown introduction to map/reduce is beyond our scope, but there are a number of useful resources online, including a page in the CouchDB wiki (*http://wiki .apache.org/couchdb/Introduction_to_CouchDB_views*) and a Java-Script-based interactive tool (*http://labs.mudynamics.com/wp-content/ uploads/2009/04/icouch.html*). The ins and outs of reducers are discussed further in "A Note on rereduce" on page 128. None of the examples in this chapter necessarily need to use the rereduce parameter, but to remind you that it exists and is very important for some situations, it is explicitly listed in all examples.

Example 3-7. Using a mapper and a reducer to count the number of messages written by date (mailboxes__count_json_mbox_by_date_time.py)

```
# -*- coding: utf-8 -*-

import sys
import couchdb
from couchdb.design import ViewDefinition
from prettytable import PrettyTable
```

```
DB = sys.argv[1]

server = couchdb.Server('http://localhost:5984')
db = server[DB]

def dateTimeCountMapper(doc):
    from dateutil.parser import parse
    from datetime import datetime as dt
    if doc.get('Date'):
        _date = list(dt.timetuple(parse(doc['Date'])))[:-3])
        yield (_date, 1)


def summingReducer(keys, values, rereduce):
    return sum(values)


view = ViewDefinition('index', 'doc_count_by_date_time', dateTimeCountMapper,
                      reduce_fun=summingReducer, language='python')
view.sync(db)

# Print out message counts by time slice such that they're
# grouped by year, month, day

fields = ['Date', 'Count']
pt = PrettyTable(fields=fields)
[pt.set_field_align(f, 'l') for f in fields]

for row in db.view('index/doc_count_by_date_time', group_level=3):
    pt.add_row(['-'.join([str(i) for i in row.key]), row.value])

pt.printt()
```

> If you need to debug mappers or reducers written in Python, you'll find
> that printing output to the console doesn't work. One approach you
> can use that does work involves appending information to a file. Just
> remember to open the file in append mode with the 'a' option: e.g.,
> open('debug.log', 'a').

To summarize, we create a view named doc_count_by_date_time that's stored in the index design document; it consists of a mapper that emits a date key for each document, and a reducer that takes whatever input it receives and returns the sum of it. The missing link you may be looking for is how the summingReducer function works. In this particular example, the reducer simply computes the sum of all values for documents that have matching keys, which amounts to counting the number of documents that have matching keys. The way that CouchDB reducers work in general is that they are passed corresponding lists of keys and values, and a custom function generally performs some aggregate operation (such as summing them up, in this case). The rereduce parameter is a device that makes incremental map/reduce possible by handling the case where the

---

results of a reducer have to themselves be reduced. No special handling of cases involving rereducing is needed for the examples in this chapter, but you can read more about rereducing in "A Note on rereduce" on page 128 or online (*http://wiki.apache .org/couchdb/Introduction_to_CouchDB_views*) if you anticipate needing it.

The `group_level` parameter is what allows us to perform frequency analyses by various date/time granularities associated with our key. Conceptually, CouchDB uses this parameter to slice the first *N* components of the key and automatically performs reduce operations on matching key/value pairs. In our situation, this means calculating sums for keys that have the first *N* matching components. Observe that if the reducer were passed the full date/time key, which is specific down to the second, we'd be querying for emails that were sent out at exactly the same time, which probably wouldn't be useful. Passing in only the first component of the date/time key would tally the number of emails sent out by year, passing in the first two components would tally the number of emails sent out by month, etc. The `group_level` keyword argument passed to the `db.view` function is how you can control what part of the key CouchDB passes into the reducer. After running the code to compute the underlying indexes, you can explore this functionality in Futon, as shown in Figure 3-5.

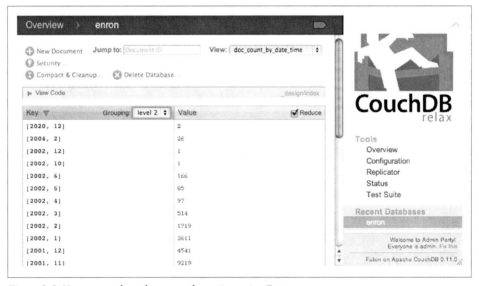

Figure 3-5. You can explore the group_by option using Futon

The amount of time it takes for `dateTimeCountMapper` to execute during the creation of the index that backs the `doc_count_by_date_time` view is on par with the previous mapping function you've seen, and it yields the ability to run a number of useful queries by altering the `group_level` parameter. Keep in mind that many alternative strategies, such as keying off of the number of milliseconds since the epoch, are also possible and may be useful for situations in which you are querying on a boundary that's not a year, month, week, etc. You'd have to emit the milliseconds since the epoch as the key in your mapper and pass in keyword arguments for `startkey` and `endkey` in `db.view`. No reducer would necessarily be needed.

What if you wanted to do time-based analysis that is independent of the day, such as the number of documents that are sent out on any given hour of the day? The grouping behavior of view queries takes advantage of the underlying structure of the B-Tree that backs a database, so you *can't* directly group by arbitrary items in the key in an analogous way to a Python list slice, such as `k[4:-2]` or `k[4:5]`. For this type of query, you'd probably want to construct a new key with a suitable prefix, such as `[hour, minute, second]`. Filtering in the client would require iterating over the entire document collection without the added benefit of having an index constructed for you for subsequent queries.

B-Trees Are the Bee's Knees?

B-Trees are the fundamental underlying data structure for CouchDB and most other database systems because they exhibit logarithmic performance for core operations (inserts, updates, deletes) over the long haul, even when continually faced with worst-case situations. B-Trees necessarily remain balanced and maintain data in sorted order. These characteristics yield efficient lookups because the underlying implementations require minimal disk reads. Given that disk seeks for traditional platter-based hard drives are still fast (on the order of low single-digit milliseconds), this means that huge volumes of data as stored by B-Trees can be accessed just as quickly.

In case you're wondering, there's no complete consensus about the etymology of the name "B-Tree," but it's generally accepted that the "B" stands for Bayer, the fellow who is credited with inventing them. There is more information about B-Trees and their common variants online than you'd probably care to read. If you decide to take the deep dive into CouchDB, it's probably worth your while to learn as much about them at the theoretical and practical implementation levels as possible since they are so integral to CouchDB's design.

Frequency by sender/recipient fields

Other metrics, such as how many messages a given person originally authored, how many direct communications occurred between any given group of people, etc., are highly relevant statistics to consider as part of email analysis. Example 3-8 demonstrates how to calculate the number of times any two people communicated by considering the To and From fields of a message. Obviously, inclusion of Cc and Bcc fields could hold special value as well, depending on the question you are asking. The only substantive difference between this listing and Example 3-6 is that the mapping function potentially yields multiple key/value pairs. You'll find that the pattern demonstrated can be minimally modified to compute many kinds of aggregate operations.

Example 3-8. Mapping and reducing by sender and recipient (mailboxes__count_json_mbox_by_sender_recipient.py)

```
# -*- coding: utf-8 -*-

import sys
import couchdb
from couchdb.design import ViewDefinition
from prettytable import PrettyTable

DB = sys.argv[1]

server = couchdb.Server('http://localhost:5984')
db = server[DB]

def senderRecipientCountMapper(doc):
    if doc.get('From') and doc.get('To'):
        for recipient in doc['To']:
            yield ([doc['From'], recipient], 1)


def summingReducer(keys, values, rereduce):
    return sum(values)


view = ViewDefinition('index', 'doc_count_by_sender_recipient',
                      senderRecipientCountMapper, reduce_fun=summingReducer,
                      language='python')
view.sync(db)

# print out a nicely formatted table
fields = ['Sender', 'Recipient', 'Count']
pt = PrettyTable(fields=fields)
[pt.set_field_align(f, 'l') for f in fields]

for row in db.view('index/doc_count_by_sender_recipient', group=True):
    pt.add_row([row.key[0], row.key[1], row.value])

pt.printt()
```

Sorting Documents by Value

CouchDB's tenacious sorting of the documents in a database by key is useful for lots of situations, but there are other occasions when you'll want to sort by value. As a case in point, it would be really useful to sort the results of Example 3-7 by frequency so that we can see the "top N" results. For small data sets, a fine option is to just perform a client-side sort yourself. Virtually every programming language has a solid implementation of the quicksort (*http://en.wikipedia.org/wiki/Quick_sort*) algorithm that exhibits reasonable combinatorics for the average case.[7]

---

7. On average, quicksort makes n*lg(n) comparisons to sort a collection in the worst case, which is about the best you can do without knowing any prior information to tailor the algorithm to the data.

For larger data sets or more niche situations, however, you may want to consider some alternatives. One approach is to transpose the reduced documents (the same ones shown in Figure 3-5, for example) and load them into another database such that the sorting can take place automatically by key. While this approach may seem a bit roundabout, it doesn't actually require very much effort to implement, and it does have the performance benefit that operations among different databases map out to different cores if the number of documents being exported is large. Example 3-9 demonstrates this approach.

Example 3-9. Sorting documents by key by using a transpose mapper and exporting to another database (mailboxes__sort_by_value_in_another_db.py)

```
# -*- coding: utf-8 -*-

import sys
import couchdb
from couchdb.design import ViewDefinition
from prettytable import PrettyTable

DB = sys.argv[1]

server = couchdb.Server('http://localhost:5984')
db = server[DB]

# Query out the documents at a given group level of interest
# Group by year, month, day

docs = db.view('index/doc_count_by_date_time', group_level=3)

# Now, load the documents keyed by [year, month, day] into a new database

db_scratch = server.create(DB + '-num-per-day')
db_scratch.update(docs)


def transposeMapper(doc):
    yield (doc['value'], doc['key'])


view = ViewDefinition('index', 'num_per_day', transposeMapper, language='python')
view.sync(db_scratch)

fields = ['Date', 'Count']
pt = PrettyTable(fields=fields)
[pt.set_field_align(f, 'l') for f in fields]

for row in db_scratch.view('index/num_per_day'):
    if row.key > 10:  # display stats where more than 10 messages were sent
        pt.add_row(['-'.join([str(i) for i in row.value]), row.key])
```

While sorting in the client and exporting to databases are relatively straightforward approaches that scale well for relatively simple situations, there's a truly industrial-strength Lucene-based solution for comprehensive indexing of all shapes and sizes. The next section investigates how to use couchdb-lucene for text-based indexing—Lucene's bread and butter—but many other possibilities, such as sorting documents by value, indexing geolocations, etc., are also well within reach.

couchdb-lucene: Full-Text Indexing and More

Lucene (*http://lucene.apache.org/java/docs/index.html*) is a Java-based search engine library for high-performance full-text indexing; its most common use is for trivially integrating keyword search capabilities into an application. The couchdb-lucene project is essentially a web service wrapper around some of Lucene's most central functionality, which enables it to index CouchDB documents. couchdb-lucene runs as a standalone Java Virtual Machine (JVM) process that communicates with CouchDB over HTTP, so you can run it on a totally separate machine if you have the hardware available.

Even a modest tutorial that scratches the surface of all that Lucene and couchdb-lucene can do for you would be wandering a little too far off the path. However, we will work through a brief example that demonstrates how to get up and running with these tools in the event that you find full-text indexing to be essential for your tasks at hand. If full-text indexing isn't something you necessarily need at this time, feel free to skip this section and come back to it later. For comparative purposes, note that it's certainly possible to perform text-based indexing by writing a simple mapping function that associates keywords and documents, like the one in Example 3-10.

Example 3-10. A mapper that tokenizes documents

```
def tokenizingMapper(doc):
    tokens = doc.split()
    for token in tokens:
        if isInteresting(token): # Filter out stop words, etc.
            yield token, doc
```

However, you'll quickly find that you need to do a lot more homework about basic Information Retrieval (IR) concepts if you want to establish a good scoring function to rank documents by relevance or anything beyond basic frequency analysis. Fortunately, the benefits of Lucene are many, and chances are good that you'll want to use couchdb-lucene instead of writing your own mapping function for full-text indexing.

> Unlike the previous sections that opted to use the couchdb module, this section uses httplib to exercise CouchDB's REST API directly and includes view functions written in JavaScript. It seems a bit convoluted to attempt otherwise.

Binary snapshots and instructions for installing couchdb-lucene are available at *http://github.com/rnewson/couchdb-lucene*. The necessary configuration details are available in the *README* file, but the short of it is that, with Java installed, you'll need to execute couchdb-lucene's run script, which fires up a web server and makes a few minor changes to CouchDB's *local.ini* configuration file so that couchdb-lucene can communicate with CouchDB over HTTP. The key configuration changes to make are documented in couchdb-lucene's *README*. Example 3-11 demonstrates.

 Windows users who are interested in acquiring a service wrapper for couchdb-lucene may want to be advised of its potential obsolescence as of October 2010 per this discussion thread: *http://www.apacheserver .net/CouchDB-lucene-windows-service-wrapper-at1031291.htm*.

Example 3-11. Configuring CouchDB to be couchdb-lucene-aware

```
[couchdb]
os_process_timeout=300000 ; increase the timeout from 5 seconds.

[external]
fti=/path/to/python /path/to/couchdb-lucene/tools/couchdb-external-hook.py

[httpd_db_handlers]
_fti = {couch_httpd_external, handle_external_req, <<"fti">>}
```

In short, we've increased the timeout to 5 minutes and defined a custom behavior called fti (full text index) that invokes functionality in a *couchdb-external-hook.py* script (supplied with couchdb-lucene) whenever an _fti context for a database is invoked. This script in turn communicates with the JVM (Java process) running Lucene to provide full-text indexing. These details are interesting, but you don't necessarily have to get bogged down with them unless that's the way you roll.

Once couchdb-lucene is up and running, try executing the script in Example 3-12, which performs a default indexing operation on the Subject field as well as the content of each document in a database. Keep in mind that with a text-based index on the subject and content of each message, you're fully capable of using the normal Lucene query syntax to gain granular control of your search. However, the default keyword capabilities are often sufficient.

Example 3-12. Using couchdb-lucene to get full-text indexing

```
# -*- coding: utf-8 -*-

import sys
import httplib
from urllib import quote
import json

DB = sys.argv[1]
QUERY = sys.argv[2]
```

```
#  The body of a JavaScript-based design document we'll create

dd = \
    {'fulltext': {'by_subject': {'index': '''function(doc) {
                                var ret=new Document();
                                ret.add(doc.Subject);
                                return ret
                        }'''},
        'by_content': {'index': '''function(doc) {
                                var ret=new Document();
                                for (var i=0; i < doc.parts.length; i++) {
                                    ret.add(doc.parts[i].content);
                                }
                                return ret
                        }'''}}}

#  Create a design document that'll be identified as "_design/lucene"
#  The equivalent of the following in a terminal:
#  $ curl -X PUT http://localhost:5984/DB/_design/lucene -d @dd.json

try:
    conn = httplib.HTTPConnection('localhost', 5984)
    conn.request('PUT', '/%s/_design/lucene' % (DB, ), json.dumps(dd))
    response = conn.getresponse()
finally:
    conn.close()

if response.status != 201:  #  Created
    print 'Unable to create design document: %s %s' % (response.status,
            response.reason)
    sys.exit()

#  Querying the design document is nearly the same as usual except that you reference
#  couchdb-lucene's _fti HTTP handler
#  $ curl http://localhost:5984/DB/_fti/_design/lucene/by_subject?q=QUERY

try:
    conn.request('GET', '/%s/_fti/_design/lucene/by_subject?q=%s' % (DB,
                quote(QUERY)))
    response = conn.getresponse()
    if response.status == 200:
        response_body = json.loads(response.read())
        print json.dumps(response_body, indent=4)
    else:
        print 'An error occurred fetching the response: %s %s' \
            % (response.status, response.reason)
finally:
    conn.close()
```

You'll certainly want to reference the online couchdb-lucene documentation (*http://github.com/rnewson/couchdb-lucene*) for the full scoop, but the gist is that you create a specially formatted design document that contains a fulltext field, which houses the name of an index and a JavaScript-based indexing function. That indexing function returns a `Document` object containing fields that Lucene should index. Note that the `Document` object is defined by `couchdb-lucene` (not CouchDB) when your index is built. A sample query result for the infamous word "raptor"[8] returns the response shown in Example 3-13. Notice that you'd use the `id` values to look up documents for display for further analysis from CouchDB directly.

Example 3-13. Sample query results for "raptor" on the Enron data set

```
/* Sample query results for
http://localhost:5984/enron/_fti/_design/lucene/by_content?q=raptor */

{ "etag" : "11b7c665b2d78be0",
  "fetch_duration" : 2,
  "limit" : 25,
  "q" : "default:raptor",
  "rows" : [ { "id" : "3b2c340c28782c8986737c35a355d0eb",
        "score" : 1.4469228982925415
      },
      { "id" : "3b2c340c28782c8986737c35a3542677",
        "score" : 1.3901585340499878
      },
      { "id" : "3b2c340c28782c8986737c35a357c6ae",
        "score" : 1.375900149345398
      },

      /* ... output truncated ... */

      { "id" : "2f84530cb39668ab3cdab83302e56d65",
        "score" : 0.8107569217681885
      }
    ],
  "search_duration" : 0,
  "skip" : 0,
  "total_rows" : 72
  }
```

Full details about the response are available in the documentation, but the most interesting part is the collection of rows containing document ID values that you can use to access the documents in CouchDB. In terms of data flow, you should note that you haven't directly interacted with `couchdb-lucene` at all, per se; you've simply defined a specially crafted design document and issued a query to CouchDB, which knows what to do based on the presence of `fulltext` and `_fti` in the design document and query, respectively. A discussion of Lucene's specific techniques for scoring documents is outside the scope of this book, but you can read more about it in its scoring documentation (*http://lucene.apache.org/java/3_0_0/scoring.html*) and, more specifically, in the Similarity (*http://lucene.apache.org/java/3_0_1/scoring.html*) class. It's unlikely that you can customize Lucene's scoring properties (should you need to do so) without

---

8. In the context of Enron, Raptors were financial devices used to hide losses. Enron used them to keep hundreds of millions in debt out of the accounting books.

modifying Lucene's source code, but you should be able to influence scoring by passing through parameters such as "boost" (*http://lucene.apache.org/java/2_4_0/queryparser syntax.html#Boosting%20a%20Term*) via the various API parameters that `couchdb-lucene` exposes, as opposed to hacking the source code.

If you're at all familiar with the term "raptor" as it relates to the Enron story, you might find the first few lines of the most highly ranked message in the search results helpful as context:

> The quarterly valuations for the assets hedged in the Raptor structure were valued through the normal quarterly revaluation process. The business units, RAC and Arthur Andersen all signed off on the initial valuations for the assets hedged in Raptor. All the investments in Raptor were on the MPR and were monitored by the business units, and we prepared the Raptor position report based upon this information....

If you're swimming in a collection of thousands of messages and aren't sure where to start looking, that simple keyword search certainly guided you to a good starting point. The subject of the message just quoted is "RE: Raptor Debris." Wouldn't it be interesting to know who else was in on that discussion thread and other threads about Raptor? Not so coincidentally, that's the topic of the next section.

Threading Together Conversations

As a first attempt at threading conversations, you might start with some basic string heuristics on the Subject header of the message and eventually get to the point where you're inspecting senders, recipients, and date stamps in an attempt to piece things together. Fortunately, mail servers are *slightly* more sophisticated than you might think and, as you know from "mbox: The Quick and Dirty on Unix Mailboxes" on page 42, there are Message-ID, In-Reply-To, and References headers that can be used to extract conversations from messages in a mailbox. A message threading algorithm commonly known as "jwz threading,"[9] takes all of this into account and provides a reasonable approach to parsing out message threads. All of the specifics for the algorithm can be found online at *http://www.jwz.org/doc/threading.html*. The implementation we'll be using is a fairly straightforward modification[10] of the one found in the Mail Trends (*http://code.google.com/p/mail-trends/*) project, which provides some other useful out-of-the-box tools. Given that no checkins for the project hosted on Google Code have occurred since early 2008, it's unclear whether Mail Trends is being actively maintained anywhere, but the project nonetheless provides a useful starting point for mail analysis, as evidenced by the salvaging of jwz threading.

---

9. The "jwz" is a reference to its author, Jamie Zawinski.

10. Namely, there were some modifications to make the code a little more object-oriented, the input/output formats were changed to consume our JSONified message objects, and the memory profile was dramatically decreased by considering only the few fields needed by the threading algorithm.

Let's go ahead and take a look at the overall workflow in Example 3-14, and then we'll dive into a few more of the details.

Example 3-14. Creating discussion threads from mbox data via "jwz threading" (mailboxes_threading.py)

```
# -*- coding: utf-8 -*-

import sys
import couchdb
from mailboxes__jwzthreading import thread, Message
from mailboxes__CouchDBBulkReader import CouchDBBulkReader
from datetime import datetime as dt
from prettytable import PrettyTable

try:
    import jsonlib2 as json
except:
    import json

DB = sys.argv[1]
NUM_PROC_THREADS = 3 # Recommendation: ~1 thread/core

# Pull the data as efficient as possible from CouchDB by using a thread
# pool to get as close as possible to being I/O bound.
# A single request to _all_docs works except that it CPU bound to a single core

now = dt.now()
print >> sys.stderr, 'Bulk reading from CouchDB...'
br = CouchDBBulkReader(DB, NUM_PROC_THREADS)
docs = br.read()
print >> sys.stderr, '\t%s' % (dt.now() - now, )

now = dt.now()
print >> sys.stderr, 'Threading in Memory...'
threads = thread([Message(doc) for doc in docs])
print >> sys.stderr, '\t%s' % (dt.now() - now, )

# Write out threading info into another database.
# Note that writes to CouchDB are serialized to append-only
# databases, so threading is unlikely to help here, and besides,
# the average document size is very small, making this a quick operation

now = dt.now()
print >> sys.stderr, 'Bulk writing to CouchDB...'
server = couchdb.Server('http://localhost:5984')
db = server.create(DB + '-threads')
results = db.update([{'thread': thread} for thread in threads],
                    all_or_nothing=True)
print >> sys.stderr, '\t%s' % (dt.now() - now, )

# Some basic stats

print >> sys.stderr, 'Total number of threads: %s' % len(threads)
print >> sys.stderr
```

```
# Compute (_id, len(thread)) tuples
# You could also compute thread length directly in CouchDB using a simple reducer
# function

stats = sorted(zip([result[1] for result in results], [len(t) for t in threads]),
               key=lambda x: x[1])

fields = ['Thread Id', 'Thread Length']
pt = PrettyTable(fields=fields)
[pt.set_field_align(f, 'l') for f in fields]

for stat in stats:
    pt.add_row(stat)

pt.printt()
```

The overall flow is that we bulk-read messages out of CouchDB, perform threading in memory, and then write out the thread information to a separate database where each thread is a document that contains references back to the original message's content. Finally, some basic statistics about the length of discussion threads are printed out. You could just as easily use a map/reduce approach to calculating statistics about thread length (see "Map/Reduce-Inspired Frequency Analysis" on page 55). A discussion thread is a document that looks like Example 3-15.

Example 3-15. Sample threading results

```
{
    "_id": "b6d4f96224bc546acd34c405e6fff62f",
    "_rev": "1-1bf63dcdd94067ad647afe2ea3ade63c",
    "thread": [
        {
            "external_id": "24a30d62545728e26eb3311d63ae6e02",
            "subject": "FW: Sitara EOL Bridge Problem Today"
        },
        {
            "external_id": "bb808c9081912f5861295bf1d105dd02",
            "subject": "FW: Sitara EOL Bridge Problem Today"
        },
        {
            "external_id": "3b2c340c28782c8986737c35a332cd88",
            "subject": "FW: Sitara EOL Bridge Problem Today"
        }
    ]
}
```

The most interesting parts of this listing are the references to `mailboxes_jwzthreading` and `CouchDBBulkReader`. The API exposed by `mailboxes_jwzthreading` simply converts each of the message documents fetched from CouchDB into a slightly different form and then passes them into the threading algorithm, which takes care of the core work and returns a convenient JSON format we can ingest back into CouchDB. The details of `mailboxes_jwzthreading` are available at *http://github.com/ptwobrussell/Mining-the -Social-Web/blob/master/python_code/mailboxes__jwzthreading.py.*

The use of `CouchDBBulkReader` could have been omitted altogether in favor of a bulk read through the `couchdb` module, but `CouchDBBulkReader` provides a significant performance boost by using an internal thread pool to dispatch multiple requests to CouchDB at the same time. The underlying issue is that CouchDB only uses a single core for a single read or a single write request to the server. This might initially strike you as odd given all of the hubbub about how Erlang—the underlying implementation language—has such extensive support for concurrency, but it's a design decision made by the maintainers of the project[11] for sensible reasons. The good news is that you can divvy out multiple requests to the server all at the same time and heat up multiple cores fairly easily. This is the approach taken by `CouchDBBulkReader`, which is introduced in Example 3-16. Briefly, an initial request is made that fetches only the ID values for every document in the database (a relatively fast operation since the amount of data that ends up being marshalled is very small), and then these IDs are sorted and chunked into equal parts. Each chunk is assigned to a thread that fetches the full document for that particular range.

As a rule of thumb, don't use more than one processing thread per core for the thread pool, and use performance-monitoring tools like top on a *nix system or Task Manager on Windows to track just how much you are taxing your system. Ideally, you'd see the `beam.smp` daemon process associated with CouchDB pegged at around 200% if you were working on a machine with two cores, which effectively makes you "CPU-bound," but anything above 150% is still a substantial improvement. You should observe that the bulk read consumes nearly all of the time required to retrieve the data, while the actual threading and writing the thread documents back to CouchDB take virtually no time at all. An interesting exercise would be to consider porting the threading algorithm into a map/reduce paradigm used by the `couchdb` module, or even rewriting it in JavaScript.

 The `threadpool` package used in Example 3-16 is available via the usual means: `easy_install threadpool`.

---

11. Fundamentally, it's unlikely that CouchDB will ever support utilizing multiple cores for a bulk write operation because of the way writes are serialized to disk. However, it's not hard to imagine a patch that takes advantage of multiple cores for certain kinds of read operations, given that the underlying data structure is a tree, which inherently lends itself to being traversed at multiple nodes.

Example 3-16. Using a thread pool to maximize read throughput from CouchDB (mailboxes__CouchDBBulkReader.py)

```python
# -*- coding: utf-8 -*-

from datetime import datetime as dt
from math import ceil
import httplib
import urllib
import time
import threadpool
try:
    import jsonlib2 as json
except:
    import json


class CouchDBBulkReader:

    def __init__(
        self,
        db,
        num_threads,
        host='localhost',
        port=5984,
        ):

        self.db = db
        self.num_threads = num_threads
        self.host = host
        self.port = port
        self.results = []

        id_buckets = self._getDocIds()
        self.pool = threadpool.ThreadPool(self.num_threads)
        requests = threadpool.makeRequests(self._getDocs, id_buckets,
                self._callback, self._errCallback)
        [self.pool.putRequest(req) for req in requests]
        self.pool.wait()

    def read(self):
        while True:
            try:
                time.sleep(0.5)
                self.pool.poll()
            except threadpool.NoResultsPending:
                return self.results
            except KeyboardInterrupt:
                print 'Keyboard interrupt. Exiting'
                sys.exit()
            finally:
                self.pool.joinAllDismissedWorkers()
```

```
# Called to quickly get all of the document ids which can be sorted and dibbied out

def _getDocIds(self):

    # Helper function to tersely compute a list of indices that evenly distribute
    # the items in it

    def partition(alist, indices):
        return [alist[i:j] for (i, j) in zip([0] + indices, indices
                + [None])][:-1]

    try:
        conn = httplib.HTTPConnection(self.host, self.port)
        conn.request('GET', '/%s/_all_docs' % (self.db, ))
        response = conn.getresponse()
        if response.status != 200:  #  OK
            print 'Unable to get docs: %s %s' % (response.status,
                    response.reason)
            sys.exit()

        ids = [i['id'] for i in json.loads(response.read())['rows']
                if not i['id'].startswith('_')]
        ids.sort()
    finally:
        conn.close()

    partition_size = int(ceil(1.0 * len(ids) / self.num_threads))
    indices = []

    _len = len(ids)
    idx = 0
    while idx < _len:
        idx += partition_size
        indices.append(idx)

    return partition(ids, indices)

def _getDocs(self, ids):
    try:
        (startkey, endkey) = (ids[0], ids[-1])
        conn = httplib.HTTPConnection(self.host, self.port)
        conn.request('GET',
                     '/%s/_all_docs?startkey="%s"&endkey="%s"&include_docs=true'
                     % (self.db, startkey, endkey))
        response = conn.getresponse()
        if response.status != 200:  #  OK
            print 'Unable to get docs: %s %s' % (response.status,
                    response.reason)
            sys.exit()
        return response.read()
    finally:
        conn.close()
```

```
def _errCallback(self, request, result):
    print 'An Error occurred:', request, result
    sys.exit()

def _callback(self, request, result):
    rows = json.loads(result)['rows']
    self.results.extend([row['doc'] for row in rows])
```

With tools in hand to compute discussion threads, let's now turn back to the Enron data.

Look Who's Talking

Running the code in Example 3-14 creates a database that provides rapid access to message ID values grouped as discussion threads. With a database already containing the original messages themselves and another Lucene-backed database containing keyword search capabilities, you can really begin to do some very interesting things. Let's now revisit Raptor from the previous section by considering the task of computing the individual sets of email addresses associated by any discussion thread where Raptor was mentioned, or, to put it another way, the various sets of people involved in discussions using this term. The resulting data structure we want to get to would look something like what's shown in Example 3-17.

Example 3-17. Ideal results from threading together discussions

```
{
    "participants : [    person-1@example.com,
                         person-2@example.com,
                         ...
                    ],
    "message_ids" : [    "id1",
                         "id2",
                         ...
                    ],
    "subject"     : "subject"
}
```

The approach we'll take involves the following three steps:

- Query `couchdb-lucene` for message IDs associated with a term of interest such as Raptor.
- Look up discussion threads associated with any of those message IDs.
- Compute the unique set of email addresses that appear in any of the header fields associated with messages in any of the threads.

Example 3-18 recycles some previous code and demonstrates one possible implementation that ties it all together.

Example 3-18. A robust approach for threading together discussion threads from mbox data (mailboxes__participants_in_conversations.py)

```python
# -*- coding: utf-8 -*-

import sys
import httplib
from urllib import quote
from urllib import urlencode
import json

DB = sys.argv[1]   # enron
QUERY = sys.argv[2]

# Query couchdb-lucene by_subject and by_content

message_ids_of_interest = []
for idx in ['by_subject', 'by_content']:

    try:
        conn = httplib.HTTPConnection('localhost', 5984)
        conn.request('GET', '/%s/_fti/_design/lucene/%s?q=%s&limit=50000' % (DB,
                    idx, quote(QUERY)))
        response = conn.getresponse()
        if response.status == 200:
            response_body = json.loads(response.read())
            message_ids_of_interest.extend([row['id'] for row in
                    response_body['rows']])
        else:
            print 'An error occurred fetching the response: %s %s' \
                % (response.status, response.reason)
            sys.exit()
    finally:
        conn.close()

# Remove any duplicates

message_ids_of_interest = list(set(message_ids_of_interest))

# Perform discussion thread filtering in memory. It's a relatively
# small amount of data

try:
    conn = httplib.HTTPConnection('localhost', 5984)
    conn.request('GET', '/%s/_all_docs?include_docs=true' % (DB + '-threads', ))
    response = conn.getresponse()
    if response.status != 200:   #  OK
        print 'Unable to get docs: %s %s' % (response.status, response.reason)
        sys.exit()

    threads = [dict([('thread_id', row['doc']['_id']), ('message_ids',
                [t['external_id'] for t in row['doc']['thread']])]) for row in
                json.loads(response.read())['rows']]
finally:
    conn.close()
```

```
# Find only the threads that have a message_id appearing in the list of message ids
# fetched from the Lucene index

threads_of_interest = [t for t in threads for message_id in t['message_ids']
                          if message_id in message_ids_of_interest]

# Remove duplicates

seen = []
idx = 0
while idx < len(threads_of_interest):
    if threads_of_interest[idx]['thread_id'] in seen:
        threads_of_interest.pop(idx)
    else:
        seen.append(threads_of_interest[idx]['thread_id'])
        idx += 1

# Cull out message ids for threads of interest

message_ids_for_threads_of_interest = [t['message_ids'] for t in
                                        threads_of_interest]

# Flatten out the list of lists into just a list and remove duplicates

message_ids_for_threads_of_interest = list(set([message_id for message_ids in
        message_ids_for_threads_of_interest for message_id in message_ids]))

# Query CouchDB for the email addresses in various headers of interest using a bulk
# request

try:
    conn = httplib.HTTPConnection('localhost', 5984)
    post_params = json.dumps({'keys': message_ids_for_threads_of_interest})
    conn.request('POST', '/%s/_all_docs?include_docs=true' % (DB, ), post_params)
    response = conn.getresponse()
    if response.status != 200:  # OK
        print 'Unable to get docs: %s %s' % (response.status, response.reason)
        sys.exit()

    full_docs = [row['doc'] for row in json.loads(response.read())['rows']]
finally:
    conn.close()

# Finally, with full messages of interest on hand, parse out headers of interest and
# and compute unique sets of email addresses for each thread by decorating
# threads_of_interest

for thread in threads_of_interest:
    participants = []
    for message_id in thread['message_ids']:
        doc = [d for d in full_docs if d['_id'] == message_id][0]
```

```
        try:
            participants.append(doc.get('From'))
            participants.extend(doc.get('To'))
            if doc.get('Cc'):
                participants.extend(doc.get('Cc'))
            if doc.get('Bcc'):
                participants.extend(doc.get('Bcc'))
        except:
            pass  # Maybe a X-To header, etc. as opposed to To?

    thread['participants'] = list(set(participants))
    thread['subject'] = doc['Subject']
print json.dumps(threads_of_interest, indent=4)
```

Sample output from the script is shown in Example 3-19.

Example 3-19. Sample results from threading discussions for a search query of "Raptor"

```
[
    {
        "thread_id": "b6d4f96224bc546acd34c405e6c471c5",
        "participants": [
            "j.kaminski@enron.com",
            "rakesh.bharati@enron.com"
        ],
        "message_ids": [
            "24a30d62545728e26eb3311d63effb47"
        ],
        "subject": "FW: Note on Valuation"
    },
    {
        "thread_id": "b6d4f96224bc546acd34c405e6dbc0d4",
        "participants": [
            "mary.fischer@enron.com",
            "danny.wilson@enron.com",
            "a..lee@enron.com",
            "john.swafford@enron.com",
            "facundo.caminos@enron.com"
        ],
        "message_ids": [
            "24a30d62545728e26eb3311d633cf6b3"
        ],
        "subject": "Tax Accruals on the Raptor Companies"
    },
    {
        "thread_id": "b6d4f96224bc546acd34c405e6eb7adf",
        "participants": [
            "mark.ruane@enron.com",
            "rick.buy@enron.com"
        ],
        "message_ids": [
            "3b2c340c28782c8986737c35a357c6ae"
        ],
        "subject": "FW: E-11 Raptor"
    },
```

```
... output truncated ...

]
```

In short, the script has provided some tools for determining who participated in what conversations based on a keyword heuristic. You could load an mbox file into a decent mail client and search out this information via a manual process, but the demonstrated approach is generally useful and could be adapted for many automated or semiautomated analyses.

Visualizing Mail "Events" with SIMILE Timeline

There are numerous ways to visualize mail data. You could bucket messages by time and present the data as a bar chart to inspect the time of day that the most mail transactions are happening, create a graph of connections among senders and recipients and filter by the discussion thread, load query results onto a time line, or use any number of other techniques. This section demonstrates out-of-the-box usage of the SIMILE Timeline (*http://simile-widgets.org/wiki/Timeline*), an easy to use (yet extremely powerful) tool for visualizing event-centric data. The SIMILE Timeline is particularly useful for exploring mail data because it allows us to view the transmission of each individual message as a unique event while also visualizing the larger discussion thread as an extended event that transpires over a longer period of time. We can also easily specify a link for each individual message so that when we click on a message in Timeline, it brings up the full text of the message in Futon.

We'll stick to pragmatic analysis approaches and avoid building a full-blown web app to visualize the mail data, but given very little additional effort, it wouldn't be difficult to construct something more robust. We'll opt to simply modify the output format from Example 3-18 so that it emits JSON that's compatible with the Timeline. From there, all that's required is pointing a simple web page to the SIMILE Event Source JSON output (*http://simile-widgets.org/wiki/Timeline_EventSources*) on your local filesystem to load up the Timeline. Sample target output is shown in Example 3-20.

Example 3-20. The data format expected by the SIMILE Timeline (mailboxes__participants_in_conversations_adapted_for_simile.py)

```
{
    "dateTimeFormat": "iso8601",
    "events": [
        {
            "start": "2002-02-06T08:20:49-08:00",
            "description": "Message involving sarah.palmer@enron.com",
            "link": "http://localhost:5984/_utils/document.html?enron/bb...",
            "durationEvent": false,
            "title": "Enron Mentions -- 02/06/02"
        },
        {
```

```
        "start": "2001-05-22T16:20:25-07:00",
        "description": "Message involving j.kaminski@enron.com, ...",
        "link": "http://localhost:5984/_utils/document.html?enron/24a...",
        "durationEvent": false,
        "title": "RE: Pricing of restriction on Enron stock"
    },
    ...
    ]
}
```

Example 3-21 demonstrates a basic augmentation to Example 3-18 that's necessary to produce output that can be consumed by the SIMILE Timeline (shown in Figure 3-6). It creates an event for each individual message in addition to an event for each discussion thread.

Example 3-21. Augmented output from Example 3-18 that emits output that can be consumed by the SIMILE Timeline

```python
# Finally, with full messages of interest on hand, parse out headers of interest
# and compute output for SIMILE Timeline

events = []
for thread in threads_of_interest:

    # Process each thread: create an event object for the thread as well as
    # for individual messages involved in the thread

    participants = []
    message_dates = []
    for message_id in thread['message_ids']:
        doc = [d for d in full_docs if d['_id'] == message_id][0]
        message_dates.append(parse(doc['Date']).isoformat())
        try:
            participants.append(doc.get('From'))
            participants.extend(doc.get('To'))
            if doc.get('Cc'):
                participants.extend(doc.get('Cc'))
            if doc.get('Bcc'):
                participants.extend(doc.get('Bcc'))
        except:
            pass  # Maybe a X-To or X-Origin header, etc. as opposed to To?

        # Append each individual message in the thread

        event = {}
        event['title'] = doc['Subject']
        event['start'] = parse(doc['Date']).isoformat()
        event['durationEvent'] = False
        event['description'] = 'Message involving ' \
            + ', '.join(list(set(participants)))
        event['link'] = 'http://localhost:5984/_utils/document.html?%s/%s' % (DB,
                doc['_id'])
        events.append(event)
```

```
    # Find start and end dates for the messages involved in the thread

    if len(thread['message_ids']) > 1:
        event = {}
        event['title'] = doc['Subject']
        message_dates.sort()
        event['start'] = parse(message_dates[0]).isoformat()
        event['end'] = parse(message_dates[-1]).isoformat()
        event['durationEvent'] = True
        event['description'] = str(len(thread['message_ids'])) \
            + ' messages in thread'
        events.append(event)  # append the thread event

if not os.path.isdir('out'):
    os.mkdir('out')

f = open(os.path.join('out', 'simile_data.json'), 'w')
f.write(json.dumps({'dateTimeFormat': 'iso8601', 'events': events}, indent=4))
f.close()

print >> sys.stderr, 'Data file written to: %s' % f.name

# Point SIMILE to the data file
```

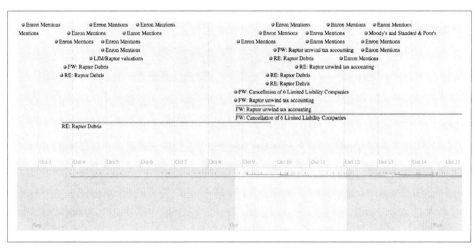

Figure 3-6. Sample results from a query for "Raptor" visualized with SIMILE Timeline: you can scroll "infinitely" in both directions

There are lots of online demonstrations of Timeline (*http://simile-widgets.org/time line/*), along with ample documentation. This simple example of plotting mail on Timeline just shows the bare minimum to get you up and running; it's just the beginning of what's possible. The "Getting Started with Timeline" tutorial (*http://www.simile-widg ets.org/wiki/Getting_Started_with_Timeline*) is a great way to begin. Assuming you have the data to back the queries it requests, the `mailboxes__participants_in_conversa tions_adapted_for_simile.py` script is turn-key in that it parses the data, dumps it into an HTML template (*http://github.com/ptwobrussell/Mining-the-Social-Web/blob/mas ter/web_code/simile/timeline.html*), and automatically opens it in your web browser. Enjoy!

Analyzing Your Own Mail Data

The Enron mail data makes for great illustrations in a chapter on mail analysis, but you'll almost certainly want to take a closer look at your own mail data. Fortunately, many popular mail clients provide an "export to mbox" option, which makes it pretty simple to get your mail data into a format that lends itself to analysis by the techniques described in this chapter. For example, in Apple Mail, you can select some number of messages, pick "Save As..." from the File menu, and then choose "Raw Message Source" as the formatting option to export the messages as an mbox file (see Figure 3-7). A little bit of searching should turn up results for how to do this in most other major clients.

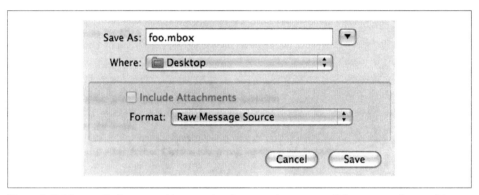

Figure 3-7. Most mail clients provide an option for exporting your mail data to an mbox archive

If you exclusively use an online mail client, you could opt to pull your data down into a mail client and export it, but you might prefer to fully automate the creation of an mbox file by pulling the data directly from the server. Just about any online mail service will support POP3 (Post Office Protocol version 3), most also support IMAP (Internet Message Access Protocol), and Python scripts for pulling down your mail aren't very hard to whip up. One particularly robust command-line tool that you can use to pull mail data from just about anywhere is *getmail (http://pyropus.ca/software/getmail/)* , which turns out to be written in Python. Two modules included in Python's standard library, `poplib` (*http://docs.python.org/library/poplib.html*) and `imaplib` (*http://docs .python.org/library/imaplib.html*), provide a terrific foundation, so you're also likely to run across lots of useful scripts if you do a bit of searching online. getmail is particularly easy to get up and running. To slurp down your Gmail inbox data, for example, you just download and install it, then set up a *getmailrc* file with a few basic options. Example 3-22 demonstrates some settings for a *nix environment. Windows users would need to change the [destination] path and [options] message_log values to valid paths.

*Example 3-22. Sample getmail settings for a *nix environment*

```
[retriever]
type = SimpleIMAPSSLRetriever
server = imap.gmail.com
username = ptwobrussell
password = blarty-blar-blar

[destination]
type = Mboxrd
path = /tmp/gmail.mbox

[options]
verbose = 2
message_log = ~/.getmail/gmail.log
```

With a configuration in place, simply invoking getmail from a terminal does the rest. Once you have a local mbox on hand, you can analyze it using the techniques you've learned in this chapter:

```
$ getmail
getmail version 4.20.0
Copyright (C) 1998-2009 Charles Cazabon.  Licensed under the GNU GPL version 2.
SimpleIMAPSSLRetriever:ptwobrussell@imap.gmail.com:993:
  msg     1/10972 (4227 bytes) from ... delivered to Mboxrd /tmp/gmail.mbox
  msg     2/10972 (3219 bytes) from ... delivered to Mboxrd /tmp/gmail.mbox
  ...
```

"Tapping into Your Gmail" on page 231 investigates using imaplib to slurp down your Gmail data and analyze it, as one part of the exercises in Chapter 7, which focuses on Google technologies.

The Graph Your (Gmail) Inbox Chrome Extension

There are several useful toolkits floating around that analyze webmail, and one of the most promising to emerge recently is the Graph Your Inbox Chrome Extension (*http://www.graphyourinbox.com*). To use this extension, you just install it, authorize it to access your mail data, run some Gmail queries, and let it take care of the rest. You can search for keywords like "pizza," time values such as "2010," or run more advanced queries such as "from:matthew@example.org" and "label:Strata". It's highly likely that this extension is only going to keep getting better, given that it's new and has been so well received thus far. Figure 3-8 shows a sample screenshot.

"Tapping into Your Gmail" on page 231 provides an overview of how to use Python's smtplib module to tap into your Gmail account (or any other mail account that speaks SMTP) and mine the textual information in messages. Be sure to check it out when you're interested in moving beyond mail header information and ready to dig into text mining.

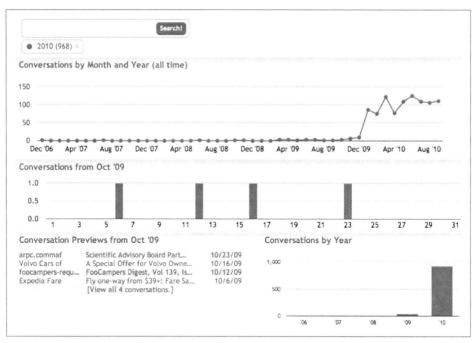

Figure 3-8. The Graph Your Inbox Chrome Extension provides a concise summary of your Gmail activity

Closing Remarks

We've covered *a lot* of ground in this chapter, but we've just barely begun to scratch the surface of what's possible with mail data. Our focus has been on mboxes, a simple and convenient file format that lends itself to high portability and easy analysis by many Python tools and packages. There's an incredible amount of open source technology available for mining mboxes, and Python is a terrific language for slicing and dicing them. A small investment in these tools and stores such as CouchDB, which lends itself to easily sharing your data, can go a long way.

## CHAPTER 4

Twitter: Friends, Followers, and Setwise Operations

Unless you've been cryogenically frozen for the past couple of years, you've no doubt heard of Twitter—a microblogging service that can be used to broadcast short (maximum 140 characters) status updates. Whether you love it, hate it, or are indifferent, it's undeniable that Twitter has reshaped the way people communicate on the Web. This chapter makes a modest attempt to introduce some rudimentary analytic functions that you can implement by taking advantage of the Twitter APIs to answer a number of interesting questions, such as:

- How many friends/followers do I have?
- Who am I following that is not following me back?
- Who is following me that I am not following back?
- Who are the friendliest and least friendly people in my network?
- Who are my "mutual friends" (people I'm following that are also following me)?
- Given all of my followers and all of their followers, what is my potential influence if I get retweeted?

 Twitter's API is constantly evolving. It is highly recommended that you follow the Twitter API account, *@TwitterAPI*, and check any differences between the text and actual behavior you are seeing against the official docs (*http://dev.twitter.com/doc*).

This chapter analyzes relationships among Twitterers, while the next chapter hones in on the actual content of tweets. The code we'll develop for this chapter is relatively robust in that it takes into consideration common issues such as the infamous Twitter rate limits (*http://dev.twitter.com/pages/rate-limiting*),[1] network I/O errors, potentially managing large volumes of data, etc. The final result is a fairly powerful command-line utility that you should be able to adapt easily for your own custom uses (*http://github.com/ptwobrussell/Mining-the-Social-Web/blob/master/python_code/TwitterSocialGraphUtility.py*).

 Having the tools on hand to harvest and mine your own tweets is essential. However, be advised that initiatives to archive historical Twitter data in the U.S. Library of Congress (*http://www.loc.gov/tweet/how-tweet-it-is.html*) may soon render the inconveniences and headaches associated with harvesting and API rate-limiting non-issues for many forms of analysis. Firms such as Infochimps (*http://infochimps.org*) are also emerging and providing a medium for acquiring various kinds of Twitter data (among other things). A query for Twitter data at Infochimps (*http://infochimps.org/search?query=twitter*) turns up everything from archives for #worldcup tweets to analyses of how smileys are used.

RESTful and OAuth-Cladded APIs

The year 2010 will be remembered by some as the transition period in which Twitter started to become "all grown up." Basic HTTP authentication got replaced with OAuth[2] (more on this shortly), documentation improved, and API statuses became transparent, among other things. Twitter search APIs that were introduced with Twitter's acquisition of Summize (*http://blog.twitter.com/2008/07/finding-perfect-match.html*) collapsed into the "traditional" REST (*http://en.wikipedia.org/wiki/Representational_State_Transfer*) API, while the streaming APIs gained increasing use for production situations. If Twitter were on the wine menu, you might pick up the 2010 bottle and say, "it was a good year—a very good year." All that said, there's a lot of useful information tucked away online, and this chapter aims not to reproduce any more of it than is absolutely necessary.

Most of the development in this chapter revolves around the social graph APIs for getting the friends and followers of a user, the API for getting extended user information (name, location, last tweet, etc.) for a list of users, and the API for getting tweet data. An entire book of its own (literally) could be written to explore additional possibilities,

---

1. At the time of this writing, Twitter limits OAuth requests to 350 per hour and anonymous requests to 150 per hour. Twitter believes that these limits should be sufficient for most every client application, and that if they're not, you're probably building your app wrong.

2. As of December 2010, Twitter implements OAuth 1.0a, but you should expect to see support for OAuth 2.0 sometime in 2011.

---

but once you've learned the ropes, your imagination will have no problems taking over. Plus, certain exercises always have to be left for the "interested reader," right?

The Python client we'll use for Twitter is quite simply named `twitter` (the same one we've already seen at work in Chapter 1). It provides a minimal wrapper around Twitter's RESTful web services. There's very little documentation about this module because you simply construct requests in the same manner that the URL is pieced together in Twitter's online documentation. For example, a request from the terminal that retrieves Tim O'Reilly's user info simply involves dispatching a request to the `/users/show` resource as a `curl` command, as follows:

```
$ curl 'http://api.twitter.com/1/users/show.json?screen_name=timoreilly'
```

 curl is a handy tool that can be used to transfer data to/from a server using a variety of protocols, and it is especially useful for making HTTP requests from a terminal. It comes standard and is usually in the PATH on most *nix systems, but Windows users may need to download and configure it (*http://curl.haxx.se/latest.cgi?curl=win32-ssl-devel-msvc*).

There are a couple of subtleties about this request. First, Twitter has a versioned API, so the appearance of `/1` as the URL context denotes that Version 1 of the API is in use. Next, a `user_id` could have been passed in instead of a `screen_name` had one been available. The mapping of the `curl` command to the equivalent Python script in Example 4-1 should be obvious.

Example 4-1. Fetching extended information about a Twitter user

```
# -*- coding: utf-8 -*-

import twitter
import json

screen_name = 'timoreilly'
t = twitter.Twitter(domain='api.twitter.com', api_version='1')
response = t.users.show(screen_name=screen_name)
print json.dumps(response, sort_keys=True, indent=4)
```

In case you haven't reviewed Twitter's online docs (*http://dev.twitter.com/doc*) yet, it's probably worthwhile to explicitly mention that the `/users/show` API call does not require authentication, and it has some specific peculiarities depending on whether a user has "protected" his tweets in the privacy settings. The `/users/lookup` API call is very similar to `/users/show` except that it requires authentication and allows you to pass in a comma-separated list of `screen_name` or `user_id` values so that you can perform batch lookups. To obtain authorization to use Twitter's API, you'll need to learn about OAuth, which is the topic of the next section.

No, You Can't Have My Password

OAuth stands for "open authorization." In an effort to be as forward-looking as possible, this section provides a very cursory overview of OAuth 2.0 (*http://tools.ietf.org/html/draft-ietf-oauth-v2-10*), an emerging authorization scheme that Facebook has already implemented from a clean slate (*http://developers.facebook.com/docs/authentication/*) (see Chapter 9) and that Twitter plans to support "soon" (*http://www.slideshare.net/episod/chirp-2010-too-many-secrets-but-never-enough-oauth-at-twitter*). It will eventually become the new industry standard. As this book was written, Twitter and many other web services support OAuth 1.0a, as defined by RFC 5849 (*http://tools.ietf.org/html/rfc5849*). However, the landscape is expected to shift, with OAuth 2.0 streamlining work for developers and promoting better user experiences (*http://hueniverse.com/2010/05/introducing-oauth-2-0/*). While the terminology and details of this section are specific to OAuth 2.0, the basic workflow involved in OAuth 1.0a is very similar. Both schemes are "three-legged" in that they involve an exchange of information (often called a "dance") among a client application that needs access to a protected resource, a resource owner such as a social network, and an end user who needs to authorize the client application to access the protected resource (without giving it a username/password combination).

 It is purely coincidence that Twitter's current (and only) API Version is 1.0 and that Twitter currently supports OAuth 1.0a. It is likely that Version 1 of Twitter's API will eventually also support OAuth 2.0 when it is ready.

So, in a nutshell, OAuth provides a way for you to authorize an application to access data you have stored away in another application without having to share your username and password. The IETF OAuth 2.0 Protocol (*http://tools.ietf.org/html/draft-ietf-oauth-v2-10*) spec isn't nearly as scary as it might sound, and you should take a little time to peruse it because OAuth is popping up everywhere—especially in the social network landscape. Here's the gist of the major steps involved:

- You (the *end user*) want to authorize an application of some sort (the *client*) to access some of your data (a *scope*) that's managed by a web service (the *resource owner*).
  - You're smart and you know better than to give the app your credentials directly.
- Instead of asking for your password, the client redirects you to the resource owner, and you authorize a scope for the client directly with the resource owner.
  - The client identifies itself with a unique *client identifier* and a way to contact it once authorization has taken place by the end user.
- Assuming the end user authorizes the client, the client is notified and given an *authorization code* confirming that the end user has authorized it to access a scope.

— But there's a small problem if we stop here: given that the client has identified itself with an identifier that is necessarily not a secret, a malicious client could have fraudulently identified itself and masqueraded as being created by a trusted publisher, effectively deceiving the end user to authorize it.

- The client presents the authorization code it just received along with its client identifier and corresponding *client secret* to the resource owner and gets back an *access token*. The combination of client identifier, client secret, and authorization code ensures that the resource owner can positively identify the client and its authorization.

   — The access token may optionally be short-lived and need to be refreshed by the client.

- The client uses the access token to make requests on behalf of the end user until the access token is revoked or expires.

Section 1.4.1 of the spec (*http://tools.ietf.org/html/draft-ietf-oauth-v2-10#section-1.4 .1*) provides more details and the basis for Figure 4-1.

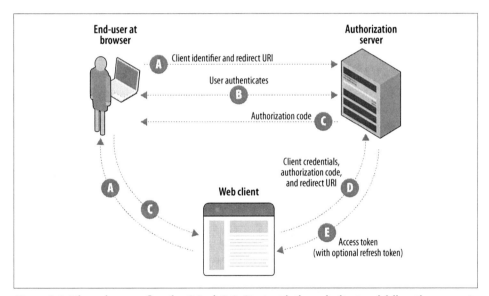

Figure 4-1. The web server flow for OAuth 2.0. Start with the web client and follow the arrows in lexographic order so that you end back at the web client after completing steps A–E.

Again, OAuth 2.0 is a relatively new beast, and as of late 2010, various details are still being hammered out before the spec is officially published as an RFC. Your best bet for really understanding it is to sweat through reading the spec, sketching out some flows, asking yourself questions, role playing as the malicious user, etc. To get a feel for some of the politics associated with OAuth, review the Ars Technica article by Ryan Paul, "Twitter: A Case Study on How to Do OAuth Wrong" (*http://arstechnica.com/*

security/guides/2010/09/twitter-a-case-study-on-how-to-do-oauth-wrong.ars). Also check out Eran Hammer-Lahav's (the first author on the OAuth 2.0 Protocol working draft) response (*http://hueniverse.com/2010/09/all-this-twitter-oauth-security-non sense/*), along with the fairly detailed rebuttal (*http://benlog.com/articles/2010/09/02/an -unwarranted-bashing-of-twitters-oauth/*) by Ben Adida, a cryptography expert.

 As a late-breaking convenience for situations that involve what Twitter calls a "single-user use case", Twitter also offers a streamlined fast track for getting the credentials you need to make requests without having to implement the entire OAuth flow. Read more about it at *http://dev.twit ter.com/pages/oauth_single_token*. This chapter and the following chapter, however, are written with the assumption that you'll want to implement the standard OAuth flow.

A Lean, Mean Data-Collecting Machine

In principle, fetching Twitter data is dirt simple: make a request, store the response, and repeat as needed. But all sorts of real-world stuff gets in the way, such as network I/O, the infamous fail whale,[3] and those pesky API rate limits. Fortunately, it's not too difficult to handle such issues, so long as you do a bit of forward planning and anticipate the things that could (and will) go wrong.

When executing a long-running program that's eating away at your rate limit, writing robust code is especially important; you want to handle any exceptional conditions that could occur, do your best to remedy the situation, and—in the event that your best just isn't good enough—save state and leave an indication of how to pick things back up where they left off. In other words, when you write data-harvesting code for a platform like Twitter, you must assume that it will throw curve balls at you. There *will* be atypical conditions you'll have to handle, and they're often more the norm than the exception.

The code we'll develop is semi-rugged in that it deals with the most common things that can go wrong and is patterned so that you can easily extend it to handle new circumstances if they arise. That said, there are two specific HTTP errors you are highly likely to encounter when harvesting even modest amounts of Twitter data: a 401 Error (Not Authorized) and a 503 Error (Over Capacity). The former occurs when you attempt to access data that a user has protected, while the latter is basically unpredictable.

Whenever Twitter returns an HTTP error, the `twitter` module throws a `TwitterHTTP Error` exception, which can be handled like any other Python exception, with a `try/ except` block. Example 4-2 illustrates a minimal code block that harvests some friend IDs and handles some of the more common exceptional conditions.

---

3. Whenever Twitter goes over capacity, an HTTP 503 error is issued. In a browser, the error page displays an image of the now infamous "fail whale." See *http://twitter.com/503*.

You'll need to create a Twitter app (*http://twitter.com/apps/new*) in order to get a consumer key and secret that can be used with the Twitter examples in this book. It's painless and only takes a moment.

Example 4-2. Using OAuth to authenticate and grab some friend data (friends_followers__get_friends.py)

```
# -*- coding: utf-8 -*-

import sys
import time
import cPickle
import twitter
from twitter.oauth_dance import oauth_dance

# Go to http://twitter.com/apps/new to create an app and get these items

consumer_key = ''
consumer_secret = ''

SCREEN_NAME = sys.argv[1]
friends_limit = 10000

(oauth_token, oauth_token_secret) = oauth_dance('MiningTheSocialWeb',
        consumer_key, consumer_secret)
t = twitter.Twitter(domain='api.twitter.com', api_version='1',
                    auth=twitter.oauth.OAuth(oauth_token, oauth_token_secret,
                    consumer_key, consumer_secret))

ids = []
wait_period = 2  # secs
cursor = -1

while cursor != 0:
    if wait_period > 3600:  # 1 hour
        print 'Too many retries. Saving partial data to disk and exiting'
        f = file('%s.friend_ids' % str(cursor), 'wb')
        cPickle.dump(ids, f)
        f.close()
        exit()

    try:
        response = t.friends.ids(screen_name=SCREEN_NAME, cursor=cursor)
        ids.extend(response['ids'])
        wait_period = 2
    except twitter.api.TwitterHTTPError, e:
        if e.e.code == 401:
            print 'Encountered 401 Error (Not Authorized)'
            print 'User %s is protecting their tweets' % (SCREEN_NAME, )
        elif e.e.code in (502, 503):
            print 'Encountered %i Error. Trying again in %i seconds' % (e.e.code,
                    wait_period)
            time.sleep(wait_period)
```

```
            wait_period *= 1.5
            continue
        elif t.account.rate_limit_status()['remaining_hits'] == 0:
            status = t.account.rate_limit_status()
            now = time.time()  # UTC
            when_rate_limit_resets = status['reset_time_in_seconds']  # UTC
            sleep_time = when_rate_limit_resets - now
            print 'Rate limit reached. Trying again in %i seconds' % (sleep_time,
                    )
            time.sleep(sleep_time)
            continue

    cursor = response['next_cursor']
    print 'Fetched %i ids for %s' % (len(ids), SCREEN_NAME)
    if len(ids) >= friends_limit:
        break

# do something interesting with the IDs

print ids
```

The `twitter.oauth` module provides `read_token_file` and `write_token_file` convenience functions that can be used to store and retrieve your OAuth token and OAuth token secret, so you don't have to manually enter in a PIN to authenticate each time.

 In OAuth 2.0 parlance, "client" describes the same role as a "consumer" in OAuth 1.0, thus the use of the variable names `consumer_key` and `consumer_secret` in the preceding listing.

There are several noteworthy items about the listing:

- You can obtain your own `consumer_key` and `consumer_secret` by registering an application with Twitter at *http://dev.twitter.com/apps/new*. These two items, along with the credentials returned through the "OAuth dance," are what enable you to provide an application with access to your account data (your friends list, in this particular example).

- The online documentation for Twitter's social graph APIs (*http://dev.twitter.com/doc/get/friends/ids*) states that requests for friend/follower data will return up to 5,000 IDs per call. In the event that there are more than 5,000 IDs to be returned, a cursor value that's not equal to zero is returned that can be used to navigate forward to the next batch. This particular example "stops short" at a maximum of 10,000 ID values, but `friends_limit` could be an arbitrarily larger number.

- Given that the `/friends/ids` resource returns up to 5,000 IDs at a time, regular user accounts could retrieve up to 1,750,000 IDs before rate limiting would kick in based on a 350 requests/hour metric. While it might be an anomaly for a user to have that many friends on Twitter, it's not at all uncommon for popular users to have many times that many followers.

- It's not clear from any official documentation or the example code itself, but ID values in the results seem to be in reverse chronological order, so the first value will be the person you most recently followed, and the last value will be the first person you followed. Requests for followers via `t.followers.ids` appear to return results in the same order.

At this point, you've only been introduced to a few Twitter APIs. These are sufficiently powerful to answer a number of interesting questions about your account or any other nonprotected account, but there are numerous other APIs out there. We'll look at some more of them shortly, but first, let's segue into a brief interlude to refactor Example 4-2.

A Very Brief Refactor Interlude

Given that virtually all interesting code listings involving Twitter data will repeatedly involve performing the OAuth dance and making robust requests that can stand up to the litany of things that you have to assume might go wrong, it's very worthwhile to establish a pattern for performing these tasks. The approach that we'll take is to isolate the OAuth logic for `login()` and `makeTwitterRequest` functions so that Example 4-2 looks like the following refactored version of Example 4-3:

Example 4-3. Example 4-2 refactored to use two common utilities for OAuth and making API requests (friends_followers__get_friends_refactored.py)

```
# -*- coding: utf-8 -*-

import sys
import time
import cPickle
import twitter
from twitter__login import login
from twitter__util import makeTwitterRequest

friends_limit = 10000

# You may need to setup your OAuth settings in twitter__login.py
t = login()

def getFriendIds(screen_name=None, user_id=None, friends_limit=10000):
    assert screen_name is not None or user_id is not None

    ids = []
    cursor = -1
    while cursor != 0:
        params = dict(cursor=cursor)
        if screen_name is not None:
            params['screen_name'] = screen_name
        else:
            params['user_id'] = user_id

        response = makeTwitterRequest(t, t.friends.ids, **params)
```

```
        ids.extend(response['ids'])
        cursor = response['next_cursor']
        print >> sys.stderr, \
            'Fetched %i ids for %s' % (len(ids), screen_name or user_id)
        if len(ids) >= friends_limit:
            break

    return ids

if __name__ == '__main__':
    ids = getFriendIds(sys.argv[1], friends_limit=10000)

    # do something interesting with the ids
    print ids
```

From here on out, we'll continue to use `twitter__login` (*http://github.com/ptwobrus sell/Mining-the-Social-Web/blob/master/python_code/twitter__login.py*) and `twit ter__util` (*http://github.com/ptwobrussell/Mining-the-Social-Web/blob/master/python _code/twitter__util.py*) to keep the examples as crisp and simple as possible. It's worthwhile to take a moment and peruse the source for these modules online before reading further. They'll appear again and again, and `twitter__util` will soon come to have a number of commonly used convenience functions in it.

The next section introduces Redis, a powerful data structures server that has quickly gained a fierce following due to its performance and simplicity.

Redis: A Data Structures Server

As we've already observed, planning ahead is important when you want to execute a potentially long-running program to scarf down data from the Web, because lots of things can go wrong. But what do you do with all of that data once you get it? You may initially be tempted to just store it to disk. In the situation we've just been looking at, that might result in a directory structure similar to the following:

```
./
screen_name1/
    friend_ids.json
    follower_ids.json
    user_info.json
screen_name2/
    ...
...
```

This looks pretty reasonable until you harvest all of the friends/followers for a very popular user—then, depending on your platform, you may be faced with a directory containing millions of subdirectories that's relatively unusable because you can't browse it very easily (if at all) in a terminal. Saving all this info to disk might also require that you maintain a registry of some sort that keeps track of all screen names, because the time required to generate a directory listing (in the event that you need one) for millions of files might not yield a desirable performance profile. If the app that uses the data then becomes threaded, you may end up with multiple writers needing to access the same file at the same time, so you'll have to start dealing with file locking and such things. That's probably not a place you want to go. All we really need in this case is a system that makes it trivially easy to store basic key/value pairs and a simple key encoding scheme—something like a disk-backed dictionary would be a good start. This next snippet demonstrates the construction of a key by concatenating a user ID, delimiter, and data structure name:

```
s = {}
s["screen_name1$friend_ids"] = [1,2,3, ...]
s["screen_name1$friend_ids"] # returns [1,2,3, ...]
```

But wouldn't it be cool if the map could automatically compute set operations so that we could just tell it to do something like:

```
s.intersection("screen_name1$friend_ids", "screen_name1$follower_ids")
```

to automatically compute "mutual friends" for a Twitterer (i.e., to figure out which of their friends are following them back)? Well, there's an open source project called Redis (*http://code.google.com/p/redis/*) that provides *exactly* that kind of capability. Redis is trivial to install, blazingly fast (written in C), scales well, is actively maintained, and has a great Python client with accompanying documentation available. Taking Redis for a test drive is as simple as installing it (*http://code.google.com/p/redis/*) and starting up the server. (Windows users can save themselves some headaches by grabbing a binary (*http://code.google.com/p/servicestack/wiki/RedisWindowsDownload*) that's maintained by servicestack.net.) Then, just run `easy_install redis` to obtain a nice Python client that provides trivial access to everything it has to offer. For example, the previous snippet translates to the following Redis code:

```
import redis

r = redis.Redis(host='localhost', port=6379, db=0) # Default params
[ r.sadd("screen_name1$friend_ids", i) for i in [1, 2, 3, ...] ]
r.smembers("screen_name1$friend_ids") # Returns [1, 2, 3, ...]
```

Note that while `sadd` and `smembers` are set-based operations, Redis includes operations specific to various other types of data structures, such as sets, lists, and hashes. The set operations turn out to be of particular interest because they provide the answers to many of the questions posed at the beginning of this chapter. It's worthwhile to take a moment to review the documentation for the Redis Python client to get a better appreciation of all it can do. Recall that you can simply execute a command like `pydoc redis.Redis` to quickly browse documentation from a terminal.

 See "Redis: under the hood" (*http://www.pauladamsmith.com/articles/redis_under_the_hood.html*) for an awesome technical deep dive into how Redis works internally.

Elementary Set Operations

The most common set operations you'll likely encounter are the union, intersection, and difference operations. Recall that the difference between a set and a list is that a set is unordered and contains only unique members, while a list is ordered and may contain duplicate members. As of Version 2.6, Python provides built-in support for sets via the set data structure. Table 4-1 illustrates some examples of common set operations for a trivially small universe of discourse involving friends and followers:

```
Friends = {Abe, Bob}, Followers = {Bob, Carol}
```

Table 4-1. Sample set operations for Friends and Followers

Operation	Result	Comment
Friends ∪ Followers	Abe, Bob, Carol	Someone's overall network
Friends ∩ Followers	Bob	Someone's mutual friends
Friends - Followers	Abe	People a person is following, but who are not following that person back
Followers - Friends	Carol	People who are following someone but are not being followed back

As previously mentioned, Redis provides native operations for computing common set operations. A few of the most relevant ones for the upcoming work at hand include:

smembers
> Returns all of the members of a set

scard
> Returns the cardinality of a set (the number of members in the set)

sinter
> Computes the intersection for a list of sets

sdiff
> Computes the difference for a list of sets

mget
> Returns a list of string values for a list of keys

mset
> Stores a list of string values against a list of keys

sadd
> Adds an item to a set (and creates the set if it doesn't already exist)

keys
> Returns a list of keys matching a regex-like pattern

Skimming the pydoc for Python's built-in set data type should convince you of the close mapping between it and the Redis APIs.

We're Gonna Analyze Like It's 1874

Although the concepts involved in set theory are as old as time itself, it is Georg Cantor who is generally credited with inventing set theory. His paper, "On a Characteristic Property of All Real Algebraic Numbers," written in 1874, formalized set theory as part of his work on answering questions related to the concept of infinity. For example:

- Are there more natural numbers (zero and the positive integers) than integers (positive and negative numbers)?

- Are there more rational numbers (numbers that can be expressed as fractions) than integers?

- Are there more irrational numbers (numbers that cannot be expressed as fractions, such as pi, $\sqrt{2}$, etc.) than rational numbers?

The gist of Cantor's work around infinity as it relates to the first two questions is that the cardinalities of the sets of natural numbers, integers, and rational numbers are all equal because you can map these numbers such that they form a sequence with a definite starting point that extends forever in *one* direction. Even though there is never an ending point, the cardinalities of these sets are said to be *countably infinite* because there is a definite sequence that could be followed deterministically if you simply had enough time to count them. The cardinality of a countably infinite set became known by mathematicians as $\aleph_0$, an official definition of infinity. Consider the following numeric patterns that convey the basic idea behind countably infinite sets. Each pattern shows a starting point that can extend infinitely:

- Natural numbers: 0, 1, 2, 3, 4, ...
- Positive integers: 1, 2, 3, 4, 5, ...
- Negative integers: -1, -2, -3, -4, -5, ...
- Integers: 0, 1, -1, 2, -2, 3, -3, 4, -4, ...
- Rational numbers: 0/0, 0/1, -1/1, -1/0, -1/-1, 0/-1, 1/-1, 1/0, 1/1, ...

Notice that the pattern for the rational numbers is that you can start at the origin of the Cartesian plane and build out a spiral in which each *x/y* coordinate pair is expressed as a fraction, which is a rational number. (The two cases where it is undefined because of division by zero are of no consequence to the cardinality of the set as a whole.)

As it runs out, however, the cardinality of the set of irrational numbers is not equal to $\aleph_0$, because it is impossible to arrange them in such a way that they are countable and form a one-to-one correspondence back to a set having cardinality $\aleph_0$. Cantor used what became known as the famous *diagonalization argument* (*http://en.wikipedia.org/wiki/Cantor's_diagonal_argument*) as the proof. The gist of the diagonalization proof is that just when you think you've mapped out a sequence that makes the irrational numbers countable, it can be shown that a whole slew of numbers are missing—and when you put these missing numbers into the sequence, there are still a slew of numbers missing. As it turns out, you can never form the one-to-one correspondence that's necessary. Thus, the cardinality of the set of irrational numbers is not the same as the cardinalities of the sets of natural numbers, positive integers, and irrational numbers, because a one-to-one correspondence from one of these sets cannot be derived.

So what is the cardinality of the set of irrational numbers? It can be shown that the power set of the set having cardinality $\aleph_0$ is the cardinality of the set of all irrational numbers. This value is known as $\aleph_1$. Further, the power set of the set having cardinality $\aleph_1$ is known as $\aleph_2$, etc. Computing the power set of a set of infinite numbers is admittedly a difficult concept to wrap one's head around, but it's one well worth pondering when you're having trouble sleeping at night.

Souping Up the Machine with Basic Friend/Follower Metrics

Redis should serve you well on your quest to efficiently process and analyze vast amounts of Twitter data for certain kinds of queries. Adapting Example 4-2 with some additional logic to house data in Redis requires only a simple change, and Example 4-4 is an update that computes some basic friend/follower statistics. Native functions in Redis are used to compute the set operations.

Example 4-4. Harvesting, storing, and computing statistics about friends and followers (friends_followers__friend_follower_symmetry.py)

```
# -*- coding: utf-8 -*-

import sys
import locale
import time
import functools
import twitter
import redis
from twitter__login import login

# A template-like function for maximizing code reuse,
# which is essentially a wrapper around makeTwitterRequest
# with some additional logic in place for interfacing with
# Redis
from twitter__util import _getFriendsOrFollowersUsingFunc

# Creates a consistent key value for a user given a screen name
from twitter__util import getRedisIdByScreenName

SCREEN_NAME = sys.argv[1]

MAXINT = sys.maxint

# For nice number formatting
locale.setlocale(locale.LC_ALL, '')

# You may need to setup your OAuth settings in twitter__login.py

t = login()
```

```
# Connect using default settings for localhost
r = redis.Redis()

# Some wrappers around _getFriendsOrFollowersUsingFunc
# that bind the first two arguments

getFriends = functools.partial(_getFriendsOrFollowersUsingFunc,
                               t.friends.ids, 'friend_ids', t, r)

getFollowers = functools.partial(_getFriendsOrFollowersUsingFunc,
                                 t.followers.ids, 'follower_ids', t, r)

screen_name = SCREEN_NAME

# get the data

print >> sys.stderr, 'Getting friends for %s...' % (screen_name, )
getFriends(screen_name, limit=MAXINT)

print >> sys.stderr, 'Getting followers for %s...' % (screen_name, )
getFollowers(screen_name, limit=MAXINT)

# use redis to compute the numbers

n_friends = r.scard(getRedisIdByScreenName(screen_name, 'friend_ids'))

n_followers = r.scard(getRedisIdByScreenName(screen_name, 'follower_ids'))

n_friends_diff_followers = r.sdiffstore('temp',
                                        [getRedisIdByScreenName(screen_name,
                                        'friend_ids'),
                                        getRedisIdByScreenName(screen_name,
                                        'follower_ids')])
r.delete('temp')

n_followers_diff_friends = r.sdiffstore('temp',
                                        [getRedisIdByScreenName(screen_name,
                                        'follower_ids'),
                                        getRedisIdByScreenName(screen_name,
                                        'friend_ids')])
r.delete('temp')

n_friends_inter_followers = r.sinterstore('temp',
        [getRedisIdByScreenName(screen_name, 'follower_ids'),
        getRedisIdByScreenName(screen_name, 'friend_ids')])
r.delete('temp')

print '%s is following %s' % (screen_name, locale.format('%d', n_friends, True))
print '%s is being followed by %s' % (screen_name, locale.format('%d',
                                      n_followers, True))
print '%s of %s are not following %s back' % (locale.format('%d',
        n_friends_diff_followers, True), locale.format('%d', n_friends, True),
        screen_name)
```

```
print '%s of %s are not being followed back by %s' % (locale.format('%d',
        n_followers_diff_friends, True), locale.format('%d', n_followers, True),
        screen_name)
print '%s has %s mutual friends' \
    % (screen_name, locale.format('%d', n_friends_inter_followers, True))
```

Aside from the use of functools.partial (*http://docs.python.org/library/functools*
.html) to create getFriends and getFollowers from a common piece of parameter-bound
code, Example 4-4 should be pretty straightforward. There's one other very subtle thing
to notice: there *isn't* a call to r.save in Example 4-4, which means that the settings in
redis.conf dictate when data is persisted to disk. By default, Redis stores data in memory
and asynchronously snapshots data to disk according to a schedule that's dictated by
whether or not a number of changes have occurred within a specified time interval. The
risk with asynchronous writes is that you might lose data if certain unexpected conditions, such as a system crash or power outage, were to occur. Redis provides an "append
only" option that you can enable in *redis.conf* to hedge against this possibility.

It is highly recommended that you enable the appendonly option in
redis.conf to protect against data loss; see the "Append Only File
HOWTO" (*http://code.google.com/p/redis/wiki/AppendOnlyFileHowto*)
for helpful details.

Consider the following output, relating to Tim O'Reilly's network of followers. Keeping
in mind that there's a rate limit of 350 OAuth requests per hour, you could expect this
code to take a little less than an hour to run, because approximately 300 API calls would
need to be made to collect all the follower ID values:

```
timoreilly is following 663
timoreilly is being followed by 1,423,704
131 of 633 are not following timoreilly back
1,423,172 of 1,423,704 are not being followed back by timoreilly
timoreilly has 532 mutual friends
```

Note that while you could choose to settle for harvesting a smaller number of followers
to avoid the rate limit–imposed wait, the API documentation does not state that taking
the first *N* pages' worth of data would yield a truly random sample, and it appears that
data is returned in reverse chronological order—so, you may not be able to extrapolate
in a predictable way whether your logic depends on it. For example, if the first 10,000
followers returned just so happened to contain the 532 mutual friends, extrapolation
from those points would result in a skewed analysis because these results are not at all
representative of the larger population. For a very popular Twitterer such as Britney
Spears, with well over 5,000,000 followers, somewhere in the neighborhood of 1,000
API calls would be required to fetch all of the followers over approximately a four-hour
period. In general, the wait is probably worth it for this kind of data, and you could use
the Twitter-streaming APIs to keep your data up-to-date so that you never have to go
through the entire ordeal again.

One common source of error for some kinds of analysis is to forget about the overall size of a population relative to your sample. For example, randomly sampling 10,000 of Tim O'Reilly's friends and followers would actually give you the full population of his friends, yet only a tiny fraction of his followers. Depending on the sophistication of your analysis, the sample size (*http://en.wikipedia.org/wiki/Sampling_(statistics)*) relative to the overall size of a population can make a difference in determining whether the outcome of an experiment is statistically significant, and the level of confidence you can have about it.

Given even these basic friend/follower stats, a couple of questions that lead us toward other interesting analyses naturally follow. For example, who are the 131 people who are not following Tim O'Reilly back? Given the various possibilities that could be considered about friends and followers, the "Who isn't following me back?" question is one of the more interesting ones and arguably can provide a lot of insight about a person's interests. So, how can we answer this question?

Staring at a list of user IDs isn't very riveting, so resolving those user IDs to actual user objects is the first obvious step. Example 4-5 extends Example 4-4 by encapsulating common error-handling code into reusable form. It also provides a function that demonstrates how to resolve those ID values to screen names using the /users/lookup API, which accepts a list of up to 100 user IDs or screen names and returns the same basic user information that you saw earlier with /users/show.

Example 4-5. Resolving basic user information such as screen names from IDs (friends_followers__get_user_info.py)

```
# -*- coding: utf-8 -*-

import sys
import json
import redis
from twitter__login import login

# A makeTwitterRequest call through to the /users/lookup
# resource, which accepts a comma separated list of up
# to 100 screen names. Details are fairly uninteresting.
# See also http://dev.twitter.com/doc/get/users/lookup
from twitter__util import getUserInfo

if __name__ == "__main__":
    screen_names = sys.argv[1:]

    t = login()
    r = redis.Redis()

    print json.dumps(
            getUserInfo(t, r, screen_names=screen_names),
            indent=4
        )
```

Although not reproduced in its entirety, the getUserInfo function that's imported from twitter__util is essentially just a makeTwitterRequest to the /users/lookup resource using a list of screen names. The following snippet demonstrates:

```
def getUserInfo(t, r, screen_names):
    info = []
    response = makeTwitterRequest(t,
                                  t.users.lookup,
                                  screen_name=','.join(screen_names)
                                  )

    for user_info in response:
        r.set(getRedisIdByScreenName(user_info['screen_name'], 'info.json'),
            json.dumps(user_info))
        r.set(getRedisIdByUserId(user_info['id'], 'info.json'),
            json.dumps(user_info))

    info.extend(response)

    return info
```

It's worthwhile to note that getUserInfo stores the same user information under two different keys: the user ID and the screen name. Storing both of these keys allows us to easily look up a screen name given a user ID value and a user ID value given a screen name. Translating a user ID value to a screen name is a particularly useful operation since the social graph APIs for getting friends and followers return only ID values, which have no intuitive value until they are resolved against screen names and other basic user information. While there is redundant storage involved in this scheme, compared to other approaches, the convenience is arguably worth it. Feel free to take a leaner approach if storage is a concern.

An example user information object for Tim O'Reilly follows in Example 4-6, illustrating the kind of information available about Twitterers. The sky is the limit with what you can do with data that's this rich. We won't mine the user descriptions and tweets of the folks who aren't following Tim back and put them in print, but you should have enough to work with should you wish to conduct that kind of analysis.

Example 4-6. Example user object represented as JSON data for Tim O'Reilly

```
{
    "id": 2384071,
    "verified": true,
    "profile_sidebar_fill_color": "e0ff92",
    "profile_text_color": "000000",
    "followers_count": 1423326,
    "protected": false,
    "location": "Sebastopol, CA",
    "profile_background_color": "9ae4e8",
    "status": {
        "favorited": false,
        "contributors": null,
        "truncated": false,
```

```
    "text": "AWESOME!! RT @adafruit: a little girl asks after seeing adafruit ...",
    "created_at": "Sun May 30 00:56:33 +0000 2010",
    "coordinates": null,
    "source": "<a href=\"http://www.seesmic.com/\" rel=\"nofollow\">Seesmic</a>",
    "in_reply_to_status_id": null,
    "in_reply_to_screen_name": null,
    "in_reply_to_user_id": null,
    "place": null,
    "geo": null,
    "id": 15008936780
  },
  "utc_offset": -28800,
  "statuses_count": 11220,
  "description": "Founder and CEO, O'Reilly Media. Watching the alpha geeks...",
  "friends_count": 662,
  "profile_link_color": "0000ff",
  "profile_image_url": "http://a1.twimg.com/profile_images/941827802/IMG_...jpg",
  "notifications": false,
  "geo_enabled": true,
  "profile_background_image_url": "http://a1.twimg.com/profile_background_...gif",
  "name": "Tim O'Reilly",
  "lang": "en",
  "profile_background_tile": false,
  "favourites_count": 10,
  "screen_name": "timoreilly",
  "url": "http://radar.oreilly.com",
  "created_at": "Tue Mar 27 01:14:05 +0000 2007",
  "contributors_enabled": false,
  "time_zone": "Pacific Time (US & Canada)",
  "profile_sidebar_border_color": "87bc44",
  "following": false
}
```

The refactored logic for handling HTTP errors and obtaining user information in batches is provided in the following sections. Note that the handleTwitterHTTPError function intentionally doesn't include error handling for every conceivable error case, because the action you may want to take will vary from situation to situation. For example, in the event of a urllib2.URLError (operation timed out) that is triggered because someone unplugged your network cable, you want to prompt the user for a specific course of action.

Example 4-5 brings to light some good news and some not-so-good news. The good news is that resolving the user IDs to user objects containing a byline, location information, the latest tweet, etc. is a treasure trove of information. The not-so-good news is that it's quite expensive to do this in terms of rate limiting, given that you can only get data back in batches of 100. For Tim O'Reilly's friends, that's only seven API calls. For his followers, however, it's over 14,000, which would take nearly two days to collect, given a rate limit of 350 calls per hour (and no glitches in harvesting).

However, given a full collection of anyone's friends and followers ID values, you *can* randomly sample and calculate measures of statistical significance to your heart's content. Redis provides the `srandmember` function that fits the bill perfectly. You pass it the name of a set, such as `timoreilly$follower_ids`, and it returns a random member of that set.

Calculating Similarity by Computing Common Friends and Followers

Another piece of low-hanging fruit that we can go after is computing the friends and followers that two or more Twitterers have in common. Within a given universe, these folks might be interesting for a couple of reasons. One reason is that they're the "common thread" connecting various disparate networks; you might interpret this to be a type of similarity metric. For example, if two users were both following a large number of the same people, you might conclude that those two users had very similar interests. From there, you might start to analyze the information embedded in the tweets of the common friends to gain more insight into what those people have in common, if anything, or make other conclusions. It turns out that computing common friends and followers is just a set operation away. Example 4-7 illustrates the use of Redis's `sinter store` function, which stores the result of a set intersection, and introduces `locale.for mat` for pretty-printing so that the output is easier to read.

Example 4-7. Finding common friends/followers for multiple Twitterers, with output that's easier on the eyes (friends_followers__friends_followers_in_common.py)

```
# -*- coding: utf-8 -*-

import sys
import redis

from twitter__util import getRedisIdByScreenName

# A pretty-print function for numbers
from twitter__util import pp

r = redis.Redis()

def friendsFollowersInCommon(screen_names):
    r.sinterstore('temp$friends_in_common',
                [getRedisIdByScreenName(screen_name, 'friend_ids')
                    for screen_name in screen_names]
                )

    r.sinterstore('temp$followers_in_common',
                [getRedisIdByScreenName(screen_name, 'follower_ids')
                    for screen_name in screen_names]
                )

    print 'Friends in common for %s: %s' % (', '.join(screen_names),
            pp(r.scard('temp$friends_in_common')))
```

```
    print 'Followers in common for %s: %s' % (', '.join(screen_names),
            pp(r.scard('temp$followers_in_common')))

    # Clean up scratch workspace

    r.delete('temp$friends_in_common')
    r.delete('temp$followers_in_common')

if __name__ == "__main__":
    if len(sys.argv) < 3:
        print >> sys.stderr, "Please supply at least two screen names."
        sys.exit(1)

    # Note:
    # The assumption is that the screen names you are
    # supplying have already been added to Redis.
    # See friends_followers__get_friends__refactored.py

    friendsFollowersInCommon(sys.argv[1:])
```

Note that although the values in the working sets are ID values, you could easily use Redis' randomkey function to sample friends and followers, and use the getUserInfo function from Example 4-5 to resolve useful information such as screen names, most recent tweets, locations, etc.

Measuring Influence

When someone shares information via a service such as Twitter, it's only natural to wonder how far the information penetrates into the overall network by means of being retweeted. It should be fair to assume that the more followers a person has, the greater the potential is for that person's tweets to be retweeted. Users who have a relatively high overall percentage of their originally authored tweets retweeted can be said to be more influential than users who are retweeted infrequently. Users who have a relatively high percentage of their tweets retweeted, even if they are not originally authored, might be said to be *mavens*—people who are exceptionally well connected and like to share information.[4] One trivial way to measure the relative influence of two or more users is to simply compare their number of followers, since every follower will have a direct view of their tweets. We already know from Example 4-6 that we can get the number of followers (and friends) for a user via the /users/lookup and /users/show APIs. Extracting that information from these APIs is trivial enough:

```
    for screen_name in screen_names:
        _json = json.loads(r.get(getRedisIdByScreenName(screen_name, "info.json")))
        n_friends, n_followers = _json['friends_count'], _json['followers_count']
```

---

4. See *The Tipping Point* by Malcolm Gladwell (Back Bay Books) for a great discourse on mavens.

Counting numbers of followers is interesting, but there's so much more that can be done. For example, a given user may not have the popularity of an information maven like Tim O'Reilly, but if you have him as a follower and he retweets you, you've suddenly tapped into a vast network of people who might just start to follow you once they've determined that you're also interesting. Thus, a much better approach that you might take in calculating users' potential influence is to not only compare their numbers of followers, but to spider out into the network a couple of levels. In fact, we can use the very same breadth-first approach that was introduced in Example 2-4.

Example 4-8 illustrates a generalized `crawl` function that accepts a list of screen names, a crawl depth, and parameters that control how many friends and followers to retrieve. The `friends_limit` and `followers_limit` parameters control how many items to fetch from the social graph APIs (in batches of 5,000), while `friends_sample` and `follow ers_sample` control how many user objects to retrieve (in batches of 100). An updated function for `getUserInfo` is also included to reflect the pass-through of the sampling parameters.

Example 4-8. Crawling friends/followers connections (friends_followers__crawl.py)

```
# -*- coding: utf-8 -*-

import sys
import redis
import functools
from twitter__login import login
from twitter__util import getUserInfo
from twitter__util import _getFriendsOrFollowersUsingFunc

SCREEN_NAME = sys.argv[1]

t = login()
r = redis.Redis()

# Some wrappers around _getFriendsOrFollowersUsingFunc that
# create convenience functions

getFriends = functools.partial(_getFriendsOrFollowersUsingFunc,
                               t.friends.ids, 'friend_ids', t, r)
getFollowers = functools.partial(_getFriendsOrFollowersUsingFunc,
                                 t.followers.ids, 'follower_ids', t, r)

def crawl(
    screen_names,
    friends_limit=10000,
    followers_limit=10000,
    depth=1,
    friends_sample=0.2, #XXX
    followers_sample=0.0,
    ):

    getUserInfo(t, r, screen_names=screen_names)
    for screen_name in screen_names:
```

```
            friend_ids = getFriends(screen_name, limit=friends_limit)
            follower_ids = getFollowers(screen_name, limit=followers_limit)

            friends_info = getUserInfo(t, r, user_ids=friend_ids,
                                    sample=friends_sample)

            followers_info = getUserInfo(t, r, user_ids=follower_ids,
                                    sample=followers_sample)

            next_queue = [u['screen_name'] for u in friends_info + followers_info]

            d = 1
            while d < depth:
                d += 1
                (queue, next_queue) = (next_queue, [])
                for _screen_name in queue:
                    friend_ids = getFriends(_screen_name, limit=friends_limit)
                    follower_ids = getFollowers(_screen_name, limit=followers_limit)

                    next_queue.extend(friend_ids + follower_ids)

                    # Note that this function takes a kw between 0.0 and 1.0 called
                    # sample that allows you to crawl only a random sample of nodes
                    # at any given level of the graph

                    getUserInfo(user_ids=next_queue)

if __name__ == '__main__':
    if len(sys.argv) < 2:
        print "Please supply at least one screen name."
    else:
        crawl([SCREEN_NAME])

        # The data is now in the system. Do something interesting. For example,
        # find someone's most popular followers as an indiactor of potential influence.
        # See friends_followers__calculate_avg_influence_of_followers.py
```

Assuming you've run `crawl` with high enough numbers for `friends_limit` and `follow ers_limit` to get all of a users' friend IDs and follower IDs, all that remains is to take a large enough random sample and calculate interesting metrics, such as the average number of followers one level out. It could also be fun to look at his top N followers to get an idea of who he might be influencing. Example 4-9 demonstrates one possible approach that pulls the data out of Redis and calculates Tim O'Reilly's most popular followers.

Example   4-9.   Calculating   a   Twitterer's   most   popular   followers (friends_followers__calculate_avg_influence_of_followers.py)

```
# -*- coding: utf-8 -*-

import sys
import json
import locale
import redis
```

```
from prettytable import PrettyTable

# Pretty printing numbers
from twitter__util import pp

# These functions create consistent keys from
# screen names and user id values
from twitter__util import getRedisIdByScreenName
from twitter__util import getRedisIdByUserId

SCREEN_NAME = sys.argv[1]

locale.setlocale(locale.LC_ALL, '')

def calculate():
    r = redis.Redis()  # Default connection settings on localhost

    follower_ids = list(r.smembers(getRedisIdByScreenName(SCREEN_NAME,
                            'follower_ids')))

    followers = r.mget([getRedisIdByUserId(follower_id, 'info.json')
                        for follower_id in follower_ids])
    followers = [json.loads(f) for f in followers if f is not None]

    freqs = {}
    for f in followers:
        cnt = f['followers_count']
        if not freqs.has_key(cnt):
            freqs[cnt] = []

        freqs[cnt].append({'screen_name': f['screen_name'], 'user_id': f['id']})

    # It could take a few minutes to calculate freqs, so store a snapshot for later use

    r.set(getRedisIdByScreenName(SCREEN_NAME, 'follower_freqs'),
          json.dumps(freqs))

    keys = freqs.keys()
    keys.sort()

    print 'The top 10 followers from the sample:'

    fields = ['Date', 'Count']
    pt = PrettyTable(fields=fields)
    [pt.set_field_align(f, 'l') for f in fields]

    for (user, freq) in reversed([(user['screen_name'], k) for k in keys[-10:]
                                    for user in freqs[k]]):
        pt.add_row([user, pp(freq)])

    pt.printt()

    all_freqs = [k for k in keys for user in freqs[k]]
    avg = reduce(lambda x, y: x + y, all_freqs) / len(all_freqs)
```

```
print "\nThe average number of followers for %s's followers: %s" \
    % (SCREEN_NAME, pp(avg))

# psyco can only compile functions, so wrap code in a function

try:
    import psyco
    psyco.bind(calculate)
except ImportError, e:
    pass  # psyco not installed

calculate()
```

 In many common number-crunching situations, the psyco (*http://psyco* *.sourceforge.net*) module can dynamically compile code and produce dramatic speed improvements. It's totally optional but definitely worth a hard look if you're performing calculations that take more than a few seconds.

Output follows for a sample size of about 150,000 (approximately 10%) of Tim O'Reilly's followers. For statistical analysis, this high of a sample size relative to the population ensures a tiny margin of error and a very high confidence (*http://en.wikipedia* *.org/wiki/Confidence_interval*) level.[5] That is, the results can be considered very representative, though not quite the same thing as the absolute truth about the population:

```
The top 10 followers from the sample:
aplusk 4,993,072
BarackObama 4,114,901
mashable 2,014,615
MarthaStewart 1,932,321
Schwarzenegger 1,705,177
zappos 1,689,289
Veronica 1,612,827
jack 1,592,004
stephenfry 1,531,813
davos 1,522,621

The average number of followers for timoreilly's followers: 445
```

Interestingly, a few familiar names show up on the list, including some of the most popular Twitterers of all time: Ashton Kutcher (@*aplusk*), Barack Obama, Martha Stewart, and Arnold Schwarzenegger, among others. Removing these top 10 followers and recalculating lowers the average number of followers of Tim's followers to approximately 284. Removing any follower with less than 10 followers of her own, however, dramatically increases the number to more than 1,000! Noting that there are tens of thousands of followers in this range and briefly perusing their profiles, however, does bring some reality into the situation: many of these users are spam accounts, users who

---

5. It's about a 0.14 margin of error for a 99% confidence level.

are protecting their tweets, etc. Culling out the top 10 followers and all followers having fewer than 10 followers of their own might be a reasonable metric to work with; doing both of these things results in a number around 800, which is still quite high. There must be something to be said for the idea of getting retweeted by a popular Twitterer who has lots of connections to other popular Twitterers.

Constructing Friendship Graphs

This chapter has used sets as the primary data structure for storing and manipulating data because we've primarily been manipulating collections of items such as ID values, and set operations have provided some powerful operations in exchange for very little effort. While there are usually a few general-purpose tools that work fairly well for most jobs, there aren't any tools that work well for every job. You have a price to pay either way; generally speaking, the price is either paid up front, when you store the data in special indexes (as you learned was the case with CouchDB in the previous chapter), or at query time, when you look it up and don't have the benefit of those indexes. If you really must have it both ways, you end up paying for it in terms of redundant storage and the complexities associated with denormalization of the data—not to mention the maintenance of the source code itself.

When you start asking questions that lend themselves to a network topology, you may want to export your Redis data into a graph database such as NetworkX (introduced back in Chapter 1). There are many possible graphs you could construct, but let's assume you're interested in analyzing the friendships that exist in someone's social network, so you want a graph indicating which people are friends with one another. Given that social graphs provide tremendous insight and that Example 4-8 already provides the machinery for crawling Twitter relationships, take some time to harvest friendship data for one or more interesting Twitterers. The remainder of this section introduces some examples for analyzing it.

Assuming you've harvested friendship data and stored it away in Redis, Example 4-10 demonstrates how to construct a graph of all the common friendships that exist for a user. Basically, you just systematically walk over all the users in a nested loop and create edges whenever a friendship exists between *any* two people in the universe being considered. Once the data is available to NetworkX, you suddenly have a full arsenal of graph algorithms and utilities at your fingertips. The next section investigates a few of the valuable things you can mine out of a friendship graph.

Example 4-10. Exporting friend/follower data from Redis to NetworkX for easy graph analytics (friends_followers__redis_to_networkx.py)

```
# -*- coding: utf-8 -*-

# Summary: Build up a digraph where an edge exists between two users
# if the source node is following the destination node
```

```
import os
import sys
import json
import networkx as nx
import redis

from twitter__util import getRedisIdByScreenName
from twitter__util import getRedisIdByUserId

SCREEN_NAME = sys.argv[1]

g = nx.Graph()
r = redis.Redis()

# Compute all ids for nodes appearing in the graph

friend_ids = list(r.smembers(getRedisIdByScreenName(SCREEN_NAME, 'friend_ids')))
id_for_screen_name = json.loads(r.get(getRedisIdByScreenName(SCREEN_NAME,
                                'info.json')))['id']
ids = [id_for_screen_name] + friend_ids

for current_id in ids:
    print >> sys.stderr, 'Processing user with id', current_id

    try:
        current_info = json.loads(r.get(getRedisIdByUserId(current_id,
                                    'info.json')))
        current_screen_name = current_info['screen_name']
        friend_ids = list(r.smembers(getRedisIdByScreenName(current_screen_name,
                            'friend_ids')))

        # filter out ids for this person if they aren't also SCREEN_NAME's friends too,
        # which is the basis of the query

        friend_ids = [fid for fid in friend_ids if fid in ids]
    except Exception, e:
        print >> sys.stderr, 'Skipping', current_id

    for friend_id in friend_ids:
        try:
            friend_info = json.loads(r.get(getRedisIdByUserId(friend_id,
                                    'info.json')))
        except TypeError, e:
            print >> sys.stderr, '\tSkipping', friend_id, 'for', current_screen_name
            continue

        g.add_edge(current_screen_name, friend_info['screen_name'])

# Pickle the graph to disk...

if not os.path.isdir('out'):
    os.mkdir('out')

filename = os.path.join('out', SCREEN_NAME + '.gpickle')
nx.write_gpickle(g, filename)
```

```
print 'Pickle file stored in: %s' % filename

# You can un-pickle like so...

# g = nx.read_gpickle(os.path.join('out', SCREEN_NAME + '.gpickle'))
```

With the task of constructing a convenient graph representation from the friendships you've crawled and stored in Redis, let's now turn to the fun part: analyzing it.

Clique Detection and Analysis

Example 4-10 provides a terse routine that demonstrates how you might go about discovering friendship cliques (*http://en.wikipedia.org/wiki/Clique*) that exist for a given user by importing data from Redis and repeatedly adding edges to the graph via the idempotent add_edge operation. For example, if Abe is friends with Bob, Carol, and Dale, and Bob and Carol are also friends, the largest ("maximum") clique in the graph exists among Abe, Bob, and Carol. If Abe, Bob, Carol, and Dale were all mutual friends, however, the graph would be fully connected, and the maximum clique would be of size 4. Adding nodes to the graph might create additional cliques, but it would not necessarily affect the size of the maximum clique in the graph. In the context of the social web, cliques are fascinating because they are representative of mutual friendships, and the maximum clique is interesting because it indicates the largest set of common friendships in the graph. Given two social networks, comparing the sizes of the maximum friendship cliques might provide a lot of insight about group dynamics, among other things.

Figure 4-2 illustrates a sample graph with the maximum clique highlighted. This graph would be said to have a *clique number* of size 4.

 Technically speaking, there is a difference between a *maximal* clique and a *maximum* clique. The maximum clique is the largest clique in the graph (or cliques in the graph, if they have the same size). A maximal clique, on the other hand, is one that is not a subgraph of another clique. The maximum clique is also a maximal clique in that it isn't a subgraph of any other clique. However, various other maximal cliques often exist in graphs and need not necessarily share any nodes with the maximum clique. Figure 4-2, for example, illustrates a maximum clique of size 4, but there are several other maximal cliques of size 3 in the graph as well.

Finding cliques is an NP-complete problem (implying an exponential runtime), but NetworkX does provide the find_cliques (*http://networkx.lanl.gov/reference/gener ated/networkx.find_cliques.html#networkx.find_cliques*) method, which delivers a solid implementation that takes care of the heavy lifting. Just be advised that it might take a long time to run as graphs get beyond a reasonably small size.

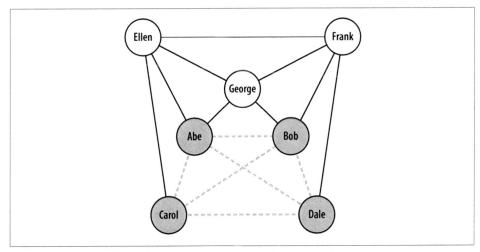

Figure 4-2. An example graph containing a maximum clique of size 4

Example 4-11 could be modified in any number of ways to compute interesting things, so long as you've first harvested the necessary friendship information. Assuming you've first constructed a graph as demonstrated in the previous section, it shows you how to use some of the NetworkX APIs for finding and analyzing cliques.

Example 4-11. Using NetworkX to find cliques in graphs (friends_followers__clique_analysis.py)

```
# -*- coding: utf-8 -*-

import sys
import json
import networkx as nx

G = sys.argv[1]

g = nx.read_gpickle(G)

# Finding cliques is a hard problem, so this could
# take awhile for large graphs.
# See http://en.wikipedia.org/wiki/NP-complete and
# http://en.wikipedia.org/wiki/Clique_problem

cliques = [c for c in nx.find_cliques(g)]

num_cliques = len(cliques)

clique_sizes = [len(c) for c in cliques]
max_clique_size = max(clique_sizes)
avg_clique_size = sum(clique_sizes) / num_cliques

max_cliques = [c for c in cliques if len(c) == max_clique_size]

num_max_cliques = len(max_cliques)
```

```
max_clique_sets = [set(c) for c in max_cliques]
people_in_every_max_clique = list(reduce(lambda x, y: x.intersection(y),
                                         max_clique_sets))

print 'Num cliques:', num_cliques
print 'Avg clique size:', avg_clique_size
print 'Max clique size:', max_clique_size
print 'Num max cliques:', num_max_cliques
print
print 'People in all max cliques:'
print json.dumps(people_in_every_max_clique, indent=4)
print
print 'Max cliques:'
print json.dumps(max_cliques, indent=4)
```

Sample output from the script follows for Tim O'Reilly's 600+ friendships and reveals some interesting insights. There are over 750,000 total cliques in the network, with an average clique size of 14 and a maximum clique size of 26. In other words, the largest number of people who are fully connected among Tim's friends is 26, and there are 6 distinct cliques of this size, as illustrated in the sample output in Example 4-12. The same individuals account for 20/26 of the population in all 6 of those cliques. You might think of these members as being especially foundational for Tim's friend network. Generally speaking, being able to discover cliques (especially maximal cliques and the maximum clique) in graphs can yield extremely powerful insight into complex data. An analysis of the similarity/diversity of tweet content among members of a large clique would be a very worthy exercise in tweet analysis. (More on tweet analysis in the next chapter.)

Example 4-12. Sample output from Example 4-11, illustrating common members of maximum cliques

```
Num cliques: 762573
Avg clique size: 14
Max clique size: 26
Num max cliques: 6

People in all max cliques:
[
    "kwerb",
    "johnbattelle",
    "dsearls",
    "JPBarlow",
    "cshirky",
    "leolaporte",
    "MParekh",
    "mkapor",
    "steverubel",
    "stevenbjohnson",
    "LindaStone",
    "godsdog",
    "Joi",
    "jayrosen_nyu",
```

```
        "dweinberger",
        "timoreilly",
        "ev",
        "jason_pontin",
        "kevinmarks",
        "Mlsif"
]

Max cliques:
[
    [
        "timoreilly",
        "anildash",
        "cshirky",
        "ev",
        "pierre",
        "mkapor",
        "johnbattelle",
        "kevinmarks",
        "MParekh",
        "dsearls",
        "kwerb",
        "Joi",
        "LindaStone",
        "dweinberger",
        "SteveCase",
        "leolaporte",
        "steverubel",
        "Borthwick",
        "godsdog",
        "edyson",
        "dangillmor",
        "Mlsif",
        "JPBarlow",
        "stevenbjohnson",
        "jayrosen_nyu",
        "jason_pontin"
    ],

    ...

]
```

Clearly, there's much more we could do than just detect the cliques. Plotting the locations of people involved in cliques on a map to see whether there's any correlation between tightly connected networks of people and geographic locale, and analyzing information in their profile data and/or tweet content are among the possibilities. As it turns out, the next chapter is all about analyzing tweets, so you might want to revisit this idea once you've read it. But first, let's briefly investigate an interesting Web API from Infochimps that we might use as a sanity check for some of the analysis we've been doing.

The Infochimps "Strong Links" API

Infochimps (*http://infochimps.org*) is an organization that provides an immense data catalog. Among its many offerings is a huge archive of historical Twitter data and various value-added APIs to operate on that data. One of the more interesting Twitter Metrics and Analytics APIs (*http://api.infochimps.com/describe/soc/net/tw*) is the Strong Links API, which returns a list of the users with whom the queried user communicates most frequently. In order to access this API, you just need to sign up for a free account to get an API key and then perform a simple GET request on a URL. The only catch is that the results provide user ID values, which must be resolved to screen names to be useful.[6] Fortunately, this is easy enough to do using existing code from earlier in this chapter. The script in Example 4-13 demonstrates how to use the Infochimps Strong Links API and uses Redis to resolve screen names from user ID values.

Example 4-13. Grabbing data from the Infochimps Strong Links API (friends_followers__infochimps_strong_links.py)

```
# -*- coding: utf-8 -*-

import sys
import urllib2
import json
import redis

from twitter__util import getRedisIdByUserId

SCREEN_NAME = sys.argv[1]
API_KEY = sys.argv[2]
API_ENDPOINT = \
    'http://api.infochimps.com/soc/net/tw/strong_links.json?screen_name=%s&apikey=%s'

r = redis.Redis()  # default connection settings on localhost

try:
    url = API_ENDPOINT % (SCREEN_NAME, API_KEY)
    response = urllib2.urlopen(url)
except urllib2.URLError, e:
    print 'Failed to fetch ' + url
    raise e

strong_links = json.loads(response.read())

# resolve screen names and print to screen:

print "%s's Strong Links" % (SCREEN_NAME, )
print '-' * 30
for sl in strong_links['strong_links']:
    if sl is None:
        continue
```

---

6. An Infochimps "Who Is" API (*http://api.infochimps.com/describe/soc/net/tw/whois*) is forthcoming and will provide a means of resolving screen names from user IDs.

```
try:
    user_info = json.loads(r.get(getRedisIdByUserId(sl[0], 'info.json')))
    print user_info['screen_name'], sl[1]
except Exception, e:
    print >> sys.stderr, "ERROR: couldn't resolve screen_name for", sl
    print >> sys.stderr, "Maybe you haven't harvested data for this person yet?"
```

What's somewhat interesting is that of the 20 individuals involved in all 6 of Tim's maximum cliques, only *@kevinmarks* appears in the results set. This seems to imply that just because you're tightly connected with friends on Twitter doesn't necessarily mean that you directly communicate with them very often. However, skipping ahead a chapter, you'll find in Table 5-2 that several of the Twitterers Tim retweets frequently do appear in the strong links list—namely, *@ahier*, *@gnat*, *@jamesoreilly*, *@pahlkadot*, *@OReillyMedia*, and *@monkchips*. (Note that *@monkchips* is second on the list of strong links, as shown in Example 4-14.) Infochimps does not declare exactly what the calculation is for its Strong Links API, except to say that it is built upon actual tweet content, analysis of which is the subject of the next chapter. The lesson learned here is that tightly connected friendship on Twitter need not necessarily imply frequent communication. (And, Infochimps provides interesting APIs that are definitely worth a look.)

Example 4-14. Sample results from the Infochimps Strong Links API from Example 4-13

```
timoreilly's Strong Links
-----------------------------
jstan 20.115004
monkchips 11.317813
govwiki 11.199023
ahier 10.485066
ValdisKrebs 9.384349
SexySEO 9.224745
tdgobux 8.937282
Scobleizer 8.406802
cheeky_geeky 8.339885
seanjoreilly 8.182084
pkedrosky 8.154991
OReillyMedia 8.086607
FOSSwiki 8.055233
n2vip 8.052422
jamesoreilly 8.015188
pahlkadot 7.811676
ginablaber 7.763785
kevinmarks 7.7423387
jcantero 7.64023
gnat 7.6349654
KentBottles 7.40848
Bill_Romanos 7.3629074
make 7.326427
carlmalamud 7.3147154
rivenhomewood 7.276802
webtechman 7.1044493
```

Interactive 3D Graph Visualization

It's a bit out of scope to take a dive into graph-layout algorithms, but it's hard to pass up an opportunity to introduce Ubigraph (*http://ubietylab.net/ubigraph/*), a 3D inter-active graph-visualization tool. While there's not really any analytical value in visual-izing a clique, it's nonetheless a good exercise to learn the ropes. Ubigraph is trivial to install and comes with bindings for a number of popular programming languages, in-cluding Python. Example 4-15 illustrates an example usage of Ubigraph for graphing the common members among the maximum cliques for a network. The bad news is that this is one of those opportunities where Windows folks will probably need to consider running a Linux-based virtual machine, since it is unlikely that there will be a build of the Ubigraph server anytime soon. The good news is that it's not very difficult to pull this together, even if you don't have advanced knowledge of Linux.

Example 4-15. Visualizing graph data with Ubigraph (friends_followers__ubigraph.py)

```
# -*- coding: utf-8 -*-

import sys
import json
import networkx as nx

# Packaged with Ubigraph in the examples/Python directory
import ubigraph

SCREEN_NAME = sys.argv[1]
FRIEND = sys.argv[2]

g = nx.read_gpickle(SCREEN_NAME + '.gpickle')

cliques = [c for c in nx.find_cliques(g) if FRIEND in c]
max_clique_size = max([len(c) for c in cliques])
max_cliques = [c for c in cliques if len(c) == max_clique_size]

print 'Found %s max cliques' % len(max_cliques)
print json.dumps(max_cliques, indent=4)

U = ubigraph.Ubigraph()
U.clear()
small = U.newVertexStyle(shape='sphere', color='#ffff00', size='0.2')
largeRed = U.newVertexStyle(shape='sphere', color='#ff0000', size='1.0')

# find the people who are common to all cliques for visualization

vertices = list(set([v for c in max_cliques for v in c]))
vertices = dict([(v, U.newVertex(style=small, label=v)) for v in vertices if v
                not in (SCREEN_NAME, FRIEND)])

vertices[SCREEN_NAME] = U.newVertex(style=largeRed, label=SCREEN_NAME)
vertices[FRIEND] = U.newVertex(style=largeRed, label=FRIEND)
```

```
for v1 in vertices:
    for v2 in vertices:
        if v1 == v2:
            continue
        U.newEdge(vertices[v1], vertices[v2])
```

All in all, you just create a graph and add vertices and edges to it. Note that unlike in NetworkX, however, nodes are not defined by their labels, so you do have to take care not to add duplicate nodes to the same graph. The preceding example demonstrates building a graph by iterating through a dictionary of vertices with minor customizations so that some nodes are easier to see than others. Following the pattern of the previous examples, this particular listing would visualize the common members of the maximum cliques shared between a particular user (Tim O'Reilly, in this case) and a friend (defined by FRIEND)—in other words, the largest clique containing two constrained nodes. Figure 4-3 shows a screenshot of Ubigraph at work. Like most everything else in this book, this is just the bare minimum of an introduction, intended to inspire you to go out and do great things with data.

Summary

This chapter only began to scratch the surface of what is possible with Twitter data, focusing primarily on the friend/follower relationships that can be discovered. A sample implementation of a command-line tool that ties all of the functionality from this chapter together is available at *http://github.com/ptwobrussell/Mining-the-Social-Web/ blob/master/python_code/TwitterSocialGraphUtility.py*, and you should be able to adapt it fairly easily for your own purposes. (If you do, please consider forking it on GitHub and making your changes available to everyone.) Some interesting ideas for fun exercises follow:

- We didn't tap into geo data in this chapter. Try plotting out a histogram of the locations your followers are from and visualize it on an online map. Chapter 6 is fairly heavy on geo data and provides a reasonable introduction to some mapping technologies you might be able to use.

- Try doing some basic frequency analysis of words that are in the description field of the user objects of your friends/followers. Chapters 7 and 8 provide tools and techniques that you might find helpful.

- Try creating a histogram of the numbers of tweets by each of your followers to see who is the chattiest. This data is available as statuses_count in user objects.

- We didn't talk about lists—a way of grouping together users, usually because of some common thread they share—in this chapter. Check out the API docs (*http: //dev.twitter.com/doc*) on list, and write some code to try to determine who has listed you (or any Twitterer you admire) and what similarities there are among the folks in the list. A good starting point is to look at the lists a person appears in directly through Twitter's public web interface.

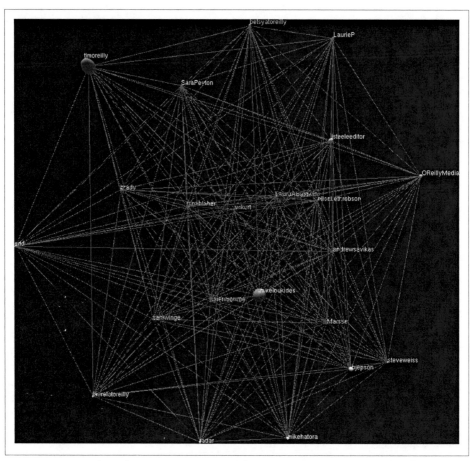

Figure 4-3. Screenshot of an interactive 3D visualization of common members appearing in the maximal cliques containing both @timoreilly and @mikeloukides (the screen shot doesn't do it justice; you really need to try this out interactively!)

CHAPTER 5

Twitter: The Tweet, the Whole Tweet, and Nothing but the Tweet

Tweet and RT were sitting on a fence. Tweet fell off.
Who was left?

In this chapter, we'll largely use CouchDB's map/reduce capabilities to exploit the entities in tweets (@mentions, #hashtags, etc.) to try to answer the question, "What's everyone talking about?" With overall throughput now far exceeding 50 million tweets per day (*http://mashable.com/2010/02/22/twitter-50-million-tweets/*) and occasional peak velocities in excess of 3,000 tweets per second (*http://blog.twitter.com/2010/06/another-big-record-part-deux.html*), there's vast potential in mining tweet content, and this is the chapter where we'll finally dig in. Whereas the previous chapter primarily focused on the social graph linkages that exist among friends and followers, this chapter focuses on learning as much as possible about Twitterers by inspecting the entities (*http://dev.twitter.com/pages/tweet_entities*) that appear in their tweets. You'll also see ties back to Redis for accessing user data you have harvested from Chapter 4 and NetworkX for graph analytics. So many tweets, so little time to mine them—let's get started!

 It is highly recommended that you read Chapters 3 and 4 before reading this chapter. Much of its discussion builds upon the foundation those chapters established, including Redis and CouchDB, which are again used in this chapter.

Pen : Sword :: Tweet : Machine Gun (?!?)

If the pen is mightier than the sword, what does that say about the tweet? There are a number of interesting incidents in which Twitter has saved lives, one of the most notorious being James Karl Buck's famous "Arrested" tweet (*http://techcrunch.com/2008/04/16/twitter-saves-man-from-egyptian-justice/*) that led to his speedy release when he was detained by Egyptian authorities. It doesn't take too much work to find evidence of similar incidents, as well as countless uses of Twitter for noble fundraising efforts and other benevolent causes. Having an outlet really can make a huge difference sometimes. More often than not, though, your home time line (tweet stream) and the public time line are filled with information that's not quite so dramatic or intriguing. At times like these, cutting out some of the cruft can help you glimpse the big picture. Given that as many as 50 percent of all tweets contain at least one entity (*http://dev.twitter .com/pages/tweet_entities*) that has been intentionally crafted by the tweet author, they make a very logical starting point for tweet analysis. In fact, Twitter has recognized their value and begun to directly expose them in the time line API calls, and in early 2010 and as the year unfolded, they increasingly became most standard throughout the entire Twitter API. Consider the tweet in Example 5-1, retrieved from a time line API call with the opt-in `include_entities=true` parameter specified in the query.

Example 5-1. A sample tweet from a search API that illustrates tweet entities

```
{
    "created_at" : "Thu Jun 24 14:21:11 +0000 2010",
    "entities" : {
                "hashtags" : [
                    {   "indices" : [ 97, 103 ],
                        "text" : "gov20"
                    },
                    {   "indices" : [ 104, 112 ],
                        "text" : "opengov"
                    }
                ],
                "urls" : [
                    {   "expanded_url" : null,
                        "indices" : [ 76, 96 ],
                        "url" : "http://bit.ly/9o4uoG"
                    }
                ],
                "user_mentions" : [
                    {   "id" : 28165790,
                        "indices" : [ 16, 28 ],
                        "name" : "crowdFlower",
                        "screen_name" : "crowdFlower"
                    }
                ]
    },
    "id" : 16932571217,
    "text" : "Great idea from @crowdflower: Crowdsourcing the Goldman ... #opengov",
    "user" : {
        "description" : "Founder and CEO, O'Reilly Media. Watching the alpha ...",
        "id" : 2384071,
        "location" : "Sebastopol, CA",
        "name" : "Tim O'Reilly",
        "screen_name" : "timoreilly",
        "url" : "http://radar.oreilly.com",
    }
}
```

By default, a tweet specifies a lot of useful information about its author via the user field in the status object, but the tweet entities provide insight into the content of the tweet itself. By briefly inspecting this one sample tweet, we can safely infer that *@timoreilly* is probably interested in the transformational topics of open government and Government 2.0, as indicated by the hashtags included in the tweet. It's probably also safe to infer that *@crowdflower* has some relation to Government 2.0 and that the URL may point to such related content. Thus, if you wanted to discover some additional information about the author of this tweet in an automated fashion, you could consider *pivoting* from *@timoreilly* over to *@crowdflower* and exploring that user's tweets or profile information, spawning a search on the hashtags included in the tweet to see what kind of other information pops up, or following the link and doing some page scraping to learn more about the underlying context of the tweet.

Given that there's so much value to be gained from analyzing tweet entities, you'll surely miss them in some APIs or from historical archives of Twitter data that are becoming more and more common to mine. Instead of manually parsing them out of the text yourself (not such an easy thing to do when tweets contain arbitrary Unicode characters), however, just `easy_install twitter-text-py`[1] so that you can focus your efforts on far more interesting problems. The script in Example 5-2 illustrates some basic usage of its `Extractor` class, which produces a structure similar to the one exposed by the time line APIs. You have everything to gain and nothing to lose by automatically embedding entities in this manner until tweet entities become the default.

 As of December 2010, tweet entities were becoming more and more common through the APIs, but were not quite officially "blessed" and the norm. This chapter was written with the assumption that you'd want to know how to parse them out for yourself, but you should realize that keeping up with the latest happenings with the Twitter API might save you some work. Manual extraction of tweet entities might also be very helpful for situations in which you're mining historical archives from organizations such as Infochimps or GNIP.

Example 5-2. Extracting tweet entities with a little help from the twitter_text package (the_tweet__extract_tweet_entities.py)

```
# -*- coding: utf-8 -*-

import sys
import json
import twitter_text
import twitter
from twitter__login import login

# Get a tweet id clicking on a status right off of twitter.com.
```

---

1. The `twitter-text-py` module is a port of the `twitter-text-rb` module (both available via GitHub), which Twitter uses in production (*http://dev.twitter.com/pages/tweet_entities*).

```
# For example, http://twitter.com/#!/timoreilly/status/17386521699024896

TWEET_ID = sys.argv[1]

# You may need to setup your OAuth settings in twitter__login.py
t = login()

def getEntities(tweet):

    # Now extract various entities from it and build up a familiar structure

    extractor = twitter_text.Extractor(tweet['text'])

    # Note that the production Twitter API contains a few additional fields in
    # the entities hash that would require additional API calls to resolve

    entities = {}
    entities['user_mentions'] = []
    for um in extractor.extract_mentioned_screen_names_with_indices():
        entities['user_mentions'].append(um)

    entities['hashtags'] = []
    for ht in extractor.extract_hashtags_with_indices():

        # massage field name to match production twitter api

        ht['text'] = ht['hashtag']
        del ht['hashtag']
        entities['hashtags'].append(ht)

    entities['urls'] = []
    for url in extractor.extract_urls_with_indices():
        entities['urls'].append(url)

    return entities


# Fetch a tweet using an API method of your choice and mixin the entities

tweet = t.statuses.show(id=TWEET_ID)

tweet['entities'] = getEntities(tweet)

print json.dumps(tweet, indent=4)
```

Now, equipped with an overview of tweet entities and some of the interesting possibilities, let's get to work harvesting and analyzing some tweets.

Analyzing Tweets (One Entity at a Time)

CouchDB makes a great storage medium for collecting tweets because, just like the email messages we looked at in Chapter 3, they are conveniently represented as JSON-based documents and lend themselves to map/reduce analysis with very little effort.

Our next example script harvests tweets from time lines, is relatively robust, and should be easy to understand because all of the modules and much of the code has already been introduced in earlier chapters. One subtle consideration in reviewing it is that it uses a simple map/reduce job to compute the maximum ID value for a tweet and passes this in as a query constraint so as to avoid pulling duplicate data from Twitter's API. See the information associated with the since_id parameter of the time line APIs for more details.

It may also be informative to note that the maximum number of most recent tweets available from the user time line is around 3,200, while the home time line[2] returns around 800 statuses; thus, it's not very expensive (in terms of counting toward your rate limit) to pull all of the data that's available. Perhaps not so intuitive when first interacting with the time line APIs is the fact that requests for data on the public time line only return 20 tweets, and those tweets are updated only every 60 seconds. To collect larger amounts of data you need to use the streaming API.

For example, if you wanted to learn a little more about Tim O'Reilly, "Silicon Valley's favorite smart guy,"[3] you'd make sure that CouchDB is running and then invoke the script shown in Example 5-3, as follows:

```
$ python the_tweet__harvest_timeline.py user 16 timoreilly
```

It'll only take a few moments while approximately 3,200 tweets' worth of interesting tidbits collect for your analytic pleasure.

Example 5-3. Harvesting tweets from a user or public time line (the_tweet__harvest_timeline.py)

```
# -*- coding: utf-8 -*-

import sys
import time
import twitter
import couchdb
from couchdb.design import ViewDefinition
from twitter__login import login
from twitter__util import makeTwitterRequest


def usage():
    print 'Usage: $ %s timeline_name [max_pages] [user]' % (sys.argv[0], )
    print
    print '\ttimeline_name in [public, home, user]'
    print '\t0 < max_pages <= 16 for timeline_name in [home, user]'
    print '\tmax_pages == 1 for timeline_name == public'
    print 'Notes:'
    print '\t* ~800 statuses are available from the home timeline.'
```

2. The Twitter API documentation states that the friend time line is similar to the home time line, except that it does not contain retweets for backward-compatibility purposes.

3. See the May 2010 cover of *Inc.* magazine (*http://www.inc.com/magazine/20100501/the-oracle-of-silicon -valley .html*).

```
    print '\t* ~3200 statuses are available from the user timeline.'
    print '\t* The public timeline updates once every 60 secs and returns 20 statuses.'
    print '\t* See the streaming/search API for additional options to harvest tweets.'

    exit()


if len(sys.argv) < 2 or sys.argv[1] not in ('public', 'home', 'user'):
    usage()
if len(sys.argv) > 2 and not sys.argv[2].isdigit():
    usage()
if len(sys.argv) > 3 and sys.argv[1] != 'user':
    usage()

TIMELINE_NAME = sys.argv[1]
MAX_PAGES = int(sys.argv[2])

USER = None

KW = {  # For the Twitter API call
    'count': 200,
    'skip_users': 'true',
    'include_entities': 'true',
    'since_id': 1,
    }
if TIMELINE_NAME == 'user':
    USER = sys.argv[3]
    KW['id'] = USER  # id or screen name
if TIMELINE_NAME == 'home' and MAX_PAGES > 4:
    MAX_PAGES = 4
if TIMELINE_NAME == 'user' and MAX_PAGES > 16:
    MAX_PAGES = 16
if TIMELINE_NAME == 'public':
    MAX_PAGES = 1

t = login()

# Establish a connection to a CouchDB database

server = couchdb.Server('http://localhost:5984')
DB = 'tweets-%s-timeline' % (TIMELINE_NAME, )

if USER:
    DB = '%s-%s' % (DB, USER)

try:
    db = server.create(DB)
except couchdb.http.PreconditionFailed, e:

    # Already exists, so append to it, keeping in mind that duplicates could occur

    db = server[DB]

    # Try to avoid appending duplicate data into the system by only retrieving tweets
    # newer than the ones already in the system. A trivial mapper/reducer combination
```

```
# allows us to pull out the max tweet id which guards against duplicates for the
# home and user timelines. It has no effect for the public timeline


def idMapper(doc):
    yield (None, doc['id'])


def maxFindingReducer(keys, values, rereduce):
    return max(values)


view = ViewDefinition('index', 'max_tweet_id', idMapper, maxFindingReducer,
                      language='python')
view.sync(db)
KW['since_id'] = int([_id for _id in db.view('index/max_tweet_id')][0].value)
# Harvest tweets for the given timeline.
# For friend and home timelines, the unofficial limitation is about 800 statuses although
# other documentation may state otherwise. The public timeline only returns 20 statuses
# and gets updated every 60 seconds.
# See http://groups.google.com/group/twitter-development-talk/browse_thread/
# thread/4678df70c301be43
# Note that the count and since_id params have no effect for the public timeline

page_num = 1
while page_num <= MAX_PAGES:
    KW['page'] = page_num
    api_call = getattr(t.statuses, TIMELINE_NAME + '_timeline')
    tweets = makeTwitterRequest(t, api_call, **KW)
    db.update(tweets, all_or_nothing=True)
    print 'Fetched %i tweets' % len(tweets)
    page_num += 1
```

Given some basic infrastructure for collecting tweets, let's start hacking to see what useful information we can discover.

Tapping (Tim's) Tweets

This section investigates a few of the most common questions that come to mind from a simple rack and stack of entities mined out of Tim O'Reilly's user time line. Although Tim has graciously agreed to being put under the microscope for educational purposes, you could easily repurpose these scripts for your own tweets or apply them to any other fascinating Twitterer. Or, you could begin with a reasonably large amount of public time line data that you've collected as your initial basis of exploration. A few interesting questions we'll consider include:

- How many of the user entities that appear most frequently in Tim's tweets are also his friends?
- What are the most frequently occurring entities that appear in Tim's tweets?
- Who does Tim retweet the most often?

- How many of Tim's tweets get retweeted?
- How many of Tim's tweets contain at least one entity?

Like so many other situations involving a relatively unknown data source, one of the first things you can do to learn more about it is to count things in it. In the case of tweet data, counting the user mentions, hashtags, and URLs are great places to start. The next section gets the ball rolling by leveraging some basic map/reduction functionality to count tweet entities. Although tweet entities already exist in time line data, some of the code examples in the rest of this chapter assume that you might have gotten the data from elsewhere (search APIs, streaming APIs, etc.). Thus, we parse out the tweet entities to maintain good and consistent form. Relying on Twitter to extract your tweet entities for you is just a couple of code tweaks away.

What entities are in Tim's tweets?

You can use CouchDB's Futon to skim Tim's user time line data one tweet at a time by browsing *http://localhost:5984/_utils*, but you'll quickly find yourself unsatisfied, and you'll want to get an overall summary of what Tim has been tweeting about, rather than a huge list of mentions of lots of specific things. Some preliminary answers are just a map/reduce job's worth of effort away and can be easily computed with the script shown in Example 5-4.

Example 5-4. Extracting entities from tweets and performing simple frequency analysis (the_tweet__count_entities_in_tweets.py)

```
# -*- coding: utf-8 -*-

import sys
import couchdb
from couchdb.design import ViewDefinition
from prettytable import PrettyTable

DB = sys.argv[1]

server = couchdb.Server('http://localhost:5984')
db = server[DB]

if len(sys.argv) > 2 and sys.argv[2].isdigit():
    FREQ_THRESHOLD = int(sys.argv[2])
else:
    FREQ_THRESHOLD = 3

# Map entities in tweets to the docs that they appear in


def entityCountMapper(doc):
    if not doc.get('entities'):
        import twitter_text

        def getEntities(tweet):
```

```
        # Now extract various entities from it and build up a familiar structure

        extractor = twitter_text.Extractor(tweet['text'])

        # Note that the production Twitter API contains a few additional fields in
        # the entities hash that would require additional API calls to resolve

        entities = {}
        entities['user_mentions'] = []
        for um in extractor.extract_mentioned_screen_names_with_indices():
            entities['user_mentions'].append(um)

        entities['hashtags'] = []
        for ht in extractor.extract_hashtags_with_indices():

            # Massage field name to match production twitter api

            ht['text'] = ht['hashtag']
            del ht['hashtag']
            entities['hashtags'].append(ht)

        entities['urls'] = []
        for url in extractor.extract_urls_with_indices():
            entities['urls'].append(url)

        return entities

    doc['entities'] = getEntities(doc)

    if doc['entities'].get('user_mentions'):
        for user_mention in doc['entities']['user_mentions']:
            yield ('@' + user_mention['screen_name'].lower(), [doc['_id'], doc['id']])
    if doc['entities'].get('hashtags'):
        for hashtag in doc['entities']['hashtags']:
            yield ('#' + hashtag['text'], [doc['_id'], doc['id']])
    if doc['entities'].get('urls'):
        for url in doc['entities']['urls']:
            yield (url['url'], [doc['_id'], doc['id']])


def summingReducer(keys, values, rereduce):
    if rereduce:
        return sum(values)
    else:
        return len(values)


view = ViewDefinition('index', 'entity_count_by_doc', entityCountMapper,
                      reduce_fun=summingReducer, language='python')
view.sync(db)

# Print out a nicely formatted table. Sorting by value in the client is cheap and easy
# if you're dealing with hundreds or low thousands of tweets
```

```
entities_freqs = sorted([(row.key, row.value) for row in
                        db.view('index/entity_count_by_doc', group=True)],
                        key=lambda x: x[1], reverse=True)

fields = ['Entity', 'Count']
pt = PrettyTable(fields=fields)
[pt.set_field_align(f, 'l') for f in fields]

for (entity, freq) in entities_freqs:
    if freq > FREQ_THRESHOLD:
        pt.add_row([entity, freq])

pt.printt()
```

Note that while it could have been possible to build a less useful index to compute frequency counts without using the **rereduce** parameter, constructing a more useful index affords the opportunity to use **rereduce**, an important consideration for any nontrivial map/reduce job.

A Note on rereduce

Example 5-4 is the first listing we've looked at that explicitly makes use of the **rereduce** parameter, so it may be useful to explain exactly what's going on there. Keep in mind that in addition to reducing the output for some number of mappers (which has necessarily been grouped by key), it's also quite possible that the reducer may be passed the output for some number of reducers to *rereduce*. In common functions such as counting things and computing sums, it may not make a difference where the input has come from, so long as a commutative operation such as addition keeps getting repeatedly applied. In some cases, however, the difference between an initial reduction and a rereduction does matter. This is where the **rereduce** parameter becomes useful.

For the summingReducer function shown in Example 5-4, consider the following sample outputs from the mapper (the actual contents of the value portion of each tuple are of no importance):

```
[ ["@foo", [x1, x2]], ["@foo", [x3, x4]], ["@bar", [x5, x6]],
  ["@foo", [x7, x8]], ("@bar", [x9, x10]] ]
```

For simplicity, let's suppose that each node in the underlying B-tree that stores these tuples is only capable of housing two items at a time (the actual value as implemented for CouchDB is well into the thousands). The reducer would conceptually operate on the following input during the first pass, when **rereduce** is false. Again, recall that the values are grouped by key:

```
# len( [ [x1, x2], [x3, x4] ] ) == 2
summingReducer(["@foo", "@foo"], [ [x1, x2], [x3, x4] ], False)

# len( [ [x7, x8] ] ) => 1
summingReducer(["@foo"], [ [x7, x8] ], False)

# len( [ [x5, x6], [x9, x10] ] ) == 2
summingReducer(["@bar", "@bar"], [ [x5, x6], [x9, x10] ], False)
```

During the next pass through the reducer, when `rereduce` is `True`, because *the reducer is operating on already reduced output that has necessarily already been grouped by key*, no comparison related to key values is necessary. Given that the previous `len` operation effectively did nothing more than count the number of occurrences of each key (a tweet entity), additional passes through the reducer now need to sum these values to compute a final tally, as is illustrated by the rereduce phase:

```
# values from previously reducing @foo keys: sum([2, 1]) == 3
summingReducer(None, [ 2, 1 ], True)

# values from previously reducing @bar keys: sum([2]) == 2
summingReducer(None, [ 2 ], True)
```

The big picture is that `len` was first used to count the number of times an entity appears, as an intermediate step; then, in a final rereduction step, the `sum` function tallied those intermediate results.

In short, the script uses a mapper to emit a tuple of the form (`entity`, [`couchdb_id`, `tweet_id`]) for each document and then uses a reducer to count the number of times each distinct entity appears. Given that you're probably working with a relatively small collection of items and that you've been introduced to some other mechanisms for sorting in Chapter 3, you then simply sort the data on the client-side and apply a frequency threshold. Example output with a threshold of 15 is shown in Table 5-1 but also displayed as a chart in Figure 5-1 so that you have a feel for the underlying distribution.

Table 5-1. Entities sorted by frequency from harvested tweets by @timoreilly

Entity	Frequency
#gov20	140
@OReillyMedia	124
#Ebook	89
@timoreilly	77
#ebooks	55
@slashdot	45
@jamesoreilly	41
#w2e	40
@gnat	38
@n2vip	37
@monkchips	33
#w2s	31
@pahlkadot	30
@dalepd	28

Entity	Frequency
#g2e	27
#ebook	25
@ahier	24
#where20	22
@digiphile	21
@fredwilson	20
@brady	19
@mikeloukides	19
#pdf10	19
@nytimes	18
#fooeast	18
@andrewsavikas	17
@CodeforAmerica	16
@make	16
@pkedrosky	16
@carlmalamud	15
#make	15
#opengov	15

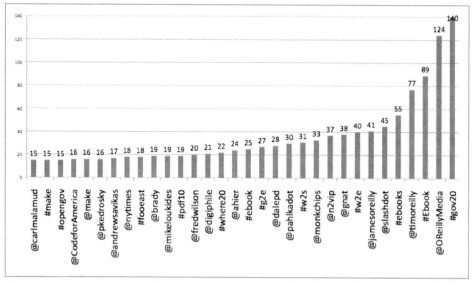

Figure 5-1. The frequency of entities that have been retweeted by @timoreilly for a sample of recent tweets

So, what's on Tim's mind these days? It's no surprise that a few of his favorite topics appear in the list—for example, #gov20 with a whopping 140 mentions, dwarfing everything else—but what may be even more intriguing is to consider some of the less obvious user mentions, which likely indicate close relationships. In fact, it may be fair to assume that Tim finds the users he mentions often interesting. You might even go as far as to infer that he is influenced by or even trusts these other users. (Many an interesting algorithm could be devised to try to determine these types of relationships, with variable degrees of certainty.) Although computing raw counts as we've done in this section is interesting, applying time-based filtering is another tempting possibility. For example, we might gain useful insight by applying a time-based filter to the map/reduce code in Example 5-4 so that we can calculate what Tim has been talking about in the past N days as opposed to over his past ~3,200 tweets, which span a nontrivial period of time. (Some Twitterers haven't even come close to tweeting 3,200 times over the course of several years.) It also wouldn't be very difficult to plot out tweets on the SIMILE Timeline that was introduced in "Visualizing Mail "Events" with SIMILE Timeline" on page 77 and browse them to get a quick gist of what Tim has been tweeting about most recently.

Do frequently appearing user entities imply friendship?

Example 4-4 provided a listing that demonstrated how to harvest a Twitterer's friends and followers, and used Redis to store the results. Assuming you've already fetched Tim's friends and followers with that listing, the results are readily available to you in Redis, and it's a fairly simple matter to compute how many of the N most frequently tweeted user entities are also Tim's friends. Example 5-5 illustrates the process of using information we already have available in Redis from Chapter 4 to resolve screen names from user IDs; Redis' in-memory set operations are used to compute which of the most frequently appearing user entities in Tim's user time line are also his friends.

Example 5-5. Finding @mention tweet entities that are also friends (the_tweet__how_many_user_entities_are_friends.py)

```
# -*- coding: utf-8 -*-

import json
import redis
import couchdb
import sys
from twitter__util import getRedisIdByScreenName
from twitter__util import getRedisIdByUserId

SCREEN_NAME = sys.argv[1]
THRESHOLD = int(sys.argv[2])

# Connect using default settings for localhost

r = redis.Redis()
```

```
# Compute screen_names for friends

friend_ids = r.smembers(getRedisIdByScreenName(SCREEN_NAME, 'friend_ids'))
friend_screen_names = []
for friend_id in friend_ids:
    try:
        friend_screen_names.append(json.loads(r.get(getRedisIdByUserId(friend_id,
                            'info.json')))['screen_name'].lower())
    except TypeError, e:
        continue # not locally available in Redis - look it up or skip it

# Pull the  list of (entity, frequency) tuples from CouchDB

server = couchdb.Server('http://localhost:5984')
db = server['tweets-user-timeline-' + SCREEN_NAME]

entities_freqs = sorted([(row.key, row.value) for row in
                        db.view('index/entity_count_by_doc', group=True)],
                        key=lambda x: x[1])

# Keep only user entities with insufficient frequencies

user_entities = [(ef[0])[1:] for ef in entities_freqs if ef[0][0] == '@'
                and ef[1] >= THRESHOLD]

# Do a set comparison

entities_who_are_friends = \
    set(user_entities).intersection(set(friend_screen_names))

entities_who_are_not_friends = \
    set(user_entities).difference(entities_who_are_friends)

print 'Number of user entities in tweets: %s' % (len(user_entities), )
print 'Number of user entities in tweets who are friends: %s' \
    % (len(entities_who_are_friends), )
for e in entities_who_are_friends:
    print '\t' + e
print 'Number of user entities in tweets who are not friends: %s' \
    % (len(entities_who_are_not_friends), )
for e in entities_who_are_not_friends:
    print '\t' + e
```

The output with a frequency threshold of 15 (shown in Example 5-6) is predictable,
yet it brings to light a couple of observations.

*Example 5-6. Sample output from Example 5-5 displaying @mention tweet entities that are also
friends of @timoreilly*

```
Number of user entities in tweets: 20
Number of user entities in tweets who are friends: 18
    ahier
    pkedrosky
    CodeforAmerica
    nytimes
```

```
        brady
        carlmalamud
        pahlkadot
        make
        jamesoreilly
        andrewsavikas
        gnat
        slashdot
        OReillyMedia
        dalepd
        mikeloukides
        monkchips
        fredwilson
        digiphile
Number of user entities in tweets who are not friends: 2
        n2vip
        timoreilly
```

All in all, there were 20 user entities who exceeded a frequency threshold of 15, and 18 of those turned out to be friends. Given that most of the people who appear in his tweets are also his friends, it's probably safe to say that there's a strong trust relationship of some kind between Tim and these individuals. Take a moment to compare this list to the results from our exercises in "Constructing Friendship Graphs" on page 108. What might be just as interesting, however, is noting that Tim himself appears as one of his most frequently tweeted-about entities, as does one other individual, @n2vip. Looking more closely at the context of the tweets involving @n2vip could be useful. Any theories on how so many user mentions could be in someone's tweet stream without them being a friend? Let's find out.

From the work you've done in Chapter 3, you already know how quick and easy it can be to apply Lucene's full-text indexing capabilities to a CouchDB database, and a minimal adaptation and extension of Example 3-12 is all that it takes to quickly hone in on tweets mentioning @n2vip. Example 5-7 demonstrates how it's done.

Example 5-7. Using couchdb-lucene to query tweet data (the_tweet__couchdb_lucene.py)

```python
# -*- coding: utf-8 -*-

import sys
import httplib
from urllib import quote
import json
import couchdb

DB = sys.argv[1]
QUERY = sys.argv[2]

#  The body of a JavaScript-based design document we'll create

dd = \
    {'fulltext': {'by_text': {'index': '''function(doc) {
                            var ret=new Document();
```

```
                    ret.add(doc.text);
                    return ret
                }'''}}}

try:
    server = couchdb.Server('http://localhost:5984')
    db = server[DB]
except couchdb.http.ResourceNotFound, e:
    print """CouchDB database '%s' not found.
Please check that the database exists and try again.""" % DB
    sys.exit(1)

try:
    conn = httplib.HTTPConnection('localhost', 5984)
    conn.request('GET', '/%s/_design/lucene' % (DB, ))
    response = conn.getresponse()
finally:
    conn.close()

# If the design document did not exist create one that'll be
# identified as "_design/lucene". The equivalent of the following
# in a terminal:
# $ curl -X PUT http://localhost:5984/DB/_design/lucene -d @dd.json
if response.status == 404:
    try:
        conn = httplib.HTTPConnection('localhost', 5984)
        conn.request('PUT', '/%s/_design/lucene' % (DB, ), json.dumps(dd))
        response = conn.getresponse()

        if response.status != 201:
            print 'Unable to create design document: %s %s' % (response.status,
                    response.reason)
            sys.exit(1)
    finally:
        conn.close()

# Querying the design document is nearly the same as usual except that you reference
# couchdb-lucene's _fti HTTP handler
# $ curl http://localhost:5984/DB/_fti/_design/lucene/by_subject?q=QUERY

try:
    conn.request('GET', '/%s/_fti/_design/lucene/by_text?q=%s' % (DB,
                    quote(QUERY)))
    response = conn.getresponse()
    if response.status == 200:
        response_body = json.loads(response.read())
    else:
        print 'An error occurred fetching the response: %s %s' \
            % (response.status, response.reason)
        print 'Make sure your couchdb-lucene server is running.'
        sys.exit(1)
finally:
    conn.close()

doc_ids = [row['id'] for row in response_body['rows']]
```

```
# pull the tweets from CouchDB and extract the text for display

tweets = [db.get(doc_id)['text'] for doc_id in doc_ids]
for tweet in tweets:
    print tweet
    print
```

Abbreviated output from the script, shown in Example 5-8, reveals that *@n2vip* appears in so many of *@timoreilly*'s tweets because the two were engaging in Twitter conversations.

Example 5-8. Sample output from Example 5-7

```
@n2vip Thanks.  Great stuff.  Passing on to the ebook team.
@n2vip I suggested it myself the other day before reading this note.
RT @n2vip Check this out if you really want to get your '#Churchill on', a ...
@n2vip Remember a revolution that began with a handful of farmers and tradesmen ...
@n2vip Good suggestion re having free sample chapters as ebooks, not just pdfs...
@n2vip I got those statistics by picking my name off the influencer list in ...
RT @n2vip An informative, non-partisan FAQ regarding Health Care Reform at ...
@n2vip Don't know anyone who is advocating that. FWIW, it was Rs who turned ...
@n2vip No, I don't.  But a lot of the people arguing against renewables seem ...
@n2vip You've obviously never read an ebook on the iPhone. It's a great reading ...
@n2vip I wasn't suggesting that insurance was the strange world, just that you ...
@n2vip In high tech, there is competition from immigrant workers. Yet these two ...
@n2vip How right you are. We really don't do a good job teaching people ...
@n2vip The climategate stuff is indeed disturbing. But I still hold by what ...
@n2vip FWIW, I usually do follow links, so do include them if appropriate. Thanks.
@n2vip I don't mind substantive disagreement - e.g. with pointers to real info ...
@n2vip Totally agree that ownership can help. But you need to understand why ...
@n2vip Maybe not completely extinct, but certainly economically extinct. E.g. ...
@n2vip I wasn't aware that it was part of a partisan agenda. Too bad, because ...
RT @n2vip if only interesed in his 'Finest Hour' speech, try this - a ...
@n2vip They matter a lot.  I was also struck by that story this morning. Oil ...
@n2vip I understand that. I guess "don't rob MYsocialized medicine to fund ...
RT @n2vip Electronic medical record efforts pushing private practice docs to ...
@n2vip I think cubesail can be deployed in 2 ways: to force quicker re-entry ...
RT @ggreenwald Wolf Blitzer has major epiphany on public opinion and HCR that ...
```

Splicing in the other half of the conversation

It appears that *@n2vip*'s many mentions are related to the fact that he engaged Tim in at least a couple of discussions, and from a quick skim of the comments, the discussions appear somewhat political in nature (which isn't terribly surprising given the high frequency of the #gov20 hashtag, noted in an exercise earlier in this chapter). An interesting follow-on exercise is to augment Example 5-7 to extract the in_reply_to_status_id fields of the tweets and reassemble a more complete and readable version of the conversations.

One technique for reconstructing the thread that minimizes the number of API calls required is to simply fetch all of *@n2vip*'s tweets that have tweet IDs greater than the minimum tweet ID in the thread of interest, as opposed to collecting individual status IDs one by one. Example 5-9 shows how this could be done.

Example 5-9. Reconstructing tweet discussion threads (the_tweet__reassemble_discussion_thread.py)

```
# -*- coding: utf-8 -*-

import sys
import httplib
from urllib import quote
import json
import couchdb
from twitter__login import login
from twitter__util import makeTwitterRequest

DB = sys.argv[1]
USER = sys.argv[2]

try:
    server = couchdb.Server('http://localhost:5984')
    db = server[DB]
except couchdb.http.ResourceNotFound, e:
    print >> sys.stderr, """CouchDB database '%s' not found.
Please check that the database exists and try again.""" % DB
    sys.exit(1)

# query by term

try:
    conn = httplib.HTTPConnection('localhost', 5984)
    conn.request('GET', '/%s/_fti/_design/lucene/by_text?q=%s' % (DB,
                 quote(USER)))
    response = conn.getresponse()
    if response.status == 200:
        response_body = json.loads(response.read())
    else:
        print >> sys.stderr, 'An error occurred fetching the response: %s %s' \
            % (response.status, response.reason)
        sys.exit(1)
finally:
    conn.close()

doc_ids = [row['id'] for row in response_body['rows']]

# pull the tweets from CouchDB

tweets = [db.get(doc_id) for doc_id in doc_ids]

# mine out the in_reply_to_status_id fields and fetch those tweets as a batch request
```

```
conversation = sorted([(tweet['_id'], int(tweet['in_reply_to_status_id']))
                        for tweet in tweets if tweet['in_reply_to_status_id']
                        is not None], key=lambda x: x[1])
min_conversation_id = min([int(i[1]) for i in conversation if i[1] is not None])
max_conversation_id = max([int(i[1]) for i in conversation if i[1] is not None])

# Pull tweets from other user using user timeline API to minimize API expenses...

t = login()

reply_tweets = []
results = []
page = 1
while True:
    results = makeTwitterRequest(t,
        t.statuses.user_timeline,
        count=200,
        # Per <http://dev.twitter.com/doc/get/statuses/user_timeline>, some
        # caveats apply with the oldest id you can fetch using "since_id"
        since_id=min_conversation_id,
        max_id=max_conversation_id,
        skip_users='true',
        screen_name=USER,
        page=page)
    reply_tweets += results
    page += 1
    if len(results) == 0:
        break

# During testing, it was observed that some tweets may not resolve or possibly
# even come back with null id values -- possibly a temporary fluke. Workaround.
missing_tweets = []
for (doc_id, in_reply_to_id) in conversation:
    try:
        print [rt for rt in reply_tweets if rt['id'] == in_reply_to_id][0]['text']
    except Exception, e:
        print >> sys.stderr, 'Refetching <<tweet %s>>' % (in_reply_to_id, )
        results = makeTwitterRequest(t, t.statuses.show, id=in_reply_to_id)
        print results['text']

    # These tweets are already on hand
    print db.get(doc_id)['text']
    print
```

A lot of this code should look familiar by now. With the ability to authenticate into Twitter's API, store and retrieve data locally, and fetch remote data from Twitter, a lot can be done with a minimal amount of "business logic." Abbreviated sample output from this script, presented in Example 5-10, follows and shows the flow of discussion between *@timoreilly* and *@n2vip*.

Example 5-10. Sample output from Example 5-9

```
Question: If all Ins. Co. suddenly became non-profit and approved ALL Dr. ...
@n2vip Don't know anyone who is advocating that. FWIW, it was Rs who turned ...

@timoreilly RT @ggreenwald Wolf Blitzer has major epiphany on public opinion ...
RT @ggreenwald Wolf Blitzer has major epiphany on public opinion and HCR that ...

@timoreilly RE: Cubesail - I don't get it, does the sail collect loose trash ...
@n2vip I think cubesail can be deployed in 2 ways: to force quicker re-entry ...

@timoreilly How are you finding % of your RT have links? What service did you ...
@n2vip I got those statistics by picking my name off the influencer list in ...

@timoreilly a more fleshed-out e-book 'teaser' chapter idea here: http://bit.ly/aML6eH
@n2vip Thanks.  Great stuff.  Passing on to the ebook team.

@timoreilly Tim, #HCR law cuts Medicare payments to fund, in part, broader ...
@n2vip I understand that. I guess "don't rob MYsocialized medicine to fund ...

@timoreilly RE: Auto Immune - a "revolution" that is measured by a hand-full ...
@n2vip Remember a revolution that began with a handful of farmers and tradesmen ...

Do oil spills in Africa not matter? http://bit.ly/bKqv01 @jaketapper @yunjid ...
@n2vip They matter a lot.  I was also struck by that story this morning. Oil ...
```

Who Does Tim Retweet Most Often?

Given the (not so) old adage that a retweet is the highest form of a compliment, another way of posing the question, "Who does Tim retweet most often?" is to ask, "Who does Tim compliment most often?" Or, because it wouldn't really make sense for him to retweet content he did not find interesting, we might ask, "Who does Tim think is talking about *stuff that matters?*" A reasonable hypothesis is that many of the user entities that appear in Tim's public time line may be references to the authors of tweets that Tim is retweeting. Let's explore this idea further and calculate how many of Tim's tweets are retweets and, of those retweets, which tweet author gets retweeted the most often. There are a number of tweet resource API methods available for collecting retweets, but given that we already have more than a few thousand tweets on hand from an earlier exercise, let's instead analyze those as a means of getting the maximum value out of our API calls.

There are a couple of basic patterns for a retweet:

- RT *@user* Mary had a little lamb
- Mary had a little lamb (via *@user*)

In either case, the meaning is simple: someone is giving *@user* credit for a particular bit of information. Example 5-11 provides a sample program that extracts the number of times Tim has retweeted other Twitterers by applying a regular expression matcher as part of a simple map/reduce routine.

Be advised that Twitter's API has been evolving quickly over the course of time this book was being written. Example 5-11 counts retweets by extracting clues such as "RT" from the tweet text itself. By the time you're reading this, there may very well be a more efficient way to compute the number of times one user has retweeted another user for some duration.

Example 5-11. Counting the number of times Twitterers have been retweeted by someone (the_tweet__count_retweets_of_other_users.py)

```python
# -*- coding: utf-8 -*-

import sys
import couchdb
from couchdb.design import ViewDefinition
from prettytable import PrettyTable

DB = sys.argv[1]

try:
    server = couchdb.Server('http://localhost:5984')
    db = server[DB]
except couchdb.http.ResourceNotFound, e:
    print """CouchDB database '%s' not found.
Please check that the database exists and try again.""" % DB
    sys.exit(1)

if len(sys.argv) > 2 and sys.argv[2].isdigit():
    FREQ_THRESHOLD = int(sys.argv[2])
else:
    FREQ_THRESHOLD = 3

# Map entities in tweets to the docs that they appear in

def entityCountMapper(doc):
    if doc.get('text'):
        import re
        m = re.search(r"(RT|via)((?:\b\W*@\w+)+)", doc['text'])
        if m:
            entities = m.groups()[1].split()
            for entity in entities:
                yield (entity.lower(), [doc['_id'], doc['id']])
        else:
            yield ('@', [doc['_id'], doc['id']])


def summingReducer(keys, values, rereduce):
    if rereduce:
        return sum(values)
    else:
        return len(values)
```

```
view = ViewDefinition('index', 'retweet_entity_count_by_doc', entityCountMapper,
                      reduce_fun=summingReducer, language='python')
view.sync(db)

# Sorting by value in the client is cheap and easy
# if you're dealing with hundreds or low thousands of tweets

entities_freqs = sorted([(row.key, row.value) for row in
                        db.view('index/retweet_entity_count_by_doc',
                        group=True)], key=lambda x: x[1], reverse=True)

fields = ['Entity', 'Count']
pt = PrettyTable(fields=fields)
[pt.set_field_align(f, 'l') for f in fields]

for (entity, freq) in entities_freqs:
    if freq > FREQ_THRESHOLD and entity != '@':
        pt.add_row([entity, freq])

pt.printt()
```

If you think the results will look almost identical to the raw entity counts computed earlier in Table 5-1, you'll be somewhat surprised. The listing in Table 5-2 also uses a threshold of 15, to juxtapose the difference.

Table 5-2. Most frequent entities appearing in retweets by @timoreilly; additional columns to illustrate normalization of retweet counts by @timoreilly

Entity	Number of times @user retweeted by @timoreilly	Total tweets ever by @user	Normalized retweet score
@monkchips	30	33215	0.000903206
@ahier	18	14849	0.001212203
@slashdot	41	22081	0.0018568
@gnat	28	11322	0.002473061
@mikeloukides	15	2926	0.005126452
@pahlkadot	16	3109	0.005146349
@oreillymedia	97	6623	0.014645931
@jamesoreilly	34	4439	0.007659383
@dalepd	16	1589	0.010069226

So, who does Tim retweet/compliment the most? Well, not so surprisingly, his company and folks closely associated with his company compose the bulk of the list, with *@oreillymedia* coming in at the top of the pack. A visual inspection of retweet tallies and raw entity tallies shows an obvious correlation. Keep in mind, however, that the results shown in the "Number of times *@user* retweeted by *@timoreilly*" column in Table 5-2 are not normalized. For example, *@dalepd* was retweeted far fewer times than *@oreillymedia*, but a brief inspection of the statuses_count field that's embedded in the user objects in tweets (among other places in the API results) reveals that @dalepd tweets far less frequently than @oreillymedia. In fact, if you normalize the data by dividing the number of retweets by the total number of tweets for each user, @dalepd just barely ranks second to @oreillymedia—meaning that Tim retweets more of his tweets than those of any other user in the table except for @oreillymedia, even though it doesn't necessarily appear that way if you sort by raw retweet frequency. Figure 5-2 illustrates this analysis as a bubble chart. Additional tinkering to determine why some folks aren't retweeted as frequently as they are mentioned would also be interesting.

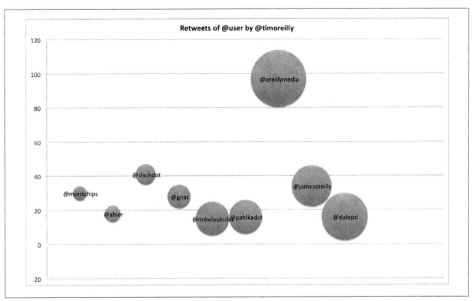

Figure 5-2. The y-axis of this bubble chart depicts the raw number of times a user has been retweeted; the area of the bubble represents a normalized score for how many times the user has been retweeted compared to the total number of times he has ever tweeted

Given that it's not too difficult to determine who Tim retweets most often, what about asking the question the other way: who retweets Tim most often? Answering this question in aggregate without a focused target population would be a bit difficult, if not impossible given the Twitter API limitations, as Tim has ~1,500,000 followers. However, it's a bit more tractable if you narrow it down to a reasonably small target population. The next section investigates some options.

What's Tim's Influence?

Asking how many of your tweets get retweeted is really just another way of measuring your own influence. If you tweet a lot and nobody retweets you, it's safe to say that your influence is pretty weak—at least as a Twitterer. In fact, it would be somewhat of a paradox to find yourself having the good fortune of many followers but not many retweets, because you generally get followers and retweets for the very same reason: you're interesting and influential!

One base metric that's quite simple and inexpensive to calculate is the ratio of tweets to retweets. A ratio of 1 would mean that every single tweet you've authored was retweeted and indicate that your influence is strong—potentially having second- and third-level effects that reach millions of unique users (literally)—while values closer to 0 show weaker influence. Of course, given the nature of Twitter, it's highly unlikely than any human user would have a tweet-to-retweet ratio of 1, if for no other reason than the mechanics of conversation (@replies) would drive the ratio downward. Twitter exposes the statuses/retweets_of_me resource, which provides the authenticating user with insight on which of her tweets have been retweeted. However, we don't have access to that API to analyze Tim's retweets, so we need to look for another outlet.

Example 5-12 takes advantage of the retweet_count field in a tweet to compute the number of tweets that have been retweeted a given number of times as part of what should now seem like a trivial map/reduce combination. Sample output formatted into a chart follows the example.

Example 5-12. Finding the tweets that have been retweeted most often (the_tweet__count_retweets_by_others.py)

```
# -*- coding: utf-8 -*-

import sys
import couchdb
from couchdb.design import ViewDefinition
from prettytable import PrettyTable
from twitter__util import pp

DB = sys.argv[1]

try:
    server = couchdb.Server('http://localhost:5984')
    db = server[DB]
except couchdb.http.ResourceNotFound, e:
    print """CouchDB database '%s' not found.
Please check that the database exists and try again.""" % DB
    sys.exit(1)

# Map entities in tweets to the docs that they appear in

def retweetCountMapper(doc):
    if doc.get('id') and doc.get('text'):
        yield (doc['retweet_count'], 1)

def summingReducer(keys, values, rereduce):
    return sum(values)

view = ViewDefinition('index', 'retweets_by_id', retweetCountMapper,
                      reduce_fun=summingReducer, language='python')
```

```
view.sync(db)

fields = ['Num Tweets', 'Retweet Count']
pt = PrettyTable(fields=fields)
[pt.set_field_align(f, 'l') for f in fields]

retweet_total, num_tweets, num_zero_retweets = 0, 0, 0
for (k,v) in sorted([(row.key, row.value) for row in
                       db.view('index/retweets_by_id', group=True)
                       if row.key is not None],
                     key=lambda x: x[0], reverse=True):
    pt.add_row([k, v])

    if k == "100+":
        retweet_total += 100*v
    elif k == 0:
        num_zero_retweets += v
    else:
        retweet_total += k*v

    num_tweets += v

pt.printt()

print '\n%s of %s authored tweets were retweeted at least once' % \
    (pp(num_tweets - num_zero_retweets), pp(num_tweets),)
print '\t(%s tweet/retweet ratio)\n' % \
      (1.0*(num_tweets - num_zero_retweets)/num_tweets,)

print 'Those %s authored tweets generated %s retweets' % (pp(num_tweets), pp(retweet_total),)
```

Figure 5-3 displays sample results from Example 5-12 that are formatted into a more compact chart that uses a logarithmic scale to squash the y-axis. Values along the x-axis correspond to the number of tweets with a given retweet value denoted by the y-axis. The total "area under the curve" is just over 3,000—the total number of tweets being analyzed. For example, just over 533 of Tim's tweets weren't retweeted at all as denoted by the far left column, 50 of his tweets were retweeted 50 times, and over 60 of his tweets were retweeted over 100 times[4] as denoted by the far right column.

The distribution isn't too surprising in that it *generally* trends according to the power law and that there are a fairly high number of tweets that went viral and were retweeted what could have been many hundreds of times. The high-level takeaways are that of over 3,000 total tweets, 2,536 of them were retweeted at least one time (a ratio of about 0.80) and generated over 50,000 retweets in all (a factor about 16).

To say the very least, the numbers confirm Tim's status as an influential information maven.

---

4. Note that as of late December 2010, the `retweet_count` field maxes out at 100. For this particular batch of data, there were 2 tweets that had been retweeted exactly 100 times, and 59 tweets that were retweeted "100+".

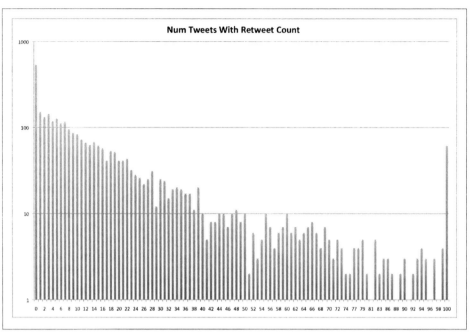

Figure 5-3. Sample results from Example 5-12

How Many of Tim's Tweets Contain Hashtags?

It seems a reasonable theory that tweets that contain hashtag entities are inherently more valuable than ones that don't because someone has deliberately gone to the trouble of embedding aggregatable information into those tweets, which essentially transforms them into semi-structured information. For example, it seems reasonable to assume that someone who averages 2+ hashtags per tweet is very interested in bridging knowledge and aware of the power of information, whereas someone who averages 0.1 hashtags per tweet probably is less so.

What's a Folksonomy?

A fundamental aspect of human intelligence is the desire to classify things and derive a hierarchy in which each element "belongs to" or is a "child" of a parent element one level higher in the hierarchy. Leaving aside philosophical debates about the difference between a taxonomy and an ontology, a *taxonomy* is essentially a hierarchical structure that classifies elements into parent/child bins. The term *folksonomy* (*http://en.wikipe dia.org/wiki/Folksonomy*) was coined around 2004 as a means of describing the universe of collaborative tagging and social indexing efforts that emerge in various ecosystems of the Web, and it's a play on words in the sense that it blends "folk" and "taxonomy." So, in essence, a folksonomy is just a fancy way of describing the decentralized universe of tags that emerges as a mechanism of *collective intelligence* when you allow people to classify content with labels.

Computing the average number of hashtags per tweet should be a cake-walk for you by now. We'll recycle some code and compute the total number of hashtags in one map/reduce phase, compute the total number of tweets in another map/reduce phase, and then divide the two numbers, as illustrated in Example 5-13.

Example 5-13. Counting hashtag entities in tweets (the_tweet__avg_hashtags_per_tweet.py)

```python
# -*- coding: utf-8 -*-

import sys
import couchdb
from couchdb.design import ViewDefinition

DB = sys.argv[1]

try:
    server = couchdb.Server('http://localhost:5984')
    db = server[DB]
except couchdb.http.ResourceNotFound, e:
    print """CouchDB database '%s' not found.
Please check that the database exists and try again.""" % DB
    sys.exit(1)

# Emit the number of hashtags in a document

def entityCountMapper(doc):
    if not doc.get('entities'):
        import twitter_text

        def getEntities(tweet):

            # Now extract various entities from it and build up a familiar structure

            extractor = twitter_text.Extractor(tweet['text'])

            # Note that the production Twitter API contains a few additional fields in
            # the entities hash that would require additional API calls to resolve

            entities = {}
            entities['user_mentions'] = []
            for um in extractor.extract_mentioned_screen_names_with_indices():
                entities['user_mentions'].append(um)

            entities['hashtags'] = []
            for ht in extractor.extract_hashtags_with_indices():

                # Massage field name to match production twitter api

                ht['text'] = ht['hashtag']
                del ht['hashtag']
                entities['hashtags'].append(ht)

            entities['urls'] = []
            for url in extractor.extract_urls_with_indices():
                entities['urls'].append(url)
```

```
        return entities

    doc['entities'] = getEntities(doc)

    if doc['entities'].get('hashtags'):
        yield (None, len(doc['entities']['hashtags']))


def summingReducer(keys, values, rereduce):
    return sum(values)


view = ViewDefinition('index', 'count_hashtags', entityCountMapper,
                    reduce_fun=summingReducer, language='python')
view.sync(db)

num_hashtags = [row for row in db.view('index/count_hashtags')][0].value

# Now, count the total number of tweets that aren't direct replies

def entityCountMapper(doc):
    if doc.get('text')[0] == '@':
        yield (None, 0)
    else:
        yield (None, 1)


view = ViewDefinition('index', 'num_docs', entityCountMapper,
                    reduce_fun=summingReducer, language='python')
view.sync(db)

num_docs = [row for row in db.view('index/num_docs')][0].value

# Finally, compute the average

print 'Avg number of hashtags per tweet for %s: %s' % \
        (DB.split('-')[-1], 1.0 * num_hashtags / num_docs,)
```

For a recent batch we fetched earlier, running this script reveals that Tim averages about 0.5 hashtags per tweet that is not a direct reply to someone. In other words, he includes a hashtag in about half of his tweets. For anyone who regularly tweets, including a hashtag that much of the time provides a substantial contribution to the overall Twitter search index and the ever-evolving folksonomy. As a follow-up exercise, it could be interesting to compute the average number of hyperlink entities per tweet, or even go so far as to follow the links and try to discover new information about Tim's interests by inspecting the title or content of the linked web pages. (In the chapters ahead, especially Chapters 7 and 8, we'll learn more about text mining, an essential skill for analyzing web pages.)

Juxtaposing Latent Social Networks (or #JustinBieber Versus #TeaParty)

One of the most fascinating aspects of data mining is that it affords you the ability to *discover* new knowledge from existing information. There really is something to be said for the old adage that "knowledge is power," and it's especially true in an age where the amount of information available is steadily growing with no indication of decline. As an interesting exercise, let's see what we can discover about some of the latent social networks that exist in the sea of Twitter data. The basic approach we'll take is to collect some focused data on two or more topics in a specific way by searching on a particular hashtag, and then apply some of the same metrics we coded up in the previous section (where we analyzed Tim's tweets) to get a feel for the similarity between the networks.

Since there's no such thing as a "stupid question," let's move forward in the spirit of famed economist Steven D. Levitt[5] and ask the question, "What do #TeaParty and #JustinBieber have in common?"[6]

Example 5-14 provides a simple mechanism for collecting approximately the most recent 1,500 tweets (the maximum currently returned by the search API) on a particular topic and storing them away in CouchDB. Like other listings you've seen earlier in this chapter, it includes simple map/reduce logic to incrementally update the tweets in the event that you'd like to run it over a longer period of time to collect a larger batch of data than the search API can give you in a short duration. You might want to investigate the streaming API (*http://dev.twitter.com/pages/streaming_api*) for this type of task.

Example 5-14. Harvesting tweets for a given query (the_tweet__search.py)

```
# -*- coding: utf-8 -*-

import sys
import twitter
import couchdb
from couchdb.design import ViewDefinition
from twitter__util import makeTwitterRequest

SEARCH_TERM = sys.argv[1]
MAX_PAGES = 15
```

---

5. Steven D. Levitt is the co-author of *Freakonomics: A Rogue Economist Explores the Hidden Side of Everything* (Harper), a book that systematically uses data to answer seemingly radical questions such as, "What do school teachers and sumo wrestlers have in common?"

6. This question was partly inspired by the interesting Radar post, "Data science democratized" (*http://radar .oreilly.com/2010/07/data-science-democratized.html*), which mentions a presentation that investigated the same question (*http://www.slideshare.net/bigdatacamp/stefan-groschupf-of-datameer-gives-lightning -talk-at-big-datacamp-4667387*).

```
KW = {
    'domain': 'search.twitter.com',
    'count': 200,
    'rpp': 100,
    'q': SEARCH_TERM,
    }

server = couchdb.Server('http://localhost:5984')
DB = 'search-%s' % (SEARCH_TERM.lower().replace('#', '').replace('@', ''), )

try:
    db = server.create(DB)
except couchdb.http.PreconditionFailed, e:

    # already exists, so append to it, and be mindful of duplicates

    db = server[DB]

t = twitter.Twitter(domain='search.twitter.com')

for page in range(1, 16):
    KW['page'] = page
    tweets = makeTwitterRequest(t, t.search, **KW)
    db.update(tweets['results'], all_or_nothing=True)
    if len(tweets['results']) == 0:
        break
    print 'Fetched %i tweets' % len(tweets['results'])
```

The following sections are based on approximately 3,000 tweets per topic and assume that you've run the script to collect data on #TeaParty and #JustinBieber (or any other topics that interest you).

 Depending on your terminal preferences, you may need to escape certain characters (such as the hash symbol) because of the way they might be interpreted by your shell. For example, in Bash, you'd need to escape a hashtag query for #TeaParty as \#TeaParty to ensure that the shell interprets the hash symbol as part of the query term, instead of as the beginning of a comment.

What Entities Co-Occur Most Often with #JustinBieber and #TeaParty Tweets?

One of the simplest yet probably most effective ways to characterize two different crowds is to examine the entities that appear in an aggregate pool of tweets. In addition to giving you a good idea of the other topics that each crowd is talking about, you can compare the entities that do co-occur to arrive at a very rudimentary similarity metric. Example 5-4 already provides the logic we need to perform a first pass at entity analysis. Assuming you've run search queries for #JustinBieber and #TeaParty, you should have two CouchDB databases called "search-justinbieber" and "search-teaparty" that you can pass in to produce your own results. Sample results for each hashtag with an entity frequency greater than 20 follow in Tables 5-3 and 5-4; Figure 5-4 displays a chart conveying the underlying frequency distributions for these tables. Because the y-axis contains such extremes, it is adjusted to be a logarithmic scale, which makes the y values easier to read.

Table 5-3. Most frequent entities appearing in tweets containing #TeaParty

Entity	Frequency
#teaparty	2834
#tcot	2426
#p2	911
#tlot	781
#gop	739
#ocra	649
#sgp	567
#twisters	269
#dnc	175
#tpp	170
#GOP	150
#iamthemob	123
#ucot	120
#libertarian	112
#obama	112
#vote2010	109
#TeaParty	106
#hhrs	104
#politics	100
#immigration	97
#cspj	96
#acon	91
#dems	82
#palin	79
#topprog	78
#Obama	74
#tweetcongress	72
#jcot	71
#Teaparty	62
#rs	60

Entity	Frequency
#oilspill	59
#news	58
#glennbeck	54
#FF	47
#liberty	47
@welshman007	45
#spwbt	44
#TCOT	43
http://tinyurl.com/24h36zq	43
#rnc	42
#military	40
#palin12	40
@Drudge_Report	39
@ALIPAC	35
#majority	35
#NoAmnesty	35
#patriottweets	35
@ResistTyranny	34
#tsot	34
http://tinyurl.com/386k5hh	31
#conservative	30
#AZ	29
#TopProg	29
@JIDF	28
@STOPOBAMA2012	28
@TheFlaCracker	28
#palin2012	28
@thenewdeal	27
#AFIRE	27
#Dems	27
#asamom	26
#GOPDeficit	25
#wethepeople	25
@andilinks	24
@RonPaulNews	24

Entity	Frequency
#ampats	24
#cnn	24
#jews	24
@First_Patriots	23
#patriot	23
#pjtv	23
@Liliaep	22
#nvsen	22
@BrnEyeSuss	21
@crispix49	21
@koopersmith	21
@Kriskxx	21
#Kagan	21
@blogging_tories	20
#cdnpoli	20
#fail	20
#nra	20
#roft	20

Table 5-4. Most frequent entities appearing in tweets containing #JustinBieber

Entity	Frequency
#justinbieber	1613
#JustinBieber	1379
@lojadoaltivo	354
@ProSieben	258
#JUSTINBIEBER	191
#Proform	191
http://migre.me/TJwj	191
#Justinbieber	107
#nowplaying	104
@justinbieber	99
#music	88
#tickets	80
@_Yassi_	78
#musicmonday	78

Entity	Frequency
#video	78
#Dschungel	74
#Celebrity	42
#beliebers	38
#BieberFact	38
@JustBieberFact	32
@TinselTownDirt	32
@rheinzeitung	28
#WTF	28
http://tinyurl.com/343kax4	28
#Telezwerge	26
#Escutando	22
#justinBieber	22
#Restart	22
#TT	22
http://bit.ly/aARD4t	21
http://bit.ly/b2Kc1L	21
#bieberblast	20
#Eclipse	20
#somebodytolove	20

What's immediately obvious is that the #TeaParty tweets seem to have a lot more area "under the curve" and a much longer tail[7] (if you can even call it a tail) than the #JustinBieber tweets. Thus, at a glance, it would seem that the average number of hashtags for #TeaParty tweets would be higher than for #JustinBieber tweets. The next section investigates this assumption, but before we move on, let's make a few more observations about these results. A cursory qualitative assessment of the results seems to indicate that the information encoded into the entities themselves is richer for #TeaParty. For example, in #TeaParty entities, we see topics such as #oilspill, #Obama, #palin, #libertarian, and @Drudge_Report, among others. In contrast, many of the most frequently occurring #JustinBieber entities are simply variations of #JustinBieber, with the rest of the hashtags being somewhat scattered and unfocused. Keep in mind, however, that this isn't all that unexpected, given that #TeaParty is a very political topic whereas #JustinBieber is associated with pop culture and entertainment.

---

7. A "long tail" or "heavy tail" refers to a feature of statistical distributions in which a significant portion (usually 50 percent or more) of the area under the curve exists within its tail. This concept is revisited as part of a brief overview of Zipf's law in "Data Hacking with NLTK" on page 205.

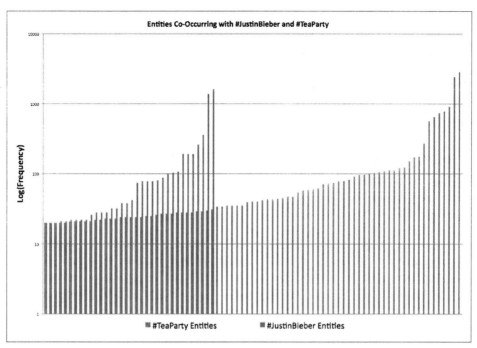

Figure 5-4. Distribution of entities co-occurring with #JustinBieber and #TeaParty

Some other observations are that a couple of user entities (*@lojadoaltivo* and *@Pro-Sieben*) appear in the top few results—higher than the "official" *@justinbieber* account itself—and that many of the entities that co-occur most often with #JustinBieber are non-English words or user entities, often associated with the entertainment industry.

Having briefly scratched the surface of a qualitative assessment, let's now return to the question of whether there are definitively more hashtags per tweet for #TeaParty than #JustinBieber.

On Average, Do #JustinBieber or #TeaParty Tweets Have More Hashtags?

Example 5-13 provides a working implementation for counting the average number of hashtags per tweet and can be readily applied to the search-justinbieber and search-teaparty databases without any additional work required.

Tallying the results for the two databases reveals that #JustinBieber tweets average around 1.95 hashtags per tweet, while #TeaParty tweets have around 5.15 hashtags per tweet. That's approximately 2.5 times more hashtags for #TeaParty tweets than #JustinBieber tweets. Although this isn't necessarily the most surprising find in the world, having firm data points on which to base further explorations or to back up conjectures is helpful: they are quantifiable results that can be tracked over time, or shared and reassessed by others.

Although the difference in this case is striking, keep in mind that the data collected is whatever Twitter handed us back as the most recent ~3,000 tweets for each topic via the search API. It isn't necessarily statistically significant, even though it is probably a very good indicator and very well may be so. Whether they realize it or not, #TeaParty Twitterers are big believers in folksonomies: they clearly have a vested interest in ensuring that their content is easily accessible and cross-referenced via search APIs and data hackers such as ourselves.

Which Gets Retweeted More Often: #JustinBieber or #TeaParty?

Earlier in this chapter, we made the reasonable conjecture that tweets that are retweeted with high frequency are likely to be more influential and more informative or editorial in nature than ones that are not. Tweets such as "Eating a pretzel" and "Aliens have just landed on the White House front lawn; we are all going to die! #fail #apocalypse" being extreme examples of content that is fairly unlikely and likely to be retweeted, respectively. How does #TeaParty compare to #JustinBieber for retweets? Analyzing @mentions from the working set of search results again produces interesting results. Truncated results showing which users have retweeted #TeaParty and #JustinBieber most often using a threshold with a frequency parameter of 10 appear in Tables 5-5 and 5-6.

Table 5-5. Most frequent retweeters of #TeaParty

Entity	Frequency
@teapartyleader	10
@dhrxsol1234	11
@HCReminder	11
@ObamaBallBuster	11
@spitfiremurphy	11
@GregWHoward	12
@BrnEyeSuss	13
@Calroofer	13
@grammy620	13
@Herfarm	14
@andilinks	16
@c4Liberty	16
@FloridaPundit	16
@tlw3	16
@Kriskxx	18
@crispix49	19
@JIDF	19

Entity	Frequency
@libertyideals	19
@blogging_tories	20
@Liliaep	21
@STOPOBAMA2012	22
@First_Patriots	23
@RonPaulNews	23
@TheFlaCracker	24
@thenewdeal	25
@ResistTyranny	29
@ALIPAC	32
@Drudge_Report	38
@welshman007	39

Table 5-6. Most frequent retweeters of #JustinBieber

Entity	Frequency
@justinbieber	14
@JesusBeebs	16
@LeePhilipEvans	16
@JustBieberFact	32
@TinselTownDirt	32
@ProSieben	122
@lojadoaltivo	189

If you do some back of the envelope analysis by running Example 5-4 on the ~3,000 tweets for each topic, you'll discover that about 1,335 of the #TeaParty tweets are retweets, while only about 763 of the #JustinBieber tweets are retweets. That's practically twice as many retweets for #TeaParty than #JustinBieber. You'll also observe that #TeaParty has a much longer tail, checking in with over 400 total retweets against #JustinBieber's 131 retweets. Regardless of statistical rigor, intuitively, those are probably pretty relevant indicators that size up the different interest groups in meaningful ways. It would seem that #TeaParty folks more consistently retweet content than #JustinBieber folks; however, of the #JustinBieber folks who do retweet content, there are clearly a few outliers who retweet much more frequently than others. Figure 5-5 displays a simple chart of the values from Tables 5-5 and 5-6. As with Figure 5-4, the *y*-axis is a log scale, which makes the chart a little more readable by squashing the frequency values to require less vertical space.

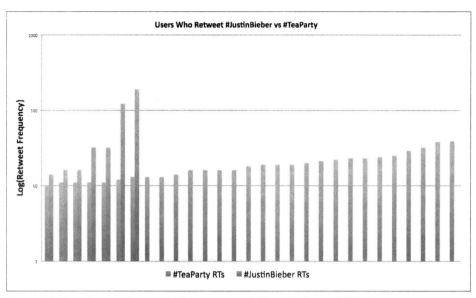

Figure 5-5. Distribution of users who have retweeted #JustinBieber and #TeaParty

How Much Overlap Exists Between the Entities of #TeaParty and #JustinBieber Tweets?

A final looming question that might be keeping you up at night is how much overlap exists between the entities parsed out of the #TeaParty and #JustinBieber tweets. Borrowing from some of the ideas in Chapter 4, we're essentially asking for the logical intersection of the two sets of entities. Although we could certainly compute this by taking the time to adapt existing Python code, it might be even easier to just capture the results of the scripts we already have on hand into two files and pass those filenames as parameters into a disposable script that provides a general-purpose facility for computing the intersection of any line-delimited file. In addition to getting the job done, this approach also leaves you with artifacts that you can casually peruse and readily share with others. Assuming you are working in a *nix shell with the script *count-entities-in-tweets.py*, one approach for capturing the entities from the #TeaParty and #JustinBieber output of Example 5-4 and storing them in sorted order follows:

```
#!/bin/bash

mkdir -p out
for db in teaparty justinbieber; do
    python the_tweet__count_entities_in_tweets.py search-$db 0 | \
    tail +3 | awk '{print $2}' | sort > out/$db.entities
done
```

After you've run this script, you can pass the two filenames into the general-purpose Python program to compute the output, as shown in Example 5-15.

Example 5-15. Computing the set intersection of lines in files (the_tweet__compute_intersection_of_lines_in_files.py)

```python
# -*- coding: utf-8 -*-

"""
Read in 2 or more files and compute the logical intersection of the lines in them
"""

import sys

data = {}
for i in range(1, len(sys.argv)):
    data[sys.argv[i]] = set(open(sys.argv[i]).readlines())

intersection = set()
keys = data.keys()
for k in range(len(keys) - 1):
    intersection = data[keys[k]].intersection(data[keys[k - 1]])

msg = 'Common items shared amongst %s:' % ', '.join(keys).strip()
print msg
print '-' * len(msg)
for i in intersection:
    print i.strip()
```

The entities shared between #JustinBieber and #TeaParty are somewhat predictable, yet interesting. Example 5-16 lists the results from our sample.

Example 5-16. Sample results from Example 5-15

```
Common items shared amongst teaparty.entities, justinbieber.entities:
-----------------------------------------------------------------
#lol
#jesus
#worldcup
#teaparty
#AZ
#milk
#ff
#guns
#WorldCup
#bp
#News
#dancing
#music
#glennbeck
http://www.linkati.com/q/index
@addthis
#nowplaying
#news
#WTF
#fail
#toomanypeople
```

```
#oilspill
#catholic
```

It shouldn't be surprising that #WorldCup, #worldcup, and #oilspill are in the results, given that they're pretty popular topics; however, having #teaparty, #glennbeck, #jesus, and #catholic show up on the list of shared hashtags might be somewhat of a surprise if you're not that familiar with the TeaParty movement. Further analysis could very easily determine exactly how strong the correlations are between the two searches by accounting for how frequently certain hashtags appear in each search. One thing that's immediately clear from these results is that none of these common entities appears in the top 20 most frequent entities associated with #JustinBieber, so that's already an indicator that they're out in the tail of the frequency distribution for #JustinBieber mentions. (And yes, having #WTF and #fail show up on the list at all, especially as a common thread between two diverse groups, is sort of funny. Experiencing frustration is, unfortunately, a common thread of humanity.) If you want to dig deeper, as a further exercise you might reuse Example 5-7 to enable full-text indexing on the tweets in order to search by keyword.

Visualizing Tons of Tweets

There are more interesting ways to visualize Twitter data than we could possibly cover in this short chapter, but that won't stop us from working through a couple of exercises with some of the more obvious approaches that provide a good foundation. In particular, we'll look at loading tweet entities into tag clouds and visualizing "connections" among users with graphs.

Visualizing Tweets with Tricked-Out Tag Clouds

Tag clouds are among the most obvious choices for visualizing the extracted entities from tweets. There are a number of interesting tag cloud widgets that you can find on the Web to do all of the hard work, and they all take the same input—essentially, a frequency distribution like the ones we've been computing throughout this chapter. But why visualize data with an ordinary tag cloud when you could use a highly customizable Flash-based *rotating* tag cloud? There just so happens to be a quite popular open source rotating tag cloud called WP-Cumulus (*http://code.google.com/p/word-cu mulus-goog-vis/wiki/UserGuide*) that puts on a nice show. All that's needed to put it to work is to produce the simple input format that it expects and feed that input format to a template containing the standard HTML boilerplate.

Example 5-17 is a trivial adaptation of Example 5-4 that illustrates a routine emitting a simple JSON structure (a list of [term, URL, frequency] tuples) that can be fed into an HTML template for WP-Cumulus. We'll pass in empty strings for the URL portion of those tuples, but you could use your imagination and hyperlink to a simple web service that displays a list of tweets containing the entities. (Recall that Example 5-7 provides just about everything you'd need to wire this up by using couchdb-lucene to perform a full-text search on tweets stored in CouchDB.) Another option might be to write a web service and link to a URL that provides any tweet containing the specified entity.

Example 5-17. Generating the data for an interactive tag cloud using WP-Cumulus (the_tweet__tweet_tagcloud_code.py)

```python
# -*- coding: utf-8 -*-

import os
import sys
import webbrowser
import json
from cgi import escape
from math import log
import couchdb
from couchdb.design import ViewDefinition

DB = sys.argv[1]
MIN_FREQUENCY = int(sys.argv[2])

HTML_TEMPLATE = '../web_code/wp_cumulus/tagcloud_template.html'
MIN_FONT_SIZE = 3
MAX_FONT_SIZE = 20

server = couchdb.Server('http://localhost:5984')
db = server[DB]

# Map entities in tweets to the docs that they appear in


def entityCountMapper(doc):
    if not doc.get('entities'):
        import twitter_text

        def getEntities(tweet):

            # Now extract various entities from it and build up a familiar structure

            extractor = twitter_text.Extractor(tweet['text'])

            # Note that the production Twitter API contains a few additional fields in
            # the entities hash that would require additional API calls to resolve

            entities = {}
            entities['user_mentions'] = []
            for um in extractor.extract_mentioned_screen_names_with_indices():
                entities['user_mentions'].append(um)

            entities['hashtags'] = []
            for ht in extractor.extract_hashtags_with_indices():

                # massage field name to match production twitter api
```

```
                    ht['text'] = ht['hashtag']
                    del ht['hashtag']
                    entities['hashtags'].append(ht)

                entities['urls'] = []
                for url in extractor.extract_urls_with_indices():
                    entities['urls'].append(url)

                return entities

            doc['entities'] = getEntities(doc)

        if doc['entities'].get('user_mentions'):
            for user_mention in doc['entities']['user_mentions']:
                yield ('@' + user_mention['screen_name'].lower(), [doc['_id'], doc['id']])
        if doc['entities'].get('hashtags'):
            for hashtag in doc['entities']['hashtags']:
                yield ('#' + hashtag['text'], [doc['_id'], doc['id']])


def summingReducer(keys, values, rereduce):
    if rereduce:
        return sum(values)
    else:
        return len(values)


view = ViewDefinition('index', 'entity_count_by_doc', entityCountMapper,
                      reduce_fun=summingReducer, language='python')
view.sync(db)

entities_freqs = [(row.key, row.value) for row in
                  db.view('index/entity_count_by_doc', group=True)]

# Create output for the WP-Cumulus tag cloud and sort terms by freq along the way

raw_output = sorted([[escape(term), '', freq] for (term, freq) in entities_freqs
                     if freq > MIN_FREQUENCY], key=lambda x: x[2])

# Implementation adapted from
# http://help.com/post/383276-anyone-knows-the-formula-for-font-s

min_freq = raw_output[0][2]
max_freq = raw_output[-1][2]


def weightTermByFreq(f):
    return (f - min_freq) * (MAX_FONT_SIZE - MIN_FONT_SIZE) / (max_freq
            - min_freq) + MIN_FONT_SIZE


weighted_output = [[i[0], i[1], weightTermByFreq(i[2])] for i in raw_output]

# Substitute the JSON data structure into the template
```

```
html_page = open(HTML_TEMPLATE).read() % \
                    (json.dumps(weighted_output),)

if not os.path.isdir('out'):
    os.mkdir('out')

f = open(os.path.join('out', os.path.basename(HTML_TEMPLATE)), 'w')
f.write(html_page)
f.close()

print 'Tagcloud stored in: %s' % f.name

# Open up the web page in your browser

webbrowser.open("file://" + os.path.join(os.getcwd(), 'out',
        os.path.basename(HTML_TEMPLATE)))
```

The most notable portion of the listing is the incorporation of the following formula (*http://help.com/post/383276-anyone-knows-the-formula-for-font-s*) that weights the tags in the cloud:

$$\frac{(f - min\_freq) * (MAX\_FONT\_SIZE - MIN\_FONT\_SIZE)}{max\_freq - min\_freq} + MIN\_FONT\_SIZE$$

This formula weights term frequencies such that they are linearly squashed between MIN_FONT_SIZE and MAX_FONT_SIZE by taking into account the frequency for the term in question along with the maximum and minimum frequency values for the data. There are many variations that could be applied to this formula, and the incorporation of logarithms isn't all that uncommon. Kevin Hoffman's paper, "In Search of the Perfect Tag Cloud" (*http://files.blog-city.com/files/J05/88284/b/insearchofperfecttagcloud.pdf*), provides a nice overview of various design decisions involved in crafting tag clouds and is a useful starting point if you're interested in taking a deeper dive into tag cloud design.

The *tagcloud_template.html* file that's referenced in Example 5-17 is fairly uninteresting and is available with this book's source code on GitHub (*http://github.com/ptwobrus sell/Mining-the-Social-Web/blob/master/web_code/wp_cumulus/tagcloud_template .html*); it is nothing more than a simple adaptation from the stock example that comes with the tag cloud's source code. Some script tags in the head of the page take care of all of the heavy lifting, and all you have to do is feed some data into a makeshift template, which simply uses string substitution to replace the %s placeholder.

Figures 5-6 and 5-7 display tag clouds for tweet entities with a frequency greater than 30 that co-occur with #JustinBieber and #TeaParty. The most obvious difference between them is how crowded the #TeaParty tag cloud is compared to the #JustinBieber cloud. The gisting of other topics associated with the query terms is also readily apparent. We already knew this from Figure 5-5, but a tag cloud conveys a similar gist and provides useful interactive capabilities to boot. Of course, there's also nothing stopping you from creating interactive Ajax Charts with tools such as Google Chart Tools (*http://code.google.com/apis/visualization/documentation/gallery.html*).

Figure 5-6. An interactive 3D tag cloud for tweet entities co-occurring with #JustinBieber

Visualizing Community Structures in Twitter Search Results

We briefly compared #JustinBieber and #TeaParty queries earlier in this chapter, and this section takes that analysis a step further by introducing a couple of visualizations from a slightly different angle. Let's take a stab at visualizing the community structures of #TeaParty and #JustinBieber Twitterers by taking the search results we've previously collected, computing friendships among the tweet authors and other entities (such as @mentions and #hashtags) appearing in those tweets, and visualizing those connections. In addition to yielding extra insights into our example, these techniques also provide useful starting points for other situations in which you have an interesting juxtaposition in mind. The code listing for this workflow won't be shown here because it's easily created by recycling code you've already seen earlier in this chapter and in previous chapters. The high-level steps involved include:

- Computing the set of screen names for the unique tweet authors and user mentions associated with the search-teaparty and search-justinbieber CouchDB databases

- Harvesting the friend IDs for the screen names with Twitter's /friends/ids resource
- Resolving screen names for the friend IDs with Twitter's /users/lookup resource (recall that there's not a direct way to look up screen names for friends; ID values must be collected and then resolved)
- Constructing a networkx.Graph by walking over the friendships and creating an edge between two nodes where a friendship exists in either direction
- Analyzing and visualizing the graphs

Figure 5-7. An interactive 3D tag cloud for tweet entities co-occurring with #TeaParty

The result of the script (*http://github.com/ptwobrussell/Mining-the-Social-Web/blob/master/python_code/*) is a pickled graph file that you can open up in the interpreter and poke around at, as illustrated in the interpreter session in Example 5-18. Because the script is essentially just bits and pieces of recycled logic from earlier examples, it's not included here in the text, but is available online (*http://github.com/ptwobrussell/Mining-the-Social-Web/blob/master/python_code/the_tweet__get_friends_for_entity_mentions_in_search_results.py*). The analysis is generated from running the script on approximately 3,000 tweets for each of the #JustinBieber and #TeaParty searches. The output from calls to nx.degree, which returns the degree[8] of each node in the graph, is omitted and rendered visually as a simple column chart in Figure 5-8.

Example 5-18. Using the interpreter to perform ad-hoc graph analysis

```
>>> import networkx as nx
>>> teaparty = nx.read_gpickle("out/search-teaparty.gpickle")
>>> justinbieber = nx.read_gpickle("out/search-justinbieber.gpickle")
>>> teaparty.number_of_nodes(), teaparty.number_of_edges()
(2262, 129812)
>>> nx.density(teaparty)
0.050763513558431887
>>> sorted(nx.degree(teaparty)
... output omitted ...
>>> justinbieber.number_of_nodes(), justinbieber.number_of_edges()
(1130, 1911)
>>> nx.density(justinbieber)
>>> 0.0029958378077553165
>>> sorted(nx.degree(teaparty))
... output omitted ...
```

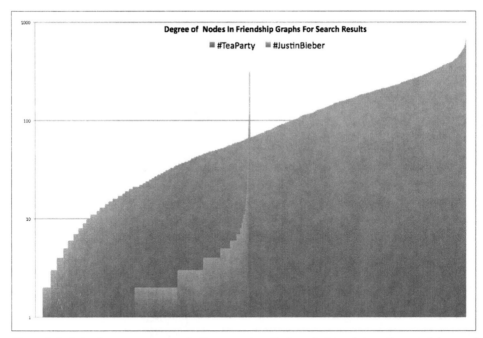

Figure 5-8. A simple way to compare the "connectedness" of graphs is to plot out the sorted degree of each node and overlay the curves

---

8. The degree of a node in an undirected graph is its total number of edges.

Without any visual representation at all, the results from the interpreter session are very telling. In fact, it's critical to be able to reason about these kinds of numbers without seeing a visualization because, more often than not, you simply won't be able to easily visualize complex graphs without a large time investment. The short story is that the density and the ratio of nodes to edges (users to friendships among them) in the #TeaParty graph vastly outstrip those for the #JustinBieber graph. However, that observation in and of itself may not be the most surprising thing. The surprising thing is the incredibly high connectedness of the nodes in the #TeaParty graph. Granted, #TeaParty is clearly an intense political movement with a relatively small following, whereas #JustinBieber is a much less concentrated entertainment topic with international appeal. Still, the overall distribution and shape of the curve for the #TeaParty results provide an intuitive and tangible view of just how well connected the #TeaParty folks really are. A 2D visual representation of the graph doesn't provide too much additional information, but the suspense is probably killing you by now, so without further ado—Figure 5-9.

Recall that *nix users can write out a Graphviz output with `nx.drawing.write_dot`, but Windows users may need to manually generate the DOT language output. See Examples 1-12 and 2-4. For large undirected graphs, you'll find Graphviz's SFDP (scalable force directed placement) (*http://www2.research.att.com/~yifanhu/PUB/peripheral .pdf*) engine invaluable. Sample usage for how you might invoke it from a command line to produce a useful layout for a dense graph follows:

```
$sfdp -Tpng -
Oteaparty -Nfixedsize=true -Nlabel='' -Nstyle=filled -Nfillcolor=red -
Nheight=0.1 -Nwidth=0.1 -Nshape=circle -Gratio=fill -Goutputorder=edgesfirst -
Gratio=fill -Gsize='10!' -Goverlap=prism teaparty.dot
```

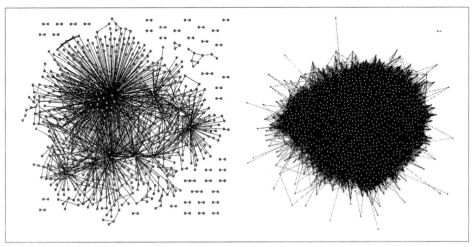

Figure 5-9. A 2D representation showcasing the connectedness of #JustinBieber (left) and #TeaParty (right) Twitterers; each edge represents a friendship that exists in at least one direction

Closing Remarks

There are a ridiculous number of obvious things you can do with tweet data, and if you get the least bit creative, the possibilities become beyond ridiculous. We've barely scratched the surface in this chapter. An entire book could quite literally be devoted to systematically working through more of the possibilities, and many small businesses focused around tweet analytics could potentially turn a fairly healthy profit by selling answers to certain classes of ad-hoc queries that customers could make. Here are interesting ideas that you could pursue:

- Define a similarity metric and use it to compare or further analyze two Twitter users or groups of users. You'll essentially be developing a profile and then measuring how well a particular user fits that profile. For example, do certain hashtags, keywords (e.g., LOL, OMG, etc.), or similar metrics appear in #JustinBieber tweets more than in more intellectual tweets like ones associated with #gov20? This question might seem obvious, but what interesting things might you learn along the way while calculating a quantifiable answer?

- Which celebrity Twitterers have a very low concentration of tweet entities yet a high tweet volume? Does this make them ramblers—you know, those folks who tweet 100 times a day about nothing in particular? Conversely, which celebrity Twitterers have a high concentration of hashtags in their tweets? What obvious comparisons can you make between the two groups?

- If you have a Twitter account and a reasonable number of tweets, consider analyzing yourself and comparing your tweet streams to those of other users. How similar are you to various Twitterers along a particular spectrum?

- We didn't broach the subject of Twitter's lists API. Can you profile various members of a list and try to discover latent social networks? For example, can you find a metric that allows you to approximate political boundaries between followers of the *@timoreilly*/healthcare and *@timoreilly*/gov20 lists?

- It might be interesting to analyze the volume of tweets or content of tweets by time of day. This is a pretty simple exercise and could incorporate the SIMILE Timeline—discussed in "Visualizing Mail "Events" with SIMILE Timeline" on page 77—for easy visualization.

- Near real-time communication is increasingly becoming the norm and Twitter provides a streaming API, which provides convenient access to much of their "fire hose." See the online streaming documentation (*http://dev.twitter.com/pages/streaming_api*) and consider checking out `tweepy` (*https://github.com/joshthecoder/tweepy*) as a terrific streaming client.

## CHAPTER 6

LinkedIn: Clustering Your Professional Network for Fun (and Profit?)

This chapter introduces techniques and considerations for mining the troves of data tucked away at LinkedIn, a popular and powerful social networking site focused on professional and business relationships. You're highly encouraged to build up a professional LinkedIn network as you follow along with this chapter, but even if you don't have a LinkedIn profile, you can still apply many of the techniques we'll explore to other domains that provide a means of exporting information similar to that you'd find in an address book. Although LinkedIn may initially seem like any other social network, the data its API provides is inherently of a different nature. Generally speaking, people who care enough to join LinkedIn are interested in the business opportunities that it provides and want their profiles to look as stellar as possible—which means ensuring that they provide ample details of a fairly personal nature conveying important business relationships, job details, etc.

Given the somewhat sensitive nature of the data, the API is somewhat different than many of the others we've looked at in this book. For example, while you can generally access all of the interesting details about *your contacts'* educational histories, previous work positions, etc., you cannot determine whether two arbitrary people are "connected," and the absence of such an API method is not accidental—this decision was made because the management team at LinkedIn strongly believes that your professional networking data is inherently private and far too valuable to open up to the same possibilities of exploitation as, say, knowledge about your Twitter or Facebook friends.[1]

Given that LinkedIn limits your access to information about your direct connections and does not lend itself to being mined as a graph, it requires that you ask different types of questions about the data that's available to you. The remainder of this chapter

---

1. LinkedIn's position was relayed in a discussion between the author and D.J. Patil, Chief Scientist, Chief Security Officer, and Senior Director—Project Analytics at LinkedIn.

introduces fundamental clustering techniques that can help you answer the following kinds of queries:

- Which of your connections are the most similar based upon a criterion like job title?
- Which of your connections have worked in companies you want to work for?
- Where do most of your connections reside geographically?

Motivation for Clustering

Given the richness of LinkedIn data, being able to answer queries about your professional networks presents some powerful opportunities. However, in implementing solutions to answer these types of questions, there are at least two common themes we'll encounter over and over again:

- It's often necessary to measure similarity between two values (usually string values), whether they're job titles, company names, professional interests, or any other field you can enter in as free text. Chapter 7 officially introduces some additional approaches and considerations for measuring similarity that you might want to also review.
- In order to cluster all of the items in a set using a similarity metric, it would be ideal to compare every member to every other member. Thus, for a set of n members, you would perform somewhere on the order of n^2 similarity computations in your algorithm for the worst-case scenario. Computer scientists call this predicament an *n-squared problem* and generally use the nomenclature $O(n^2)$ to describe it;[2] conversationally, you'd say it's a "Big-O of *n*-squared" problem. However, $O(n^2)$ problems become intractable for very large values of n. Most of the time, the use of the term "intractable" means you'd have to wait years (or even hundreds of years) for a solution to be computed—or, at any rate, "too long" for the solution to be useful.

These two issues inevitably come up in any discussion involving what is known as the *approximate matching problem*,[3] which is a very well-studied (but still difficult and messy) problem that's ubiquitous in nearly any industry.

---

2. Technically speaking, it is sometimes more precise to describe the time complexity of a problem as $\Theta(n^2)$, because $O(n^2)$ represents a worst case, whereas $\Theta(n^2)$ represents a tighter bound for the expected performance. In other words, $\Theta(n^2)$ says that it's not just an n^2 problem in the worst case, it's an n^2 problem in the best case, too. However, our objective in this chapter isn't to analyze the runtime complexity of algorithms (a difficult subject in and of itself), and we'll stick with the more common $O(n^2)$ notation and describing the worst case.

3. Also commonly called fuzzy matching, clustering, and/or deduplication, among many other things. Trying to perform approximate matching on multiple fields (records) is commonly referred to as the "record linkage" problem.

Techniques for approximate matching are a fundamental part of any legitimate data miner's tool belt, because in nearly any sector of any industry—ranging from defense intelligence to fraud detection at a bank to local landscaping companies—there can be a truly immense amount of semi-standardized relational data that needs to be analyzed (whether the people in charge realize it or not). What generally happens is that a company establishes a database for collecting some kind of information, but not every field is enumerated into some predefined universe of valid answers. Whether it's because the application's user interface logic wasn't designed properly, because some fields just don't lend themselves to having static predetermined values, or because it was critical to the user experience that users be allowed to enter whatever they'd like into a text box, the result is always the same: you eventually end up with a lot of semistandardized data, or "dirty records." While there might be a total of N distinct string values for a particular field, some number of these string values will actually relate the same concept. Duplicates can occur for various reasons: erroneous misspellings, abbreviations or shorthand, differences in the case of words, etc.

Although it may not be obvious, this is exactly the situation we're faced with in mining LinkedIn data: LinkedIn members are able to enter in their professional information as free text, which results in a certain amount of unavoidable variation. For example, if you wanted to examine your professional network and try to determine where most of your connections work, you'd need to consider common variations in company names. Even the simplest of company names have a few common variations you'll almost certainly encounter. For example, it should be obvious to most people that "Google" is an abbreviated form of "Google, Inc.", but even these kinds of simple variations in naming conventions must be explicitly accounted for during standardization efforts. In standardizing company names, a good starting point is to first consider suffixes such as ", Inc.", ", LLC", etc. Assuming you had a comma-separated values (CSV) file of contacts that you'd exported from LinkedIn, you might start out by doing some basic normalization and then printing out selected entities from a histogram, as illustrated in Example 6-1.

The two primary ways you can access your LinkedIn data are by either exporting it as address book data, which maintains very basic information such as name, job title, company, and contact information, or using the LinkedIn API to programmatically exploit the full details of your contacts. While using the API provides access to everything that would be visible to you as an authenticated user browsing profiles at *http:// linkedin.com*, we can get all of the job title details we need for this first exercise by exporting address book information. (We'll use LinkedIn APIs later in this chapter, in "Fetching Extended Profile Information" on page 188.) In case it's not obvious how to export your connections, Figure 6-1 provides some visual cues that show you how to make it happen. We'll be using Python's csv module to parse the exported data; to ensure compatibility with the upcoming code listing, choose the "Outlook CSV" option.

Example 6-1. Simple normalization of company suffixes from address book data (linkedin__analyze_companies.py)

```
# -*- coding: utf-8 -*-

import sys
import nltk
import csv
from prettytable import PrettyTable

CSV_FILE = sys.argv[1]

# Handle any known abbreviations,
# strip off common suffixes, etc.

transforms = [(', Inc.', ''), (', Inc', ''), (', LLC', ''), (', LLP', '')]

csvReader = csv.DictReader(open(CSV_FILE), delimiter=',', quotechar='"')
contacts = [row for row in csvReader]
companies = [c['Company'].strip() for c in contacts if c['Company'].strip() != '']

for i in range(len(companies)):
    for transform in transforms:
        companies[i] = companies[i].replace(*transform)

pt = PrettyTable(fields=['Company', 'Freq'])
pt.set_field_align('Company', 'l')
fdist = nltk.FreqDist(companies)
[pt.add_row([company, freq]) for (company, freq) in fdist.items() if freq > 1]
pt.printt()
```

However, you'd need to get a little more sophisticated to handle more complex situations, such as the various manifestations of company names like O'Reilly Media that you might encounter. For example, you might see this company's name represented as O'Reilly & Associates, O'Reilly Media, O'Reilly, Inc.,[4] or just O'Reilly. The very same problem presents itself in considering job titles, except that it can get a lot messier because job titles are so much more variable. Table 6-1 lists a few job titles you're likely to encounter in a software company that include a certain amount of natural variation. How many distinct roles do you see for the 10 distinct titles that are listed?

Table 6-1. Example job titles for the technology industry

Job Title
Chief Executive Officer
President/CEO
President & CEO

---

4. If you think this is starting to sound complicated, just consider the work taken on by Dun & Bradstreet (*http://www.dnb.com/us/*) (the "Who's Who" of company information), the company that is blessed with the challenge of maintaining a worldwide directory that identifies companies spanning multiple languages from all over the globe.

Job Title
CEO
Developer
Software Developer
Software Engineer
Chief Technical Officer
President
Senior Software Engineer

Figure 6-1. To export your connections, click on Contacts, choose My Connections from the pop-up menu, and then click on the "Export connections" link on the following screen

While it's certainly possible to define a list of aliases or abbreviations that equate titles like CEO and Chief Executive Officer, it may not be very practical to manually define lists that equate titles such as Software Engineer and Developer for the general case in all possible domains. However, for even the messiest of fields in a worst-case scenario, it shouldn't be too difficult to implement a solution that condenses the data to the point that it's manageable for an expert to review it, and then feed it back into a program that can apply it in much the same way that the expert would have done. More times than not, this is actually the approach that organizations prefer since it allows humans to briefly insert themselves into the loop to perform quality control.

Clustering Contacts by Job Title

Now that you can (hopefully) better appreciate the nature of the record-matching problem, let's collect some real-world data from LinkedIn and start hacking out clusters. A few reasons you might be interested in mining your LinkedIn data are because you want to take an honest look at whether your networking skills have been helping you to meet the "right kinds of people," or because you want to approach contacts who will most likely fit into a certain socioeconomic bracket with a particular kind of business enquiry or proposition. The remainder of this section systematically works through some exercises in clustering your contacts by job title.

Standardizing and Counting Job Titles

An obvious starting point when working with a new data set is to count things, and this situation is no different. This section introduces a pattern for transforming common job titles and then performs a basic frequency analysis.

Assuming you have a reasonable number of exported contacts, the minor nuances among job titles that you'll encounter may actually be surprising, but before we get into that, let's put together some code that establishes some patterns for normalizing record data and takes a basic inventory sorted by frequency. Example 6-2 inspects job titles and prints out frequency information for the titles themselves and for individual tokens that occur in them. If you haven't already, you'll need to **easy_install pretty table** , a package that you can use to produce nicely formatted tabular output.

Example 6-2. Standardizing common job titles and computing their frequencies (linkedin__analyze_titles.py)

```
# -*- coding: utf-8 -*-

import sys
import nltk
import csv
from prettytable import PrettyTable

CSV_FILE = sys.argv[1]

transforms = [
    ('Sr.', 'Senior'),
    ('Sr', 'Senior'),
    ('Jr.', 'Junior'),
    ('Jr', 'Junior'),
    ('CEO', 'Chief Executive Officer'),
```

```
        ('COO', 'Chief Operating Officer'),
        ('CTO', 'Chief Technology Officer'),
        ('CFO', 'Chief Finance Officer'),
        ('VP', 'Vice President'),
    ]

csvReader = csv.DictReader(open(CSV_FILE), delimiter=',', quotechar='"')
contacts = [row for row in csvReader]

# Read in a list of titles and split apart
# any combined titles like "President/CEO"
# Other variations could be handled as well such
# as "President & CEO", "President and CEO", etc.

titles = []
for contact in contacts:
    titles.extend([t.strip() for t in contact['Job Title'].split('/')
                   if contact['Job Title'].strip() != ''])

# Replace common/known abbreviations

for i in range(len(titles)):
    for transform in transforms:
        titles[i] = titles[i].replace(*transform)

# Print out a table of titles sorted by frequency

pt = PrettyTable(fields=['Title', 'Freq'])
pt.set_field_align('Title', 'l')
titles_fdist = nltk.FreqDist(titles)
[pt.add_row([title, freq]) for (title, freq) in titles_fdist.items() if freq > 1]
pt.printt()

# Print out a table of tokens sorted by frequency

tokens = []
for title in titles:
    tokens.extend([t.strip(',') for t in title.split()])
pt = PrettyTable(fields=['Token', 'Freq'])
pt.set_field_align('Token', 'l')
tokens_fdist = nltk.FreqDist(tokens)
[pt.add_row([token, freq]) for (token, freq) in tokens_fdist.items() if freq > 1
 and len(token) > 2]
pt.printt()
```

In short, the code reads in CSV records and makes a mild attempt at normalizing them by splitting apart combined titles that use the forward slash (like a title of "President/ CEO") and replacing known abbreviations. Beyond that, it just displays the results of a frequency distribution of both full job titles and individual tokens contained in the job titles. This is nothing new, but it is useful as a starting template and provides you with some reasonable insight into how the data breaks down. Sample results are shown in Example 6-3.

Example 6-3. Sample results for Example 6-2

Title	Freq
Chief Executive Officer	16
Senior Software Engineer	12
Owner	9
Software Engineer	9

...

Token	Freq
Engineer	44
Software	31
Senior	27
Manager	26
Chief	24
Officer	12
Director	11

...

What's interesting is that the sample results show that the most common job title based on exact matches is "Chief Executive Officer," while the most common token in the job titles is "Engineer." Although "Engineer" is not a constituent token of the most common job title, it does appear in a large number of job titles (for example, "Senior Software Engineer" and "Software Engineer," which show up near the top of the job titles list). In analyzing job title or address book data, this is precisely the kind of insight that motivates the need for an approximate matching or clustering algorithm. The next section investigates further.

Common Similarity Metrics for Clustering

The most substantive decision that needs to be made in taking a set of strings—job titles, in this case—and clustering them in a useful way is which underlying similarity metric to use. There are myriad string similarity metrics available, and choosing the one that's most appropriate for your situation largely depends on the nature of your objective. A few of the common similarity metrics that might be helpful in comparing job titles follow:

Edit distance

Edit distance, also known as Levenshtein (*http://en.wikipedia.org/wiki/Vladimir _Levenshtein*) distance, is a simple measure of how many insertions, deletions, and replacements it would take to convert one string into another. For example, the cost of converting "dad" into "bad" would be one replacement operation and would yield a value of 1. NLTK provides an implementation of edit distance via the `nltk.metrics.distance.edit_distance` function. Note that the actual edit distance between two strings is often different from the number of operations required to *compute* the edit distance; computation of edit distance is usually on the order of *M*N* operations for strings of length *M* and *N*.

n-gram similarity

An *n*-gram is just a terse way of expressing each possible consecutive sequence of *n* tokens from a text, and it provides the foundational data structure for computing collocations. Peek ahead to "Bigram Analysis" on page 224 for an extended discussion of *n*-grams and collocations.

There are many variations of *n*-gram similarity, but consider the straightforward case of computing all possible bigrams for the tokens of two strings, and scoring the similarity between the strings by counting the number of common bigrams between them. Example 6-4 demonstrates.

Example 6-4. Using NLTK to compute bigrams in the interpreter

```
>>> ceo_bigrams = nltk.bigrams("Chief Executive Officer".split(), pad_right=True, \
... pad_left=True)
>>> ceo_bigrams
[(None, 'Chief'), ('Chief', 'Executive'), ('Executive', 'Officer'),
('Officer', None)]
>>> cto_bigrams = nltk.bigrams("Chief Technology Officer".split(), pad_right=True, \
... pad_left=True)
>>> cto_bigrams
[(None, 'Chief'), ('Chief', 'Technology'), ('Technology', 'Officer'),
('Officer', None)]
>>> len(set(ceo_bigrams).intersection(set(cto_bigrams)))
2
```

Note that the use of the keyword arguments `pad_right` and `pad_left` intentionally allows for leading and trailing tokens to match. The effect of padding is to allow bigrams such as (None, 'Chief') to emerge, which are important matches across job titles. NLTK provides a fairly comprehensive array of bigram and trigram scoring functions via the `BigramAssociationMeasures` and `TrigramAssociationMeas ures` classes defined in `nltk.metrics.association` module.

Jaccard distance

The Jaccard metric expresses the similarity of two sets and is defined by |*Set1 intersection Set2*|/|*Set1 union Set2*|. In other words, it's the number of items in common between the two sets divided by the total number of distinct items in the two sets. Peek ahead to "How the Collocation Sausage Is Made: Contingency Tables and Scoring Functions" on page 228 for an extended discussion. In general, you'll compute Jaccard similarity by using *n*-grams, including unigrams (single tokens), to measure the similarity of two strings. An implementation of Jaccard distance is available at `nltk.metrics.distance.jaccard_distance` and could be implemented as:

```
len(X.union(Y)) - len(X.intersection(Y)))/float(len(X.union(Y)))
```

where X and Y are sets of items.

MASI distance

The MASI[5] distance metric is a weighted version of Jaccard similarity that adjusts the score to result in a smaller distance than Jaccard when a partial overlap between sets exists. MASI distance is defined in NLTK as `nltk.metrics.distance.masi_dis tance`, which can be implemented as:

```
1 - float(len(X.intersection(Y)))/float(max(len(X),len(Y)))
```

where X and Y are sets of items. Example 6-5 and the sample results in Table 6-2 provide some data points that may help you better understand this metric.

Example 6-5. Using built-in distance metrics from NLTK to compare small sets of items (linkedin__distances.py)

```
# -*- coding: utf-8 -*-

from nltk.metrics.distance import jaccard_distance, masi_distance
from prettytable import PrettyTable

fields = ['X', 'Y', 'Jaccard(X,Y)', 'MASI(X,Y)']
pt = PrettyTable(fields=fields)
[pt.set_field_align(f, 'l') for f in fields]

for z in range(4):
    X = set()
    for x in range(z, 4):
        Y = set()
        for y in range(1, 3):
            X.add(x)
            Y.add(y)
            pt.add_row([list(X), list(Y), round(jaccard_distance(X, Y), 2),
                        round(masi_distance(X, Y), 2)])
pt.printt()
```

Notice that whenever the two sets are either completely disjoint or equal—i.e., when one set is totally subsumed[6] by the other—the MASI distance works out to be the same value as the Jaccard distance. However, when the sets overlap only partially, the MASI distance works out to be higher than the Jaccard distance. It's worth considering whether you think MASI will be more effective than Jaccard distance for the task of scoring two arbitrary job titles and clustering them together if the similarity (distance) between them exceeds a certain threshold. The table of sample results in Table 6-2 tries to help you wrap your head around how MASI compares to plain old Jaccard.

---

5. Measuring Agreement on Set-Valued Items. See *http://www.cs.columbia.edu/~becky/pubs/lrec06masi.pdf*.

6. `def subsumed(X,Y): return X.union_update(Y) == X or Y.union_update(X) == Y`

Table 6-2. A comparison of Jaccard and MASI distances for two small sets of items as emitted from Example 6-5

X	Y	Jaccard (X,Y)	MASI (X,Y)
[0]	[1]	1.0	1.0
[0]	[1, 2]	1.0	1.0
[0, 1]	[1]	0.5	0.5
[0, 1]	[1, 2]	0.67	0.5
[0, 1, 2]	[1]	0.67	0.67
[0, 1, 2]	[1, 2]	0.33	0.33
[0, 1, 2, 3]	[1]	0.75	0.75
[0, 1, 2, 3]	[1, 2]	0.5	0.5
[1]	[1]	0.0	0.0
[1]	[1, 2]	0.5	0.5
[1, 2]	[1]	0.5	0.5
[1, 2]	[1, 2]	0.0	0.0
[1, 2, 3]	[1]	0.67	0.67
[1, 2, 3]	[1, 2]	0.33	0.33
[2]	[1]	1.0	1.0
[2]	[1, 2]	0.5	0.5
[2, 3]	[1]	1.0	1.0
[2, 3]	[1, 2]	0.67	0.5
[3]	[1]	1.0	1.0
[3]	[1, 2]	1.0	1.0

While the list of interesting similarity metrics could go on and on, there's quite literally an ocean of literature about them online, and it's easy enough to plug in and try out different similarity heuristics once you have a better feel for the data you're mining. The next section works up a script that clusters job titles using the MASI similarity metric.

A Greedy Approach to Clustering

Given MASI's partiality to partially overlapping terms, and that we have insight suggesting that overlap in titles is important, let's try to cluster job titles by comparing them to one another using MASI distance, as an extension of Example 6-2. Example 6-6 clusters similar titles and then displays your contacts accordingly. Take a look at the code—especially the nested loop invoking the DISTANCE function that makes a greedy decision—and then we'll discuss.

Example 6-6. Clustering job titles using a greedy heuristic (linkedin__cluster_contacts_by_title.py)

```python
# -*- coding: utf-8 -*-

import sys
import csv
from nltk.metrics.distance import masi_distance

CSV_FILE = sys.argv[1]

DISTANCE_THRESHOLD = 0.34
DISTANCE = masi_distance

def cluster_contacts_by_title(csv_file):

    transforms = [
        ('Sr.', 'Senior'),
        ('Sr', 'Senior'),
        ('Jr.', 'Junior'),
        ('Jr', 'Junior'),
        ('CEO', 'Chief Executive Officer'),
        ('COO', 'Chief Operating Officer'),
        ('CTO', 'Chief Technology Officer'),
        ('CFO', 'Chief Finance Officer'),
        ('VP', 'Vice President'),
        ]

    seperators = ['/', 'and', '&']

    csvReader = csv.DictReader(open(csv_file), delimiter=',', quotechar='"')
    contacts = [row for row in csvReader]

# Normalize and/or replace known abbreviations
# and build up list of common titles

    all_titles = []
    for i in range(len(contacts)):
        if contacts[i]['Job Title'] == '':
            contacts[i]['Job Titles'] = ['']
            continue
        titles = [contacts[i]['Job Title']]
        for title in titles:
            for seperator in seperators:
                if title.find(seperator) >= 0:
                    titles.remove(title)
                    titles.extend([title.strip() for title in title.split(seperator)
                                   if title.strip() != ''])

        for transform in transforms:
            titles = [title.replace(*transform) for title in titles]
        contacts[i]['Job Titles'] = titles
        all_titles.extend(titles)

    all_titles = list(set(all_titles))
```

```
    clusters = {}
    for title1 in all_titles:
        clusters[title1] = []
        for title2 in all_titles:
            if title2 in clusters[title1] or clusters.has_key(title2) and title1 \
               in clusters[title2]:
                continue
            distance = DISTANCE(set(title1.split()), set(title2.split()))
            if distance < DISTANCE_THRESHOLD:
                clusters[title1].append(title2)

# Flatten out clusters

    clusters = [clusters[title] for title in clusters if len(clusters[title]) > 1]

# Round up contacts who are in these clusters and group them together

    clustered_contacts = {}
    for cluster in clusters:
        clustered_contacts[tuple(cluster)] = []
        for contact in contacts:
            for title in contact['Job Titles']:
                if title in cluster:
                    clustered_contacts[tuple(cluster)].append('%s %s.'
                        % (contact['First Name'], contact['Last Name'][0]))

    return clustered_contacts

if __name__ == '__main__':
    clustered_contacts = cluster_contacts_by_title(CSV_FILE)

    for titles in clustered_contacts:
        common_titles_heading = 'Common Titles: ' + ', '.join(titles)
        print common_titles_heading

        descriptive_terms = set(titles[0].split())
        for title in titles:
            descriptive_terms.intersection_update(set(title.split()))
        descriptive_terms_heading = 'Descriptive Terms: ' \
            + ', '.join(descriptive_terms)
        print descriptive_terms_heading
        print '-' * max(len(descriptive_terms_heading), len(common_titles_heading))
        print '\n'.join(clustered_contacts[titles])
        print
```

The code listing starts by separating out combined titles using a list of common conjunctions and then normalizes common titles. Then, a nested loop iterates over all of the titles and clusters them together according to a thresholded MASI similarity metric. This tight loop is where most of the real action happens in the listing: it's where each title is compared to each other title. If the distance between any two titles as determined by a similarity heuristic is "close enough," we *greedily* group them together. In this context, being "greedy" means that the first time we are able to determine that an item might fit in a cluster, we go ahead and assign it without further considering whether there might be a better fit, or making any attempt to account for such a better fit if one appears later. Although incredibly pragmatic, this approach produces very reasonable results. Clearly, the choice of an effective similarity heuristic is critical, but given the nature of the nested loop, the fewer times we have to invoke the scoring function, the better. More will be said about this consideration in the next section, but do note that we do use some conditional logic to try to avoid repeating unnecessary calculations if possible.

The rest of the listing just looks up contacts with a particular job title and groups them for display, but there is one other interesting nuance involved in computing clusters: *you often need to assign each cluster a meaningful label.* The working implementation computes labels by taking the setwise intersection of terms in the job titles for each cluster, which seems reasonable given that it's the most obvious common thread. Your mileage is sure to vary with other approaches.

The types of results you might expect from this code are useful in that they group together individuals who are likely to share common responsibilities in their job duties. This information might be useful for a variety of reasons, whether you're planning an event that includes a "CEO Panel," trying to figure out who can best help you to make your next career move, or trying to determine whether you are *really* well-enough connected to other similar professionals given your own job responsibilities. Abridged results for a sample network are presented in Example 6-7.

Example 6-7. Sample output for Example 6-6

```
Common Titles: Chief Executive Officer,
               Chief Finance Officer,
               Chief Technology Officer,
               Chief Operations Officer
Descriptive Terms: Chief, Officer
-----------------------------------------
Gregg P.
Scott S.
Mario G.
Brian F.
Damien K.
Chris A.
Trey B.
Emil E.
Dan M.
Tim E.
John T. H.


...


Common Titles: Consultant,
               Software Engineer,
               Software Engineer
Descriptive Terms: Software, Engineer
-----------------------------------------
```

Kent L.
Paul C.
Rick C.
James B.
Alex R.
Marco V.
James L.
Bill T.

...

Scalable clustering sure ain't easy

It's important to note that *in the worst case*, the nested loop executing the DISTANCE calculation from Example 6-6 would require it to be invoked in what we've already mentioned is $O(n^2)$ time complexity—in other words, len(all_titles)*len(all_titles) times. A nested loop that compares every single item to every single other item for clustering purposes is *not* a scalable approach for a very large value of n, but given that the unique number of titles for your professional network is not likely to be very large, it shouldn't impose a performance constraint. It may not seem like a big deal—after all, it's just a nested loop—but the crux of an $O(n^2)$ algorithm is that the number of comparisons required to process an input set increases exponentially in proportion to the number of items in the set. For example, a small input set of 100 job titles would require only 10,000 scoring operations, while 10,000 job titles would require 100,000,000 scoring operations. The math doesn't work out so well and eventually buckles, even when you have a lot of hardware to throw at it.

Your initial reaction when faced with what seems like a predicament that scales exponentially will probably be to try to reduce the value of n as much as possible. But most of the time you won't be able to reduce it enough to make your solution scalable as the size of your input grows, because you still have an $O(n^2)$ algorithm. What you really want to do is figure out a way to come up with an algorithm that's on the order of $O(k*n)$, where k is much smaller than n and represents a manageable amount of overhead that grows much more slowly than the rate of n's growth. But as with any other engineering decision, there are performance and quality trade-offs to be made in all corners of the real world, and *it sure ain't easy* to strike the right balance. In fact, many data-mining companies that have successfully implemented scalable record-matching analytics at a high degree of fidelity consider their specific approaches to be proprietary information (trade secrets), since they result in definite business advantages. (More times than you'd think, it's not the ability to solve a problem that really matters, but the ability to implement it in a particular manner that can be taken to the market.)

For situations in which an $O(n^2)$ algorithm is simply unacceptable, one variation to the working example that you might try is rewriting the nested loops so that a random sample is selected for the scoring function, which would effectively reduce it to $O(k*n)$, if k were the sample size. As the value of the sample size approaches n, however, you'd expect the runtime to begin approaching the $O(n^2)$ runtime. Example 6-8 shows how that sampling technique might look in code; the key changes to the previous listing are highlighted in bold. The key takeaway is that for each invocation of the outer loop, we're executing the inner loop a much smaller, fixed number of times.

Example 6-8. A small modification to an excerpt of Example 6-6 that incorporates random sampling to improve performance

```
# ...snip ...

all_titles = list(set(all_titles))
clusters = {}
for title1 in all_titles:
    clusters[title1] = []
    for sample in range(SAMPLE_SIZE):
        title2 = all_titles[random.randint(0, len(all_titles)-1)]
        if title2 in clusters[title1] or clusters.has_key(title2) and title1 \
            in clusters[title2]:
            continue
        distance = DISTANCE(set(title1.split()), set(title2.split()))
        if distance < DISTANCE_THRESHOLD:
            clusters[title1].append(title2)

# ...snip ...
```

Another approach you might consider is to randomly sample the data into n bins (where n is some number that's generally less than or equal to the square root of the number of items in your set), perform clustering within each of those individual bins, and then optionally merge the output. For example, if you had one million items, an $O(n^2)$ algorithm would take a trillion logical operations, whereas binning the one million items into 1,000 bins containing 1,000 items each and clustering each individual bin would require only a billion operations. (That's 1,000*1,000 comparisons for each bin for all 1,000 bins.) A billion is still a large number, but it's three orders of magnitude smaller than a trillion, and that's nothing to sneeze at.

There are many other approaches in the literature besides sampling or binning that could be far better at reducing the dimensionality of a problem. For example, you'd ideally compare every item in a set, and at the end of the day, the particular technique you'll end up using to avoid an $O(n^2)$ situation for a large value of n will vary based upon real-world constraints and insights you're likely to gain through experimentation and domain-specific knowledge. As you consider the possibilities, keep in mind that the field of machine learning offers many techniques that are designed to combat exactly these types of scale problems by using various sorts of probabilistic models and sophisticated sampling techniques. The next section introduces a fairly intuitive and well-known clustering algorithm called k-means, which is a general-purpose unsupervised approach for clustering a multidimensional space. We'll be using this technique later to cluster your contacts by geographic location.

Intelligent clustering enables compelling user experiences

It's easy to get so caught up in the data-mining techniques themselves that you lose sight of the business case that motivated them in the first place. Simple clustering techniques can create incredibly compelling user experiences (all over the place) by leveraging results even as simple as the job title ones we just produced. Figure 6-2 demonstrates a powerful alternative view of your data via a simple tree widget that could be used as part of a navigation pane or faceted display for filtering search criteria. Assuming that the underlying similarity metrics you've chosen have produced meaningful clusters, a simple hierarchical display that presents data in logical groups with a count of the items in each group can streamline the process of finding information, and power intuitive workflows for almost any application where a lot of skimming would otherwise be required to find the results.

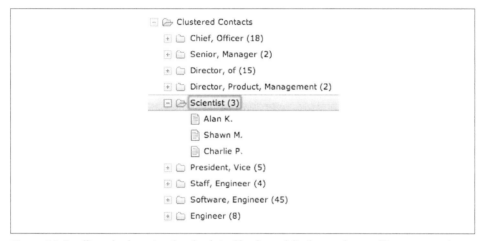

Figure 6-2. Intelligently clustering data lends itself to faceted displays and compelling user experiences

The code to create a simple navigational display can be surprisingly simple, given the maturity of Ajax toolkits and other UI libraries. For example, Example 6-9 shows a simple web page that is all that's required to populate the Dojo tree widget (*http://docs .dojocampus.org/dijit/Tree*) shown in Figure 6-2 using a makeshift template.

Example 6-9. A template for a Dojo tree widget, as displayed in Figure 6-2—just add data and watch it go!

```
<!DOCTYPE HTML PUBLIC "-//W3C//DTD HTML 4.01//EN"
        "http://www.w3.org/TR/html4/strict.dtd">
<html>
<head>
    <title>Clustered Contacts</title>
    <link rel="stylesheet"
        href="http://ajax.googleapis.com/ajax/libs/dojo/1.5/dojo/resources/dojo.css">
    <link rel="stylesheet"
        href="http://ajax.googleapis.com/ajax/libs/dojo/1.5/dijit/themes/claro/claro.css">
```

```
    <script src="http://ajax.googleapis.com/ajax/libs/dojo/1.5/dojo/dojo.xd.js"
        type="text/javascript" djConfig="parseOnLoad:true"></script>

    <script language="JavaScript" type="text/javascript">
        dojo.require("dojo.data.ItemFileReadStore");
        dojo.require("dijit.Tree");
        dojo.require("dojo.parser");
    </script>

    <script language="JavaScript" type="text/javascript">
        var data = %s; //substituted by Python
    </script>

</head>
<body class="claro">
    <div dojoType="dojo.data.ItemFileReadStore" jsId="jobsStore"
        data="data"></div>

    <div dojoType="dijit.Tree" id="mytree" store="jobsStore"
        label="Clustered Contacts" openOnClick="true">
    </div>
</body>
</html>
```

The data value that's substituted into the template is a simple JSON structure, which we can obtain easily enough by modifying the output from Example 6-6, as illustrated in Example 6-10.

Example 6-10. Munging the clustered_contacts data that's computed in Example 6-6 to produce JSON that's consumable by Dojo's tree widget

```
import json
import webbrowser
import os

data = {"label" : "name", "temp_items" : {}, "items" : []}
for titles in clustered_contacts:
    descriptive_terms = set(titles[0].split())
    for title in titles:
        descriptive_terms.intersection_update(set(title.split()))
    descriptive_terms = ', '.join(descriptive_terms)

    if data['temp_items'].has_key(descriptive_terms):
        data['temp_items'][descriptive_terms].extend([{'name' : cc } for cc
            in clustered_contacts[titles]])
    else:
        data['temp_items'][descriptive_terms] = [{'name' : cc } for cc
            in clustered_contacts[titles]]

for descriptive_terms in data['temp_items']:
    data['items'].append({"name" : "%s (%s)" % (descriptive_terms,
        len(data['temp_items'][descriptive_terms]),),),
```

```
            "children" : [i for i in
                data['temp_items'][descriptive_terms]]})

del data['temp_items']

# Open the template and substitute the data

if not os.path.isdir('out'):
    os.mkdir('out')

TEMPLATE = os.path.join(os.getcwd(), '..', 'web_code', 'dojo', 'dojo_tree.html')
OUT = os.path.join('out', 'dojo_tree.html')

t = open(TEMPLATE).read()
f = open(OUT, 'w')
f.write(t % json.dumps(data, indent=4))
f.close()

webbrowser.open("file://" + os.path.join(os.getcwd(), OUT))
```

There's incredible value in being able to create user experiences that present data in intuitive ways that power workflows. Something as simple as an intelligently crafted hierarchical display can inadvertently motivate users to spend more time on a site, discover more information than they normally would, and ultimately realize more value in the services the site offers.

Hierarchical and k-Means Clustering

Example 6-6 introduced a greedy approach to clustering, but there are at least two other common clustering techniques that you should know about: hierarchical clustering and *k*-means clustering. Hierarchical clustering is superficially similar to the greedy heuristic we have been using, while *k*-means clustering is radically different. We'll primarily focus on *k*-means throughout the rest of this chapter, but it's worthwhile to briefly introduce the theory behind both of these approaches since you're very likely to encounter them during literature review and research. An excellent implementation of both of these approaches is available via the `cluster` module that you can `easy_install`, so please go ahead and take a moment to do that.

Hierarchical clustering

Hierarchical clustering is a deterministic and exhaustive technique, in that it computes the full matrix of distances between all items and then walks through the matrix clustering items that meet a minimum distance threshold. It's *hierarchical* in that walking over the matrix and clustering items together naturally produces a tree structure that expresses the relative distances between items. In the literature, you may see this technique called *agglomerative*, because the leaves on the tree represent the items that are being clustered, while nodes in the tree agglomerate these items into clusters.

This technique is similar to but not fundamentally the same as the approach used in Example 6-6, which uses a greedy heuristic to cluster items instead of successively building up a hierarchy. As such, the actual wall clock time (the amount of time it takes for the code to run) for hierarchical clustering may be a bit longer, and you may need to tweak your scoring function and distance threshold. However, the use of dynamic programming (*http://en.wikipedia.org/wiki/Dynamic_programming*) and other clever bookkeeping techniques can result in substantial savings in wall clock execution time, depending on the implementation. For example, given that the distance between two items such as job titles is almost certainly going to be symmetric, you should only have to compute one half of the distance matrix instead of the full matrix. Even though the time complexity of the algorithm as a whole is still $O(n^2)$, only 0.5^*n^2 units of work are being performed instead of n^2 units of work.

If we were to rewrite Example 6-6 to use the cluster module, the nested loop performing the clustering DISTANCE computation would be replaced with something like the code in Example 6-11.

Example 6-11. A minor modification to Example 6-6 that uses cluster.HierarchicalClustering instead of a greedy heuristic (linkedin__cluster_contacts_by_title_hac.py)

```
# ... snip ...

# Import the goods
from cluster import HierarchicalClustering

# Define a scoring function
def score(title1, title2):
    return DISTANCE(set(title1.split()), set(title2.split()))

# Feed the class your data and the scoring function
hc = HierarchicalClustering(all_titles, score)

# Cluster the data according to a distance threshold
clusters = hc.getlevel(DISTANCE_THRESHOLD)

# Remove singleton clusters
clusters = [c for c in clusters if len(c) > 1]

# ... snip ...
```

If you're very interested in variations on hierarchical clustering, be sure to check out the HierarchicalClustering class' setLinkageMethod method, which provides some subtle variations on how the class can compute distances between clusters. For example, you can specify whether distances between clusters should be determined by calculating the shortest, longest, or average distance between any two clusters. Depending on the distribution of your data, choosing a different linkage method can potentially produce quite different results. Figure 6-3 displays a portion of a professional network as a radial tree layout and a dendogram using Protovis (*http://vis.stanford.edu/proto vis/*), a powerful HTML5-based visualization toolkit. The radial tree layout is more space-efficient and probably a better choice for this particular data set, but a dendogram (*http://en.wikipedia.org/wiki/Dendrogram*) would be a great choice if you needed to easily find correlations between each level in the tree (which would correspond to each level of agglomeration in hierarchical clustering) for a more complex set of data. Both of the visualizations presented here are essentially just static incarnations of the interactive tree widget from Figure 6-2. As they show, an amazing amount of information becomes apparent when you are able to look at a simple image of your professional network.[7]

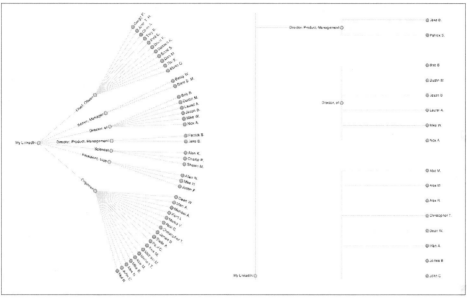

Figure 6-3. A Protovis radial tree layout of contacts clustered by job title (left), and a slice of the same data presented as a dendogram (right)

k-means clustering

Whereas hierarchical clustering is a deterministic technique that exhausts the possibilities and is an $O(n^2)$ approach, *k*-means clustering generally executes on the order of $O(k^*n)$ times. The substantial savings in performance come at the expense of results that are approximate, but they still have the potential to be quite good. The idea is that you generally have a multidimensional space containing *n* points, which you cluster into *k* clusters through the following series of steps:

---

7. linkedin__cluster_contacts_by_title_hac.py   (*https://github.com/ptwobrussell/Mining-the-Social-Web/blob/master/python_code/linkedin__cluster_contacts_by_title_hac.py*) provides a minimal adaptation of Example 6-6 that demonstrates how to produce output that could be consumed by Protovis.

1. Randomly pick *k* points in the data space as initial values that will be used to compute the *k* clusters: K_1, K_2, ..., K_k.

2. Assign each of the *n* points to a cluster by finding the nearest K_n—effectively creating *k* clusters and requiring *k**n comparisons.

3. For each of the *k* clusters, calculate the centroid (*http://en.wikipedia.org/wiki/Centroid*), or the mean of the cluster, and reassign its K_i value to be that value. (Hence, you're computing "*k*-means" during each iteration of the algorithm.)

4. Repeat steps 2–3 until the members of the clusters do not change between iterations. Generally speaking, relatively few iterations are required for convergence.

Because *k*-means may not be all that intuitive at first glance, Figure 6-4 displays each step of the algorithm as presented in the online "Tutorial on Clustering Algorithms" (*http://home.dei.polimi.it/matteucc/Clustering/tutorial_html/AppletKM.html*), which features an interactive Java applet. The sample parameters used involve 100 data points and a value of 3 for the parameter *k*, which means that the algorithm will produce three clusters. The important thing to note at each step is the location of the squares, and which points are included in each of those three clusters as the algorithm progresses. The algorithm only takes nine steps to complete.

Although you could run *k*-means on points in two dimensions or two thousand dimensions, the most common range is usually somewhere on the order of tens of dimensions, with the most common cases being two or three dimensions. When the dimensionality of the space you're working in is relatively small, *k*-means can be an effective clustering technique because it executes fairly quickly and is capable of producing very reasonable results. You do, however, need to pick an appropriate value for *k*, which is not always obvious. The next section demonstrates how to fetch more extended profile information for your contacts, which bridges this discussion with a follow-up exercise devoted to geographically clustering your professional network by applying *k*-means.

Fetching Extended Profile Information

Although the earlier exercises in this chapter were interesting, sooner rather than later, you'll want to begin using the LinkedIn APIs to mine the full richness of the data that's available to you. As you'd expect, there's a basic developer opt-in process where you register to get authorization credentials; you'll want to visit *http://developer.linkedin.com* and read up on the full details, but Figure 6-5 demonstrates the broad strokes. Once you have credentials, the overall process is similar to that of any other social network that requires you to do the OAuth dance to access APIs: you request API credentials, get back a token and secret, and then use these values to ultimately get the coveted access token that can be used when sending requests. Of course, most of the gory details will be abstracted away since we'll be using the `linkedin` Python module to do most of the tedious work for us. Just `easy_install python-linkedin`.

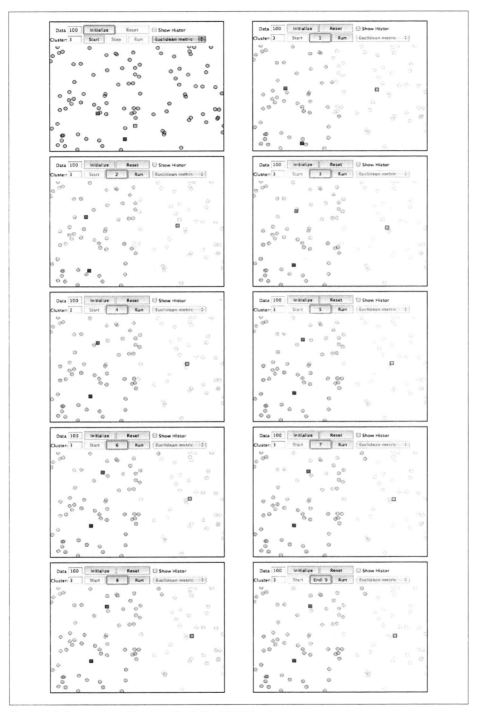

Figure 6-4. Progression of k-means for k=3 with 100 points

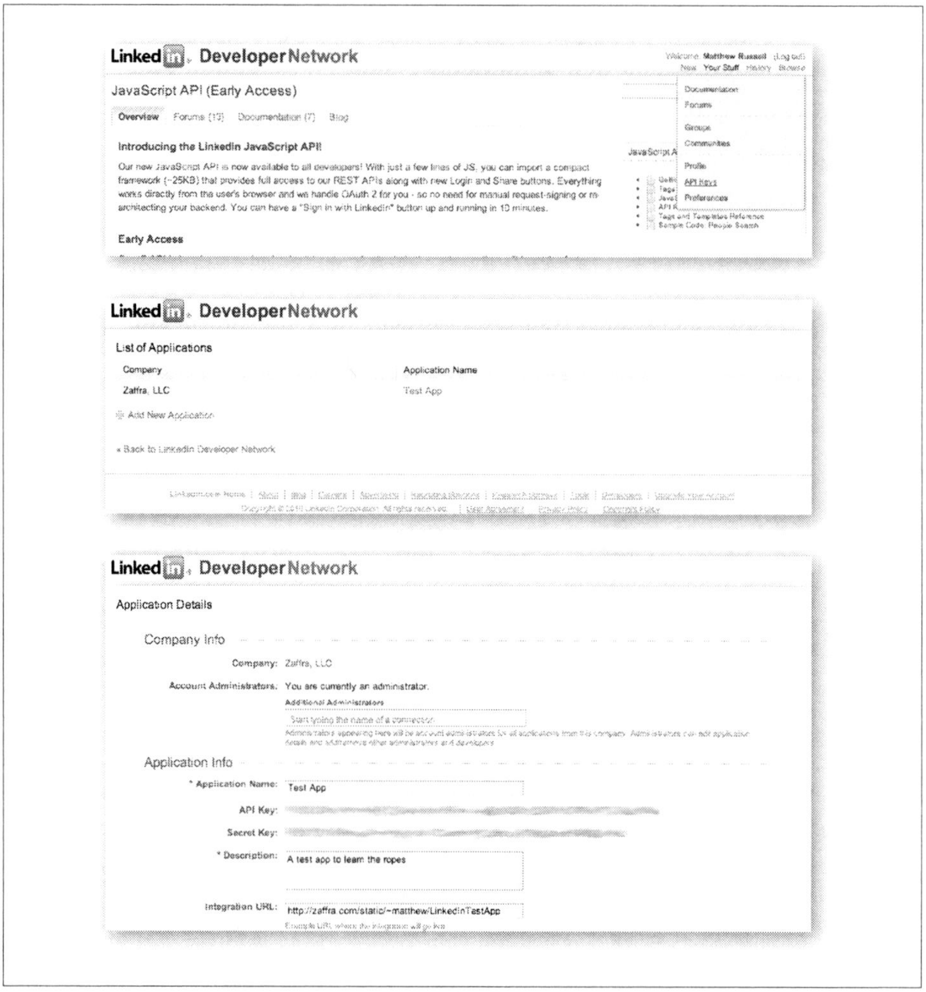

Figure 6-5. Basic steps involved in getting LinkedIn API credentials: from http://developer.linkedin.com, pick "Your Stuff"→"API Keys" (top), then create a new app (middle), and finally set up your app parameters and take note of your API key and secret (bottom)

Once the linkedin package is installed, the following script (Example 6-12) is a working template that you can use to get logged in and start accessing your professional network at the API level. The linkedin package is still somewhat nascent, so the process may be a little more streamlined by the time you read this.[8]

---

8. As of October 2010, LinkedIn is rolling out an OAuth 2 implementation (http://blog.linkedin.com/2010/10/06/linkedin-oauth2/). The linkedin module as of version 1.6 implements OAuth 1.0a as outlined in http://developer.linkedin.com/docs/.

Example 6-12. Harvesting extended profile information for your LinkedIn contacts (linkedin__get_connections.py)

```
# -*- coding: utf-8 -*-

import os
import sys
import webbrowser
import cPickle
from linkedin import linkedin

KEY = sys.argv[1]
SECRET = sys.argv[2]

# Parses out oauth_verifier parameter from window.location.href and
# displays it for the user

RETURN_URL = 'http://miningthesocialweb.appspot.com/static/linkedin_oauth_helper.html'


def oauthDance(key, secret, return_url):
    api = linkedin.LinkedIn(key, secret, return_url)

    result = api.requestToken()

    if not result:
        print >> sys.stderr, api.requestTokenError()
        return None

    authorize_url = api.getAuthorizeURL()

    webbrowser.open(authorize_url)

    oauth_verifier = raw_input('PIN number, bro: ')

    result = api.accessToken(verifier=oauth_verifier)
    if not result:
        print >> sys.stderr, 'Error: %s\nAborting' % api.getRequestTokenError()
        return None

    return api


# First, do the oauth_dance

api = oauthDance(KEY, SECRET, RETURN_URL)

# Now do something like get your connections:

if api:
    connections = api.GetConnections()
else:
    print >> sys.stderr, 'Failed to aunthenticate. You need to learn to dance'
    sys.exit(1)
```

```
# Be careful - this type of API usage is "expensive".
# See http://developer.linkedin.com/docs/DOC-1112

print >> sys.stderr, 'Fetching extended connections...'

extended_connections = [api.GetProfile(member_id=c.id, url=None, fields=[
    'first-name',
    'last-name',
    'current-status',
    'educations',
    'specialties',
    'interests',
    'honors',
    'positions',
    'industry',
    'summary',
    'location',
    ]) for c in connections]

# Store the data

if not os.path.isdir('out'):
    os.mkdir('out')

f = open('out/linkedin_connections.pickle', 'wb')
cPickle.dump(extended_connections, f)
f.close()

print >> sys.stderr, 'Data pickled to out/linkedin_connections.pickle'
```

Note that unlike Twitter, LinkedIn requires that you specify your own URL for capturing the OAuth verifier (access token) that's needed for authorizing a command-line client like the Python program we're running. The web page template in Example 6-13 is available at GitHub (*http://github.com/ptwobrussell/Mining-the-Social-Web/blob/master/web_code/linkedin/linkedin_oauth_helper.html*) and demonstrates how to extract that information and present it to the user in a Twitter-esque manner, in case you're curious.

Example 6-13. A sample template that extracts the LinkedIn OAuth verifier and displays it for you

```
<!DOCTYPE HTML PUBLIC "-//W3C//DTD HTML 4.01//EN"
        "http://www.w3.org/TR/html4/strict.dtd">
<html>
<head>
    <title>LinkedIn OAuth Helper</title>

    <script src="http://ajax.googleapis.com/ajax/libs/dojo/1.5/dojo/dojo.xd.js"
        type="text/javascript"></script>
    <script type="text/javascript">
        dojo.ready(function() {
            var q = dojo.queryToObject(window.location.search.slice(1));
            dojo.byId("oauth_verifier").innerHTML = q.oauth_verifier;
        });
    </script>
```

```
</head>
<body>
    <div>
        Type the following identifier into the prompt in your terminal:
        <strong><span id="oauth_verifier"></span></strong>
    </div>
</body>
</html>
```

That's basically all you need to know to get up and running with the linkedin package, but there are a couple of other important considerations for using the API. Perhaps the most pertinent is that LinkedIn's rate-throttling limits (*http://developer.linkedin.com/docs/DOC-1112*) are a little more complex than what you may have seen elsewhere. Applications you build have a total daily rate limit, individual users of your applications have rate limits, and you as a developer have another rate limit in most situations. Beyond that, there are different rate limits depending on the particular API and whether the users of an application are accessing their own data or data for folks in their networks. Once you meet or exceed the rate limit, you have to wait until midnight Pacific Standard Time (PST) for it to reset. Example 6-12 demonstrates how to get the "mini-profiles" for users via GetConnections, and how to fetch full public profile details by passing in arguments to GetProfile. The rate limits don't really afford you the ability to accumulate large piles of data via long-running processes, so the remaining samples in this chapter don't use techniques such as using a thread pool to speed up fetching data. You can easily stand by for the minute or so it will take to max out your rate limit if you're the type who likes to spend all your money at one place.

Geographically Clustering Your Network

With the know-how to access extended LinkedIn profile information, and a working knowledge of common clustering algorithms, all that's left is to introduce a nice visualization that puts it all together. The next section applies *k*-means to the problem of clustering your professional contacts and plots them out in Google Earth. The section after it introduces an alternative visualization called a *Dorling Cartogram* (*http://vis.stanford.edu/protovis/ex/cartogram.html*), which is essentially a geographically clustered bubble chart that lets you easily visualize how many of your contacts live in each state. Ironically, it doesn't explicitly use a clustering algorithm like *k*-means at all, but it still produces intuitive results that are mapped out in 2D space, and it conveys a semblance of geographic clustering and frequency information.

Mapping Your Professional Network with Google Earth

An interesting exercise in seeing *k*-means in action is to use it to visualize and cluster your professional LinkedIn network by putting it on a map—or the globe, if you're a fan of Google Earth. In addition to the insight gained by visualizing how your contacts are spread out, you can analyze clusters by using your contacts, the distinct employers of your contacts, or the distinct metro areas in which your contacts reside as a basis. All three approaches might yield results that are useful for different purposes. Through the LinkedIn API, you can fetch location information that describes the major metropolitan area, such as "Greater Nashville Area," in which each of your contacts resides, which with a bit of munging is quite adequate for geocoding the locations back into coordinates that we can plot in a tool like Google Earth

The primary things that must be done in order to get the ball rolling include:

- Parsing out the geographic location from each of your contacts' public profiles. Example 6-12 demonstrates how to fetch this kind of information.

- Geocoding the locations back into coordinates. The approach we'll take is to easy_install geopy and let it handle all the heavy lifting. There's a nice getting-started guide (*http://code.google.com/p/geopy/wiki/GettingStarted*) available online; depending on your choice of geocoder, you may need to request an API key from a service provider such as Google or Yahoo!.

- Feeding the geocoordinates into the KMeansClustering class of the cluster module to calculate clusters.

- Constructing KML that can be fed into a visualization tool like Google Earth.

Lots of interesting nuances and variations become possible once you have the basic legwork of Example 6-14 in place. The linkedin__kml_utility that's referenced is pretty uninteresting and just does some XML munging; you can view the details on GitHub (*http://github.com/ptwobrussell/Mining-the-Social-Web/blob/master/python _code/linkedin__kml_utility.py*).

 Recall from "Plotting geo data via microform.at and Google Maps" on page 33 that you can point Google Maps to an addressable URL pointing to a KML file if you'd prefer not to download and use Google Earth.

Example 6-14. Geocoding the locations of your LinkedIn contacts and exporting them to KML (linkedin__geocode.py)

```
# -*- coding: utf-8 -*-

import os
import sys
import cPickle
from urllib2 import HTTPError
from geopy import geocoders
from cluster import KMeansClustering, centroid

# A very uninteresting helper function to build up an XML tree

from linkedin_kml_utility import createKML

K = int(sys.argv[1])
```

```
# Use your own API key here if you use a geocoding service
# such as Google or Yahoo!

GEOCODING_API_KEY = sys.argv[2]

CONNECTIONS_DATA = sys.argv[3]

OUT = "clusters.kmeans.kml"

# Open up your saved connections with extended profile information

extended_connections = cPickle.load(open(CONNECTIONS_DATA))
locations = [ec.location for ec in extended_connections]
g = geocoders.Yahoo(GEOCODING_API_KEY)

# Some basic transforms may be necessary for geocoding services to function properly
# Here are a few examples that seem to cause problems for Yahoo. You'll probably need
# to add your own.

transforms = [('Greater ', ''), (' Area', ''), ('San Francisco Bay',
              'San Francisco')]

# Tally the frequency of each location

coords_freqs = {}
for location in locations:

    # Avoid unnecessary I/O

    if coords_freqs.has_key(location):
        coords_freqs[location][1] += 1
        continue
    transformed_location = location

    for transform in transforms:
        transformed_location = transformed_location.replace(*transform)
        while True:
            num_errors = 0
            try:

                # This call returns a generator

                results = g.geocode(transformed_location, exactly_one=False)
                break
            except HTTPError, e:
                num_errors += 1
                if num_errors >= 3:
                    sys.exit()
                print >> sys.stderr, e
                print >> sys.stderr, 'Encountered an urllib2 error. Trying again...'
        for result in results:

            # Each result is of the form ("Description", (X,Y))
```

```
            coords_freqs[location] = [result[1], 1]
            break

# Here, you could optionally segment locations by continent
# country so as to avoid potentially finding a mean in the middle of the ocean
# The k-means algorithm will expect distinct points for each contact so build out
# an expanded list to pass it

expanded_coords = []
for label in coords_freqs:
    ((lat, lon), f) = coords_freqs[label]
    expanded_coords.append((label, [(lon, lat)] * f))  # Flip lat/lon for Google Earth

# No need to clutter the map with unnecessary placemarks...

kml_items = [{'label': label, 'coords': '%s,%s' % coords[0]} for (label,
            coords) in expanded_coords]

# It could also be interesting to include names of your contacts on the map for display

for item in kml_items:
    item['contacts'] = '\n'.join(['%s %s.' % (ec.first_name, ec.last_name[0])
                        for ec in extended_connections if ec.location
                        == item['label']])

cl = KMeansClustering([coords for (label, coords_list) in expanded_coords
                    for coords in coords_list])

centroids = [{'label': 'CENTROID', 'coords': '%s,%s' % centroid(c)} for c in
            cl.getclusters(K)]

kml_items.extend(centroids)
kml = createKML(kml_items)

if not os.path.isdir('out'):
    os.mkdir('out')

f = open("out/" + OUT, 'w')
f.write(kml)
f.close()

print >> sys.stderr, 'Data pickled to out/' + OUT
```

 Location values returned as part of LinkedIn profile information are generally of the form "Greater Nashville Area," and a certain amount of munging is necessary in order to extract the city name. The approach presented here is imperfect, and you may have to tweak it based upon what you see happening with your data to achieve total accuracy.

As in Example 6-6, most of the work involved in getting to the point where the results can be visualized is data-processing boilerplate. The most interesting details are tucked away inside of KMeansClustering's getclusters method call, toward the end of the listing. The approach demonstrated groups your contacts by location, clusters them, and then uses the results of the clustering algorithm to compute the centroids. Figure 6-6 illustrates sample results from running the code in Example 6-14.

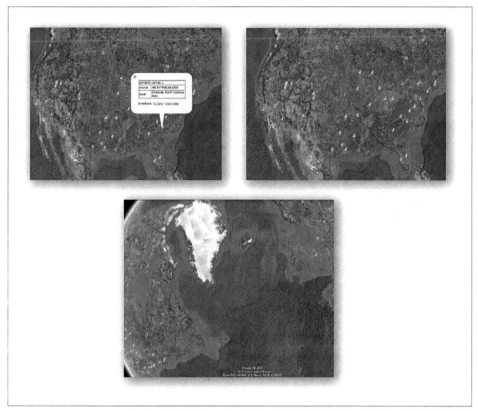

Figure 6-6. From top left to bottom: 1) clustering contacts by location so that you can easily see who lives/works in what city, 2) finding the centroids of three clusters computed by k-means, 3) don't forget that clusters could span countries or even continents when trying to find an ideal meeting location!

Just visualizing your network can be pretty interesting, but computing the geographic centroids of your professional network can also open up some intriguing possibilities. For example, you might want to compute candidate locations for a series of regional workshops or conferences. Alternatively, if you're in the consulting business and have a hectic travel schedule, you might want to plot out some good locations for renting a little home away from home. Or maybe you want to map out professionals in your network according to their job duties, or the socioeconomic bracket they're likely to fit in based on their job titles and experience. Beyond the numerous options opened up by visualizing your professional network's location data, geographic clustering lends itself to many other possibilities, such as supply chain management and Travelling Salesman (*http://en.wikipedia.org/wiki/Travelling_salesman_problem*) types of problems.

Mapping Your Professional Network with Dorling Cartograms

Protovis (*http://vis.stanford.edu/protovis/*), a cutting-edge HTML5-based visualization toolkit introduced in Chapter 7, includes a visualization called a Dorling Cartogram, which is essentially a geographically clustered bubble chart. Whereas a more traditional cartogram might convey information by distorting the geographic boundaries of a state on a map, a Dorling Cartogram places a uniform shape such as a circle on the map approximately where the actual state would be located, and encodes information using the circumference (and often the color) of the circle, as demonstrated in Figure 6-7. They're a great visualization tool because they allow you to use your instincts about where information should appear on a 2D mapping surface, and they are able to encode parameters using very intuitive properties of shapes, like area and color.

 Protovis also includes several other visualizations that convey geographical information, such as heatmaps (*http://vis.stanford.edu/protovis/ex/ heatmap.html*), symbol maps (*http://vis.stanford.edu/protovis/ex/symbol .html*), and chloropleth maps (*http://vis.stanford.edu/protovis/ex/choro pleth.html*). See "A Tour Through the Visualization Zoo" (*http://queue .acm.org/detail.cfm?id=1805128*) for an overview of these and many other visualizations that may be helpful.

All that said, assuming you've followed along with Example 6-14 and successfully geocoded your contacts from the location data provided by LinkedIn, a minimal adjustment to the script to produce a slightly different output is all that's necessary to power a Protovis Dorling Cartogram visualization.[9] A modified version of the canonical Dorling Cartogram example is available at GitHub (*http://github.com/ptwobrussell/Mining -the-Social-Web/blob/master/python_code/linkedin__create_dorling_cartogram_output .py*) and should produce a visualization similar to Figure 6-7. The sample code connects the dots to produce a useful visualization, but there's a lot more that you could do to soup it up, such as adding event handlers to display connection information when you click on a particular state. As was pointed out in the Warning just after Example 6-14, the geocoding approach implemented here is necessarily imperfect and may require some tweaking.

Closing Remarks

This chapter covered some serious ground, introducing fundamental clustering techniques and applying them to your professional network data on LinkedIn in a variety of ways. As in the other chapters, we just touched the tip of the iceberg; there are many other interesting things that you can do with your LinkedIn data that were not

---

9. The Protovis Dorling Cartogram visualization currently is implemented to handle locations in the United States only.

introduced in this chapter. Take some time to explore the extended profile information that you have available. It could be interesting to try to correlate where people work versus where they went to school and/or analyze whether people tend to relocate into and out of certain areas, but keep in mind that your tool belt contains lots of other tools by now that don't necessarily have to include geo data or clustering. If you do continue to look at geo data, one of the many projects you might want to check out is an emerging open framework called geodict (*http://petewarden.typepad.com/searchbrowser/2010/10/geodict-an-open-source-tool-for-extracting-locations-from-text.html*).

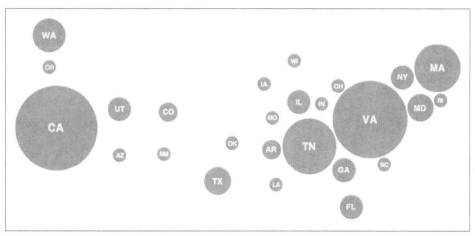

Figure 6-7. A Dorling Cartogram that uses the area of a circle to convey the number of colleagues that reside in each state; color could have been used to denote another variable, such as the unemployment rate associated with the state or your colleagues' job turnover rates, as determined by mining extended profile information

## CHAPTER 7

Google+: TF-IDF, Cosine Similarity, and Collocations

Initial printings of this book from February 2011 through February 2012 featured Google Buzz as the backdrop for data in this chapter. This chapter has been fully revised (with as few changes made as possible) to now feature Google+ instead. Example files have been updated and renamed with the *plus_* prefix, but previous *buzz_* example files are still available online with the other example code.

This short chapter begins our journey into text mining,[1] and it's something of an inflection point in this book. Earlier chapters have mostly focused on analyzing structured or semi-structured data such as records encoded as microformats, relationships among people, or specially marked #hashtags in tweets. However, this chapter begins munging and making sense of textual information in documents by introducing Information Retrieval (IR) theory fundamentals such as TF-IDF, cosine similarity, and collocation detection. As you may have already inferred from the chapter title, Google+ (*http://plus .google.com*) initially serves as our primary source of data because it's inherently social, easy to harvest,[2] and has a lot of potential for the social web. Toward the end of this chapter, we'll also look at what it takes to tap into your Gmail data. In the chapters ahead, we'll investigate mining blog data and other sources of free text, as additional forms of text analytics such as entity extraction and the automatic generation of abstracts are introduced. There's no real reason to introduce Google+ earlier in the book than blogs (the topic of Chapter 8), other than the fact that Google+ *activities* (notes) fill an interesting niche somewhere between Twitter and blogs, so this ordering

1. This book avoids splitting hairs over exactly what differences could be implied by common phrases such as "text mining," "unstructured data analytics" (UDA), or "information retrieval," and simply treats them as essentially the same thing.

2. There's also somewhat of a play on words here, since Google is so well known for its search capabilities and this chapter hones in on fundamental document-centric search techniques.

facilitates telling a story from cover to cover. All in all, the text-mining techniques you'll learn in any chapter of this book could just as easily be applied to any other chapter.

Wherever possible we won't reinvent the wheel and implement analysis tools from scratch, but we will take a couple of "deep dives" when particularly foundational topics come up that are essential to an understanding of text mining. The Natural Language Toolkit (NLTK), a powerful technology that you may recall from some opening examples in Chapter 1, provides many of the tools. Its rich suites of APIs can be a bit overwhelming at first, but don't worry: text analytics is an incredibly diverse and complex field of study, but there are lots of powerful fundamentals that can take you a long way without too significant of an investment. This chapter and the chapters after it aim to hone in on those fundamentals.

 A full-blown introduction to NLTK is outside the scope of this book, but you can review the full text of *Natural Language Processing with Python: Analyzing Text with the Natural Language Toolkit* (O'Reilly) online (*http://www.nltk.org/book*). Paper copies are also available at *http://oreilly.com/catalog/9780596516499*.

Harvesting Google+ Data

Anyone with a Gmail account can trivially create a Google+ account and start collaborating with friends. From a product standpoint, Google+ has evolved rapidly and used some of the most compelling features (and anti-features) of existing social network platforms (such as Twitter and Facebook) in carving out its own set of unique features. A full overview of Google+ isn't in scope for this chapter, and you can easily read about it (or sign up) online to learn more. Suffice it to say that Google+ has leveraged tried and true features of existing social networks such as marking content with hashtags and maintaining a profile according to customizable privacy settings with additional novelties such as a fresh take on content sharing called "circles," video chats called "hangouts," and extensive integration with other Google services such as Gmail contacts and Picasa web albums.

In Google+ API (*https://developers.google.com/+/api/*) parlance, social interactions are framed in terms of people, activities, and comments. An *activity* is a note that could just as long as a blog post, but could also be void of any real textual meaning because it's essentially just a pointer to multimedia data such as photos or videos. For the purposes of this chapter, we'll be focusing on harvesting and analyzing Google+ activity data that is textual and intended to convey the same kind of meaning that you might encounter in a tweet, blog post, or Facebook status update. If you haven't signed up for Google+ yet, it's worth taking the time to do so, as well as spending a few moments to familiarize yourself with a Google+ profile. One of the easiest ways to find someone on Google+ is to just search for them at *http://plus.google.com/*. (Unfortunately, as of early 2012, there doesn't appear to be a way to use somebody's Gmail username to look up someone on Google+.) For example, searching for "Tim O'Reilly" produces the results shown in Figure 7-1, which easily surfaces his public profile page at *https:// plus.google.com/107033731246200681024/*.

Figure 7-1. Searching for Tim O'Reilly on Google+ easily surfaces a pointer to his public profile along with several other Tim O'Reilly Google+ members.

Let's now fetch some data from Tim O'Reilly's public profile by getting your development environment situated. In order to get started collecting Google+ data with Python, there are only a couple of prerequisites involved:

- Install Google's Python API client via `easy_install --upgrade google-api-python-client`, which should take care of satisfying the various dependencies involved in interacting with the Google+ (and other Google services) APIs.

- Go to *https://code.google.com/apis/console*, and enable Google Plus API Access under the Services menu item.

- Finally, take note of the API key that's available by accessing the API Access menu item.

You should assume that the textual data exposed as Google+ activities contains markup, escaped HTML entities, etc., so a little bit of additional filtering is needed to clean it up. Example 7-1 provides an example session demonstrating how to fetch and distill plain text suitable for mining some good text content out of a Google+ user's public profile data. Although this first example illustrates the use of CouchDB as an optional storage medium, we'll be making a transition away from CouchDB in this chapter in favor of storing a JSON archive of the data, so that we can hone in on text-mining techniques, as opposed to discussing storage considerations. If you're interested in a more aggressive use of CouchDB and useful add-ons like `couchdb-lucene`, revisit the earlier chapters of this book.

Example 7-1. Harvesting Google+ data (plus__get_activities.py)

```
# -*- coding: utf-8 -*-

import os
import sys
import httplib2
import json
import apiclient.discovery
from BeautifulSoup import BeautifulStoneSoup
from nltk import clean_html

USER_ID=sys.argv[1] # Tim O'Reilly's Google+ id is '107033731246200681024'

API_KEY=""

MAX_RESULTS = 200 # May actually get slightly more

# Helper function for removing html and converting escaped entities.
# Returns UTF-8

def cleanHtml(html):
  if html == "": return ""

  return BeautifulStoneSoup(clean_html(html),
          convertEntities=BeautifulStoneSoup.HTML_ENTITIES).contents[0]

service = apiclient.discovery.build('plus', 'v1', http=httplib2.Http(),
                                    developerKey=API_KEY)

activities_resource = service.activities()
request = activities_resource.list(
  userId=USER_ID,
  collection='public',
  maxResults='100') # Max allowed per API

activities = []

while request != None and len(activities) < MAX_RESULTS:

  activities_document = request.execute()

  if 'items' in activities_document:

    for activity in activities_document['items']:

      if activity['object']['objectType'] == 'note' and \
         activity['object']['content'] != '':

        activity['title'] = cleanHtml(activity['title'])
        activity['object']['content'] = cleanHtml(activity['object']['content'])
        activities.append(activity)
```

```
    request = service.activities().list_next(request, activities_document)

# Store out to a local file as json data if you prefer

if not os.path.isdir('out'):
    os.mkdir('out')

filename = os.path.join('out', USER_ID + '.plus')
f = open(filename, 'w')
f.write(json.dumps(activities, indent=2))
f.close()

print >> sys.stderr, str(len(activities)), "activities written to", f.name

# Or store it somewhere like CouchDB like so...

# server = couchdb.Server('http://localhost:5984')
# DB = 'plus-' + USER_ID
# db = server.create(DB)
# db.update(activities, all_or_nothing=True)
```

Now that you have the tools to fetch and store Google+ data, let's start analyzing it.

Data Hacking with NLTK

NLTK is written such that you can explore data very easily and begin to form some impressions without a lot of upfront investment. Before skipping ahead, though, consider following along with the interpreter session in Example 7-2 to get a feel for some of the powerful functionality that NLTK provides right out of the box. Don't forget that you can use the built-in `help` function to get more information whenever you need it. For example, `help(nltk)` would provide documentation on the NLTK package. Also keep in mind that not all of the functionality from the interpreter session is intended for incorporation into production software, since output is written through standard output and not capturable into a data structure such as a list. In that regard, methods such as `nltk.text.concordance` are considered "demo functionality." Speaking of which, many of NLTK's modules have a `demo` function that you can call to get some idea of how to use the functionality they provide, and the source code for these demos is a great starting point for learning how to use new APIs. For example, you could run `nltk.text.demo()` in the interpreter to get some additional insight into capabilities provided by the `nltk.text` module. We'll take a closer look at how some of this demonstration functionality works over the coming pages.

The examples throughout this chapter, including the following interpreter session, use the `split` method to tokenize text. Chapter 8 introduces more sophisticated approaches for tokenization that may work better.

Example 7-2. Hacking on Google Plus data in the interpreter with NLTK. Example 7-1 produces a data archive in the out directory from where you ran the script.

```
>>> import nltk
>>> import json
>>> data = json.loads(open("out/107033731246200681024.plus").read())
>>> all_content = " ".join([ a['object']['content'] for a in data ])
>>> len(all_content)
203026
>>> tokens = all_content.split()
>>> text = nltk.Text(tokens)
>>> text.concordance("open")
Building index...
Displaying 12 of 12 matches:
 . Part of what matters so much when open source, the web, and open data meet
 much when open source, the web, and open data meet government is that practic
 government to provide a platform to open and share freely downloadable GIS da
s bill to prevent NIH from mandating open access to federally funded research.
 agencies such as the NIH to mandate open access to research that is funded by
lly like + John Tolva 's piece about open government in Chicago. It ties toget
orce. Analysis builds new processes. open data builds businesses." I haven't s
e in. We wanted reading to remain as open as it did when printed books ruled t
 a stand for reading portability and open access. Offer books in multiple open
open access. Offer books in multiple open formats, DRM-free, and from multiple
hat story redefined free software as open source, and the world hasn't been th
g behind them. Thinking deeply about open source and the internet got me think
>>> text.collocations()
Building collocations list
AlhambraPatternsAndTextures AlhambraPatternsAndTextures;
OccupyWallStreet OccupyWallStreet; PopupCrecheShops PopupCrecheShops;
Wall Street; Maker Faire; Mini Maker; New York; Bay Mini; East Bay;
United States; Ada Lovelace; hedge fund; Faire East; Steve Jobs; 21st
century; Silicon Valley; sales tax; Jennifer Pahlka; Mike Loukides;
data science
>>> fdist = text.vocab()
Building vocabulary index...
>>> fdist["open"]
11
>>> fdist["source"]
5
>>> fdist["web"]
6
>>> fdist["2.0"]
4
>>> len(tokens)
33280
>>> len(fdist.keys()) # unique tokens
8598
>>> [w for w in fdist.keys()[:100] \
... if w.lower() not in nltk.corpus.stopwords.words('english')]
[u'one', u'-', u'new', u'+', u'like', u'government', u'would', u'people', u'get',
 u'data', u'make', u'really', u'also', u'many', u'"It's", u'business', u'I'm", u'it's",
 u'much', u'way', u'AlhambraPatternsAndTextures', u'book', u'see', u'work', u'great',
 u'market']
```

```
>>> [w for w in fdist.keys() if len(w) > 15 and not w.startswith("http")]
[u'one', u'-', u'new', u'+', u'like', u'government', u'would', u'people', u'get', u'data',
 u'make', u'really', u'also', u'many', u"It's", u'business', u"I'm", u"it's", u'much',
 u'way', u'AlhambraPatternsAndTextures', u'book', u'see', u'work', u'great', u'market']
>>> [w for w in fdist.keys() if len(w) > 15 and not w.startswith("http")]
[u'AlhambraPatternsAndTextures', u'OccupyWallStreet', u'PopupCrecheShops',
 u'#OccupyWallStreet', u'"CurrentCapacity"', u'"DesignCapacity"', u'"LegacyBatteryInfo"',
 u'"unconferences,"', u'@OReillyMedia#Ebook', u'@josephjesposito', u'@netgarden(come-on,',
 u'@oreillymedia"deal', u'Administration\u2014which', u'Amazon-California',
 u'Community-generated', u'Frisch(12:00-1:00)',u'Internet-related', u'Representatives.[10]',
 u'Republican-controlled', u'Twitter,@_vrajesh', u"administration's", u'all-encompassing',
 u'augmented-reality', u'books-to-diapers-to-machetes', u'brain-wave-sensing',
 u'brick-and-mortar', u'codeforamerica.org', u'continuously-updated', u'crimespotting.org',
 u'disobedience\u2014including', u'dolphin-slaughter', u'community-driven',
 u'connect-the-dots', u'entertainment-sector', u'government-funded', u'informationdiet.com',
 u'instantaneously.', u'little-mentioned', u'micro-entrepreneurship.', u'nineteenth-century',
 u'opsociety.org/securedonation.htm', u'problem/solution/explanation', u'problematically,',
 u'reconceptualization', u'responsibility."',u'scientifically-literate', u'self-employment,',
 u'subscription-based', u'technology-based', u'transportation.)', u'two-dimensional,',
 u'unintentionally?', u'watercolor-style',
 u'{"Amperage"=18446744073709548064,"Flags"=4,"Capacity"=4464,"Current"=2850,"Voltage"=7362,
 "Cycle', u'\u201cverbivocovisual\u201d']
>>> len([w for w in fdist.keys() if w.startswith("http")])
98
>>> for rank, word in enumerate(fdist): print rank, word, fdist[word]
0 the 1815
1 of 1017
2 to 988
3 and 701
4 a 699
5 in 546
6 that 535
7 is 413
... output truncated ...
```

> You may need to run nltk.download('stopwords') to download NLTK's
> stopwords data if you haven't already installed it. If possible, it is rec-
> ommended that you just run nltk.download() to install all of the NLTK
> data.

The last command in the interpreter session lists the words from the frequency distribution, sorted by frequency. Not surprisingly, common words like "the," "to," and
"of"—stopwords—are the most frequently occurring, but there's a steep decline and
the distribution has a very long tail. We're working with a small sample of text data,
but this same property will hold true for any frequency analysis of natural language.
Zipf's law (*http://en.wikipedia.org/wiki/Zipf's_law*), a well-known empirical law of natural language, asserts that a word's frequency within a corpus is inversely proportional
to its rank in the frequency table. What this means is that if the most frequently occurring term in a corpus accounts for N% of the total words, the second most frequently
occurring term in the corpus should account for (N/2)% of the words, the third most
frequent term for (N/3)% of the words, etc. When graphed, such a distribution (even

for a small sample of data) shows a curve that hugs each axis, as you can see in Figure 7-2. An important observation is that most of the area in such a distribution lies in its tail, which for a corpus large enough to span a reasonable sample of a language is always quite long. If you were to plot this kind of distribution on a chart where each axis was scaled by a logarithm, the curve would approach a straight line for a representative sample size.

Figure 7-2. The frequency distribution for terms appearing in a small sample of Google+ data "hugs" each axis

Zipf's law gives you insight into what a frequency distribution for words appearing in a corpus should look like, and it provides some rules of thumb that can be useful in estimating frequency. For example, if you know that there are a million (non-unique) words in a corpus, and you assume that the most frequently used word (usually "the," in English) accounts for 7% of the words,[3] you could derive the total number of logical calculations an algorithm performs if you were to consider a particular slice of the terms from the frequency distribution. Sometimes, this kind of simple arithmetic on the back of a napkin is all that it takes to sanity-check assumptions about a long-running wall-clock time, or confirm whether certain computations on a large enough data set are even tractable.

---

3. The word "the" accounts for 7% of the tokens in the Brown Corpus (*http://en.wikipedia.org/wiki/Brown _Corpus*) and provides a reasonable starting point for a corpus if you don't know anything else about it.

Text Mining Fundamentals

Although rigorous approaches to natural language processing (NLP) that include such things as sentence segmentation, tokenization, word chunking, and entity detection are necessary in order to achieve the deepest possible understanding of textual data, it's helpful to first introduce some fundamentals from Information Retrieval theory. The remainder of this chapter introduces some of its more foundational aspects, including TF-IDF, the cosine similarity metric, and some of the theory behind collocation detection. Chapter 8 provides a deeper discussion of NLP.

> If you want to dig deeper into IR theory, the full text of *Introduction to Information Retrieval* is available online (*http://nlp.stanford.edu/IR -book/information-retrieval-book.html*) and provides more information than you could ever want to know about the field.

A Whiz-Bang Introduction to TF-IDF

Information retrieval is an extensive field with many specialties. This discussion narrows in on TF-IDF, one of the most fundamental techniques for retrieving relevant documents from a corpus. TF-IDF stands for *term frequency-inverse document frequency* and can be used to query a corpus by calculating normalized scores that express the relative importance of terms in the documents. Mathematically, TF-IDF is expressed as the product of the term frequency and the inverse document frequency, *tf_idf = tf*idf*, where the term `tf` represents the importance of a term in a specific document, and `idf` represents the importance of a term relative to the entire corpus. Multiplying these terms together produces a score that accounts for both factors and has been an integral part of every major search engine at some point in its existence. To get a more intuitive idea of how TF-IDF works, let's walk through each of the calculations involved in computing the overall score.

For simplicity in illustration, suppose you have a corpus containing three sample documents and terms are calculated by simply breaking on whitespace, as illustrated in Example 7-3.

Example 7-3. Sample data structures used in illustrations throughout this chapter

```
corpus = {
        'a' : "Mr. Green killed Colonel Mustard in the study with the candlestick. \
            Mr. Green is not a very nice fellow.",
        'b' : "Professor Plumb has a green plant in his study.",
        'c' : "Miss Scarlett watered Professor Plumb's green plant while he was away \
            from his office last week."
}
```

```
terms = {
        'a' : [ i.lower() for i in corpus['a'].split() ],
        'b' : [ i.lower() for i in corpus['b'].split() ],
        'c' : [ i.lower() for i in corpus['c'].split() ]
       }
```

A term's frequency could simply be represented as the number of times it occurs in the text, but it is more commonly the case that it is normalized by taking into account the total number of terms in the text, so that the overall score accounts for document length relative to a term's frequency. For example, the term "green" (once normalized to low-ercase) occurs twice in corpus['a'] and only once in corpus['b'], so corpus['a'] would produce a higher score if frequency were the only scoring criterion. However, if you normalize for document length, corpus['b'] would have a slightly higher term fre-quency score for "green" (1/9) than corpus['a'] (2/19), because corpus['b'] is shorter than corpus['a']—even though "green" occurs more frequently in corpus['a']. Thus, a common technique for scoring a compound query such as "Mr. Green" is to sum the term frequency scores for each of the query terms in each document, and return the documents ranked by the summed term frequency score.

The previous paragraph is actually not as confusing as it sounds; for example, querying our sample corpus for "Mr. Green" would return the normalized scores reported in Table 7-1 for each document.

Table 7-1. Sample term frequency scores for "Mr. Green"

Document	tf(Mr.)	tf(Green)	Sum
corpus['a']	2/19	2/19	4/19 (0.2105)
corpus['b']	0	1/9	1/9 (0.1111)
corpus['c']	0	1/16	1/16 (0.0625)

For this contrived example, a cumulative term frequency scoring scheme works out and returns corpus['a'] (the document that we'd expect it to return), since corpus['a'] is the only one that contains the compound token "Mr. Green". However, a number of problems could have emerged because the term frequency scoring model looks at each document as an unordered collection of words. For example, queries for "Green Mr." or "Green Mr. Foo" would have returned the exact same scores as the query for "Mr. Green", even though neither of those compound tokens appear in the sample sentences. Additionally, there are a number of scenarios that we could easily contrive to illustrate fairly poor results from the term frequency ranking technique by exploiting the fact that trailing punctuation is not properly handled, and the context around tokens of interest is not taken into account by the calculations.

Considering term frequency alone turns out to be a common problem when scoring on a document-by-document basis because it doesn't account for very frequent words that are common across many documents. Meaning, all terms are weighted equally regardless of their actual importance. For example, "the green plant" contains the stopword "the", which skews overall term frequency scores in favor of corpus['a'] because "the" appears twice in that document, as does "green". In contrast, in corpus['c'] "green" and "plant" each appear only once. Consequently, the scores would break down as shown in Table 7-2, with corpus['a'] ranked as more relevant than corpus['c'] even though intuition might lead you to believe that ideal query results probably shouldn't have turned out that way. (Fortunately, however, corpus['b'] still ranks highest.)

Table 7-2. Sample term frequency scores for "the green plant"

Document	tf(the)	tf(green)	tf(plant)	Sum
corpus['a']	2/19	2/19	0	4/19 (0.2105)
corpus['b']	0	1/9	1/9	2/9 (0.2222)
corpus['c']	0	1/16	1/16	1/8 (0.125)

Toolkits such as NLTK provide lists of stopwords that can be used to filter out terms such as "the", "a", "and", etc., but keep in mind that there may be terms that evade even the best stopword lists and yet still are quite common to specialized domains. The inverse document frequency metric is a calculation that provides a generic normalization metric for a corpus, and accounts for the appearance of common terms across a set of documents by taking into consideration the total number of documents in which a query term ever appears. The intuition behind this metric is that it produces a higher value if a term is somewhat uncommon across the corpus than if it is very common, which helps to account for the problem with stopwords we just investigated. For example, a query for "green" in the corpus of sample documents should return a lower inverse document frequency score than "candlestick", because "green" appears in every document while "candlestick" appears in only one. Mathematically, the only nuance of interest for the inverse document frequency calculation is that a logarithm is used to squash the result into a compressed range (as shown in Figure 7-3) since its usual application is in multiplying it against term frequency as a scaling factor.

At this point, we've come full circle and devised a way to compute a score for a multi-term query that accounts for the frequency of terms appearing in a document, the length of the document in which any particular term appears, and the overall uniqueness of the terms across documents in the entire corpus. In other words, tf-idf = tf*idf. Example 7-4 is a naive implementation of this discussion that should help solidify the concepts described. Take a moment to review it, and then we'll discuss a few sample queries.

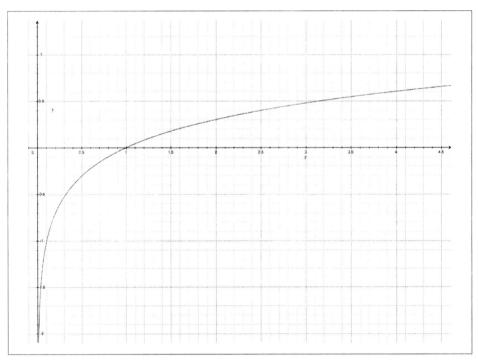

Figure 7-3. The logarithm squashes a large range of values into a more compressed space

Example 7-4. Running TF-IDF on sample data (plus__tf_idf.py)

```python
# -*- coding: utf-8 -*-

import sys
from math import log

QUERY_TERMS = sys.argv[1:]


def tf(term, doc, normalize=True):
    doc = doc.lower().split()
    if normalize:
        return doc.count(term.lower()) / float(len(doc))
    else:
        return doc.count(term.lower()) / 1.0


def idf(term, corpus):
    num_texts_with_term = len([True for text in corpus if term.lower()
                              in text.lower().split()])

    # tf-idf calc involves multiplying against a tf value less than 0, so it's important
    # to return a value greater than 1 for consistent scoring. (Multiplying two values
    # less than 1 returns a value less than each of them)
```

```
    try:
        return 1.0 + log(float(len(corpus)) / num_texts_with_term)
    except ZeroDivisionError:
        return 1.0


def tf_idf(term, doc, corpus):
    return tf(term, doc) * idf(term, corpus)


corpus = \
    {'a': 'Mr. Green killed Colonel Mustard in the study with the candlestick. \
Mr. Green is not a very nice fellow.',
     'b': 'Professor Plumb has a green plant in his study.',
     'c': "Miss Scarlett watered Professor Plumb's green plant while he was away \
from his office last week."}

# Score queries by calculating cumulative tf_idf score for each term in query

query_scores = {'a': 0, 'b': 0, 'c': 0}
for term in [t.lower() for t in QUERY_TERMS]:
    for doc in sorted(corpus):
        print 'TF(%s): %s' % (doc, term), tf(term, corpus[doc])
    print 'IDF: %s' % (term, ), idf(term, corpus.values())
    print

    for doc in sorted(corpus):
        score = tf_idf(term, corpus[doc], corpus.values())
        print 'TF-IDF(%s): %s' % (doc, term), score
        query_scores[doc] += score
    print

print "Overall TF-IDF scores for query '%s'" % (' '.join(QUERY_TERMS), )
for (doc, score) in sorted(query_scores.items()):
    print doc, score
```

Although we're working on a trivially small scale, the calculations involved work the same for larger data sets. Table 7-3 is a consolidated adaptation of the program's output for three sample queries that involve four distinct terms:

- "green"
- "Mr. Green"
- "the green plant"

Even though the IDF calculations for terms are for the entire corpus, they are displayed on a per-document basis so that you can easily verify TF-IDF scores by skimming a single row and multiplying two numbers. Again, it's worth taking a few minutes to understand the data in the table so that you have a good feel for the way the calculations work. It's remarkable just how powerful TF-IDF is, given that it doesn't account for the proximity or ordering of words in a document.

Table 7-3. Calculations involved in TF-IDF sample queries, as computed by Example 7-4

Document	tf(mr.)	tf(green)	tf(the)	tf(plant)
corpus['a']	0.1053	0.1053	1.1053	0
corpus['b']	0	0.1111	0	0.1111
corpus['c']	0	0.0625	0	0.0625

	idf(mr.)	idf(green)	idf(the)	idf(plant)
corpus['a']	2.0986	1.0	2.099	1.4055
corpus['b']	2.0986	1.0	2.099	1.4055
corpus['c']	2.0986	1.0	2.099	1.4055

	tf-idf(mr.)	tf-idf(green)	tf-idf(the)	tf-idf(plant)
corpus['a']	0.2209	0.1053	0.2209	0
corpus['b']	0	0.1111	0	0.1562
corpus['c']	0	0.0625	0	0.0878

The same results for each query are shown in Table 7-4, with the TF-IDF values summed on a per-document basis.

Table 7-4. Summed TF-IDF values for sample queries as computed by Example 7-4

Query	corpus['a']	corpus['b']	corpus['c']
green	0.1053	**0.1111**	0.0625
Mr. Green	0.2209 + 0.1053 = **0.3262**	0 + 0.1111 = 0.1111	0 + 0.0625 = 0.0625
the green plant	0.2209 + 0.1053 + 0 = **0.3262**	0 + 0.1111 + 0.1562 = 0.2673	0 + 0.0625 + 0.0878 = 0.1503

From a qualitative standpoint, the query results seem reasonable. The corpus['b'] document is the winner for the query "green", with corpus['a'] just a hair behind. In this case, the deciding factor was the length of corpus['b'] being much smaller than corpus['a']: the normalized TF score tipped in favor of corpus['b'] for its one occurrence of "green", even though "Green" appeared in corpus['a'] two times. Since "green" appears in all three documents, the net effect of the IDF term in the calculations was a wash. Do note, however, that if we had returned 0.0 instead of 1.0 for IDF calculations, as is done in some implementations, the TF-IDF scores for "green" would have been 0.0 for all three documents. Depending on the particular situation, it may be better to return 0.0 for the IDF scores rather than 1.0. For example, if you had 100,000 documents and "green" appeared in all of them, you'd almost certainly consider it to be a stopword and want to remove its effects in a query entirely.

A very worthwhile exercise to consider is why corpus['a'] scored highest for "the green plant" as opposed to corpus['b'], which at first blush, might have seemed a little more obvious.

A finer point to observe is that the sample implementation provided in Example 7-4 adjusts the IDF score by adding a value of 1.0 to the logarithm calculation, for the purposes of illustration and because we're dealing with a trivial document set. Without the 1.0 adjustment in the calculation, it would be possible to have the idf function return values that are less than 1.0, which would result in two fractions being multiplied in the TF-IDF calculation. Since multiplying two fractions together results in a value smaller than either of them, this turns out to be an easily overlooked edge case in the TF-IDF calculation. Recall that the intuition behind the TF-IDF calculation is that we'd like to be able to multiply two terms in a way that consistently produces larger TF-IDF scores for more-relevant queries than for less-relevant queries.

Querying Google+ Data with TF-IDF

Let's apply TF-IDF to the Google+ data we collected earlier and see how it works out as a tool for querying the data. NLTK provides some abstractions that we can use instead of rolling our own, so there's actually very little to do now that you understand the underlying theory. The listing in Example 7-5 assumes you saved the Google+ data as a JSON file, and it allows you to pass in multiple query terms that are used to score the documents by relevance.

Example 7-5. Querying Google+ data with TF-IDF (plus__tf_idf_nltk.py)

```
# -*- coding: utf-8 -*-

import sys
import json
import nltk

# Load in unstructured data from wherever you've saved it

DATA = sys.argv[1]
data = json.loads(open(DATA).read())

QUERY_TERMS = sys.argv[2:]

activities = [activity['object']['content'].lower().split() \
                for activity in data \
                    if activity['object']['content'] != ""]

# Provides tf/idf/tf_idf abstractions

tc = nltk.TextCollection(activities)

relevant_activities = []
```

```
for idx in range(len(activities)):
    score = 0
    for term in [t.lower() for t in QUERY_TERMS]:
        score += tc.tf_idf(term, activities[idx])
    if score > 0:
        relevant_activities.append({'score': score, 'title': data[idx]['title'],
                                    'url': data[idx]['url']})

# Sort by score and display results

relevant_activities = sorted(relevant_activities, key=lambda p: p['score'], reverse=True)
for activity in relevant_activities:
    print activity['title']
    print '\tLink: %s' % (activity['url'], )
    print '\tScore: %s' % (activity['score'], )
```

Sample query results for "SOPA", a controversial piece of proposed legislation, on Tim O'Reilly's Google+ data are shown in Example 7-6.

Example 7-6. Sample results from Example 7-5

```
I think the key point of this piece by +Mike Loukides, that PIPA and SOPA provide a
"right of ext...
    Link: https://plus.google.com/107033731246200681024/posts/ULi4RYpvQGT
    Score: 0.0805961208217
Learn to Be a Better Activist During the SOPA Blackouts +Clay Johnson has put together
an awesome...
    Link: https://plus.google.com/107033731246200681024/posts/hrC5aj7gS6v
    Score: 0.0255051015259
SOPA and PIPA are bad industrial policy There are many arguments against SOPA and PIPA
that are b...
    Link: https://plus.google.com/107033731246200681024/posts/LZs8TekXK2T
    Score: 0.0227351539694
Further thoughts on SOPA, and why Congress shouldn't listen to lobbyists Colleen Taylor
of GigaOM...
    Link: https://plus.google.com/107033731246200681024/posts/5Xd3VjFR8gx
    Score: 0.0112879721039
```

Given a search term, being able to narrow in on three Google+ content items ranked by relevance is of tremendous benefit when analyzing unstructured text data. Try out some other queries and qualitatively review the results to see for yourself how well the TF-IDF metric works, keeping in mind that the absolute values of the scores aren't really important—it's the ability to find and sort documents by relevance that matters. Then, begin to ponder the gazillion ways that you could tune or augment this metric to be even more effective. (After all, every data hacker has to complete this exercise at some point in life.) One obvious improvement that's left as an exercise for the reader is to stem verbs so that variations in tense, grammatical role, etc., resolve to the same stem and can be more accurately accounted for in similarity calculations. The nltk.stem module provides easy-to-use implementations for several common stemming algorithms.

Finding Similar Documents

Once you've queried and discovered documents of interest, one of the next things you might want to do is find similar documents. Whereas TF-IDF can provide the means to narrow down a corpus based on search terms, cosine similarity is one of the most common techniques for comparing documents to one another, which is the essence of finding a similar document. An understanding of cosine similarity requires a brief introduction to vector space models, which is the topic of the next section.

The Theory Behind Vector Space Models and Cosine Similarity

While it has been emphasized that TF-IDF models documents as unordered collections of words, another convenient way to model documents is with a model called a *vector space*. The basic theory behind a vector space model is that you have a large multidimensional space that contains one vector for each document, and the distance between any two vectors indicates the similarity of the corresponding documents. One of the most beautiful things about vector space models is that you can also represent a query as a vector and find the most relevant documents for the query by finding the document vectors with the shortest distance to the query vector. Although it's virtually impossible to do this subject justice in a short section, it's important to have a basic understanding of vector space models if you have any interest at all in text mining or the IR field. If you're not interested in the background theory and want to jump straight into implementation details on good faith, feel free to skip ahead to the next section.

 This section assumes a basic understanding of trigonometry. If your trigonometry skills are a little rusty, consider this section a great opportunity to brush up on high school math.

First, it might be helpful to clarify exactly what is meant by the term "vector," since there are so many subtle variations associated with it across various fields of study. Generally speaking, a vector is a list of numbers that expresses both a direction relative to an origin and a magnitude, which is the distance from that origin. A vector can very naturally be represented as a line segment between the origin and a point in an N-dimensional space by drawing a line between the origin and the point. To illustrate, imagine a document that is defined by only two terms ("Open", "Web"), with a corresponding vector of (0.45, 0.67), where the values in the vector are values such as TF-IDF scores for the terms. In a vector space, this document could be represented in two dimensions by a line segment extending from the origin at (0,0) to the point at (0.45, 0.67). In reference to an x/y plane, the x-axis would represent "Open", the y-axis would represent "Web", and the vector from (0,0) to (0.45, 0.67) would represent the document in question. However, interesting documents generally contain hundreds of terms at a minimum, but the same fundamentals apply for modeling documents in these higher-dimensional spaces; it's just harder to visualize.

Try making the transition from visualizing a document represented by a vector with two components to a document represented by three dimensions, such as ("Open", "Web", "Government"). Then consider taking a leap of faith and accepting that although it's hard to visualize, it is still possible to have a vector represent additional dimensions that you can't easily sketch out or see. If you're able to do that, you should have no problem believing the same vector operations that can be applied to a 2-dimensional space can be equally as well applied to a 10-dimensional space or a 367-dimensional space. Figure 7-4 shows an example vector in 3-dimensional space.

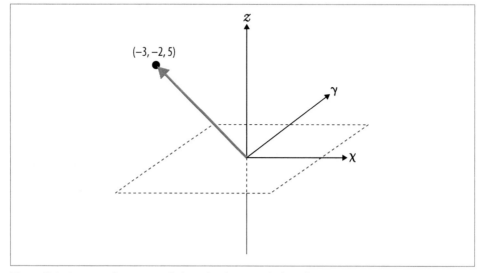

Figure 7-4. An example vector with the value (–3, –2, 5) plotted in 3D space

Given that it's possible to model documents as term-centric vectors, with each term in the document represented by its corresponding TF-IDF score, the task then is to determine what metric best represents the similarity between two documents. As it turns out, the cosine of the angle between any two vectors is a valid metric for comparing them and is known as the *cosine similarity* of the vectors. Although perhaps not yet intuitive, years of scientific research have demonstrated that computing the cosine similarity of documents represented as term vectors is a very effective metric. (It does suffer from many of the same problems as TF-IDF, though; see "Before You Go Off and Try to Build a Search Engine..." on page 236 for a very brief synopsis.) Building up a rigorous proof of the details behind the cosine similarity metric would be beyond the scope of this book, but the gist is that the cosine of the angle between any two vectors indicates the similarity between them and is equivalent to the dot product of their unit vectors. Intuitively, it might be helpful to consider that the closer two vectors are to one another, the smaller the angle between them will be, and thus the larger the cosine of the angle between them will be. Two identical vectors would have an angle of 0 degrees and a similarity metric of 1.0, while two vectors that are orthogonal to one another would have an angle of 90 degrees and a similarity metric of 0.0. The following sketch attempts to demonstrate:

$\vec{doc1} \cdot \vec{doc2} = \|doc1\| \cdot \|doc2\| \cdot \cos \Theta$	Given (by trigonometry)
$\dfrac{\vec{doc1} \cdot \vec{doc2}}{\|doc1\| \cdot \|doc2\|} = \cos \Theta$	By division
$\hat{doc1} \cdot \hat{doc2} = \cos \Theta$	By definition of 'unit vector'
$\hat{doc1} \cdot \hat{doc2} = \text{Similarity (doc1, doc2)}$	By substitution (assume: $\cos \Theta$ = Similarity (doc1, doc2))

Recalling that a unit vector has a length of 1.0 (by definition), the beauty of computing document similarity with unit vectors is that they're already normalized against what might be substantial variations in length. Given that brief math lesson, you're probably ready to see some of this in action. That's what the next section is all about.

Clustering Posts with Cosine Similarity

If you don't care to remember anything else from the previous section, just remember this: to compute the similarity between two documents, you really just need to produce a term vector for each document and compute the dot product of the unit vectors for those documents. Conveniently, NLTK exposes the nltk.cluster.util.cosine_dis tance(v1,v2) function for computing cosine similarity, so it really is pretty straightforward to compare documents. As Example 7-7 shows, all of the work involved is in producing the appropriate term vectors; in short, it computes term vectors for a given pair of documents by assigning TF-IDF scores to each component in the vectors. Because the exact vocabularies of the two documents are probably not identical, however, placeholders with a value of 0.0 must be left in each vector for words that are missing from the document at hand but present in the other one. The net effect is that you end up with two vectors of identical length with components ordered identically that can be used to perform the vector operations.

For example, suppose document1 contained the terms *(A, B, C)* and had the corresponding vector of TF-IDF weights *(0.10, 0.15, 0.12)*, while document2 contained the terms *(C, D, E)* with the corresponding vector of TF-IDF weights *(0.05, 0.10, 0.09)*. The derived vector for document1 would be *(0.10, 0.15, 0.12, 0.0, 0.0)*, and the derived vector for document2 would be *(0.0, 0.0, 0.05, 0.10, 0.09)*. Each of these vectors could be passed into NLTK's cosine_distance function, which yields the cosine similarity. Internally, cosine_distance uses the numpy module to *very* efficiently compute the dot product of the unit vectors, and that's the result. Although the code in this section reuses the TF-IDF calculations that were introduced previously, the exact scoring function could be any useful metric. TF-IDF (or some variation thereof), however, is quite common for many implementations and provides a great starting point.

Example 7-7 illustrates an approach for using cosine similarity to find the most similar document to each document in a corpus of Google+ data. It should apply equally as well to any other type of unstructured data, such as blog posts, books, etc.

Example 7-7. Finding similar documents using cosine similarity (plus__cosine_similarity.py)

```
# -*- coding: utf-8 -*-

import sys
import json
import nltk

# Load in textual data from wherever you've saved it

DATA = sys.argv[1]
data = json.loads(open(DATA).read())

all_posts = [post['object']['content'].lower().split()
             for post in data
                 if post['object']['content'] != '']

# Provides tf/idf/tf_idf abstractions for scoring

tc = nltk.TextCollection(all_posts)

# Compute a term-document matrix such that td_matrix[doc_title][term]
# returns a tf-idf score for the term in the document

td_matrix = {}
for idx in range(len(all_posts)):
    post = all_posts[idx]
    fdist = nltk.FreqDist(post)

    doc_title = data[idx]['title']
    url = data[idx]['url']
    td_matrix[(doc_title, url)] = {}

    for term in fdist.iterkeys():
        td_matrix[(doc_title, url)][term] = tc.tf_idf(term, post)

# Build vectors such that term scores are in the same positions...

distances = {}
for (title1, url1) in td_matrix.keys():

    distances[(title1, url1)] = {}
    (max_score, most_similar) = (0.0, ('', ''))

    for (title2, url2) in td_matrix.keys():

        # Take care not to mutate the original data structures
        # since we're in a loop and need the originals multiple times
```

```
        terms1 = td_matrix[(title1, url1)].copy()
        terms2 = td_matrix[(title2, url2)].copy()

        # Fill in "gaps" in each map so vectors of the same length can be computed

        for term1 in terms1:
            if term1 not in terms2:
                terms2[term1] = 0

        for term2 in terms2:
            if term2 not in terms1:
                terms1[term2] = 0

        # Create vectors from term maps

        v1 = [score for (term, score) in sorted(terms1.items())]
        v2 = [score for (term, score) in sorted(terms2.items())]

        # Compute similarity amongst documents

        distances[(title1, url1)][(title2, url2)] = \
            nltk.cluster.util.cosine_distance(v1, v2)

        if url1 == url2:
            continue

        if distances[(title1, url1)][(title2, url2)] > max_score:
            (max_score, most_similar) = (distances[(title1, url1)][(title2,
                                          url2)], (title2, url2))

    print '''Most similar to %s (%s)
\t%s (%s)
\tscore %d
''' % (title1, url1,
        most_similar[0], most_similar[1], max_score)
```

If you've found this discussion of cosine similarity interesting, recall that *the best part is that querying a vector space is the very same operation as computing the similarity between documents, except that instead of comparing just document vectors, you compare your query vector and the document vectors.* In terms of implementation, that means constructing a vector containing your query terms and comparing it to each document in the corpus. Be advised, however, that the approach of directly comparing a query vector to every possible document vector is not a good idea for even a corpus of modest size. You'd need to make some very good engineering decisions involving the appropriate use of indexes to achieve a scalable solution. (Just a little something to consider before you go off and build the next great search engine.)

Visualizing Similarity with Graph Visualizations

Like just about everything else in this book, there's certainly more than one way to visualize the similarity between items. The approach introduced in this section is to use graph-like structures, where a link between documents encodes a measure of the similarity between them. This situation presents an excellent opportunity to introduce more visualizations from Protovis (*http://vis.stanford.edu/protovis/*), an HTML5-based visualization toolkit produced by the Stanford Visualization Group. Protovis is specifically designed with the interests of data scientists in mind, offers a familiar declarative syntax, and achieves a nice middle ground between high-level and low-level interfaces. A minimal (uninteresting) adaptation to Example 7-7 is all that's needed to emit a collection of nodes and edges that can be used to produce visualizations similar to those in the Protovis examples gallery (*http://vis.stanford.edu/protovis/ex/*). A nested loop can compute the similarity between the working sample of Google+ data from this chapter, and linkages between items may be determined based upon a simple statistical thresholding criterion. The details associated with munging the data and tweaking the Protovis example templates won't be presented here, but the code is available for download online (*http://github.com/ptwobrussell/Mining-the-Social-Web/blob/master/python_code/plus__cosine_similarity_protovis_output.py*).

The code produces the arc diagram presented in Figure 7-5 and the matrix diagram in Figure 7-6. The arc diagram produces arcs between nodes if there is a linkage between them, scales nodes according to their degree, and sorts the nodes such that clutter is minimized and it's easy to see which of them have the highest number of connections. Titles are displayed vertically, but they could be omitted because a tool tip displays the title when the mouse hovers over a node. Clicking on a node opens a new browser window that points to the activity represented by that node. Additional bells and whistles, such as event handlers, coloring the arcs based on the similarity scores, and tweaking the parameters for this visualization, would not be very difficult to implement (and a fun way to spend a rainy day).

A complementary display to an arc diagram is a matrix diagram, with the color intensity of each cell varying as a function of the strength of the correlation of similarity score; a darker cell represents higher similarity. The diagonal in the matrix in Figure 7-6 has been omitted since we're not interested in having our eye drawn to those cells, even though the similarity scores for the diagonal would be perfect. Hovering over a cell displays a tool tip with the similarity score. An advantage of matrix diagrams is that there's no potential for messy overlap between edges that represent linkages. A commonly cited disadvantage of arc diagrams is that path finding is difficult, but in this particular situation, path finding isn't that important, and besides, it can still be accomplished if desired. Depending on your personal preferences and the data you're trying to visualize, either or both of these approaches could be appropriate.

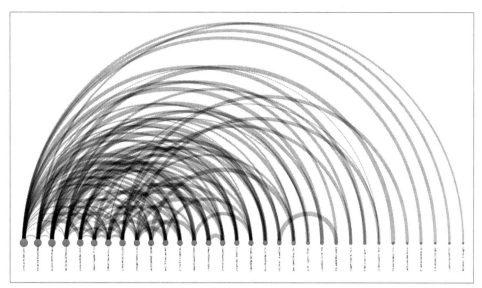

Figure 7-5. A Protovis arc diagram displaying the linkages between Google+ activities

Figure 7-6. A Protovis matrix diagram displaying linkages between Google+ activities

Bigram Analysis

As previously mentioned, one issue that is frequently overlooked in unstructured text processing is the tremendous amount of information gained when you're able to look at more than one token at a time, because so many concepts we express are phrases and not just single words. For example, if someone were to tell you that a few of the most common terms in a post are "open", "source", and "government", could you necessarily say that the text is probably about "open source", "open government", both, or neither? If you had a priori knowledge of the author or content, you could probably make a good guess, but if you were relying totally on a machine to try to *classify* the nature of a document as being about collaborative software development or transformational government, you'd need to go back to the text and somehow determine which of the words most frequently occur after "open"—i.e., you'd like to find the *collocations* that start with the token "open".

Recall from Chapter 6 that an *n*-gram is just a terse way of expressing each possible consecutive sequence of *n* tokens from a text, and it provides the foundational data structure for computing collocations. There are always (*n*-1) *n*-grams for any value of *n*, and if you were to consider all of the bigrams (2-grams) for the sequence of tokens ["Mr.", "Green", "killed", "Colonel", "Mustard"], you'd have four possibilities: [("Mr.", "Green"), ("Green", "killed"), ("killed", "Colonel"), ("Colonel", "Mustard")]. You'd need a larger sample of text than just our sample sentence to determine collocations, but assuming you had background knowledge or additional text, the next step would be to statistically analyze the bigrams in order to determine which of them are likely to be collocations.

It's worth noting that the storage necessary for persisting an *n*-gram model requires space for $(T{-}1)^*n$ tokens (which is practically T^*n), where T is the number of tokens in question and n is defined by the size of the desired *n*-gram. As an example, assume a document contains 1,000 tokens and requires around 8 KB of storage. Storing all bigrams for the text would require roughly double the original storage, or 16 KB, as you would be storing 999^*2 tokens plus overhead. Storing all trigrams for the text (998^*3 tokens plus overhead) would require roughly triple the original storage, or 24 KB. Thus, without devising specialized data structures or compression schemes, the storage costs for *n*-grams can be estimated as *n* times the original storage requirement for any value of *n*.

n-grams are very simple yet very powerful as a technique for clustering commonly co-occurring words. If you compute all of the *n*-grams for even a small value of *n*, you're likely to discover that some interesting patterns emerge from the text itself with no additional work required. For example, in considering the bigrams for a sufficiently long text, you're likely to discover the proper names, such as "Mr. Green" and "Colonel Mustard", concepts such as "open source" or "open government", and so forth. Similar patterns emerge when you consider frequent trigrams and *n*-grams for values of *n* slightly larger than three. In fact, computing bigrams in this way produces essentially the same results as the `collocations` function that you ran in an earlier interpreter session, except that some additional statistical analysis takes into account the use of rare words. As you already know from the interpreter session we looked at earlier in this chapter (Example 7-2), NLTK takes care of most of the effort in computing *n*-grams, discovering collocations from text, discovering the context in which a token has been used, etc. Example 7-8 demonstrates.

Example 7-8. Using NLTK to compute bigrams and collocations for a sentence

```
>>> import nltk
>>> nltk.ngrams("Mr. Green killed Colonel Mustard in the study with the \
... candlestick. Mr. Green is not a very nice fellow.".split(), 2)
[('Mr.', 'Green'), ('Green', 'killed'), ('killed', 'Colonel'),
 ('Colonel', 'Mustard'), ('Mustard', 'in'), ('in', 'the'),
 ('the', 'study'), ('study', 'with'), ('with', 'the'),
 ('the', 'candlestick.'), ('candlestick.', 'Mr.'), ('Mr.', 'Green'),
 ('Green', 'is'), ('is', 'not'), ('not', 'a'), ('a', 'very'),
 ('very', 'nice'), ('nice', 'fellow.')]
>>> txt = nltk.Text("Mr. Green killed Colonel Mustard in the study with the\
... candletick. Mr. Green is not a very nice fellow.".split())
>>> txt.collocations()
Building collocations list
Mr. Green
```

Recall that the only drawback to using built-in demo functionality such as `nltk.Text.collocations` is that these functions don't return data structures that you can store and manipulate. Whenever you run into such a situation, just take a look at the source code, which is usually pretty easy to adapt for your own purposes. Example 7-9 illustrates how you could compute the collocations and concordance indexes for a collection of tokens and maintain control of the results.

Example 7-9. Using NLTK to compute collocations in a similar manner to the nltk.Text.collocations demo functionality (plus_collocations.py)

```
# -*- coding: utf-8 -*-

import sys
import json
import nltk

# Load in human readable text from wherever you've saved it

DATA = sys.argv[1]
N = 25
data = json.loads(open(DATA).read())

all_tokens = [token for activity in data for token in activity['object']['content'
            ].lower().split()]
```

```
finder = nltk.BigramCollocationFinder.from_words(all_tokens)
finder.apply_freq_filter(2)
finder.apply_word_filter(lambda w: w in nltk.corpus.stopwords.words('english'))
scorer = nltk.metrics.BigramAssocMeasures.jaccard
collocations = finder.nbest(scorer, N)

for collocation in collocations:
    c = ' '.join(collocation)
    print c
```

In short, the implementation loosely follows NLTK's collocations demo function. It filters out bigrams that don't appear more than a minimum number of times (two, in this case) and then applies a scoring metric to rank the results. In this instance, the scoring function is the well-known *Jaccard Index*, as defined by nltk.metrics.Bigram AssocMeasures.jaccard. A *contingency table* is used by the BigramAssocMeasures class to rank the co-occurrence of terms in any given bigram as compared to the possibilities of other words that could have appeared in the bigram. Conceptually, the Jaccard Index measures similarity of sets, and in this case, the sample sets are specific comparisons of bigrams that appeared in the text. The details of how contingency tables and Jaccard values are calculated is arguably an advanced topic, but the next section, "How the Collocation Sausage Is Made: Contingency Tables and Scoring Functions" on page 228, provides an extended discussion of those details since they're critical to a good understanding of collocation detection.

In the meantime, though, let's examine Example 7-10. This example shows some output from Tim's Google+ data that should make it pretty apparent that returning scored bigrams is immensely more powerful than only returning tokens, because of the additional context that grounds the terms in meaning.

Example 7-10. Sample results from Example 7-9

```
ada lovelace
jennifer pahlka
hod lipson
pine nuts
safe, welcoming
1st floor,
5 southampton
7ha cost:
bcs, 1st
borrow 42
broadcom masters
building, 5
date: friday
disaster relief
dissolvable sugar
do-it-yourself festival,
dot com
fabric samples
finance protection
london, wc2e
maximizing shareholder
```

```
patron profiles
portable disaster
rural co
vat tickets:
```

Keeping in mind that no special heuristics or tactics that could have inspected the text for proper names based on Title Case were employed, it's actually quite amazing that so many proper names and common phrases were sifted out of the data. There's still a certain amount of inevitable noise in the results because we have not yet made any effort to clean punctuation from the tokens, but for the small amount of work we've put in, the results are really quite good. This might be a good time to mention that even if reasonably good natural language processing capabilities were employed, it might still be difficult to eliminate all the noise from the results of textual analysis. Getting comfortable with the noise and finding heuristics to control it is a good idea until you get to the point where you're willing to make a significant investment in obtaining the perfect results that a well-educated human would be able to pick out from the text.

Hopefully, the primary observation you're making at this point is that with very little effort and time invested, we've been able to use another very basic technique to draw out some pretty powerful meaning from some free text data, and *the results seem to be pretty representative of what we already suspect should be true.* This is encouraging, because it suggests that applying the same technique to anyone else's Google+ data (or any other kind of unstructured text, for that matter) would potentially be just as informative, giving you a quick glimpse into key items that are being discussed. And just as importantly, while the data in this case probably confirms a few things you may already know about Tim O'Reilly, you may have learned a couple of new things, too—one of which is that he might just have a sweet spot for Ada Lovelace as evidenced by "ada lovelace" showing up in the collocation results. While it would be easy enough to use the concordance, a regular expression, or even the Python string type's built-in find method to find posts relevant to "ada lovelace", let's instead take advantage of the code we developed in Example 7-5 and use TF-IDF to query for "ada lovelace." What comes back? Survey says:

```
I just got an email from +Suw Charman about Ada Lovelace Day,
and thought I'd share it here, sinc...
    Link: https://plus.google.com/107033731246200681024/posts/1XSAkDs9b44
    Score: 0.198150014715
```

And there you have it. The "ada lovelace" query leads us to some content about Ada Lovelace Day. You've effectively started with a nominal (if that) understanding of the text, narrowed in on some interesting topics using collection analysis, and searched the text for one of those interesting topics using TF-IDF. There's no reason you couldn't also use cosine similarity at this point to find the most similar post to the one about the lovely Ada Lovelace (or whatever it is that you're keen to investigate).

How the Collocation Sausage Is Made: Contingency Tables and Scoring Functions

 This section dives into some of the more technical details of how `Bigram CollocationFinder`—the Jaccard scoring function from Example 7-9—works. If this is your first reading of the chapter or you're not interested in these details, feel free to skip this section and come back to it later.

A common data structure that's used to compute metrics related to bigrams is the *contingency table*. The purpose of a contingency table is to compactly express the frequencies associated with the various possibilities for appearance of different terms of a bigram. Take a look at the bold entries in Table 7-5, where *token1* expresses the existence of *token1* in the bigram, and *~token1* expresses that *token1* does not exist in the bigram.

Table 7-5. Contingency table example—values in italics represent "marginals," and values in bold represent frequency counts of bigram variations

	token1	~token1	
token2	**frequency(token1, token2)**	**frequency(~token1, token2)**	*frequency(*, token2)*
~token2	**frequency(token1, ~token2)**	**frequency(~token1, ~token2)**	
	*frequency(token1, *)*		*frequency(*, *)*

Although there are a few details associated with which cells are significant for which calculations, hopefully it's not difficult to see that the four middle cells in the table express the frequencies associated with the appearance of various tokens in the bigram. The values in these cells can compute different similarity metrics that can be used to score and rank bigrams in order of likely significance, as was the case with the previously introduced Jaccard Index, which we'll dissect in just a moment. First, however, let's briefly discuss how the terms for the contingency table are computed.

The way that the various entries in the contingency table are computed is directly tied to which data structures you have precomputed or otherwise have available. If you assume that you only have available a frequency distribution for the various bigrams in the text, the way to calculate *frequency(token1, token2)* is a direct lookup, but what about *frequency(~token1, token2)*? With no other information available, you'd need to scan *every single bigram* for the appearance of *token2* in the second slot and subtract *frequency(token1, token2)* from that value. (Take a moment to convince yourself that this is true if it isn't obvious.)

However, if you assume that you have a frequency distribution available that counts the occurrences of each individual token in the text (the text's unigrams) in addition to a frequency distribution of the bigrams, there's a *much less expensive* shortcut you can take that involves two lookups and an arithmetic operation. Subtract the number of times that *token2* appeared as a unigram from the number of times the bigram *(token1, token2)* appeared, and you're left with the number of times the bigram *(~token1, token2)* appeared. For example, if the bigram *("mr.", "green")* appeared three times and the unigram *("green")* appeared seven times, it must be the case that the bigram *(~"mr.", "green")* appeared four times (where *~"mr."* literally means "any token other than 'mr.'"). In Table 7-5, the expression *frequency(*, token2)* represents the unigram *token2* and is referred to as a *marginal* because it's noted in the margin of the table as a shortcut. The value for *frequency(token1, *)* works the same way in helping to compute *frequency(token1, ~token2)*, and the expression *frequency(*, *)* refers to any possible unigram and is equivalent to the total number of tokens in the text. Given *frequency(token1, token2)*, *frequency(token1, ~token2)*, and *frequency(~token1, token2)*, the value of *frequency(*, *)* is necessary to calculate *frequency(~token1, ~token2)*.

Although this discussion of contingency tables may seem somewhat tangential, it's an important foundation for understanding different scoring functions. For example, consider the Jaccard Index. Conceptually, it expresses the similarity of two sets and is defined by:

$$\frac{|\text{Set1} \cap \text{Set2}|}{|\text{Set1} \cup \text{Set2}|}$$

In other words, that's the number of items in common between the two sets divided by the total number of distinct items in the combined sets. It's worth taking a moment to ponder this simple yet effective calculation. If *Set1* and *Set2* were identical, the union and the intersection of the two sets would be equivalent to one another, resulting in a ratio of 1.0. If both sets were completely different, the numerator of the ratio would be 0, resulting in a value of 0.0. Then there's everything else in between. The Jaccard Index as applied to a particular bigram expresses the ratio between the frequency of a particular bigram and the sum of the frequencies with which any bigram containing a term in the bigram of interest appears. One interpretation of that metric might be that the higher the ratio is, the more likely it is that *(token1, token2)* appears in the text, and hence, the more likely it is that the collocation "token1 token2" expresses a meaningful concept.

The selection of the most appropriate scoring function is usually determined based upon knowledge about the characteristics of the underlying data, some intuition, and sometimes a bit of luck. Most of the association metrics defined in `nltk.metrics.asso ciations` are discussed in Chapter 5 of Christopher Manning and Hinrich Schuetze's *Foundations of Statistical Natural Language Processing* (MIT Press), which is conveniently available online (*http://nlp.stanford.edu/fsnlp/promo/colloc.pdf*) and serves as a useful reference for the descriptions that follow. An in-depth discussion of these metrics is outside the scope of this book, but the promotional chapter just mentioned provides a detailed account with in-depth examples. The Jaccard Index, Dice's coefficient, and the likelihood ratio are good starting points if you find yourself needing to build your own collocation detector. They are described, along with some other key terms, in the list that follows:

Raw frequency

As its name implies, raw frequency is the ratio expressing the frequency of a particular *n*-gram divided by the frequency of all *n*-grams. It is useful for examining the overall frequency of a particular collocation in a text.

Jaccard Index

The Jaccard Index is a ratio that measures the similarity between sets. As applied to collocations, it is defined as the frequency of a particular collocation divided by the total number of collocations that contain at least one term in the collocation of interest. It is useful for determining the likelihood of whether the given terms actually form a collocation, as well as ranking the likelihood of probable collocations. Using notation consistent with previous explanations, this formulation would be mathematically defined as:

$$\frac{\text{frequency(token1, token2)}}{\text{frequency(token1, token2)} + \text{frequency(\~token1, token2)} + \text{frequency(token1, \~token2)}}$$

Dice's coefficient

Dice's coefficient is extremely similar to the Jaccard Index. The fundamental difference is that it weights agreements among the sets twice as heavily as Jaccard. It is defined mathematically as:

$$\frac{2*\text{frequency(token1, token2)}}{\text{frequency(*, token2)} + \text{frequency(token1, *)}}$$

Mathematically, it can be shown fairly easily that:

$$\text{Dice} = \frac{2 * \text{Jaccard}}{1 + \text{Jaccard}}$$

You might choose to use this metric instead of the Jaccard Index when it's more important to bias the score in favor of instances in which the collocation "token1 token2" appears.

Likelihood ratio

This metric is yet another approach to hypothesis testing that is used to measure the independence between terms that may form a collocation. It's been shown to be a more appropriate approach for collocation discovery than the chi-square test in the general case, and it works well on data that includes many infrequent collocations. The particular calculations involved in computing likelihood estimates for collocations as implemented by NLTK assume a binomial distribution (*http://en.wikipedia.org/wiki/Binomial_distribution*), where the parameters governing the distribution are calculated based upon the number of occurrences of collocations and constituent terms.

Chi-square

Like Student's t-score, this metric is commonly used for testing independence between two variables and can be used to measure whether two tokens are collocations based upon Pearson's chi-square test of statistical significance. Generally speaking, the differences obtained from applying the t-test and chi-square test are not substantial. The advantage of chi-square testing is that unlike t-testing, it does not assume an underlying normal distribution; for this reason, chi-square testing is more commonly used.

Student's t-score

Traditionally, Student's t-score has been used for hypothesis testing, and as applied to *n*-gram analysis, t-scores can be used for testing the hypothesis of whether two terms are collocations. The statistical procedure for this calculation uses a standard distribution per the norm for t-testing. An advantage of the t-score values as opposed to raw frequencies is that a t-score takes into account the frequency of a bigram relative to its constituent components. This characteristic facilitates ranking the strengths of collocations. A criticism of the t-test is that it necessarily assumes that the underlying probability distribution for collocations is normal, which is not often the case.

Pointwise Mutual Information

Pointwise Mutual Information (PMI) is a measure of how much information is gained about a particular word if you also know the value of a neighboring word. To put it another way, how much one word can tell you about another. Ironically (in the context of the current discussion), the calculations involved in computing the PMI lead it to score high-frequency words lower than low-frequency words, which is opposite of the desired effect. Therefore, it is a good measure of independence but not a good measure of dependence (i.e., a less than ideal choice for scoring collocations). It has also been shown that sparse data is a particular stumbling block for PMI scoring, and that other techniques such as the likelihood ratio tend to outperform it.

Tapping into Your Gmail

Google+ is a great source of clean textual data that you can mine, but it's just one of many starting points. Since this chapter showcases Google technology, this section provides a brief overview of how to tap into your Gmail data so that you can mine the text of what may be many thousands of messages in your inbox. If you haven't read Chapter 3 yet, recall that it's devoted to mail analysis but focuses primarily on the structured data features of mail messages, such as the participants in mail threads. The techniques outlined in that chapter could be easily applied to Gmail messages, and vice versa.

Accessing Gmail with OAuth

In early 2010, Google announced OAuth access to IMAP and SMTP in Gmail (*http:// googlecode.blogspot.com/2010/03/oauth-access-to-imapsmtp-in-gmail.html*). This was a significant announcement because it officially opened the door to "Gmail as a platform," enabling third-party developers to build apps that can access your Gmail data without you needing to give them your username and password. This section won't get into the particular nuances of how Xoauth, Google's particular implementation of OAuth (*http://code.google.com/apis/accounts/docs/OAuth.html*), works (see "No, You Can't Have My Password" on page 86 for a terse introduction to OAuth). Instead, it focuses on getting you up and running so that you can access your Gmail data, which involves just a few simple steps:

- Select the "Enable IMAP" option under the "Forwarding and POP/IMAP" tab in your Gmail Account Settings.
- Visit the Google Mail Xoauth Tools wiki page (*http://code.google.com/p/google -mail-xoauth-tools/wiki/XoauthDotPyRunThrough*), download the xoauth.py command-line utility, and follow the instructions to generate an OAuth token and secret for an "anonymous" consumer.[4]
- Install python-oauth2 (*http://github.com/simplegeo/python-oauth2/*) via easy_install oauth2 and use the template in Example 7-11 to establish a connection.

Example 7-11. A template for connecting to IMAP using OAuth (plus__gmail_template.py)

```
# -*- coding: utf-8 -*-

import sys
import oauth2 as oauth
import oauth2.clients.imap as imaplib

# See http://code.google.com/p/google-mail-xoauth-tools/wiki/
#     XoauthDotPyRunThrough for details on xoauth.py

OAUTH_TOKEN = sys.argv[1]  # obtained with xoauth.py
OAUTH_TOKEN_SECRET = sys.argv[2]  # obtained with xoauth.py
GMAIL_ACCOUNT = sys.argv[3]  # example@gmail.com

url = 'https://mail.google.com/mail/b/%s/imap/' % (GMAIL_ACCOUNT, )

# Standard values for Gmail's Xoauth
consumer = oauth.Consumer('anonymous', 'anonymous')
token = oauth.Token(OAUTH_TOKEN, OAUTH_TOKEN_SECRET)
```

---

4. If you're just hacking your own Gmail data, using the anonymous consumer credentials generated from xoauth.py is just fine; you can always register and create a "trusted" client application (*http://code.google .com/apis/accounts/docs/RegistrationForWebAppsAuto.html*) when it becomes appropriate to do so.

```
conn = imaplib.IMAP4_SSL('imap.googlemail.com')
conn.debug = 4  # set to the desired debug level
conn.authenticate(url, consumer, token)

conn.select('INBOX')

# access your INBOX data
```

Once you're able to access your mail data, the next step is to fetch and parse some message data.

Fetching and Parsing Email Messages

The IMAP protocol is a fairly finicky and complex beast, but the good news is that you don't have to know much of it to search and fetch mail messages. imaplib-compliant examples are readily available online (*http://www.doughellmann.com/PyMOTW/imaplib/*), and one of the more common operations you'll want to do is search for messages. There are various ways that you can construct an IMAP query. An example of how you'd search for messages from a particular user is conn.search(None, '(FROM "me")'), where None is an optional parameter for the character set and '(FROM "me")' is a search command to find messages that you've sent yourself (Gmail recognizes "me" as the authenticated user). A command to search for messages containing "foo" in the subject would be '(SUBJECT "foo")', and there are *many* additional possibilities that you can read about in Section 6.4.4 of RFC 3501 (*http://www.faqs.org/rfcs/rfc3501.html*), which defines the IMAP specification. imaplib returns a search response as a tuple that consists of a status code and a string of space-separated message IDs wrapped in a list, such as ('OK', ['506 527 566']). You can parse out these ID values to fetch RFC 822-compliant (*http://www.faqs.org/rfcs/rfc822.html*) mail messages, but alas, there's additional work involved to parse the content of the mail messages into a usable form. Fortunately, with some minimal adaptation, we can reuse the code from Example 3-3, which used the email module to parse messages into a more readily usable form, to take care of the uninteresting email-parsing cruft that's necessary to get usable text from each message. Example 7-12 illustrates.

Example 7-12. A simple workflow for extracting the bodies of Gmail messages returned from a search (plus__search_and_parse_mail.py)

```
# -*- coding: utf-8 -*-

import oauth2 as oauth
import oauth2.clients.imap as imaplib

import os
import sys
import email
import quopri
import json
from BeautifulSoup import BeautifulSoup
```

```
# See http://code.google.com/p/google-mail-xoauth-tools/wiki/
#    XoauthDotPyRunThrough for details on xoauth.py

OAUTH_TOKEN = sys.argv[1]  # obtained with xoauth.py
OAUTH_TOKEN_SECRET = sys.argv[2]  # obtained with xoauth.py
GMAIL_ACCOUNT = sys.argv[3]  # example@gmail.com
Q = sys.argv[4]

url = 'https://mail.google.com/mail/b/%s/imap/' % (GMAIL_ACCOUNT, )

# Authenticate with OAuth

# Standard values for Gmail's xoauth implementation
consumer = oauth.Consumer('anonymous', 'anonymous')
token = oauth.Token(OAUTH_TOKEN, OAUTH_TOKEN_SECRET)
conn = imaplib.IMAP4_SSL('imap.googlemail.com')
conn.debug = 4
conn.authenticate(url, consumer, token)

# Select a folder of interest

conn.select('INBOX')

# Repurpose scripts from "Mailboxes: Oldies but Goodies"


def cleanContent(msg):

    # Decode message from "quoted printable" format

    msg = quopri.decodestring(msg)

    # Strip out HTML tags, if any are present

    soup = BeautifulSoup(msg)
    return ''.join(soup.findAll(text=True))


def jsonifyMessage(msg):
    json_msg = {'parts': []}
    for (k, v) in msg.items():
        json_msg[k] = v.decode('utf-8', 'ignore')

    # The To, CC, and Bcc fields, if present, could have multiple items
    # Note that not all of these fields are necessarily defined

    for k in ['To', 'Cc', 'Bcc']:
        if not json_msg.get(k):
            continue
        json_msg[k] = json_msg[k].replace('\n', '').replace('\t', '').replace('\r'
                , '').replace(' ', '').decode('utf-8', 'ignore').split(',')

    try:
        for part in msg.walk():
            json_part = {}
```

```
                if part.get_content_maintype() == 'multipart':
                    continue
                json_part['contentType'] = part.get_content_type()
                content = part.get_payload(decode=False).decode('utf-8', 'ignore')
                json_part['content'] = cleanContent(content)

                json_msg['parts'].append(json_part)
        except Exception, e:
            sys.stderr.write('Skipping message - error encountered (%s)' % (str(e), ))
        finally:
            return json_msg


# Consume a query from the user. This example illustrates searching by subject

(status, data) = conn.search(None, '(SUBJECT "%s")' % (Q, ))
ids = data[0].split()

messages = []
for i in ids:
    try:
        (status, data) = conn.fetch(i, '(RFC822)')
        messages.append(email.message_from_string(data[0][1]))
    except Exception, e:
        'Print error fetching message %s. Skipping it.' % (i, )

jsonified_messages = [jsonifyMessage(m) for m in messages]

# Separate out the text content from each message so that it can be analyzed

content = [p['content'] for m in jsonified_messages for p in m['parts']]

# Note: Content can still be quite messy and contain lots of line breaks and other quirks

if not os.path.isdir('out'):
    os.mkdir('out')

filename = os.path.join('out', GMAIL_ACCOUNT.split("@")[0] + '.gmail.json')
f = open(filename, 'w')
f.write(json.dumps(jsonified_messages))
f.close()

print >> sys.stderr, "Data written out to", f.name
```

Once you've successfully parsed out the text from the body of a Gmail message, some additional work will be required to cleanse the text to the point that it's suitable for a nice display or advanced NLP, as illustrated in Chapter 8, but not much effort is required to get it to the point where it's clean enough for collocation analysis. In fact, the results of Example 7-12 can be fed almost directly into Example 7-9 to produce a list of collocations from the search results. A very interesting visualization exercise would be to create a graph plotting the strength of linkages between messages based on the number of bigrams they have in common, as determined by a custom metric.

Before You Go Off and Try to Build a Search Engine...

While this chapter has hopefully given you some good insight into how to extract useful information from unstructured text, it's barely scratched the surface of the most fundamental concepts, both in terms of theory and engineering considerations. Information retrieval is literally a multibillion-dollar industry, so you can only imagine the amount of combined investment that goes into both the theory and implementations that work at scale to power search engines such as Google and Yahoo!. This section is a modest attempt to make sure you're aware of some of the inherent limitations of TF-IDF, cosine similarity, and other concepts introduced in this chapter, with the hopes that it will be beneficial in shaping your overall view of this space.

While TF-IDF is a powerful tool that's easy to use, our specific implementation of it has a few important limitations that we've conveniently overlooked but that you should consider. One of the most fundamental is that it treats a document as a bag of words, which means that the order of terms in both the document and the query itself does not matter. For example, querying for "Green Mr." would return the same results as "Mr. Green" if we didn't implement logic to take the query term order into account or interpret the query as a phrase as opposed to a pair of independent terms. But obviously, the order in which terms appear is very important.

Even if you carry out an *n*-gram analysis to account for collocations and term ordering, there's still the underlying issue that TF-IDF assumes that all tokens with the same text value mean the same thing. Clearly, however, this need not be the case. Any homonym of your choice is a counterexample, and there are plenty of them, and even words that do mean the same thing can connote slightly different meanings depending on the exact context in which they are used. A key difference in a traditional keyword search technology based on TF-IDF principles and a more advanced semantic search engine is that the semantic search engine would necessarily allow you to ground your search terms in a particular meaning by defining context. For example, you might be able to specify that the term you are searching for should be interpreted as a person, location, organization, or other specific type of entity. Being able to ground search terms in specific contexts is a very active area of research at the moment.

Cosine similarity suffers from many of the same flaws as TF-IDF. It does not take into account the context of the document or the term order from the *n*-gram analysis, and it assumes that terms appearing close to one another in vector space are necessarily similar, which is certainly not always the case. The obvious counterexample is homonyms, which may mean quite different things but are interpreted as the same term since they have the same text values. Our particular implementation of cosine similarity also hinges on TF-IDF scoring as its means of computing the relative importance of words in documents, so the TF-IDF errors have a cascading effect.

You've probably also realized that there can be a lot of pesky details that have to be managed in analyzing unstructured text, and these details turn out to be pretty important for state-of-the-art implementations. For example, string comparisons are case-sensitive, so it's important to normalize terms so that frequencies can be calculated as accurately as possible. But blindly normalizing to lowercase, for example, can also potentially complicate the situation, since the case used in certain words and phrases can be important. "Mr. Green" and "Web 2.0" are two examples worth considering. In the case of "Mr. Green", maintaining the title case in "Green" could potentially be advantageous since it could provide a useful clue to a query algorithm that it's not referring to an adjective and is likely part of a noun phrase. We'll briefly touch on this topic again in Chapter 8 when NLP is discussed, since it's ultimately the *context* in which "Green" is being used that is lost with the bag-of-words approach, whereas more advanced parsing with NLP has the potential to preserve that context.

Another consideration that's rooted more in our particular implementation than a general characteristic of TF-IDF itself is that our use of split to tokenize the text may leave trailing punctuation on tokens that can affect tabulating frequencies. For example, in the earlier working example, corpus['b'] ends with the token "study", which is not the same as the token "study" that appears in corpus['a'] (the token that someone would probably be more likely to query). In this instance, the trailing period on the token affects both the TF and the IDF calculations.

 You might consider stemming words so that common variations of the same word are essentially treated as the same term instead of different terms. Check out the nltk.stem package for several good stemming implementations.

Finally, there are plenty of engineering considerations to ponder should you decide to implement a solution that you plan to take into a production situation. The use of indexes and caching are critical considerations for obtaining reasonable query times on even moderately large data sets. The ability to analyze truly massive amounts of textual data in batch-processing systems such as Hadoop,[5] even on reasonably priced cloud infrastructures such as Amazon's Elastic Compute Cloud, can be quite expensive and require the budget of a medium-sized corporation.

Closing Remarks

This chapter introduced some of the fundamentals of IR theory: TF-IDF, cosine similarity, and collocations. Given the immense power of search providers like Google, it's easy to forget that these foundational search techniques even exist. However, understanding them yields insight into the assumptions and limitations of the commonly accepted status quo for search, while also clearly differentiating the state-of-the-art entity-centric techniques that are emerging. (Chapter 8 introduces a fundamental

---

5. If Hadoop interests you, you might want to check out Dumbo (*http://github.com/klbostee/dumbo/wiki/building-and-installing*), a project that allows you to write and run Hadoop programs in Python.

paradigm shift away from the tools in this chapter and should make the differences more pronounced than they may seem if you haven't read that material yet.) If you'd like to try applying the techniques from this chapter to the Web (in general), you might want to check out Scrapy (*http://scrapy.org*), an easy-to-use and mature web scraping and crawling framework.

## CHAPTER 8

Blogs et al.: Natural Language Processing (and Beyond)

This chapter is a modest attempt to introduce Natural Language Processing (NLP) and apply it to the unstructured data in blogs. In the spirit of the prior chapters, it attempts to present the minimal level of detail required to empower you with a solid general understanding of an inherently complex topic, while also providing enough of a technical drill-down that you'll be able to immediately get to work mining some data. Although we've been regularly cutting corners and taking a Pareto-like approach—giving you the crucial 20% of the skills that you can use to do 80% of the work—the corners we'll cut in this chapter are especially pronounced because NLP is just that complex. No chapter out of any book—or any small multivolume set of books, for that matter, could possibly do it justice. This chapter is a pragmatic introduction that'll give you enough information to do some pretty amazing things, like automatically generating abstracts from documents and extracting lists of important entities, but we will not journey very far into topics that would require multiple dissertations to sort out.

Although it's not absolutely necessary that you have read Chapter 7 before you dive into this chapter, it's highly recommended that you do so. A good understanding of Natural Language Processing presupposes an appreciation and working knowledge of some of the fundamental strengths and weaknesses of TF-IDF, vector space models, etc. In that regard, these two chapters have a somewhat tighter coupling than most other chapters in this book. The specific data source that's used in this chapter is blogs, but as was the case in Chapter 7, just about any source of text could be used. Blogs just happen to be a staple in the social web (*http://radar.oreilly.com/2010/10/why-blogging-still-matters.html*) that are inherently well suited to text mining. And besides, the line between blog posts and articles is getting quite blurry (*http://www.slate.com/id/2271184/pagenum/all/*) these days!

NLP: A Pareto-Like Introduction

The opening section of this chapter is mostly an expository discussion that attempts to illustrate the difficulty of NLP and give you a good understanding of how it differs from the techniques introduced in previous chapters. The section after it, however, gets right to business with some sample code to get you on your way.

Syntax and Semantics

You may recall from Chapter 7 that perhaps the most fundamental weaknesses of TF-IDF and cosine similarity are that these models inherently don't require a deep *semantic* understanding of the data. Quite the contrary, the examples in that chapter were able to take advantage of very basic syntax that separated tokens by whitespace to break an otherwise opaque document into a bag of tokens and use frequency and simple statistical similarity metrics to determine which tokens were likely to be important in the data. Although you can do some really amazing things with these techniques, they don't really give you any notion of what any given token means in the context in which it appears in the document. Look no further than a sentence containing a homograph (*http://en.wikipedia.org/wiki/Homograph*)[1] such as "fish" or "bear" as a case in point; either one could be a noun or a verb.

NLP is inherently complex and difficult to do even reasonably well, and completely nailing it for a large set of commonly spoken languages may very well be the problem of the century. After all, a complete mastery of NLP is practically synonymous with acing the Turing Test (*http://en.wikipedia.org/wiki/Turing_test*), and to the most careful observer, a computer program that achieves this demonstrates an uncanny amount of human-like intelligence. Whereas structured or semi-structured sources are essentially collections of records with some presupposed meaning given to each field that can immediately be analyzed, there are more subtle considerations to be handled with natural language data for even the seemingly simplest of tasks. For example, let's suppose you're given a document and asked to count the number of sentences in it. It's a trivial task if you're a human and have just a basic understanding of English grammar, but it's another story entirely for a machine, which will require a complex and detailed set of instructions to complete the same task.

The encouraging news is that machines can detect the ends of sentences on relatively well-formed data very quickly and with nearly perfect accuracy. However, even if you've accurately detected all of the sentences, there's still a lot that you probably don't know about the ways that words or phrases are used in those sentences. For example, consider the now classic circa-1990 phrase, "That's the bomb" (*http://www.nydaily news.com/archives/entertainment/1997/06/08/1997-06-08_that_s_the_bomb__kids_*

---

1. A homonym is a special case of a homograph. Two words are homographs if they have the same spelling. Two words are homonyms if they have the same spelling and the same pronunciation. For some reason, "homonym" seems more common in parlance than "homograph" even if it's being misused.

---

slang.html).[2] It's a trivially parseable sentence consisting of almost nothing except a subject, predicate, and object. However, without additional context, even if you have perfect information about the components of the sentence—you have no way of knowing the meaning of the word "bomb"—it could be "something really cool," or a nuke capable of immense destruction. The point is that even with perfect information about the structure of a sentence, you may still need additional context outside the sentence to interpret it. In this case, you need to resolve what the pronoun "that" really refers to[3] and do some inferencing about whether "that" is likely to be a dangerous weapon or not. Thus, as an overly broad generalization, we can say that NLP is fundamentally about taking an opaque document that consists of an ordered collection of symbols adhering to proper *syntax* and a well-defined *grammar*, and ultimately deducing the associated *semantics* that are associated with those symbols.

A Brief Thought Exercise

Let's get back to the task of detecting sentences, the first step in most NLP pipelines, to illustrate some of the complexity involved in NLP. It's deceptively easy to overestimate the utility of simple rule-based heuristics, and it's important to work through an exercise so that you realize what some of the key issues are and don't waste time trying to reinvent the wheel.

Your first attempt at solving the sentence detection problem might be to just count the periods, question marks, and exclamation points in the sentence. That's the most obvious heuristic for starting out, but it's quite crude and has the potential for producing an extremely high margin of error. Consider the following (pretty unambiguous) accusation:

> "Mr. Green killed Colonel Mustard in the study with the candlestick. Mr. Green is not a very nice fellow."

Simply tokenizing the sentence by splitting on punctuation (specifically, periods) would produce the following result:

```
>>> txt = "Mr. Green killed Colonel Mustard in the study with the \
... candlestick. Mr. Green is not a very nice fellow."
>>> txt.split(".")
['Mr', 'Green killed Colonel Mustard in the study with the candlestick',
 'Mr', 'Green is not a very nice fellow', '']
```

It should be immediately obvious that performing sentence detection by blindly breaking on periods without incorporating some notion of context or higher-level information is insufficient. In this case, the problem is the use of "Mr.", a valid abbreviation that's commonly used in the English language. Although we already know from

---

2. See also Urban Dictionary's definitions for bomb (_http://www.urbandictionary.com/define.php?term=bomb_).

3. Resolving pronouns is called anaphora resolution (_http://en.wikipedia.org/wiki/Anaphora_(linguistics)_), a topic that's well outside the scope of this book.

Chapter 7 that *n*-gram analysis of this sample would likely tell us that "Mr. Green" is really one collocation or *chunk* (a compound token containing whitespace), if we had a larger amount of text to analyze, it's not hard to imagine other edge cases that would be difficult to detect based on the appearance of collocations. Thinking ahead a bit, it's also worth pointing out that finding the key topics in a sentence isn't easy to accomplish with trivial logic either. As an intelligent human, you can easily discern that the key topics in our sample might be "Mr. Green", "Colonel Mustard", "the study", and "the candlestick", but training a machine to tell you the same things is a complex task. A few obvious possibilities are probably occurring to you, such as doing some 'Title Case' detection with a regular expression, constructing a list of common abbreviations to parse out the proper noun phrases, and applying some variation of that logic to the problem of finding end-of-sentence boundaries to prevent yourself from getting into trouble on that front.

OK, sure. Those things will work for some examples, but what's the margin of error going to be like for arbitrary English text? How forgiving is your algorithm for poorly formed English text; highly abbreviated information such as text messages or tweets; or (gasp) other romantic languages, such as Spanish, French, or Italian? There are no simple answers here, and that's why text analytics is such an important topic in an age where the amount of accessible textual data is literally increasing every second. These things aren't pointed out to discourage you. They're actually mentioned to motivate you to keep trying when times get tough because this is an inherently difficult space that no one has completely conquered yet. Even if you do feel deflated, you won't feel that way for long because NLTK actually performs reasonably well out-of-the-box for many situations involving arbitrary text, as we'll see in the next section.

A Typical NLP Pipeline with NLTK

This section interactively walks you through a session in the interpreter to perform NLP with NLTK. The NLP pipeline we'll follow is typical and resembles the following high-level flow:

> End of Sentence (EOS) Detection→
> Tokenization→
> Part-of-Speech Tagging→
> Chunking→
> Extraction

We'll use the following sample text for purposes of illustration: "Mr. Green killed Colonel Mustard in the study with the candlestick. Mr. Green is not a very nice fellow." Remember that even though you have already read the text and understand that it's composed of two sentences and all sorts of other things, it's merely an opaque string value to a machine at this point. Let's look at the steps we need to work through in more detail:

EOS detection

This step breaks a text into a collection of meaningful sentences. Since sentences generally represent logical units of thought, they tend to have a predictable syntax that lends itself well to further analysis. Most NLP pipelines you'll see begin with this step because tokenization (the next step) operates on individual sentences. Breaking the text into paragraphs or sections might add value for certain types of analysis, but it is unlikely to aid in the overall task of EOS detection. In the interpreter, you'd parse out a sentence with NLTK like so:

```
>>> import nltk
>>> txt = "Mr. Green killed Colonel Mustard in the study with the candlestick. \
... Mr. Green is not a very nice fellow."
>>> sentences = nltk.tokenize.sent_tokenize(txt)
>>> sentences
['Mr. Green killed Colonel Mustard in the study with the candlestick.',
 'Mr. Green is not a very nice fellow.']
```

We'll talk a little bit more about what is happening under the hood with sent_token ize in the next section. For now, we'll accept at face value that proper sentence detection has occurred for arbitrary text—a clear improvement over breaking on characters that are likely to be punctuation marks.

Tokenization

This step operates on individual sentences, splitting them into tokens. Following along in the example interpreter session, you'd do the following:

```
>>> tokens = [nltk.tokenize.word_tokenize(s) for s in sentences]
>>> tokens
[['Mr.', 'Green', 'killed', 'Colonel', 'Mustard', 'in', 'the', 'study', 'with',
  'the', 'candlestick', '.'],
 ['Mr.', 'Green', 'is', 'not', 'a', 'very', 'nice', 'fellow', '.']]
```

Note that for this simple example, tokenization appeared to do the same thing as splitting on whitespace, with the exception that it tokenized out end-of-sentence markers (the periods) correctly. As we'll see in a later section, though, it can do a bit more if we give it the opportunity, and we already know that distinguishing between whether a period is an end of sentence marker or part of an abbreviation isn't always trivial.

POS tagging

This step assigns part-of-speech information to each token. In the example interpreter session, you'd run the tokens through one more step to have them decorated with tags:

```
>>> pos_tagged_tokens = [nltk.pos_tag(t) for t in tokens]
>>> pos_tagged_tokens
[[('Mr.', 'NNP'), ('Green', 'NNP'), ('killed', 'VBD'), ('Colonel', 'NNP'),
  ('Mustard', 'NNP'), ('in', 'IN'), ('the', 'DT'), ('study', 'NN'),
  ('with', 'IN'), ('the', 'DT'), ('candlestick', 'NN'), ('.', '.')],
 [('Mr.', 'NNP'), ('Green', 'NNP'), ('is', 'VBZ'), ('not', 'RB'), ('a', 'DT'),
  ('very', 'RB'), ('nice', 'JJ'), ('fellow', 'JJ'), ('.', '.')]]
```

You may not intuitively understand all of these tags, but they do represent part-of-speech information. For example, 'NNP' indicates that the token is a noun that is part of a noun phrase, 'VBD' indicates a verb that's in simple past tense, and 'JJ' indicates an adjective. The Penn Treebank Project (*http://www.cis.upenn.edu/~tree bank/*) provides a full summary (*http://www.ling.upenn.edu/courses/Fall_2003/ ling001/penn_treebank_pos.html*) of the part-of-speech tags that could be returned. With POS tagging completed, it should be getting pretty apparent just how powerful analysis can become. For example, by using the POS tags, we'll be able to chunk together nouns as part of noun phrases and then try to reason about what types of entities they might be (e.g., people, places, organizations, etc.).

Chunking

This step involves analyzing each tagged token within a sentence and assembling compound tokens that express logical concepts—quite a different approach than statistically analyzing collocations. It is possible to define a custom grammar through NLTK's chunk.RegexpParser, but that's beyond the scope of this chapter; see Chapter 9 ("Building Feature Based Grammars") of *Natural Language Processing with Python* (O'Reilly), available online at *http://nltk.googlecode.com/svn/ trunk/doc/book/ch09.html*, for full details. Besides, NLTK exposes a function that combines chunking with named entity extraction, which is the next step.

Extraction

This step involves analyzing each chunk and further tagging the chunks as named entities, such as people, organizations, locations, etc. The continuing saga of NLP in the interpreter demonstrates:

```
>>> ne_chunks = nltk.batch_ne_chunk(pos_tagged_tokens)
>>> ne_chunks
[Tree('S', [Tree('PERSON', [('Mr.', 'NNP')]), Tree('PERSON', [('Green', 'NNP')]),
    ('killed', 'VBD'),
 Tree('ORGANIZATION', [('Colonel', 'NNP'), ('Mustard', 'NNP')]), ('in', 'IN'),
    ('the', 'DT'), ('study', 'NN'), ('with', 'IN'), ('the', 'DT'),
    ('candlestick', 'NN'), ('.', '.')]),
 Tree('S', [Tree('PERSON', [('Mr.', 'NNP')]), Tree('ORGANIZATION',
    [('Green', 'NNP')]), ('is', 'VBZ'), ('not', 'RB'),
 ('a', 'DT'), ('very', 'RB'), ('nice', 'JJ'), ('fellow', 'JJ'), ('.', '.')])]
>>> ne_chunks[0].draw() # You can draw each chunk in the tree
```

Don't get too wrapped up in trying to decipher exactly what the tree output means just yet. In short, it has chunked together some tokens and attempted to classify them as being certain types of entities. (You may be able to discern that it has identified "Mr. Green" as a person, but unfortunately categorized "Colonel Mustard" as an organization.) Figure 8-1 illustrates the effect of calling draw() on the results from nltk.batch_ne_chunk.

As interesting as it would be to continue talking about the intricacies of NLP, producing a state-of-the-art NLP stack or even taking much of a deeper dive into NLTK for the purposes of NLP isn't really our purpose here. The background in this section is provided to motivate an appreciation for the difficulty of the task and to encourage you to review the aforementioned NLTK book (*http://www.nltk.org/book*) or one of the many other plentiful resources available online if you'd like to pursue the topic further. As a bit of passing advice, if your business (or idea) depends on a *truly state-of-the-art* NLP stack, strongly consider purchasing a license to a turn-key product from a commercial or academic institution instead of trying to home-brew your own. There's a lot you can do on your own with open source software, and that's a great place to start, but as with anything else, the investment involved can be significant if you have to make numerous improvements that require specialized consulting engagements. NLP is still very much an active field of research, and the cutting edge is nowhere near being a commodity just yet.

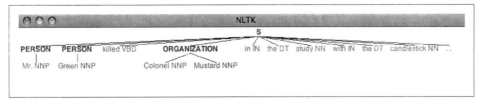

Figure 8-1. NLTK can interface with drawing toolkits so that you can inspect the chunked output in a more intuitive visual form than the raw text output you see in the interpreter

Unless otherwise noted, the remainder of this chapter assumes you'll be using NLTK "as-is" as well. (If you had a PhD in computational linguistics or something along those lines, you'd be more than capable of modifying NLTK for your own needs and would probably be reading much more scholarly material than this chapter.)

With that brief introduction to NLP concluded, let's get to work mining some blog data.

Sentence Detection in Blogs with NLTK

Given that sentence detection is probably the first task you'll want to ponder when building an NLP stack, it makes sense to start there. Even if you never complete the remaining tasks in the pipeline, it turns out that EOS detection alone yields some powerful possibilities such as document summarization, which we'll be considering as a follow-up exercise. But first, we'll need to fetch some high-quality blog data. Let's use the tried and true `feedparser` module, which you can `easy_install` if you don't have it already, to fetch some posts from the O'Reilly Radar blog (*http://radar.oreilly.com*). The listing in Example 8-1 fetches a few posts and saves them to a local file as plain old JSON, since nothing else in this chapter hinges on the capabilities of a more advanced storage medium, such as CouchDB. As always, you can choose to store the posts anywhere you'd like.

Example 8-1. Harvesting blog data by parsing feeds (blogs_and_nlp__get_feed.py)

```python
# -*- coding: utf-8 -*-

import os
import sys
from datetime import datetime as dt
import json
import feedparser
from BeautifulSoup import BeautifulStoneSoup
from nltk import clean_html



# Example feed:
# http://feeds.feedburner.com/oreilly/radar/atom
FEED_URL = sys.argv[1]


def cleanHtml(html):
    return BeautifulStoneSoup(clean_html(html),
                             convertEntities=BeautifulStoneSoup.HTML_ENTITIES).contents[0]


fp = feedparser.parse(FEED_URL)

print "Fetched %s entries from '%s'" % (len(fp.entries[0].title), fp.feed.title)

blog_posts = []
for e in fp.entries:
    blog_posts.append({'title': e.title, 'content'
                        : cleanHtml(e.content[0].value), 'link': e.links[0].href})

if not os.path.isdir('out'):
    os.mkdir('out')

out_file = '%s__%s.json' % (fp.feed.title, dt.utcnow())
f = open(os.path.join(os.getcwd(), 'out', out_file), 'w')
f.write(json.dumps(blog_posts))
f.close()

print >> sys.stderr, 'Wrote output file to %s' % (f.name, )
```

Obtaining our unstructured text from a reputable source affords us the luxury of assuming good English grammar; hopefully this also means that one of NLTK's out-of-the-box sentence detectors will work reasonably well. There's no better way to find out than hacking some code to see what happens, so go ahead and take a gander at the code listing in Example 8-2. It introduces the sent_tokenize and word_tokenize methods, which are aliases for NLTK's currently recommended sentence detector and word tokenizer. A brief discussion of the listing is provided afterward.

Example 8-2. Using NLTK's NLP tools to parse blog data (blogs_and_nlp__sentence_detection.py)

```python
# -*- coding: utf-8 -*-

import sys
import json
import nltk

# Load in output from blogs_and_nlp__get_feed.py

BLOG_DATA = sys.argv[1]
blog_data = json.loads(open(BLOG_DATA).read())

# Customize your list of stopwords as needed. Here, we add common
# punctuation and contraction artifacts

stop_words = nltk.corpus.stopwords.words('english') + [
    '.',
    ',',
    '--',
    '\'s',
    '?',
    ')',
    '(',
    ':',
    '\'',
    '\'re',
    '"',
    '-',
    '}',
    '{',
    ]

for post in blog_data:
    sentences = nltk.tokenize.sent_tokenize(post['content'])

    words = [w.lower() for sentence in sentences for w in
                nltk.tokenize.word_tokenize(sentence)]

    fdist = nltk.FreqDist(words)

    # Basic stats

    num_words = sum([i[1] for i in fdist.items()])
    num_unique_words = len(fdist.keys())

    # Hapaxes are words that appear only once

    num_hapaxes = len(fdist.hapaxes())

    top_10_words_sans_stop_words = [w for w in fdist.items() if w[0]
                                        not in stop_words][:10]

    print post['title']
    print '\tNum Sentences:'.ljust(25), len(sentences)
    print '\tNum Words:'.ljust(25), num_words
```

```
print '\tNum Unique Words:'.ljust(25), num_unique_words
print '\tNum Hapaxes:'.ljust(25), num_hapaxes
print '\tTop 10 Most Frequent Words (sans stop words):\n\t\t', \
    '\n\t\t'.join(['%s (%s)'
        % (w[0], w[1]) for w in top_10_words_sans_stop_words])
print
```

The first things you're probably wondering about are the sent_tokenize and word_token ize calls. NLTK provides several options for tokenization, but it provides "recommen-dations" as to the best available via these aliases. At the time of this writing (you can double-check this with pydoc at any time), the sentence detector is the PunktSentence Tokenizer and the word tokenizer is the TreebankWordTokenizer. Let's take a brief look at each of these.

Internally, the PunktSentenceTokenizer relies heavily on being able to detect abbrevia-tions as part of collocation patterns, and it uses some regular expressions to try to intelligently parse sentences by taking into account common patterns of punctuation usage. A full explanation of the innards of the PunktSentenceTokenizer's logic is outside the scope of this book, but Tibor Kiss and Jan Strunk's original paper, "Unsupervised Multilingual Sentence Boundary Detection" (*http://www.linguistics.ruhr-uni-bochum .de/~strunk/ks2005FINAL.pdf*) discusses its approach, is highly readable, and you should take some time to review it. As we'll see in a bit, it is possible to instantiate the PunktSentenceTokenizer with sample text that it trains on to try to improve its accuracy. The type of underlying algorithm that's used is an *unsupervised learning algorithm*; it does not require you to explicitly mark up the sample training data in any way. Instead, the algorithm inspects certain *features* that appear in the text itself, such as the use of capitalization, the co-occurrences of tokens, etc., to derive suitable parameters for breaking the text into sentences.

While NLTK's WhitespaceTokenizer, which creates tokens by breaking a piece of text on whitespace, would have been the simplest word tokenizer to introduce, you're al-ready familiar with some of the shortcomings of blindly breaking on whitespace. In-stead, NLTK currently recommends the TreebankWordTokenizer, a word tokenizer that operates on sentences and uses the same conventions as the Penn Treebank Project.[4] The one thing that may catch you off guard is that the TreebankWordTokenizer's toke-nization (*http://www.cis.upenn.edu/~treebank/tokenization.html*) does some less-than-obvious things, such as separately tagging components in contractions and nouns having possessive forms. For example, the parsing for the sentence "I'm hungry," would yield separate components for "I" and "'m", maintaining a distinction between the subject and verb for "I'm". As you might imagine, finely grained access to this kind of grammatical information can be quite valuable when it's time to do advanced analysis that scrutinizes relationships between subjects and verbs in sentences.

---

4. "Treebank" is a very specific term that refers to a corpus that's been specially tagged with advanced linguistic information. In fact, the reason such a corpus is called a "treebank" is to emphasize that it's a bank (think: collection) of sentences that have been parsed into trees adhering to a particular grammar.

If you have a lot of trouble with advanced word tokenizers such as NLTK's `TreebankWordTokenizer` or `PunktWordTokenizer`, it's fine to default back to the `WhitespaceTokenizer` until you decide whether it's worth the investment to use a more advanced tokenizer. In fact, in some cases using a more straightforward tokenizer can be advantageous. For example, using an advanced tokenizer on data that frequently inlines URLs might be a bad idea, because these tokenizers do not recognize URLs out of the box and will mistakenly break them up into multiple tokens. It's not in the scope of this book to implement a custom tokenizer, but there are lots of online sources you can consult if this is something you're interested in attempting.

Given a sentence tokenizer and a word tokenizer, we can first parse the text into sentences and then parse each sentence into tokens. Note that while this approach is fairly intuitive, it can have a subtle Achilles' heel in that errors produced by the sentence detector propagate forward and can potentially bound the upper limit of the quality that the rest of the NLP stack can produce. For example, if the sentence tokenizer mistakenly breaks a sentence on the period after "Mr." that appears in a section of text such as "Mr. Green killed Colonel Mustard in the study with the candlestick", it may not be possible to extract the entity "Mr. Green" from the text unless specialized repair logic is in place. Again, it all depends on the sophistication of the full NLP stack and how it accounts for error propagation. The out-of-the-box `PunktSentenceTokenizer` is trained on the Penn Treebank corpus and performs quite well. The end goal of the parsing is to instantiate a handy-dandy `FreqDist` object, which expects a list of tokens. The remainder of the code in Example 8-2 is straightforward usage of a few of the commonly used NLTK APIs.

The aim of this section was to familiarize you with the first step involved in building an NLP pipeline. Along the way, we developed a few metrics that make a feeble attempt at characterizing some blog data. Our pipeline doesn't involve part-of-speech tagging or chunking (yet), but it should give you a basic understanding of some concepts and get you thinking about some of the subtler issues involved. While it's true that we could have simply split on whitespace, counted terms, tallied the results, and still gained a lot of information from the data, it won't be long before you'll be glad that you took these initial steps toward a deeper understanding of the data. To illustrate one possible application for what you've just learned, in the next section, we'll look at a simple document summarization algorithm that relies on little more than sentence segmentation and frequency analysis.

Summarizing Documents

Although it may not be immediately obvious, just being able to perform reasonably good sentence detection as part of an NLP approach to mining unstructured data can enable some pretty powerful text-mining capabilities, such as crude but very reasonable attempts at document summarization. There are numerous possibilities and approaches, but one of the simplest to get started with dates all the way back to the April 1958 issue of *IBM Journal*. In the seminal article entitled "The Automatic Creation of Literature Abstracts," H.P. Luhn describes a technique that essentially boils down to filtering out sentences containing frequently occurring words that appear near one another.

The original paper is easy to understand and is rather interesting; Luhn actually describes how he prepared punch cards in order to run various tests with different parameters! It's amazing to think that what we can implement in a few dozen lines of Python on a cheap piece of commodity hardware, he probably labored over for hours and hours to program into a gargantuan mainframe. Example 8-3 provides a basic implementation of Luhn's algorithm for document summarization. A brief analysis of the algorithm appears in the next section. Before skipping ahead to that discussion, first take a moment to trace through the code and see whether you can determine how it works.

Example 8-3. A document summarization algorithm (blogs_and_nlp__summarize.py)

```
# -*- coding: utf-8 -*-

import sys
import json
import nltk
import numpy

N = 100  # Number of words to consider
CLUSTER_THRESHOLD = 5  # Distance between words to consider
TOP_SENTENCES = 5  # Number of sentences to return for a "top n" summary

# Approach taken from "The Automatic Creation of Literature Abstracts" by H.P. Luhn

def _score_sentences(sentences, important_words):
    scores = []
    sentence_idx = -1

    for s in [nltk.tokenize.word_tokenize(s) for s in sentences]:

        sentence_idx += 1
        word_idx = []

        # For each word in the word list...
        for w in important_words:
            try:
                # Compute an index for where any important words occur in the sentence
```

```
            word_idx.append(s.index(w))
        except ValueError, e: # w not in this particular sentence
            pass

    word_idx.sort()

    # It is possible that some sentences may not contain any important words at all
    if len(word_idx)== 0: continue

    # Using the word index, compute clusters by using a max distance threshold
    # for any two consecutive words

    clusters = []
    cluster = [word_idx[0]]
    i = 1
    while i < len(word_idx):
        if word_idx[i] - word_idx[i - 1] < CLUSTER_THRESHOLD:
            cluster.append(word_idx[i])
        else:
            clusters.append(cluster[:])
            cluster = [word_idx[i]]
        i += 1
    clusters.append(cluster)

    # Score each cluster. The max score for any given cluster is the score
    # for the sentence

    max_cluster_score = 0
    for c in clusters:
        significant_words_in_cluster = len(c)
        total_words_in_cluster = c[-1] - c[0] + 1
        score = 1.0 * significant_words_in_cluster \
            * significant_words_in_cluster / total_words_in_cluster

        if score > max_cluster_score:
            max_cluster_score = score

    scores.append((sentence_idx, score))

return scores

def summarize(txt):
    sentences = [s for s in nltk.tokenize.sent_tokenize(txt)]
    normalized_sentences = [s.lower() for s in sentences]

    words = [w.lower() for sentence in normalized_sentences for w in
            nltk.tokenize.word_tokenize(sentence)]

    fdist = nltk.FreqDist(words)

    top_n_words = [w[0] for w in fdist.items()
            if w[0] not in nltk.corpus.stopwords.words('english')][:N]

    scored_sentences = _score_sentences(normalized_sentences, top_n_words)
```

```
# Summarization Approach 1:
# Filter out non-significant sentences by using the average score plus a
# fraction of the std dev as a filter

avg = numpy.mean([s[1] for s in scored_sentences])
std = numpy.std([s[1] for s in scored_sentences])
mean_scored = [(sent_idx, score) for (sent_idx, score) in scored_sentences
               if score > avg + 0.5 * std]

# Summarization Approach 2:
# Another approach would be to return only the top N ranked sentences

top_n_scored = sorted(scored_sentences, key=lambda s: s[1])[-TOP_SENTENCES:]
top_n_scored = sorted(top_n_scored, key=lambda s: s[0])

# Decorate the post object with summaries

return dict(top_n_summary=[sentences[idx] for (idx, score) in top_n_scored],
            mean_scored_summary=[sentences[idx] for (idx, score) in mean_scored])


if __name__ == '__main__':

    # Load in output from blogs_and_nlp__get_feed.py

    BLOG_DATA = sys.argv[1]
    blog_data = json.loads(open(BLOG_DATA).read())

    for post in blog_data:

        post.update(summarize(post['content']))

        print post['title']
        print '-' * len(post['title'])
        print
        print '-------------'
        print 'Top N Summary'
        print '-------------'
        print ' '.join(post['top_n_summary'])
        print
        print '-------------------'
        print 'Mean Scored Summary'
        print '-------------------'
        print ' '.join(post['mean_scored_summary'])
        print
```

As example input/output, we'll use Tim O'Reilly's Radar post, "The Louvre of the
Industrial Age" (*http://radar.oreilly.com/2010/07/louvre-industrial-age-henry-ford
.html*). It's around 460 words long and is reprinted here so that you can compare the
sample output from the two summarization attempts in the listing:

> This morning I had the chance to get a tour of The Henry Ford Museum in Dearborn,
> MI, along with Dale Dougherty, creator of Make: and Makerfaire, and Marc Greuther,
> the chief curator of the museum. I had expected a museum dedicated to the auto industry,

but it's so much more than that. As I wrote in my first stunned tweet, "it's the Louvre of the Industrial Age."

When we first entered, Marc took us to what he said may be his favorite artifact in the museum, a block of concrete that contains Luther Burbank's shovel, and Thomas Edison's signature and footprints. Luther Burbank was, of course, the great agricultural inventor who created such treasures as the nectarine and the Santa Rosa plum. Ford was a farm boy who became an industrialist; Thomas Edison was his friend and mentor. The museum, opened in 1929, was Ford's personal homage to the transformation of the world that he was so much a part of. This museum chronicles that transformation.

The machines are astonishing—steam engines and coal-fired electric generators as big as houses, the first lathes capable of making other precision lathes (the makerbot of the 19th century), a ribbon glass machine that is one of five that in the 1970s made virtually all of the incandescent lightbulbs in the world, combine harvesters, railroad locomotives, cars, airplanes, even motels, gas stations, an early McDonalds' restaurant and other epiphenomena of the automobile era.

Under Marc's eye, we also saw the transformation of the machines from purely functional objects to things of beauty. We saw the advances in engineering—the materials, the workmanship, the design, over a hundred years of innovation. Visiting The Henry Ford, as they call it, is a truly humbling experience. I would never in a hundred years have thought of making a visit to Detroit just to visit this museum, but knowing what I know now, I will tell you confidently that it is as worth your while as a visit to Paris just to see the Louvre, to Rome for the Vatican Museum, to Florence for the Uffizi Gallery, to St. Petersburg for the Hermitage, or to Berlin for the Pergamon Museum. This is truly one of the world's great museums, and the world that it chronicles is our own.

I am truly humbled that the Museum has partnered with us to hold Makerfaire Detroit on their grounds. If you are anywhere in reach of Detroit this weekend, I heartily recommend that you plan to spend both days there. You can easily spend a day at Makerfaire, and you could easily spend a day at The Henry Ford. P.S. Here are some of my photos from my visit. (More to come soon. Can't upload many as I'm currently on a plane.)

Filtering sentences using an average score and standard deviation yields a summary of around 170 words:

This morning I had the chance to get a tour of The Henry Ford Museum in Dearborn, MI, along with Dale Dougherty, creator of Make: and Makerfaire, and Marc Greuther, the chief curator of the museum. I had expected a museum dedicated to the auto industry, but it's so much more than that. As I wrote in my first stunned tweet, "it's the Louvre of the Industrial Age. This museum chronicles that transformation. The machines are astonishing - steam engines and coal fired electric generators as big as houses, the first lathes capable of making other precision lathes (the makerbot of the 19th century), a ribbon glass machine that is one of five that in the 1970s made virtually all of the incandescent lightbulbs in the world, combine harvesters, railroad locomotives, cars, airplanes, even motels, gas stations, an early McDonalds' restaurant and other epiphenomena of the automobile era. You can easily spend a day at Makerfaire, and you could easily spend a day at The Henry Ford.

An alternative summarization approach, which considers only the top *N* sentences (where *N* = 5 in this case), produces a slightly more abridged result of around 90 words. It's even more succinct, but arguably still a pretty informative distillation:

> This morning I had the chance to get a tour of The Henry Ford Museum in Dearborn, MI, along with Dale Dougherty, creator of Make: and Makerfaire, and Marc Greuther, the chief curator of the museum. I had expected a museum dedicated to the auto industry, but it's so much more than that. As I wrote in my first stunned tweet, "it's the Louvre of the Industrial Age. This museum chronicles that transformation. You can easily spend a day at Makerfaire, and you could easily spend a day at The Henry Ford.

As in any other situation involving analysis, there's a lot of insight to be gained from visually inspecting the summarizations in relation to the full text. Outputting a simple markup format that can be opened by virtually any web browser is as simple as adjusting the final portion of the script that performs the output to do some string substitution. Example 8-4 illustrates one possibility.

Example 8-4. Augmenting the output of Example 8-3 to produce HTML markup that lends itself to analyzing the summarization algorithm's results (blogs_and_nlp__summarize_markedup_output.py)

```
# -*- coding: utf-8 -*-

import os
import sys
import json
import nltk
import numpy
from blogs_and_nlp__summarize import summarize

HTML_TEMPLATE = """<html>
    <head>
        <title>%s</title>
        <meta http-equiv="Content-Type" content="text/html; charset=UTF-8"/>
    </head>
    <body>%s</body>
</html>"""

if __name__ == '__main__':

    # Load in output from blogs_and_nlp__get_feed.py

    BLOG_DATA = sys.argv[1]
    blog_data = json.loads(open(BLOG_DATA).read())

    # Marked up version can be written out to disk

    if not os.path.isdir('out/summarize'):
        os.makedirs('out/summarize')

    for post in blog_data:

        post.update(summarize(post['content']))
```

```
# You could also store a version of the full post with key sentences markedup
# for analysis with simple string replacement...

for summary_type in ['top_n_summary', 'mean_scored_summary']:
    post[summary_type + '_marked_up'] = '<p>%s</p>' % (post['content'], )
    for s in post[summary_type]:
        post[summary_type + '_marked_up'] = \
        post[summary_type + '_marked_up'].replace(s, \
          '<strong>%s</strong>' % (s, ))

    filename = post['title'] + '.summary.' + summary_type + '.html'
    f = open(os.path.join('out', 'summarize', filename), 'w')
    html = HTML_TEMPLATE % (post['title'] + \
      ' Summary', post[summary_type + '_marked_up'],)

    f.write(html.encode('utf-8'))
    f.close()

    print >> sys.stderr, "Data written to", f.name
```

The resulting output is the full text of the document with sentences comprising the
summary highlighted in bold, as displayed in Figure 8-2. As you explore alternative
techniques for summarization, a quick glance between browser tabs can give you an
intuitive feel for the similarity between the summarization techniques. The primary
difference illustrated here is a fairly long (and descriptive) sentence near the middle of
the document, beginning with the words "The machines are astonishing".

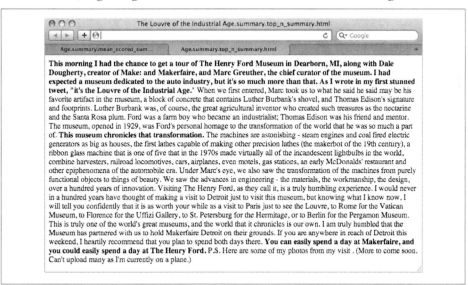

*Figure 8-2. The text from an O'Reilly Radar blog post with the most important sentences as determined
by a summarization algorithm conveyed in bold*

The next section presents a brief discussion of Luhn's approach.

Analysis of Luhn's Summarization Algorithm

The basic premise behind Luhn's algorithm is that the important sentences in a document will be the ones that contain frequently occurring words. However, there are a few details worth pointing out. First, not all frequently occurring words are important; generally speaking, stopwords are filler and are hardly ever of interest for analysis. Keep in mind that although we do filter out common stopwords in the sample implementation, it may be possible to create a custom list of stopwords for any given blog or domain with additional a priori knowledge, which might further bolster the strength of this algorithm or any other algorithm that assumes stopwords have been filtered. For example, a blog written exclusively about baseball might so commonly use the word "baseball" that you should consider adding it to a stopword list, even though it's not a general-purpose stopword. (As a side note, it would be interesting to incorporate TF-IDF into the scoring function for a particular data source as a means of accounting for common words in the parlance of the domain.)

Assuming that a reasonable attempt to eliminate stopwords has been made, the next step in the algorithm is to choose a reasonable value for N and choose the top N words as the basis of analysis. Note that the latent assumption behind this algorithm is that these top N words are sufficiently descriptive to characterize the nature of the document, and that for any two sentences in the document, the sentence that contains more of these words will be considered more descriptive. All that's left after determining the "important words" in the document is to apply a heuristic to each sentence and filter out some subset of sentences to use as a summarization or abstract of the document. Scoring each sentence takes place in the function score_sentences. This is where most of the interesting action happens in the listing.

In order to score each sentence, the algorithm in score_sentences applies a simple distance threshold to cluster tokens, and scores each cluster according to the following formula:

$$\frac{(\text{significant words in cluster})^2}{\text{total words in cluster}}$$

The final score for each sentence is equal to the highest score for any cluster appearing in the sentence. Let's consider the high-level steps involved in score_sentences for an example sentence to see how this approach works in practice:

Input: Sample sentence

```
['Mr.', 'Green', 'killed', 'Colonel', 'Mustard', 'in', 'the', 'study',
'with', 'the', 'candlestick', '.']
```

Input: List of important words

```
['Mr.', 'Green', 'Colonel', 'Mustard', 'candlestick']
```

Input/Assumption: Cluster threshold (distance)

    3

Intermediate Computation: Clusters detected
```
[ ['Mr.', 'Green', 'killed', 'Colonel', 'Mustard'], ['candlestick'] ]
```
Intermediate Computation: Cluster scores
```
[ 3.2, 1 ] # Computation: [ (4*4)/5, (1*1)/1]
```
Output: Sentence score
```
3.2 # max([3.2, 1])
```

The actual work done in `score_sentences` is just bookkeeping to detect the clusters in the sentence. A cluster is defined as a sequence of words containing two or more important words, where each important word is within a distance threshold of its nearest neighbor. While Luhn's paper suggests a value of 4 or 5 for the distance threshold, we used a value of 3 for simplicity in this example; thus, the distance between 'Green' and 'Colonel' was sufficiently bridged, and the first cluster detected consisted of the first five words in the sentence. Note that had the word "study" also appeared in the list of important words, the entire sentence (except the final punctuation) would have emerged as a cluster.

Once each sentence has been scored, all that's left is to determine which sentences to return as a summary. The sample implementation provides two approaches. The first approach uses a statistical threshold to filter out sentences by computing the mean and standard deviation for the scores obtained, while the latter simply returns the top N sentences. Depending on the nature of the data, your mileage will probably vary, but you should be able to tune the parameters to achieve reasonable results with either. One nice thing about using the top N sentences is that you have a pretty good idea about the maximum length of the summary. Using the mean and standard deviation could potentially return more sentences than you'd prefer, if a lot of sentences contain scores that are relatively close to one another.

Luhn's algorithm is simple to implement and plays to the usual strength of frequently appearing words being descriptive of the overall document. However, keep in mind that like many of the IR approaches we explored in the previous chapter, Luhn's algorithm makes no attempt to understand the data at a deeper semantic level. It directly computes summarizations as a function of frequently occurring words, and it isn't terribly sophisticated in how it scores sentences. Still, as was the case with TF-IDF, this makes it all the more amazing that it can perform as well as it seems to perform on randomly selected blog data.

When weighing the pros and cons of implementing a much more complicated approach, it's worth reflecting on the effort that would be required to improve upon a reasonable summarization such as that produced by Luhn's algorithm. Sometimes, a crude heuristic is all you really need to accomplish your goal. At other times, however, you may need something more state of the art. The tricky part is computing the cost-benefit analysis of migrating from the crude heuristic to the state-of-the-art solution. Many of us tend to be overly optimistic about the relative effort involved.

Entity-Centric Analysis: A Deeper Understanding of the Data

Throughout this chapter, it's been implied that analytic approaches that exhibit a deeper understanding of the data can be dramatically more powerful than approaches that simply treat each token as an opaque symbol. But what does "a deeper understanding" of the data really mean? One interpretation is being able to detect the entities in documents and using those entities as the basis of analysis, as opposed to document-centric analysis involving keyword searches or interpreting a search input as a particular type of entity and customizing results accordingly. Although you may not have thought about it in those terms, this is precisely what emerging technologies such as WolframAlpha do at the presentation layer. For example, a search for "tim o'reilly" in WolframAlpha returns results that imply an understanding that the entity being searched for is a person; you don't just get back a list of documents containing the keywords (see Figure 8-3). Regardless of the internal technique that's used to accomplish this end, the resulting user experience is dramatically more powerful because the results conform to a format that more closely satisfies the user's expectations.

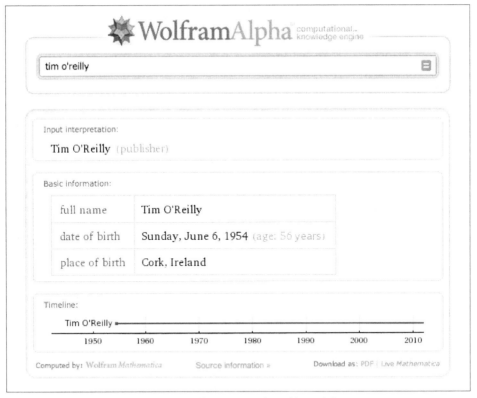

Figure 8-3. Sample results for a "tim o'reilly" query with WolframAlpha

Although it's beyond the scope of this chapter to ponder the various possibilities of entity-centric analysis, it's well within our scope and quite appropriate to present a means of extracting the entities from a document, which can then be used for various analytic purposes. Assuming the sample flow of an NLP pipeline as presented earlier in this chapter, one approach you could take would be to simply extract all the nouns and noun phrases from the document and index them as entities appearing in the documents—the important underlying assumption being that nouns and noun phrases (or some carefully constructed subset thereof) qualify as entities of interest. This is actually a very fair assumption to make and a good starting point for entity-centric analysis, as the following sample listing demonstrates. Note that for results annotated according to Penn Treebank conventions, any tag beginning with 'NN' is some form of a noun or noun phrase. A full listing of the Penn Treebank Tags (*http://bulba.sdsu .edu/jeanette/thesis/PennTags.html*) is available online.

Example 8-5 analyzes the part-of-speech tags that are applied to tokens, and identifies nouns and noun phrases as entities. In data-mining parlance, finding the entities in a text is called *entity extraction*.

Example 8-5. Extracting entities from a text with NLTK (blogs_and_nlp__extract_entities.py)

```
# -*- coding: utf-8 -*-

import sys
import nltk
import json

# Load in output from blogs_and_nlp__get_feed.py

BLOG_DATA = sys.argv[1]
blog_data = json.loads(open(BLOG_DATA).read())

for post in blog_data:

    sentences = nltk.tokenize.sent_tokenize(post['content'])
    tokens = [nltk.tokenize.word_tokenize(s) for s in sentences]
    pos_tagged_tokens = [nltk.pos_tag(t) for t in tokens]

    # Flatten the list since we're not using sentence structure
    # and sentences are guaranteed to be separated by a special
    # POS tuple such as ('.', '.')

    pos_tagged_tokens = [token for sent in pos_tagged_tokens for token in sent]

    all_entity_chunks = []
    previous_pos = None
    current_entity_chunk = []
    for (token, pos) in pos_tagged_tokens:

        if pos == previous_pos and pos.startswith('NN'):
            current_entity_chunk.append(token)
        elif pos.startswith('NN'):
            if current_entity_chunk != []:
```

```
                # Note that current_entity_chunk could be a duplicate when appended,
                # so frequency analysis again becomes a consideration

                all_entity_chunks.append((' '.join(current_entity_chunk), pos))
            current_entity_chunk = [token]

        previous_pos = pos

    # Store the chunks as an index for the document
    # and account for frequency while we're at it...

    post['entities'] = {}
    for c in all_entity_chunks:
        post['entities'][c] = post['entities'].get(c, 0) + 1

    # For example, we could display just the title-cased entities

    print post['title']
    print '-' * len(post['title'])
    proper_nouns = []
    for (entity, pos) in post['entities']:
        if entity.istitle():
            print '\t%s (%s)' % (entity, post['entities'][(entity, pos)])
    print
```

 You may recall from the description of "extraction" in "A Typical NLP
Pipeline with NLTK" on page 242 that NLTK provides an
nltk.batch_ne_chunk function that attempts to extract named entities
from POS-tagged tokens. You're welcome to use this capability directly,
but you may find that your mileage varies with the out-of-the-box models that back the implementation. A discussion of improving the implementation that ships with NLTK is outside the scope of this chapter.

Sample output for the listing is presented in Example 8-6. It provides results that are
quite meaningful and would make great suggestions for tags by an intelligent blogging
platform. For a larger corpus than we're working with in this example, a tag cloud
would also be an obvious candidate for visualizing the data. (Recall that "Visualizing
Tweets with Tricked-Out Tag Clouds" on page 158 introduced an easy-to-use but very
powerful tag cloud that you could easily adapt to work here.)

Example 8-6. Sample results from Example 8-5

```
The Louvre of the Industrial Age
---------------------------------
    Paris (1)
    Henry Ford Museum (1)
    Vatican Museum (1)
    Museum (1)
    Thomas Edison (2)
    Hermitage (1)
```

```
Uffizi Gallery (1)
Ford (2)
Santa Rosa (1)
Dearborn (1)
Makerfaire (1)
Berlin (1)
Marc (2)
Makerfaire (1)
Rome (1)
Henry Ford (1)
Ca (1)
Louvre (1)
Detroit (2)
St. Petersburg (1)
Florence (1)
Marc Greuther (1)
Makerfaire Detroit (1)
Luther Burbank (2)
Make (1)
Dale Dougherty (1)
Louvre (1)
```

Could we have discovered the same list of terms by more blindly analyzing the lexical characteristics (such as use of capitalization) of the sentence? Perhaps, but keep in mind that this technique can also capture nouns and noun phrases that are not indicated by title case. Case is indeed an important *feature* of the text that can generally be exploited to great benefit, but there are other interesting entities in the sample text that are all lowercase (for example, "chief curator", "locomotives", and "lightbulbs").

Although the list of entities certainly doesn't convey the overall meaning of the text as effectively as the summary we computed earlier, identifying these entities can be extremely valuable for analysis since *they have meaning at a semantic level and are not just frequently occurring words*. In fact, the frequencies of most of the terms displayed in the sample output are quite low. Nevertheless, they're important because they have a grounded meaning in the text—namely, they're people, places, things, or ideas, which are generally the substantive information in the data.

It's not much of a leap at this point to think that it would be another major step forward to take into account the verbs and compute triples of the form subject-verb-object so that you know which entities are interacting with which other entities, and the nature of those interactions. Such triples would lend themselves to visualizing object graphs of documents, which could potentially be skimmed much faster than reading the documents themselves. Better yet, imagine taking multiple object graphs derived from a set of documents and merging them to get the gist of the larger corpus. This exact technique is very much an area of active research and has tremendous applicability for virtually any situation suffering from the information-overload problem. But as will be illustrated, it's an excruciating problem for the general case and not for the faint of heart.

Assuming a part-of-speech tagger has identified the following parts of speech from a sentence and emitted output such as [('Mr.', 'NNP'), ('Green', 'NNP'), ('killed',

'VBD'), ('Colonel', 'NNP'), ('Mustard', 'NNP'), ...], an index storing subject-predicate-object tuples of the form ('Mr. Green', 'killed', 'Colonel Mustard') would be easy to compute. However, the reality of the situation is that you're very unlikely to run across actual POS-tagged data with that level of simplicity—unless you're planning to mine children's books (something that's not actually a bad idea for beginners). For example, consider the tagging emitted from NLTK for the first sentence from the blog post printed earlier in this chapter as an arbitrary and realistic piece of data you might like to translate into an object graph:

> This morning I had the chance to get a tour of The Henry Ford Museum in Dearborn, MI, along with Dale Dougherty, creator of Make: and Makerfaire, and Marc Greuther, the chief curator of the museum.

The simplest possible triple that you might expect to distill from that sentence is ('I', 'get', 'tour'), but even if you got that back, it wouldn't convey that Dale Dougherty also got the tour, or that Mark Greuther was involved. The POS-tagged data should make it pretty clear that it's not quite so straightforward to arrive at any of those interpretations, either, because the sentence has a very rich structure:

```
[(u'This', 'DT'), (u'morning', 'NN'), (u'I', 'PRP'), (u'had', 'VBD'), (u'the', 'DT'),
(u'chance', 'NN'), (u'to', 'TO'), (u'get', 'VB'), (u'a', 'DT'), (u'tour', 'NN'),
(u'of', 'IN'), (u'The', 'DT'), (u'Henry', 'NNP'), (u'Ford', 'NNP'), (u'Museum', 'NNP'),
(u'in', 'IN'), (u'Dearborn', 'NNP'), (u',', ','), (u'MI', 'NNP'), (u',', ','),
(u'along', 'IN'), (u'with', 'IN'), (u'Dale', 'NNP'), (u'Dougherty', 'NNP'), (u',',
','), (u'creator', 'NN'), (u'of', 'IN'), (u'Make', 'NNP'), (u':', ':'), (u'and', 'CC'),
(u'Makerfaire', 'NNP'), (u',', ','), (u'and', 'CC'), (u'Marc', 'NNP'), (u'Greuther',
'NNP'), (u',', ','), (u'the', 'DT'), (u'chief', 'NN'), (u'curator', 'NN'), (u'of',
'IN'), (u'the', 'DT'), (u'museum', 'NN'), (u'.', '.')]
```

It's doubtful whether even a state-of-the-art solution would be capable of emitting meaningful triples in this case, given the complex nature of the predicate "had a chance to get a tour", and that the other actors involved in the tour are listed in a phrase appended to the end of the sentence. Strategies for constructing these triples are well outside the scope of this book, but in theory, you should be able to use reasonably accurate POS tagging information to take a good stab at it. The difficulty of this task was pointed out not to discourage you, but to provide a realistic view of the complexity of NLP in general so that you know what you're getting into when you decide to tackle the problem of computing triples for the general case. It can be a lot of work, but the results are well worth it.

All that said, the good news is that you can actually do a lot of interesting things by distilling just the entities from text and using them as the basis of analysis, as demonstrated earlier. You can very easily produce triples from text on a per-sentence basis, where the "predicate" of each triple is a notion of a generic relationship signifying that the subject and object "interacted" with one another. Example 8-7 is a refactoring of Example 8-5 that collects entities on a per-sentence basis, which could be quite useful for computing the interactions between entities using a sentence as a context window.

Example 8-7. Discovering interactions between entities (blogs_and_nlp__extract_interactions.py)

```
# -*- coding: utf-8 -*-

import sys
import nltk
import json

def extract_interactions(txt):
    sentences = nltk.tokenize.sent_tokenize(txt)
    tokens = [nltk.tokenize.word_tokenize(s) for s in sentences]
    pos_tagged_tokens = [nltk.pos_tag(t) for t in tokens]

    entity_interactions = []
    for sentence in pos_tagged_tokens:

        all_entity_chunks = []
        previous_pos = None
        current_entity_chunk = []

        for (token, pos) in sentence:

            if pos == previous_pos and pos.startswith('NN'):
                current_entity_chunk.append(token)
            elif pos.startswith('NN'):
                if current_entity_chunk != []:
                    all_entity_chunks.append((' '.join(current_entity_chunk),
                            pos))
                current_entity_chunk = [token]

            previous_pos = pos

        if len(all_entity_chunks) > 1:
            entity_interactions.append(all_entity_chunks)
        else:
            entity_interactions.append([])

    assert len(entity_interactions) == len(sentences)

    return dict(entity_interactions=entity_interactions,
                sentences=sentences)

if __name__ == '__main__':

    # Read in output from blogs_and_nlp__get_feed.py

    BLOG_DATA = sys.argv[1]
    blog_data = json.loads(open(BLOG_DATA).read())

    # Display selected interactions on a per-sentence basis

    for post in blog_data:

        post.update(extract_interactions(post['content']))
```

```
print post['title']
print '-' * len(post['title'])
for interactions in post['entity_interactions']:
    print '; '.join([i[0] for i in interactions])
print
```

The results from this listing, presented in Example 8-8, highlight something very important about the nature of unstructured data analysis: it's messy!

Example 8-8. Sample output from Example 8-7

```
The Louvre of the Industrial Age
---------------------------------
morning; chance; tour; Henry Ford Museum; Dearborn; MI; Dale Dougherty; creator;
Make; Makerfaire; Marc Greuther; chief curator

tweet; Louvre

"; Marc; artifact; museum; block; contains; Luther Burbank; shovel; Thomas Edison…

Luther Burbank; course; inventor; treasures; nectarine; Santa Rosa

Ford; farm boy; industrialist; Thomas Edison; friend

museum; Ford; homage; transformation; world

machines; steam; engines; coal; generators; houses; lathes; precision; lathes;
makerbot; century; ribbon glass machine; incandescent; lightbulbs; world; combine;
harvesters; railroad; locomotives; cars; airplanes; gas; stations; McDonalds;
restaurant; epiphenomena

Marc; eye; transformation; machines; objects; things

advances; engineering; materials; workmanship; design; years

years; visit; Detroit; museum; visit; Paris; Louvre; Rome; Vatican Museum; Florence;
Uffizi Gallery; St. Petersburg; Hermitage; Berlin

world; museums

Museum; Makerfaire Detroit

reach; Detroit; weekend

day; Makerfaire; day
```

A certain amount of noise in the results is almost inevitable, but realizing results that are highly intelligible and useful—even if they do contain a manageable amount of noise—is a very worthy aim. The amount of effort required to achieve pristine results that are nearly noise-free can be immense. In fact, in most situations, this is downright impossible because of the inherent complexity involved in natural language and the limitations of most currently available toolkits, such as NLTK. If you are able to make certain assumptions about the domain of the data or have expert knowledge of the

---

nature of the noise, you may be able to devise heuristics that are effective without risking an unacceptable amount of potential information loss. But it's a fairly difficult proposition.

Still, the interactions do provide a certain amount of "gist" that's valuable. For example, how closely would your interpretation of "morning; chance; tour; Henry Ford Museum; Dearborn; MI; Dale Dougherty; creator; Make; Makerfaire; Marc Greuther; chief curator" align with the meaning in the original sentence?

As was the case with our previous adventure in summarization, displaying markup that can be visually skimmed for inspection is also quite handy. A simple modification to the script's output is all that's necessary to produce the result shown in Figure 8-4 (see Example 8-9).

Example 8-9. Modification of script from Example 8-7 (blogs_and_nlp__extract_interactions_markedup_output.py)

```
# -*- coding: utf-8 -*-

import os
import sys
import nltk
import json
from blogs_and_nlp__extract_interactions import extract_interactions

HTML_TEMPLATE = """<html>
    <head>
        <title>%s</title>
        <meta http-equiv="Content-Type" content="text/html; charset=UTF-8"/>
    </head>
    <body>%s</body>
</html>"""

if __name__ == '__main__':

    # Read in output from blogs_and_nlp__get_feed.py

    BLOG_DATA = sys.argv[1]
    blog_data = json.loads(open(BLOG_DATA).read())

    # Marked up version can be written out to disk

    if not os.path.isdir('out/interactions'):
        os.makedirs('out/interactions')

    for post in blog_data:

        post.update(extract_interactions(post['content']))

        # Display output as markup with entities presented in bold text

        post['markup'] = []
```

```
for sentence_idx in range(len(post['sentences'])):

    s = post['sentences'][sentence_idx]
    for (term, _) in post['entity_interactions'][sentence_idx]:
        s = s.replace(term, '<strong>%s</strong>' % (term, ))

    post['markup'] += [s]

filename = post['title'] + '.entity_interactions.html'
f = open(os.path.join('out', 'interactions', filename), 'w')
html = HTML_TEMPLATE % (post['title'] + ' Interactions', ' '.join(post['markup']),)
f.write(html.encode('utf-8'))
f.close()

print >> sys.stderr, "Data written to", f.name
```

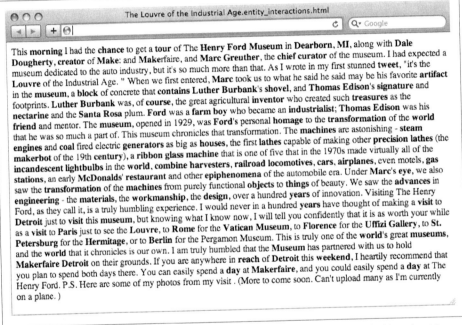

Figure 8-4. Sample HTML output that displays entities identified in the text in bold so that it's easy to visually skim the content for its key concepts

As a consideration for the "interested reader," it would be worthwhile to perform additional analyses to identify the sets of interactions for a larger body of text and to find co-occurrences in the interactions. You could also very easily adapt some of the Graphviz or Protovis output from Chapter 1 to visualize a graph of the interactions where edges don't necessary have any labels. The example file *http://github.com/ptwobrussell/ Mining-the-Social-Web/blob/master/python_code/introduction__retweet_visualization .py* would make a very good starting point.

Even without knowing the specific nature of the interaction, there's still a lot of value in just knowing the subject and the object. And if you're feeling ambitious and are comfortable with a certain degree of messiness and lack of precision, by all means you can attempt to fill in the missing verbs!

Quality of Analytics

When you've done a lot of data mining, you'll eventually want to start quantifying the quality of your analytics. This is especially the case with text mining. For example, if you began customizing the basic algorithm for extracting the entities from unstructured text, how would you know whether your algorithm was getting more or less performant with respect to the quality of the results? While you could manually inspect the results for a small corpus and tune the algorithm until you were satisfied with them, you'd still have a devil of a time determining whether your analytics would perform well on a much larger corpus or a different class of document altogether—hence, the need for a more automated process.

An obvious starting point is to randomly sample some documents and create a "golden set" of entities that you believe are absolutely crucial for a good algorithm to extract from them and use this list as the basis of evaluation. Depending on how rigorous you'd like to be, you might even be able to compute the *sample error* and use a statistical device called a confidence interval[5] to predict the *true error* with a sufficient degree of confidence for your needs.

However, what exactly is the calculation you should be computing based on the results of your extractor and golden set in order to compute accuracy? A very common calculation for measuring accuracy is called the *F1 score*, which is defined in terms of two concepts called *precision* and *recall*[6] as:

$$F = 2 \cdot \frac{\text{precision} \cdot \text{recall}}{\text{precision} + \text{recall}}$$

where:

$$\text{precision} = \frac{TP}{TP + FP}$$

---

5. Plenty of information regarding confidence intervals (*http://en.wikipedia.org/wiki/Confidence_interval*) is readily available online.

6. More precisely, F1 is said to be the *harmonic mean* of precision and recall, where the harmonic mean of any two numbers, x and y, is defined as:

$$H = 2 * \frac{x * y}{x + y}$$

You can read more about why it's the "harmonic" mean by reviewing the definition of a harmonic number (*http://en.wikipedia.org/wiki/Harmonic_number*).

and:

$$recall = \frac{TP}{TP + FN}$$

In the current context, precision is a measure of exactness that reflects "false positives," and recall is a measure of completeness that reflects "true positives." The following list clarifies the meaning of these terms in relation to the current discussion in case they're unfamiliar or confusing:

True positives (TP)
     Terms that were correctly identified as entities

False positives (FP)
     Terms that were identified as entities but should not have been

True negatives (TN)
     Terms that were not identified as entities and should not have been

False negatives (FN)
     Terms that were not identified as entities but should have been

Given that precision is a measure of exactness that quantifies false positives, it is defined as *precision = TP / (TP + FP)*. Intuitively, if the number of false positives is zero, the exactness of the algorithm is perfect and the precision yields a value of 1.0. Conversely, if the number of false positives is high and begins to approach or surpass the value of true positives, precision is poor and the ratio approaches zero. As a measure of completeness, recall is defined as *TP / (TP + FN)* and yields a value of 1.0, indicating perfect recall, if the number of false negatives is zero. As the number of false negatives increases, recall approaches zero. Note that by definition, F1 yields a value of 1.0 when precision and recall are both perfect, and approaches zero when both precision and recall are poor. Of course, what you'll find out in the wild is that it's generally a trade-off as to whether you want to boost precision or recall, because it's very difficult to have both. If you think about it, this makes sense because of the trade-offs involved with false positives and false negatives (see Figure 8-5).

To put all of this into perspective, let's consider the classic (by now anyway) sentence, "Mr. Green killed Colonel Mustard in the study with the candlestick" and assume that an expert has determined that the key entities in the sentence are "Mr. Green", "Colonel Mustard", "study", and "candlestick". Assuming your algorithm identified these four terms and only these four terms, you'd have 4 true positives, 0 false positives, 5 true negatives ("killed", "with", "the", "in", "the"), and 0 false negatives. That's perfect precision and perfect recall, which yields an F1 score of 1.0. Substituting various values into the precision and recall formulas is straightforward and a worthwhile exercise if this is your first time encountering these terms. For example, what would the precision, recall, and F1 score have been if your algorithm had identified "Mr. Green", "Colonel", "Mustard", and "candlestick"?

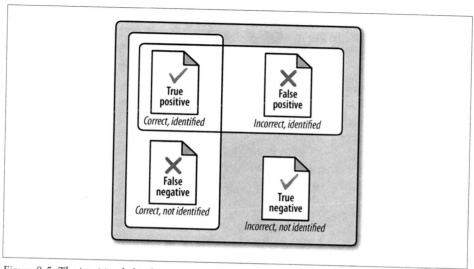

Figure 8-5. The intuition behind true positives, false positives, true negatives, and false negatives

As somewhat of an aside, you might find it interesting to know that many of the most compelling technology stacks used by commercial businesses in the NLP space use advanced statistical models to process natural language according to supervised learning algorithms. A *supervised learning algorithm* is essentially an approach in which you provide training samples of the form [(input1, output1), (input2, output2), ..., (inputN, outputN)] to a model such that the model is able to predict the tuples with reasonable accuracy. The tricky part is ensuring that the trained model generalizes well to inputs that have not yet been encountered. If the model performs well for training data but poorly on unseen samples, it's usually said to suffer from the problem of *overfitting* the training data. A common approach for measuring the efficacy of a model is called *cross-validation*. With this approach, a portion of the training data (say, one-third) is reserved exclusively for the purpose of testing the model, and only the remainder is used for training the model.

Closing Remarks

This chapter introduced the bare essentials of advanced unstructured data analytics, and demonstrated how to use NLTK to go beyond the sentence parsing that was introduced in Chapter 7, putting together the rest of an NLP pipeline and extraction entities from text. The field of computational linguistics is still quite nascent, and nailing the problem of NLP for most of the world's most commonly spoken languages is arguably the problem of the century. Push NLTK to its limits, and when you need more performance or quality, consider rolling up your sleeves and digging into some of the academic literature. It's admittedly a daunting task, but a truly worthy problem if you are interested in tackling it.

If you'd like to expand on the contents of this chapter, consider using NLTK's word-stemming tools to try to compute (entity, stemmed predicate, entity) tuples, building upon the code in Example 8-7. You might also look into WordNet (*http://wordnet .princeton.edu/*), a tool that you'll undoubtedly run into sooner rather than later, to discover additional meaning about the items in the tuples. If you find yourself with copious free time on your hands, consider taking a look at some of the many popular commenting APIs, such as DISQUS (*http://groups.google.com/group/disqus-dev/web/ api-1-1*), and try to incorporate the NLP techniques we've covered into the comments streams for blog posts. Crafting a WordPress plug-in that intelligently suggests tags based upon the entities that are extracted from a draft blog post would also be a great way to spend an evening or weekend.

## CHAPTER 9

Facebook: The All-in-One Wonder

From the standpoint of the social web, Facebook truly is an all-in-one wonder. Given that its more than 500 million users can update their public statuses to let their friends know what they're doing/thinking/etc., exchange lengthier messages in a fashion similar to emailing back and forth, engage in real-time chat, organize and share their photos, "check in" to physical locales, and do about a dozen other things via the site, it's not all that surprising that Facebook edged out Google (*http://techcrunch.com/2010/12/29/hitwise-facebook-overtakes-google-to-become-most-visited-website-in-2010/*) as the most visited website as 2010 came to a close. Figure 9-1 shows a chart that juxtaposes Google and Facebook visiting figures just in case there's any doubt in your mind. This is particularly exciting because where there are a lot of regular users, there's lots of interesting data. In this chapter, we'll take advantage of Facebook's incredibly powerful APIs for mining this data to discover your most connected friends, cluster your friends based on common interests, and get a quick indicator of what the people in your social network are talking about.

We'll start with a brief overview of common Facebook APIs, then quickly transition into writing some scripts that take advantage of these APIs so that we can analyze and visualize some of your social data. Virtually all of the techniques we've applied in previous chapters could be applied to your Facebook data, because the Facebook platform is so rich and diverse. As in most of the other chapters, we won't be able to cover all of the ground that could possibly be covered: a small tome could be devoted just to the many interesting applications and data-mining contraptions you could build on such a rich platform that gives you access to so many details about the people closest to you. As with any other rich developer platform, make sure that any techniques you apply from this chapter in production applications take into account users' privacy, and remember to review Facebook's developer principles and policies (*http://developers.facebook.com/policy/*) regularly so as to avoid any unexpected surprises when rolling out your application to the rest of the world.

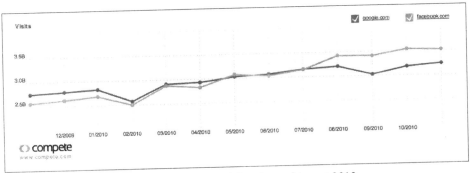

Figure 9-1. Total monthly visits of Facebook and Google as of August 2010

Tapping into Your Social Network Data

This section provides a brief overview of how to complete Facebook's OAuth 2.0 flow for a desktop application to get you an access token, then quickly transitions into some data-gathering exercises. To keep this chapter as simple as possible, we won't discuss building a Facebook application: there are plenty of tutorials online that can teach you how to do that, and introducing Facebook application development would require an overview of a server platform such as Google App Engine (GAE), since Facebook apps must be externally hosted in your own server environment. However, a GAE version of the scripts that are presented in this chapter is available for download at *http://github .com/ptwobrussell/Mining-the-Social-Web/tree/master/web_code/facebook_gae_demo _app* . It's easy to deploy and is a bona fide Facebook application that you can use as a starting point once you decide that you're ready to go down that path and convert your scripts into deployable apps.

From Zero to Access Token in Under 10 Minutes

As with any other OAuth-enabled app, to get started you'll need to acquire an application ID and secret to use for authorization, opt into the developer community, and create an "application." The following list summarizes the main steps, and some visual cues are provided in Figure 9-2:

- First, if you don't already have one, you'll need to set up a Facebook account. Just go to *http://facebook.com* and sign up to join the party.
- Next, you'll need to install the Developer application by visiting *http://www.face book.com/developers* and clicking through the request to install the application.
- Once the Developer application is installed, you can click the "Set Up New Application" button to create your application.

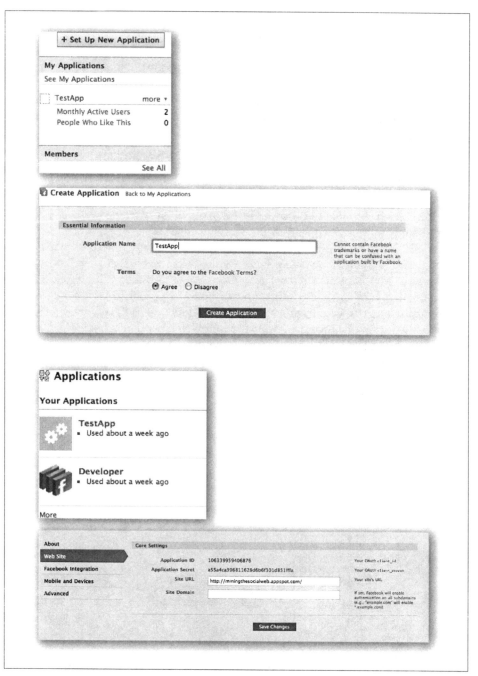

Figure 9-2. From top to bottom: a) the button you'll click from http://www.facebook.com/developers to set up a new application, b) the dialog you'll complete to give your app a name and acknowledge the terms of service, c) your application now appears in the list of applications, and d) your app's settings, including your OAuth 2.0 app ID and secret

- Once you've completed the security check, your app will have an ID and secret that you can use to complete the steps involved in Facebook's OAuth 2.0 implementation, and you'll be presented with a form that you'll need to fill out to specify your application's Web Site settings. Just enter the URL that you eventually plan to use for hosting your app as the Site URL and include the same domain as the Site Domain. Facebook uses your Web Site settings as part of the OAuth flow, and you'll receive an error message during the OAuth dance if they're not filled out appropriately.

It may not be obvious, but perhaps the simplest way for you to get back to your development application once you've left it is to just return to *http://facebook.com/develop ers* (requires a login).

With the basic details of application registration out of the way, the next step is writing a script that handles authentication and gets you an access token that you can use to access APIs. The overall flow for the process is actually a little simpler than what you've seen in previous chapters involving Twitter and LinkedIn. Our script will pop open a web browser, you'll sign into your Facebook account, and then it'll present a special code (your access token) that you'll copy/paste into a prompt so that it can be saved out to disk and used in future requests. Example 9-1 illustrates the process and is nothing more than a cursory implementation of the flow described in "Desktop Application Authentication" (*http://developers.facebook.com/docs/authentication/desktop*). A brief review of Facebook's authentication (*http://developers.facebook.com/docs/authentica tion/*) documentation may be helpful; refer back to "No, You Can't Have My Password" on page 86 if you haven't read it already. However, note that the flow implemented in Example 9-1 for a desktop application is a little simpler than the flow involved in authenticating a web app.

Example 9-1. Getting an OAuth 2.0 access token for a desktop app (facebook_login.py)

```
# -*- coding: utf-8 -*-

import os
import sys
import webbrowser
import urllib


def login():

    # Get this value from your Facebook application's settings

    CLIENT_ID = ''

    REDIRECT_URI = \
        'http://miningthesocialweb.appspot.com/static/facebook_oauth_helper.html'

    # You could customize which extended permissions are being requested on the login
    # page or by editing the list below. By default, all the ones that make sense for
    # read access as described on http://developers.facebook.com/docs/authentication/
```

```python
    # are included. (And yes, it would be probably be ridiculous to request this much
    # access if you wanted to launch a successful production application.)

    EXTENDED_PERMS = [
        'user_about_me',
        'friends_about_me',
        'user_activities',
        'friends_activities',
        'user_birthday',
        'friends_birthday',
        'user_education_history',
        'friends_education_history',
        'user_events',
        'friends_events',
        'user_groups',
        'friends_groups',
        'user_hometown',
        'friends_hometown',
        'user_interests',
        'friends_interests',
        'user_likes',
        'friends_likes',
        'user_location',
        'friends_location',
        'user_notes',
        'friends_notes',
        'user_online_presence',
        'friends_online_presence',
        'user_photo_video_tags',
        'friends_photo_video_tags',
        'user_photos',
        'friends_photos',
        'user_relationships',
        'friends_relationships',
        'user_religion_politics',
        'friends_religion_politics',
        'user_status',
        'friends_status',
        'user_videos',
        'friends_videos',
        'user_website',
        'friends_website',
        'user_work_history',
        'friends_work_history',
        'email',
        'read_friendlists',
        'read_requests',
        'read_stream',
        'user_checkins',
        'friends_checkins',
        ]

args = dict(client_id=CLIENT_ID, redirect_uri=REDIRECT_URI,
        scope=','.join(EXTENDED_PERMS), type='user_agent', display='popup'
        )
```

```
webbrowser.open('https://graph.facebook.com/oauth/authorize?'
                + urllib.urlencode(args))

# Optionally, store your access token locally for convenient use as opposed
# to passing it as a command line parameter into scripts...

access_token = raw_input('Enter your access_token: ')

if not os.path.isdir('out'):
    os.mkdir('out')

filename = os.path.join('out', 'facebook.access_token')
f = open(filename, 'w')
f.write(access_token)
f.close()

print >> sys.stderr, \
        "Access token stored to local file: 'out/facebook.access_token'"

    return access_token

if __name__ == '__main__':
    login()
```

One important detail you're probably wondering about is the definition of EXTEN
DED_PERMS, and a brief explanation is certainly in order. The first time you try to log in
to the application, it'll notify you that the application is requesting lots of *extended
permissions* so that you can have maximum flexibility in accessing the data that's available to you (Figure 9-3). The details of extended permissions are described in Facebook's authentication documentation (*http://developers.facebook.com/docs/authentica
tion/*), but the short story is that, by default, applications can only access some basic
data from user profiles—such as name, gender, and profile picture—and explicit permissions must be granted to access additional data. *The subtlety to observe here is that
you might be able to see certain details about your friends, such as things that they "like"
or activity on their walls through your normal Facebook account, but your app cannot
access these same details unless you have granted it explicit permission to do so.* In other
words, there's a difference between what you'll see in your friends' profiles when signed
in to facebook.com and the data you'll get back when requesting information through
the API. This is because it's Facebook (not you) who is exercising the platform to get
data when you're logged in to facebook.com, but it's you (as a developer) who is requesting data when you build your app.

> If your app does not request extended permissions to access data but
> tries to access it anyway, you may get back empty data objects as op-
> posed to an explicit error message.

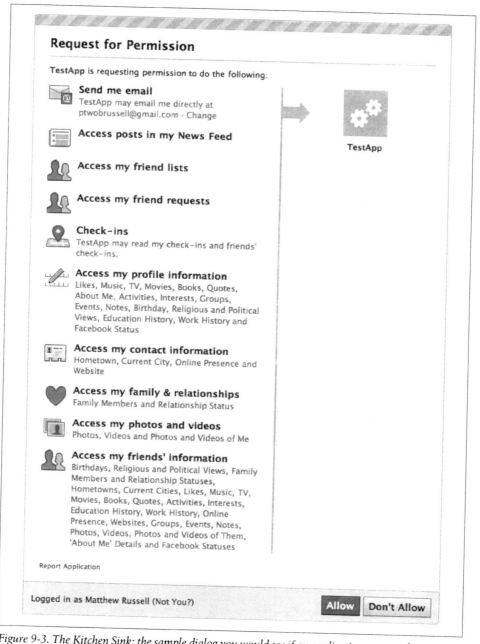

Figure 9-3. The Kitchen Sink: the sample dialog you would see if an application requested permission to access everything available to it

The Facebook platform's documentation is continually evolving, and they may not tell you everything you need to know about extended permissions. For example, it appears that in order to access religious or political information for friends (your friends_religion_politics extended permission), those friends must have your app installed and have explicitly authorized access to this data as well via their user_religion_politics extended permission.

Now, outfitted with a shiny new access token that has permissions to access all of your data, it's time to move on to more interesting things.

Facebook's Query APIs

As you've probably heard, the Facebook developer ecosystem is complex, continually evolving,[1] and filled with many twists and turns involving the most sophisticated privacy controls (*http://www.facebook.com/privacy/explanation.php*) the Web has ever seen. In addition to sporting a standard battery of REST APIs (*http://developers.facebook.com/docs/reference/rest/*) and a more advanced SQL-like language for querying data in a manner similar to SQL called Facebook Query Language (*http://developers.facebook.com/docs/reference/fql/*) (FQL), Facebook unveiled the Graph API and the Open Graph protocol (*http://opengraphprotocol.org*) (OGP) in April 2010 at the F8 conference. In short, OGP is a mechanism that enables you to make any web page an object in a rich social graph by injecting some RDFa (*http://www.w3.org/TR/xhtml-rdfa -primer/*) (more on this in a moment) metadata into the page, and the Graph API is a simple and intuitive mechanism for querying the graph. Each object has a particular type. At the time of this writing, the Graph API supports the following types of objects, as described in the Graph API Reference (*http://developers.facebook.com/docs/reference/ api/*):

Album
> A photo album

Application
> An individual application registered on the Facebook Platform

Checkin
> A check-in made through Facebook Places

Event
> A Facebook event

Group
> A Facebook group

---

1. It's a good idea to bookmark and keep an eye on the developer roadmap (*http://developers.facebook.com/ roadmap*) to stay up to date.

Link
> A shared link

Note
> A Facebook note

Page
> A Facebook page

Photo
> An individual photo

Post
> An individual entry in a profile's feed

Status Message
> A status message on a user's wall

Subscription
> An individual subscription from an application to get real-time updates for an object type

User
> A user profile

Video
> An individual video

The Graph API Reference (*http://developers.facebook.com/docs/reference/api/*) contains detailed documentation for each object type, describing the types of properties and connections you can expect to exist for each object.

Example 9-2 is the canonical example from the documentation that demonstrates how to turn the IMDB's page on *The Rock* into an object in the Open Graph protocol as part of an XHTML document that uses namespaces. These bits of metadata have great potential once realized at a massive scale, because they enable a URI like *http://www.imdb.com/title/tt0117500* to unambiguously represent any web page—whether it's for a person, company, product, etc.—in a machine-readable way and furthers the vision for a semantic web.

Example 9-2. Sample RDFa for the Open Graph protocol

```
<html xmlns:og="http://ogp.me/ns#">
<head>
<title>The Rock (1996)</title>
<meta property="og:title" content="The Rock" />
<meta property="og:type" content="movie" />
<meta property="og:url" content="http://www.imdb.com/title/tt0117500/" />
<meta property="og:image" content="http://ia.media-imdb.com/images/rock.jpg" />
...
</head>
...
</html>
```

When considering the possibilities with OGP, be forward-thinking and creative, but bear in mind that it's brand new and still evolving. As it relates to the semantic web and web standards in general, consternation about the use of "open" (*http://techcrunch .com/2010/04/23/facebook-open-graph/*) has surfaced and various kinks in the spec are still being worked out (*http://groups.google.com/group/open-graph-protocol/browse _thread/thread/cc03368ef0d12c1a*) It is essentially a single-vendor effort, and it's little more than on par with the capabilities of meta elements (*http://en.wikipedia.org/wiki/ Meta_element*) from the much earlier days of the Web. In effect, OGP is really more of a snowflake than a standard at this moment, but the potential is in place for that to change, and many exciting things may happen as the future unfolds and innovation takes place. We'll return to the topic of the semantic web in Chapter 10, where we briefly discuss its vast potential. Let's now turn back and hone in on how to put the Graph API to work by building a simple Facebook app to mine social data.

 Because of the titular similarity, it's easy to confuse Google's Social Graph API (*http://socialgraph-resources.googlecode.com/svn/trunk/sam ples/findyours.html*) with Facebook's Graph API, even though they are quite different.

At its core, the Graph API is incredibly simple: substitute an object's ID in the URI *http(s)://graph.facebook.com/ID* to fetch details about the object. For example, fetching the URL *http://graph.facebook.com/http://www.imdb.com/title/tt0117500* in your web browser would return the response in Example 9-3.

Example 9-3. A sample response for an Open Graph query to http://graph.facebook.com/http:// www.imdb.com/title/tt0117500

```
{
    "id": "114324145263104",
    "name": "The Rock (1996)",
    "picture": "http://profile.ak.fbcdn.net/hprofile-ak-snc4/hs344.snc4/41581...jpg",
    "link": "http://www.imdb.com/title/tt0117500/",
    "category": "Movie",
    "description": "Directed by Michael Bay.  With Sean Connery, Nicolas Cage, ...",
    "likes" : 3
}
```

If you inspect the source for the URL *http://www.imdb.com/title/tt0117500*, you'll find that fields in the response correspond to the data in the meta tags of the page, and this is no coincidence. The delivery of rich metadata in response to a simple query is the whole idea behind the way OGP is designed to work. Where it gets more interesting is when you explicitly request additional metadata for an object in the page by appending the query string parameter metadata=1 to the request. A sample response for the query *https://graph.facebook.com/114324145263104?metadata=1* is shown in Example 9-4.

Example 9-4. A sample response for an Open Graph query to http://graph.facebook.com/http://www.imdb.com/title/tt0117500?metadata=1 with the optional metadata included

```
{
    "id": "118133258218514",
    "name": "The Rock (1996)",
    "picture": "http://profile.ak.fbcdn.net/hprofile-ak-snc4/..._s.jpg",
    "link": "http://www.imdb.com/title/tt0117500",
    "category": "Movie",
    "website": "http://www.imdb.com/title/tt0117500",
    "description": "Directed by Michael Bay.  With Sean Connery, Nicolas Cage, ...",
    "likes": 3,
    "metadata": {
        "connections": {
            "feed": "http://graph.facebook.com/http://www.imdb.com/title/tt0117500/feed",
            "posts": "http://graph.facebook.com/http://www.imdb.com/title/tt0117500/posts",
            "tagged": "http://graph.facebook.com/http://www.imdb.com/title/tt0117500/tagged",
            "statuses": "http://graph.facebook.com/http://www.imdb.com/title/...",
            "links": "http://graph.facebook.com/http://www.imdb.com/title/tt0117500/links",
            "notes": "http://graph.facebook.com/http://www.imdb.com/title/tt0117500/notes",
            "photos": "http://graph.facebook.com/http://www.imdb.com/title/tt0117500/photos",
            "albums": "http://graph.facebook.com/http://www.imdb.com/title/tt0117500/albums",
            "events": "http://graph.facebook.com/http://www.imdb.com/title/tt0117500/events",
            "videos": "http://graph.facebook.com/http://www.imdb.com/title/tt0117500/videos"
        },
        "fields": [
            {
                "name": "id",
                "description": "The Page's ID. Publicly available. A JSON string."
            },
            {
                "name": "name",
                "description": "The Page's name. Publicly available. A JSON string."
            },
            {
                "name": "category",
                "description": "The Page's category. Publicly available. A JSON string."
            },
            {
                "name": "likes",
                "description": "\\* The number of users who like the Page..."
            }
        ]
    },
    "type": "page"
}
```

The items in `metadata.connections` are pointers to other nodes in the graph that you can crawl to get to other interesting bits of data. For example, you could follow the "photos" link to pull down photos associated with the movie, and potentially walk links associated with the photos to discover who posted them or see comments that might have been made about them. In case it hasn't already occurred to you, you are also an object in the graph. Try visiting the same URL prefix, but substitute in your own Facebook ID or username as the URL context and see for yourself. Given that you are the logical center of your own social network, we'll be revisiting this possibility at length throughout the rest of this chapter. The next section digs deeper into Graph API queries, and the section after it takes a closer look at FQL queries.

Exploring the Graph API one connection at a time

Facebook no longer maintains (*http://github.com/facebook/python-sdk/*) an official Python SDK for the Graph API; however, a community-fork of that same repository that appears to be actively maintained is available and can be easily installed by downloading and executing the standard `python setup.py install` command or, directly from GitHub with `pip` as follows: `pip install -e git+git://github.com/pythonforfa cebook/facebook-sdk.git#egg=git-latest` (keeping in mind that you may have to first `easy_install pip` if you don't already have it.) There are several nice examples (*https: //github.com/pythonforfacebook/facebook-sdk/tree/master/examples*) of how you could use this module to quickly get through the OAuth dance and build a full-blown Facebook app that's hosted on a platform like Google App Engine. We'll just be narrowing in on some particular portions of the `GraphAPI` class (defined in *facebook.py*), which we'll use in standalone scripts. A few of these methods follow:

- `get_object(self, id, **args)`
  Example: `get_object("me", metadata=1)`
- `get_objects(self, id, **args)`
  Example: `get_objects(["me", "some_other_id"], metadata=1)`
- `get_connections(self, id, connection_name, **args)`
  Example: `get_connections("me", "friends", metadata=1)`
- `request(self, path, args=None, post_args=None)`
  Example: `request("search", {"q" : "programming", "type" : "group"})`

 Unlike with other social networks, there don't appear to be clearly published guidelines about Facebook API rate limits. Although the availability of the APIs seems to be quite generous, you should still carefully design your application to use the APIs as little as possible and handle any/all error conditions, just to be on the safe side. The closest thing to guidelines you're likely to find as of late 2010 are developer discussions in forums (*http://forum.developers.facebook .net/viewtopic.php?pid=221976*).

The most common (and often, the only) keyword argument you'll probably use is `metadata=1`, in order to get back the connections associated with an object in addition to just the object details themselves. Take a look at Example 9-5, which introduces the `GraphAPI` class and uses its `get_objects` method to query for "programming groups". It relays an important characteristic about the sizes of the result sets you may get for many types of requests.

Example 9-5. Querying the Open Graph for "programming" groups (facebook__graph_query.py)

```
# -*- coding: utf-8 -*-

import sys
import json
import facebook
import urllib2
from facebook__login import login

try:
    ACCESS_TOKEN = open('out/facebook.access_token').read()
    Q = sys.argv[1]
except IOError, e:
    try:

        # If you pass in the access token from the Facebook app as a command line
        # parameter, be sure to wrap it in single quotes so that the shell
        # doesn't interpret any characters in it

        ACCESS_TOKEN = sys.argv[1]
        Q = sys.argv[2]
    except:
        print >> sys.stderr, \
            "Could not either find access token in 'facebook.access_token' or parse args."
        ACCESS_TOKEN = login()
        Q = sys.argv[1]

LIMIT = 100

gapi = facebook.GraphAPI(ACCESS_TOKEN)

# Find groups with the query term in their name

group_ids = []
i = 0
while True:
    results = gapi.request('search', {
        'q': Q,
        'type': 'group',
        'limit': LIMIT,
        'offset': LIMIT * i,
        })
    if not results['data']:
        break

    ids = [group['id'] for group in results['data'] if group['name'
        ].lower().find('programming') > -1]

    # once groups stop containing the term we are looking for in their name, bail out

    if len(ids) == 0:
        break
    group_ids += ids

    i += 1
```

```
if not group_ids:
    print 'No results'
    sys.exit()

# Get details for the groups

groups = gapi.get_objects(group_ids, metadata=1)

# Count the number of members in each group. The FQL API documentation at
# http://developers.facebook.com/docs/reference/fql/group_member hints that for
# groups with more than 500 members, we'll only get back a random subset of up
# to 500 members.

for g in groups:
    group = groups[g]
    conn = urllib2.urlopen(group['metadata']['connections']['members'])
    try:
        members = json.loads(conn.read())['data']
    finally:
        conn.close()
    print group['name'], len(members)
```

Sample results for the query for "programming" are presented in Example 9-6, and it's no coincidence that the upper bound of the result sets approaches 500. As the comment in the code notes, the FQL documentation states that when you query the group_mem ber table, your results will be limited to 500 total items. Unfortunately, the Graph API documentation is still evolving and, at the time of this writing, similar warnings are not documented (although they hopefully will be soon). In counting the members of groups, the takeaway is that you'll often be working with a reasonably sized random sample. "Visualizing Your Entire Social Network" on page 290 describes a different scenario in which a somewhat unexpected truncation of results occurs, and how to work around this by dispatching multiple queries.

Example 9-6. Sample results from Example 9-5

```
Graffiti Art Programming 492
C++ Programming 495
Basic Programming 495
Programming 215
C Programming 493
C programming language 492
Programming 490
ACM Programming Competitors 496
programming 494
COMPUTER PROGRAMMING 494
Programming with Python 494
Game Programming 494
ASLMU Programming 494
Programming 352
Programming 450
Programmation - Programming 480
```

A sample web application (*http://miningthesocialweb.appspot.com*) that encapsulates most of the example code from this chapter and uses the same basic pattern is hosted on GAE, if you'd like to take it for a spin before laying down some code of your own. Figure 9-4 illustrates the results of our sample query for "programming" groups. Recall that you can install and fully customize the GAE-powered Facebook app yourself if that's a better option for you than running scripts from a local console. In terms of productivity, it's probably best to develop with local scripts and then roll functionality into the GAE codebase once it's ready so as to maintain a speedy development cycle.

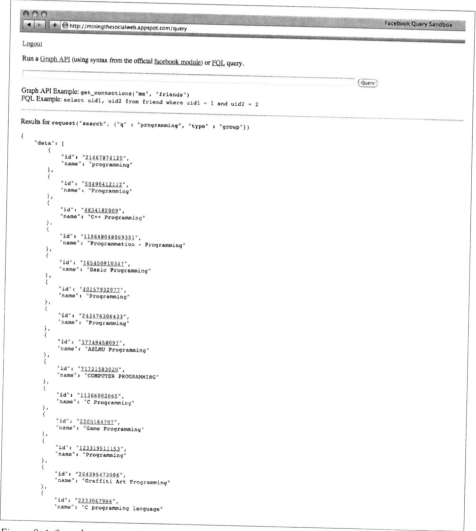

Figure 9-4. Sample query and results for "programming" groups—you can click on the links to crawl through to the next level of the graph

Slicing and dicing data with FQL

As you learned in the previous section, there's not much overhead involved in writing simple routines to interact with the Graph API, because objects in the graph are simple and you're passed URLs that you can use as-is to walk the object's connections. For more advanced types of queries or certain workflows, however, you may find FQL to be a better fit for the problem. Extensive FQL documentation exists online (*http:// developers.facebook.com/docs/reference/fql/*). I won't go into too much depth here since the online documentation is authoritative and constantly evolving with the platform, but the gist is predictable if you're familiar with basic SQL syntax. FQL queries have the form `select [fields] from [table] where [conditions]`, but various restrictions apply that prevent FQL from being anything more than a carefully selected small subset of SQL. For example, only one table name can appear in the `from` clause, and the conditions that can appear in the `where` clause are limited (but usually adequate) and must be marked as indexed fields in the FQL documentation. In terms of executing FQL queries on the Facebook platform at a 50,000-foot level, all that's necessary is to send your FQL queries to one of two API endpoints: *https://api.facebook.com/method/fql .query* or *https://api.facebook.com/method/fql.multiquery*. The difference between them is discussed next.

Example 9-7 illustrates a simple FQL query that fetches the names, genders, and relationship statuses of the currently logged-in user's friends.

Example 9-7. A nested FQL query that ties together user and connection data

```
select name, sex, relationship_status from user where uid in
    (select target_id from connection where source_id = me() and target_type = 'user')
```

This *nested query* works by first executing the subquery:

```
select target_id from connection where source_id = me() and target_type = 'user'
```

which produces a list of user ID values. The special `me()` directive is a convenient shortcut that corresponds to the currently logged-in user's ID, and the `connection` table is designed to enable queries where you are looking up the currently logged-in user's friends. Note that while most connections stored in the connection table (*http://devel opers.facebook.com/docs/reference/fql/connection*) are among users, other types of connections may exist among users and other object types, such as `'page'`, so the presence of a `target_type` filter is important. The outer query is then evaluated, which resolves to:

```
select name, sex, relationship_status from user where uid in ( ... )
```

from the user (*http://developers.facebook.com/docs/reference/fql/user*) table. The FQL user (*http://developers.facebook.com/docs/reference/fql/user*) table has a wealth of information that can enable many interesting types of analysis on your friends. Check it out.

The general form of the results set from this FQL query is shown in Example 9-8.

Example 9-8. Sample FQL results query

```
[
    {
        "name": "Matthew Russell",
        "relationship_status": "Married",
        "sex": "male"
    },
    ...
]
```

An FQL *multiquery* works in essentially the same way, except that you can run multiple queries and reference query results as table names using the hash symbol. Example 9-9 is an equivalent FQL multiquery to the nested query shown previously.

Example 9-9. An FQL multiquery that ties together user and connections data

```
{
    "name_sex_relationships" : "select name, sex, relationship_status from user \
        where uid in (select target_id from #ids)",
    "ids" : "select target_id from connection where source_id = me() \
        and target_type = 'user'"
}
```

Note that whereas the single list of objects is returned from the nested query, the results from both components of the FQL multiquery are returned, as Example 9-10 demonstrates.

Example 9-10. Sample FQL multiquery results

```
[
    {
        "fql_result_set": [
            {
                "target_id": -1
            },
            ...
        ],
        "name": "ids"
    },
    {
        "fql_result_set": [
            {
                "name": "Matthew Russell",
                "relationship_status": "Married",
                "sex": "male"
            },
            ...
        ],
        "name" : "name_sex_relationships"
    }
]
```

Programmatically, the query logic is pretty simple and can be wrapped up into a small class. Example 9-11 demonstrates an FQL class that can take a query from the command line and run it. Here are a couple of sample queries that you could try running:

```
$ python facebook__fql_query.py 'select name, sex, relationship_status
from user where uid in (select target_id from connection
where source_id = me())'
```

```
$ python facebook__fql_query.py '{"name_sex_relationships" : "select name,
sex, relationship_status from user where uid in (select target_id from #ids)",
"ids" : "select target_id from connection where source_id = me()"}'
```

Example 9-11. Encapsulating FQL queries with a small Python class abstraction (facebook__fql_query.py)

```python
# -*- coding: utf-8 -*-

import sys
from urllib import urlencode
import json
import urllib2
from facebook__login import login


class FQL(object):

    ENDPOINT = 'https://api.facebook.com/method/'

    def __init__(self, access_token=None):
        self.access_token = access_token

    def _fetch(cls, url, params=None):
        conn = urllib2.urlopen(url, data=urlencode(params))
        try:
            return json.loads(conn.read())
        finally:
            conn.close()

    def query(self, q):
        if q.strip().startswith('{'):
            return self.multiquery(q)
        else:
            params = dict(query=q, access_token=self.access_token, format='json')
            url = self.ENDPOINT + 'fql.query'
            return self._fetch(url, params=params)

    def multiquery(self, q):
        params = dict(queries=q, access_token=self.access_token, format='json')
        url = self.ENDPOINT + 'fql.multiquery'
        return self._fetch(url, params=params)


# Sample usage...
```

```
if __name__ == '__main__':
    try:
        ACCESS_TOKEN = open('out/facebook.access_token').read()
        Q = sys.argv[1]
    except IOError, e:
        try:

            # If you pass in the access token from the Facebook app as a command line
            # parameter, be sure to wrap it in single quotes so that the shell
            # doesn't interpret any characters in it. You may also need to escape
            # the # character

            ACCESS_TOKEN = sys.argv[1]
            Q = sys.argv[2]
        except IndexError, e:
            print >> sys.stderr, \
                "Could not either find access token in 'facebook.access_token'
                    or parse args."
            ACCESS_TOKEN = login()
            Q = sys.argv[1]

    fql = FQL(access_token=ACCESS_TOKEN)
    result = fql.query(Q)
    print json.dumps(result, indent=4)
```

The sample GAE app (*http://miningthesocialweb.appspot.com/*) provided as part of this chapter's source code detects and runs FQL queries as well as Graph API queries, so you can use it as a sort of playground to experiment with FQL. With some basic infrastructure for executing queries now in place, the next section walks through some use cases for building data-powered visualizations and UI widgets.

Visualizing Facebook Data

This section lays down some templates and introduces some good starting points for analyzing and visualizing Facebook data. If you've been following along, you now have the basic tools you need to get at anything the platform can provide. The types of exercises we'll explore in this section include:

- Visualizing all the mutual friendships in your social network
- Visualizing the mutual friendships within specific groups and for arbitrary criteria, such as gender
- Building a simple data-driven game that challenges you to identify friends based on where they live now and their hometowns

The list of possibilities goes on and on, and with the necessary boilerplate intact, you'll have no trouble customizing the scripts we'll write to solve a variety of other problems.

Visualizing Your Entire Social Network

This section works through the process of fetching friendship information from your Facebook account and visualizing it in interesting and useful ways, with an angle toward using the JavaScript InfoVis Toolkit (*http://thejit.org/*) (JIT). The JIT offers some great example templates that can easily be customized to whip up an interactive visualization.

Visualizing with RGraphs

An RGraph (*http://en.wikipedia.org/wiki/Radial_tree*)[2] is a network visualization that organizes the display by laying out nodes in concentric circles, starting from the center. RGraphs are available in many visualization toolkits, including the JIT. It's worth taking a moment to explore the JIT's RGraph examples to familiarize yourself with the vast possibilities it offers.

 Protovis' Node-Link tree (*http://vis.stanford.edu/protovis/ex/tree.html*), that was introduced in "Hierarchical and k-Means Clustering" on page 185, is essentially the same core visualization, but the JIT is also worth having on hand and provides more interactive out-of-the-box examples that you might find easier to pick up and run with. Having options is not a bad thing.

As you well know by this point in the book, most of the effort involved in connecting the dots between fetching raw Facebook data and visualizing it is the munging that's necessary to get it into a format that's consumable by the visualization. One of the data formats accepted by the RGraph and other JIT graph visualizations is a predictable JSON structure that consists of a list of objects, each of which represents a node and its adjacencies. Example 9-12 conveys the general concept so that you have an idea of our end goal. This structure shows that "Matthew" is connected to three other nodes identified by ID values as defined by `adjacencies`. The `data` field provides additional information about "Matthew" and, in this case, conveys a human-readable label about his three connections along with what appears to be a normalized popularity score.

Example 9-12. Sample input that can be consumed by the JIT's RGraph visualization

```
[
    {
        "adjacencies": [
            "2",
            "3",
            "4",
            ...
        ],
```

2. Also commonly called radial graphs, radial trees, radial maps, and many other things that don't necessarily include the term "radial" or "radius."

```
    "data": {
        "connections": "Mark<br>Luke<br>John",
        "normalized_popularity": 0.0079575596817,
        "sex" : "male"
    },
    "id": "1",
    "name": "Matthew"
},
...
]
```

Let's compute the *mutual friendships* that exist within your network of friends and visualize this data as an RGraph. In other words, we'll be computing all the friendships that exist within your friend network, which should give us a good idea of who is popular in your network as well as who isn't so very well connected. There's potential value in knowing both of these things. At an abstract level, we just need to run a few FQL queries to gather the data: one to calculate the IDs of your friends, another to connect your friends in the graph, and a final query to grab any pertinent details we'd like to lace into the graph, such as names, birthdays, etc. The following queries convey the idea:

Get friend IDs

```
q = "select target_id from connection where \
    source_id = me() and target_type = 'user'"
my_friends = [str(t['target_id']) for t in fql.query(q)]
```

Calculate mutual friendships

```
q = "select uid1, uid2 from friend where uid1 in (%s) and uid2 in (%s)" %
    (",".join(my_friends), ",".join(my_friends),)
mutual_friendships = fql(q)
```

Grab additional details to decorate the graph

```
q = "select uid, first_name, last_name, sex from user where uid in (%s)" %
    (",".join(my_friends),)
names = dict([(unicode(u["uid"]), u["first_name"] + " " +
    u["last_name"][0] + ".") for u in fql(q)])
```

That's the gist, but there is one not-so-well-documented detail that you may discover: if you pass even a modest number of ID values into the second step when computing the mutual friendships, you'll find that you get back arbitrarily truncated results. This isn't completely unwarranted, given that you are asking the Facebook platform to execute what's logically an $O(n^2)$ operation on your behalf (a nested loop that compares all your friends to one another), but the fact that you get back any data at all instead of receiving an error message kindly suggesting that you pass in less data might catch you off guard.

 Just like everything else in the world, the Facebook platform isn't perfect. Give credit where credit is due, and file bug reports as needed.

Fortunately, there's a fix for this situation: just batch in the data through several queries and aggregate it all. In code, that might look something like this:

```
mutual_friendships = []
N = 50
for i in range(len(my_friends)/N +1):
    q = "select uid1, uid2 from friend where uid1 in (%s) and uid2 in (%s)" % \
        (",".join(my_friends), ",".join(my_friends[i*N:(i+1)*N]),)
    mutual_friendships += fql(query=q)
```

Beyond that potential snag, the rest of the logic involved in producing the expected output for the RGraph visualization is pretty straightforward and follows the pattern just discussed. Example 9-13 demonstrates a working example that puts it all together and produces additional JavaScript output that can be used for other analysis.

Example 9-13. Harvesting and munging friends data for the JIT's RGraph visualization (facebook__get_friends_rgraph.py)

```
# -*- coding: utf-8 -*-

import os
import sys
import json
import webbrowser
import shutil
from facebook__fql_query import FQL
from facebook__login import login

HTML_TEMPLATE = '../web_code/jit/rgraph/rgraph.html'
OUT = os.path.basename(HTML_TEMPLATE)

try:
    ACCESS_TOKEN = open('out/facebook.access_token').read()
except IOError, e:
    try:

        # If you pass in the access token from the Facebook app as a command line
        # parameter, be sure to wrap it in single quotes so that the shell
        # doesn't interpret any characters in it. You may also need to escape
        # the # character

        ACCESS_TOKEN = sys.argv[1]
    except IndexError, e:
        print >> sys.stderr, \
            "Could not either find access token in 'facebook.access_token' or parse args."
        ACCESS_TOKEN = login()

fql = FQL(ACCESS_TOKEN)

# get friend ids

q = \
    'select target_id from connection where source_id = me() and target_type =\'user\''
my_friends = [str(t['target_id']) for t in fql.query(q)]
```

```
# now get friendships among your friends. note that this api appears to return
# arbitrarily truncated results if you pass in more than a couple hundred friends
# into each part of the query, so we perform (num friends)/N queries and aggregate
# the results to try and get complete results
# Warning: this can result in a several API calls and a lot of data returned that
# you'll have to process

mutual_friendships = []
N = 50
for i in range(len(my_friends) / N + 1):
    q = 'select uid1, uid2 from friend where uid1 in (%s) and uid2 in (%s)' \
        % (','.join(my_friends), ','.join(my_friends[i * N:(i + 1) * N]))
    mutual_friendships += fql.query(q)


# get details about your friends, such as first and last name, and create an accessible map
# note that not every id will necessarily information so be prepared to handle those cases
# later

q = 'select uid, first_name, last_name, sex from user where uid in (%s)' \
    % (','.join(my_friends), )
results = fql.query(q)
names = dict([(unicode(u['uid']), u['first_name'] + ' ' + u['last_name'][0] + '.'
            ) for u in results])

sexes = dict([(unicode(u['uid']), u['sex']) for u in results])

# consolidate a map of connection info about your friends.

friendships = {}
for f in mutual_friendships:
    (uid1, uid2) = (unicode(f['uid1']), unicode(f['uid2']))
    try:
        name1 = names[uid1]
    except KeyError, e:
        name1 = 'Unknown'
    try:
        name2 = names[uid2]
    except KeyError, e:
        name2 = 'Unknown'

    if friendships.has_key(uid1):
        if uid2 not in friendships[uid1]['friends']:
            friendships[uid1]['friends'].append(uid2)
    else:
        friendships[uid1] = {'name': name1, 'sex': sexes.get(uid1, ''),
                             'friends': [uid2]}

    if friendships.has_key(uid2):
        if uid1 not in friendships[uid2]['friends']:
            friendships[uid2]['friends'].append(uid1)
    else:
        friendships[uid2] = {'name': name2, 'sex': sexes.get(uid2, ''),
                             'friends': [uid1]}

# Emit JIT output for consumption by the visualization
```

```
jit_output = []
for fid in friendships:
    friendship = friendships[fid]
    adjacencies = friendship['friends']

    connections = '<br>'.join([names.get(a, 'Unknown') for a in adjacencies])
    normalized_popularity = 1.0 * len(adjacencies) / len(friendships)
    sex = friendship['sex']
    jit_output.append({
        'id': fid,
        'name': friendship['name'],
        'data': {'connections': connections, 'normalized_popularity'
                : normalized_popularity, 'sex': sex},
        'adjacencies': adjacencies,
        })

# Wrap the output in variable declaration and store into
# a file named facebook.rgraph.js for consumption by rgraph.html

if not os.path.isdir('out'):
    os.mkdir('out')

# HTML_TEMPLATE references some dependencies that we need to
# copy into out/

shutil.rmtree('out/jit', ignore_errors=True)

shutil.copytree('../web_code/jit',
                'out/jit')

html = open(HTML_TEMPLATE).read() % (json.dumps(jit_output),)
f = open(os.path.join(os.getcwd(), 'out', 'jit', 'rgraph', OUT), 'w')
f.write(html)
f.close()

print >> sys.stderr, 'Data file written to: %s' % f.name

# Write out another file that's standard JSON for additional analysis
# and potential use later (by facebook_sunburst.py, for example)

json_f = open(os.path.join('out', 'facebook.friends.json'), 'w')
json_f.write(json.dumps(jit_output, indent=4))
json_f.close()

print 'Data file written to: %s' % json_f.name

# Open up the web page in your browser

webbrowser.open('file://' + f.name)
```

 If you have a very large friends network, you may need to filter the friends you visualize by a meaningful criterion that makes the results more manageable. See Example 9-16 for an example of filtering by group by interactively prompting the user for input.

If all goes according to plan, you'll have an interactive visualization of your entire social network on hand. Figure 9-5 illustrates what this might look like for a very large social network. The next section introduces some techniques for paring down the output to something more manageable.

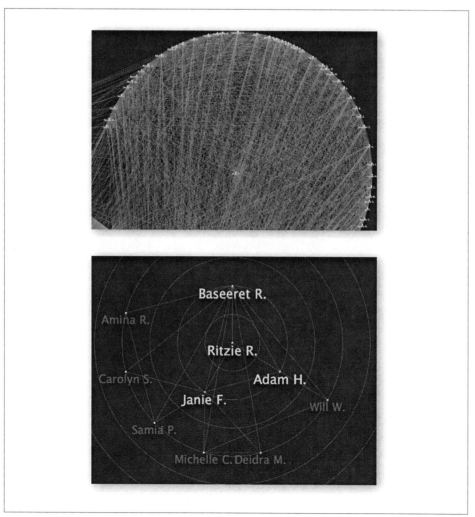

Figure 9-5. A sample RGraph computed with Facebook data for a fairly large network of 500+ people, per Example 9-13 (top), and a much smaller RGraph of mutual friends who are members of a particular group, as computed by Example 9-16 later in this chapter (bottom)

Visualizing with a Sunburst

A Sunburst visualization (*http://www.cc.gatech.edu/gvu/ii/sunburst/*) is a space-filling visualization for rendering hierarchical structures such as trees. It gets its name from its resemblance to sunburst images, such as the one on the flag of the Imperial Japanese Army, as shown in Figure 9-6. The JIT's Sunburst (*http://thejit.org/static/v20/Jit/Exam ples/Sunburst/example2.html*) implementation is as powerful as it is beautiful. Like the RGraph, it consumes a simple graph-like JSON structure and exposes handy event handlers. But while a Sunburst visualization consumes essentially the same data structure as an RGraph, its layout yields additional insight almost immediately. You can easily see the relative degrees of intermediate nodes in the tree based upon how much area is taken up by each layer in the Sunburst. For example, it's not difficult to adapt the JIT's example implementation to render a useful interactive visualization of even a quite large social network, along with what relative share of the population fits a given criterion, such as gender. In fact, that's exactly what is depicted in Figure 9-6. It shows that about two-thirds of the members of this social network are female, with each of those members appearing adjacent to that portion of the sector.

Example 9-14 demonstrates how to take the sample output from Example 9-13 and transform it such that it can be consumed by a JIT Sunburst that segments your social network by gender. Note that the `$angularWidth` parameter is a relative measure of the angle used by each level of the tree, and is used by the script to scale the sector (*http:// en.wikipedia.org/wiki/Circular_sector*). The area that each friend consumes is scaled according to their popularity and provides an intuitive visual indicator. Friends who have privacy settings in place to prevent API access to gender information will have gender values of an empty string and are simply ignored.[3] The interactive version of the visualization also displays a tool tip that shows a person's mutual friends whenever you hover over a slice, as shown in Figure 9-6, so that you can narrow in on people and get more specific.

Example 9-14. Harvesting and munging data for the JIT's Sunburst visualization (facebook__sunburst.py)

```
# -*- coding: utf-8 -*-

import os
import sys
import json
import webbrowser
import shutil
from copy import deepcopy

HTML_TEMPLATE = '../web_code/jit/sunburst/sunburst.html'
OUT = os.path.basename(HTML_TEMPLATE)
```

---

3. Also commonly called "pie piece."

```
# Reuses out/facebook.friends.json written out by
# facebook__get_friends_rgraph.py
DATA = sys.argv[1]
data = json.loads(open(DATA).read())

# Define colors to be used in the visualization
# for aesthetics

colors = ['#FF0000', '#00FF00', '#0000FF']

# The primary output to collect input

jit_output = {
    'id': 'friends',
    'name': 'friends',
    'data': {'$type': 'none'},
    'children': [],
    }

# A convenience template

template = {
    'id': 'friends',
    'name': 'friends',
    'data': {'connections': '', '$angularWidth': 1, '$color': ''},
    'children': [],
    }

i = 0
for g in ['male', 'female']:

    # Create a gender object

    go = deepcopy(template)
    go['id'] += '/' + g
    go['name'] += '/' + g
    go['data']['$color'] = colors[i]

    # Find friends by each gender

    friends_by_gender = [f for f in data if f['data']['sex'] == g]
    for f in friends_by_gender:

        # Load friends into the gender object

        fo = deepcopy(template)
        fo['id'] = f['id']
        fo['name'] = f['name']
        fo['data']['$color'] = colors[i % 3]
        fo['data']['$angularWidth'] = len(f['adjacencies'])  # Rank by global popularity
        fo['data']['connections'] = f['data']['connections']  # For the tooltip

        go['children'].append(fo)
```

```
    jit_output['children'].append(go)
    i += 1

# Emit the output expected by the JIT Sunburst

if not os.path.isdir('out'):
    os.mkdir('out')

# HTML_TEMPLATE references some dependencies that we need to
# copy into out/

shutil.rmtree('out/jit', ignore_errors=True)

shutil.copytree('../web_code/jit',
                'out/jit')


html = open(HTML_TEMPLATE).read() % (json.dumps(jit_output),)
f = open(os.path.join(os.getcwd(), 'out', 'jit', 'sunburst', OUT), 'w')
f.write(html)
f.close()

print 'Data file written to: %s' % f.name

# Open up the web page in your browser

webbrowser.open('file://' + f.name)
```

Although the sample implementation only groups friends by gender and popularity, you could produce a consumable JSON object that's representative of a tree with multiple levels, where each level corresponds to a different criterion. For example, you could visualize first by gender, and then by relationship status to get an intuitive feel for how those two variables correlate in your social network.

Visualizing with spreadsheets (the old-fashioned way)

Although you might be envisioning yourself creating lots of sexy visualizations with great visual appeal in the browser, it'a far more likely that you'll want to visualize data the old-fashioned way: in a spreadsheet. Assuming you saved the JSON output that powered the RGraph in the previous section into a local file, you could very easily crunch the numbers and produce a simple CSV format that you can load into a spreadsheet to quickly get the gist of what the distribution of your friendships looks like— i.e., a histogram showing the popularity of each of the friends in your social network. Example 9-15 demonstrates how to quickly transform the data into a readily consumable CSV format.

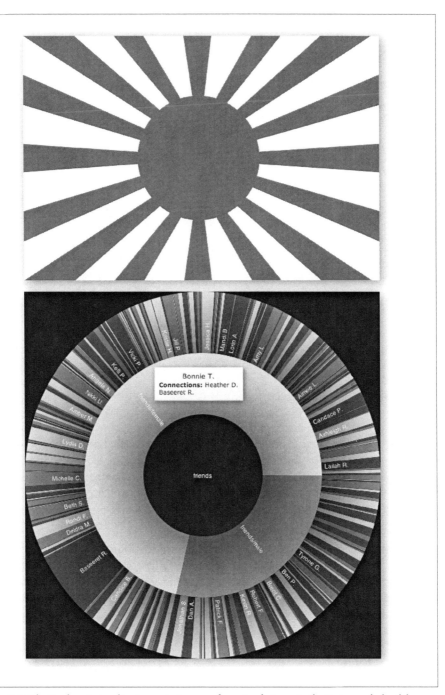

Figure 9-6. The Sunburst visualization gets its name from its obvious similarity to symbols of the sun, like that on the flag of the Japanese Imperial Army (top). This particular visualization demonstrates that about 2/3 of the friends network is female and about 1/3 is male (bottom).

Example 9-15. Exporting data so that it can easily be loaded into a spreadsheet for analysis (facebook__popularity_spreadsheet.py)

```
# -*- coding: utf-8 -*-

import os
import sys
import json
import operator

# Reuses out/facebook.friends.json written out by
# facebook__get_friends_rgraph.py
DATA = open(sys.argv[1]).read()
data = json.loads(DATA)

popularity_data = [(f['name'], len(f['adjacencies'])) for f in data]
popularity_data = sorted(popularity_data, key=operator.itemgetter(1))

csv_data = []
for d in popularity_data:
    csv_data.append('%s\t%s' % (d[0], d[1]))

if not os.path.isdir('out'):
    os.mkdir('out')

filename = os.path.join('out', 'facebook.spreadsheet.csv')
f = open(filename, 'w')
f.write('\n'.join(csv_data))
f.close()

print 'Data file written to: %s' % filename
```

Visualizing the data as a histogram yields interesting results because it provides a quick image of how connected people are in the network. For example, if the network were perfectly connected, the distribution would be flat. In Figure 9-7, you can see that the second most popular person in the network has around half as many connections as the most popular person in the network, and the rest of the relationships in the network roughly follow a Zipf-like distribution[4] with a long tail that very closely fits to a logarithmic trendline.

A logarithmic distribution isn't all that unexpected for a fairly large and diverse social network. It's inevitable that there will be a few highly connected individuals, with the majority of folks having relatively few connections with one another compared to the most popular individuals. In line with the Pareto principle, or the 80-20 rule (*http://en .wikipedia.org/wiki/Pareto_principle*), in this instance, we might say that "20% of the people have 80% of the friends."

---

4. This concept was introduced in "Data Hacking with NLTK" on page 205.

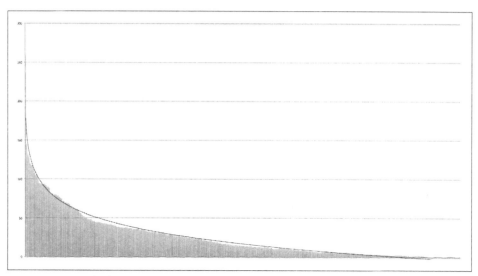

Figure 9-7. Sample distribution of popularity in a Facebook friends network with a logarithmic trendline (names omitted to protect the innocent)

Visualizing Mutual Friendships Within Groups

The sample implementation provided in Example 9-13 attempts to visualize all the mutual friendships in your social network. If you are running it in a modern browser with good support for the canvas element, the JIT holds up surprisingly well for even huge graphs. A click handler is included in the sample implementation: it displays the selected node's connections and a normalized popularity score (calculated as the number of connections divided by the total number of connections in your network) below the graph. Viewing your entire friend network is surely interesting, but sooner rather than later you'll want to filter your friends by some meaningful criteria and analyze smaller graphs.

There are lots of great filtering options available if your objective is to build out a nice user interface around a small web app, but we'll take the simplest possible approach and filter the JSON output produced from Example 9-13 according to a specifiable group criterion. Groups are the most logical starting point, and Example 9-16 demonstrates how to implement this additional functionality. An advantage of filtering the output from your global friendship network is that you'll retain the complete "connec tions" data for the rest of the network, so you'll still be able to keep track of what other friends a person is connected to even if those friends aren't in the group. Keep in mind that the possibilities for additional group analysis are vast: you could analyze whether your male friends are more connected than your female friends, perform clique analysis as described in "Clique Detection and Analysis" on page 110, or any number of other possibilities.

Example 9-16. Harvesting and munging data to visualize mutual friends with a particular group (facebook__filter_rgraph_output_by_group.py)

```
# -*- coding: utf-8 -*-

import os
import sys
import json
import facebook
import webbrowser
import shutil
from facebook__fql_query import FQL
from facebook__login import login

HTML_TEMPLATE = '../web_code/jit/rgraph/rgraph.html'
OUT = os.path.basename(HTML_TEMPLATE)

# Reuses out/facebook.friends.json written out by
# facebook__get_friends_rgraph.py

DATA = sys.argv[1]
rgraph = json.loads(open(DATA).read())

try:
    ACCESS_TOKEN = open('out/facebook.access_token').read()
except IOError, e:
    try:

        # If you pass in the access token from the Facebook app as a command line
        # parameter, be sure to wrap it in single quotes so that the shell
        # doesn't interpret any characters in it. You may also need to escape
        # the # character.

        ACCESS_TOKEN = sys.argv[2]
    except IndexError, e:
        print >> sys.stderr, \
            "Could not either find access token in 'facebook.access_token' or parse args."
        ACCESS_TOKEN = login()

gapi = facebook.GraphAPI(ACCESS_TOKEN)

groups = gapi.get_connections('me', 'groups')

# Display groups and prompt the user

for i in range(len(groups['data'])):
    print '%s) %s' % (i, groups['data'][i]['name'])

choice = int(raw_input('Pick a group, any group: '))
gid = groups['data'][choice]['id']

# Find the friends in the group

fql = FQL(ACCESS_TOKEN)
q = \
```

```
    """select uid from group_member where gid = %s and uid in
(select target_id from connection where source_id = me() and target_type = 'user')
""" \
    % (gid, )

uids = [u['uid'] for u in fql.query(q)]

# Filter the previously generated output for these ids

filtered_rgraph = [n for n in rgraph if n['id'] in uids]

# Trim down adjancency lists for anyone not appearing in the graph.
# Note that the full connection data displayed as HTML markup
# in "connections" is still preserved for the global graph.

for n in filtered_rgraph:
    n['adjacencies'] = [a for a in n['adjacencies'] if a in uids]

if not os.path.isdir('out'):
    os.mkdir('out')

# HTML_TEMPLATE references some dependencies that we need to
# copy into out/

shutil.rmtree('out/jit', ignore_errors=True)

shutil.copytree('../web_code/jit',
                'out/jit')

html = open(HTML_TEMPLATE).read() % (json.dumps(filtered_rgraph),)
f = open(os.path.join(os.getcwd(), 'out', 'jit', 'rgraph', OUT), 'w')
f.write(html)
f.close()

print 'Data file written to: %s' % f.name

# Open up the web page in your browser

webbrowser.open('file://' + f.name)
```

A sample graph for a group who attended the same elementary school is illustrated in Figure 9-5.

It would no doubt be interesting to compare the connectedness of different types of groups, identify which friends participate in the most groups to which you also belong, etc. But don't spend all of your time in one place; the possibilities are vast.

If you're using a modern browser that supports the latest and greatest canvas element, you may be able to adapt the following JavaScript code to save your graph as an image:

```
//grab the canvas element
var canvas = document.getElementById("infovis-canvas");
//now prompt a file download
window.location = canvas.toDataURL("image/png");
```

Where Have My Friends All Gone? (A Data-Driven Game)

There are a number of interesting variables that you could correlate for analysis, but everyone loves a good game every once in a while. This section lays the foundation for a simple game you can play to see how well you know your friends, by grouping them such that their hometowns and current locations are juxtaposed. We'll be reusing the tree widget from "Intelligent clustering enables compelling user experiences" on page 183 as part of this exercise, and most of the effort will be put into the grunt work required to transform data from an FQL query into a suitable format. Because the grunt work is mostly uninteresting cruft, we'll save some trees by displaying only the FQL query and the final format. As always, the full source is available online at *http://github.com/ptwobrussell/Mining-the-Social-Web/blob/master/python_code/linke din__get_friends_current_locations_and_hometowns.py*.

The FQL query we'll run to get the names, current locations, and hometowns is simple and should look fairly familiar to previous FQL queries:

```
q = """select name, current_location, hometown_location from user where uid in
    (select target_id from connection where source_id = me())"""
results = fql(query=q)
```

Example 9-17 shows the final format that feeds the tree widget once you've invested the sweat equity in massaging it into the proper format, and Example 9-18 shows the Python code to generate it.

Example 9-17. Target JSON that needs to be produced for consumption by the Dojo tree widget

```
{
    "items": [
        {
            "name": " Alabama (2)",
            "children": [
                {
                    "state": " Alabama",
                    "children": [
                        {
                            "state": " Tennessee",
                            "name": "Nashville, Tennessee (1)",
                            "children": [
                                {
                                    "name": "Joe B."
                                }
                            ]
                        }
                    ],
                    "name": "Prattville, Alabama (1)",
                    "num_from_hometown": 1
                }
            ]
        },
```

```
{
    "name": " Alberta (1)",
    "children": [
        {
            "state": " Alberta",
            "children": [
                {
                    "state": " Alberta",
                    "name": "Edmonton, Alberta (1)",
                    "children": [
                        {
                            "name": "Gina F."
                        }
                    ]
                }
            ],
            "name": "Edmonton, Alberta (1)",
            "num_from_hometown": 1
        }
    ]
},
...
],
"label": "name"
}
```

The final widget ends up looking like Figure 9-8, a hierarchical display that groups your friends first by where they are currently located and then by their hometowns. In Figure 9-8, Jess C. is currently living in Tuscaloosa, AL but grew up in Princeton, WV. Although we're correlating two harmless variables here, this exercise helps you quickly determine where most of your friends are located and gain insight into who has migrated from his hometown and who has stayed put. It's not hard to imagine deviations that are more interesting or faceted displays that introduce additional variables, such as college attended, professional affiliation, or marital status.

A simple FQL query is all that it took to fetch the essential data, but there's a little work involved in rolling up data items to populate the hierarchical tree widget. The source code for the tree widget itself is identical to that in "Intelligent clustering enables compelling user experiences" on page 183, and all that's necessary in order to visualize the data is to capture it into a file and point the tree widget to it. A fun improvement to the user experience might be integrating Google Maps with the widget so that you can quickly bring up locations you're unfamiliar with on a map. Adding age and gender information into this display could also be interesting if you want to dig deeper or take another approach to clustering. Emitting some KML in a fashion similar to that described in "Geographically Clustering Your Network" on page 193 and visualizing it in Google Earth might be another possibility worth considering, depending on your objective.

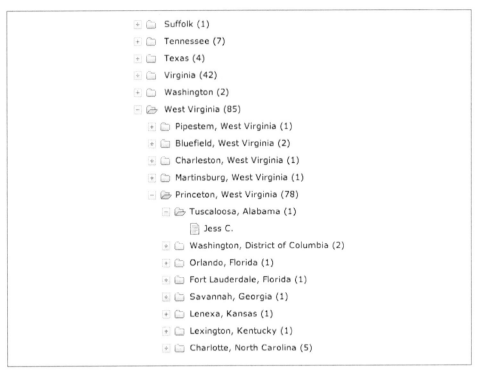

Figure 9-8. How well do you know your friends? Find out by playing the smash hit, "Where are they now?", a game that's just as informative as it is fun!

Example 9-18. Harvesting data and computing the target JSON as displayed in Example 9-17 (facebook__get_friends_current_locations_and_hometowns.py)

```python
import sys
import json
import facebook
from facebook__fql_query import FQL
from facebook__login import login

try:
    ACCESS_TOKEN = open("facebook.access_token").read()
except IOError, e:
    try:
        # If you pass in the access token from the Facebook app as a command-line
        # parameter, be sure to wrap it in single quotes so that the shell
        # doesn't interpret any characters in it. You may also need to escape
        # the # character.
        ACCESS_TOKEN = sys.argv[1]
    except IndexError, e:
        print >> sys.stderr, "Could not either find access token" + \
            in 'facebook.access_token' or parse args. Logging in..."
        ACCESS_TOKEN = login()
```

```
# Process the results of the following FQL query to create JSON output suitable for
# consumption by a simple hierarchical tree widget:

fql = FQL(ACCESS_TOKEN)

q = \
    """select name, current_location, hometown_location from user where uid in
        (select target_id from connection where source_id = me() and target_type =
            'user')"""
results = fql.query(q)

# First, read over the raw FQL query and create two hierarchical maps that group
# people by where they live now and by their hometowns. We'll simply tabulate
# frequencies, but you could easily grab additional data in the FQL query and use it
# for many creative situations.

current_by_hometown = {}
for r in results:
    if r['current_location'] != None:
        current_location = r['current_location']['city'] + ', ' \
            + r['current_location']['state']
    else:
        current_location = 'Unknown'

    if r['hometown_location'] != None:
        hometown_location = r['hometown_location']['city'] + ', ' \
            + r['hometown_location']['state']
    else:
        hometown_location = 'Unknown'

    if current_by_hometown.has_key(hometown_location):
        if current_by_hometown[hometown_location].has_key(current_location):
            current_by_hometown[hometown_location][current_location] += \
                [r['name']]
        else:
            current_by_hometown[hometown_location][current_location] = \
                [r['name']]
    else:
        current_by_hometown[hometown_location] = {}
        current_by_hometown[hometown_location][current_location] = \
            [r['name']]

# There are a lot of different ways you could slice and dice the data now that
# it's in a reasonable data structure. Let's create a hierarchical
# structure that lends itself to being displayed as a tree.

items = []
for hometown in current_by_hometown:
    num_from_hometown = sum([len(current_by_hometown[hometown][current])
                            for current in current_by_hometown[hometown]])
    name = '%s (%s)' % (hometown, num_from_hometown)
    try:
        hometown_state = hometown.split(',')[1]
    except IndexError:
        hometown_state = hometown
```

```
        item = {'name': name, 'state': hometown_state,
                'num_from_hometown': num_from_hometown}

    item['children'] = []
    for current in current_by_hometown[hometown]:
        try:
            current_state = current.split(',')[1]
        except IndexError:
            current_state = current

        item['children'].append({'name': '%s (%s)' % (current,
                                len(current_by_hometown[hometown][current])),
                                'state': current_state, 'children'
                                : [{'name': f[:f.find(' ') + 2] + '.'}
                                for f in
                                current_by_hometown[hometown][current]]})

        # Sort items alphabetically by state. Further roll-up by state could
        # be done here if desired.

    item['children'] = sorted(item['children'], key=lambda i: i['state'])
    items.append(item)

# Optionally, roll up outer-level items by state to create a better user experience
# in the display. Alternatively, you could just pass the current value of items in
# the final statement that creates the JSON output for smaller data sets.

items = sorted(items, key=lambda i: i['state'])
all_items_by_state = []
grouped_items = []
current_state = items[0]['state']
num_from_state = items[0]['num_from_hometown']
for item in items:
    if item['state'] == current_state:
        num_from_state += item['num_from_hometown']
        grouped_items.append(item)
    else:
        all_items_by_state.append({'name': '%s (%s)' % (current_state,
                num_from_state), 'children': grouped_items})
        current_state = item['state']
        num_from_state = item['num_from_hometown']
        grouped_items = [item]
all_items_by_state.append({'name': '%s (%s)' % (current_state,
                        num_from_state), 'children': grouped_items})

# Finally, emit output suitable for consumption by a hierarchical tree widget

print json.dumps({'items': all_items_by_state, 'label': 'name'},
indent=4)
```

Visualizing Wall Data As a (Rotating) Tag Cloud

As with any other source of unstructured data, analyzing the language used on your wall or in your news feed can be an interesting proposition. There are a number of tag cloud widgets that you can find on the Web, and they all take the same input—essentially, a frequency distribution. But why visualize data with an ordinary tag cloud when you could use a customizable and interactive tag cloud? Recall that there just so happens to be a quite popular open source rotating tag cloud called WP-Cumulus (*http://code.google.com/p/word-cumulus-goog-vis/wiki/UserGuide*) that puts on quite a nice show.[5] All that's needed to put it to work is to produce the simple input format that it expects, and feed that input format into a template with the standard HTML boilerplate in it. For brevity, the boilerplate won't be repeated here. See *http://github .com/ptwobrussell/Mining-the-Social-Web/blob/master/web_code/dojo/facebook.cur rent_locations_and_hometowns.html*.

Example 9-19 presents some minimal logic to grab several pages of news data and compute a simple JSON structure that's a list of [`term, URL, frequency`] tuples that can be fed into an HTML template. We'll pass in empty strings for the URL portion of those tuples, but with a little extra work, you could introduce additional logic that maintains a map of which terms appeared in which posts so that the terms in the tag cloud could point back to source data. Note that since we're fetching multiple pages of data from the Graph API in this example, we've simply opted to interface directly with the API endpoint for your Facebook wall (*http://www.facebook.com/help/?page= 820*).

Example 9-19. Harvesting and munging data for visualization as a WP-Cumulus tag cloud (facebook__tag_cloud.py)

```
# -*- coding: utf-8 -*-

import os
import sys
import urllib2
import json
import webbrowser
import nltk
from cgi import escape
from facebook__login import login

try:
    ACCESS_TOKEN = open('out/facebook.access_token').read()
except IOError, e:
    try:

        # If you pass in the access token from the Facebook app as a command line
        # parameter, be sure to wrap it in single quotes so that the shell doesn't
        # interpret any characters in it. You may also need to escape the # character
```

---

5. It was introduced in "Visualizing Tweets with Tricked-Out Tag Clouds" on page 158.

```
        ACCESS_TOKEN = sys.argv[1]
    except IndexError, e:
        print >> sys.stderr, \
            "Could not find local access token or parse args. Logging in..."
        ACCESS_TOKEN = login()

BASE_URL = 'https://graph.facebook.com/me/home?access_token='
HTML_TEMPLATE = '../web_code/wp_cumulus/tagcloud_template.html'
OUT_FILE = 'out/facebook.tag_cloud.html'
NUM_PAGES = 5
MIN_FREQUENCY = 3
MIN_FONT_SIZE = 3
MAX_FONT_SIZE = 20

# Loop through the pages of connection data and build up messages

url = BASE_URL + ACCESS_TOKEN
messages = []
current_page = 0
while current_page < NUM_PAGES:
    data = json.loads(urllib2.urlopen(url).read())
    messages += [d['message'] for d in data['data'] if d.get('message')]
    current_page += 1
    url = data['paging']['next']

# Compute frequency distribution for the terms

fdist = nltk.FreqDist([term for m in messages for term in m.split()])

# Customize a list of stop words as needed

stop_words = nltk.corpus.stopwords.words('english')
stop_words += ['&', '.', '?', '!']

# Create output for the WP-Cumulus tag cloud and sort terms by freq along the way

raw_output = sorted([[escape(term), '', freq] for (term, freq) in fdist.items()
                    if freq > MIN_FREQUENCY and term not in stop_words],
                    key=lambda x: x[2])

# Implementation adapted from
# http://help.com/post/383276-anyone-knows-the-formula-for-font-s

min_freq = raw_output[0][2]
max_freq = raw_output[-1][2]


def weightTermByFreq(f):
    return (f - min_freq) * (MAX_FONT_SIZE - MIN_FONT_SIZE) / (max_freq
            - min_freq) + MIN_FONT_SIZE


weighted_output = [[i[0], i[1], weightTermByFreq(i[2])] for i in raw_output]
```

```
# Substitute the JSON data structure into the template

html_page = open(HTML_TEMPLATE).read() % (json.dumps(weighted_output), )

f = open(OUT_FILE, 'w')
f.write(html_page)
f.close()

print 'Date file written to: %s' % f.name

# Open up the web page in your browser

webbrowser.open('file://' + os.path.join(os.getcwd(), OUT_FILE))
```

Figure 9-9 shows some sample results. The data for this tag cloud was collected during a Boise State versus Virginia Tech football game. Not surprisingly, the most common word in news feeds is "I". All in all, that's not a lot of effort to produce a quick visualization of what people are talking about on your wall, and you could easily extend it to get the gist of any other source of textual data. If you want to pursue automatic construction of a tag cloud with interesting content, however, you might want to consider incorporating some of the more advanced filtering and NLP techniques introduced earlier in the book. This way, you're specifically targeting terms that are likely to be entities as opposed to performing simple frequency analysis. Recall that Chapter 8 provided a fairly succinct overview of how you might go about accomplishing such an objective.

Closing Remarks

You can literally do just about anything social that you can imagine on Facebook, and the vast amounts of data that it exposes through powerful APIs provide huge opportunities for creating smart and amazing data-driven applications. The cursory treatment we've given the Facebook platform in this chapter doesn't even scratch the surface of the possibilities, but it hopefully has given you a lot of tools that you can use to dig deeper and perhaps become the creator of the next great (data-driven) Facebook app.

As a further exercise, you could consider visualizing the unstructured text on your friends' walls or group walls with a tag cloud, but applying the kinds of entity-centric analytics that were introduced in Chapter 8 instead of using the trivial tokenization scheme we used in this chapter. It could also be interesting to dig into the structured data available via the Graph API to discover the chattiest person in your network based on the number of overall statuses or comments that your friends post. Another great idea would be to try to cluster your friends based on what they *Like*, and then analyze those preferences in a pivot table (*http://en.wikipedia.org/wiki/Pivot_table*) or graph them.

Figure 9-9. A rotating tag cloud that's highly customizable and requires very little effort to get up and running

## CHAPTER 10

The Semantic Web: A Cocktail Discussion

While the previous chapters attempted to provide an overview of the social web and motivate you to get busy hacking on data, it seems appropriate to wrap up with a brief postscript on the semantic web. This short discussion makes no attempt to regurgitate the reams of interesting mailing list discussions, blog posts, and other sources of information that document the origin of the Web, how it has revolutionized just about everything in our lives in under two decades, and how the semantic web has always been a part of that vision. It does, however, aim to engage you in something akin to a cocktail discussion that, while glossing over a lot of the breadth and depth of these issues, hopefully excites you about the possibilities that lie ahead.

An Evolutionary Revolution?

Let's start out by dissecting the term "semantic web." Given that the Web is all about sharing information and that a working definition of *semantics* is "enough meaning to result in an action,"[1] it's not a very big leap to deduce that the semantic web is mostly about representing knowledge in a very meaningful way. But let's take that one step further and not assume that it's a human who is consuming the information that's represented. Let's consider the possibilities that could be realized if information were shared in a fully *machine-understandable way*—a way that is unambiguous enough that a reasonably sophisticated user agent like a web robot could extract, interpret, and use the information to make important decisions. Some steps have been made in this direction: for instance, we discussed how microformats already make this possible for certain domains in Chapter 2, and in Chapter 9 we looked at how Facebook is aggressively bootstrapping an explicit graph construct into the Web with its Open Graph

---

1. As defined in *Programming the Semantic Web* (*http://oreilly.com/catalog/9780596153823/*) , by Toby Segaran, Jamie Taylor, and Colin Evans (O'Reilly).

protocol. But before we get too pie-in-the-sky, let's back up for just a moment and reflect on how we got to where we are right now.

The Internet is just a network of networks,[2] and what's very fascinating about it from a technical standpoint is how layers of increasingly higher-level protocols build on top of lower-level protocols to ultimately produce a fault-tolerant worldwide computing infrastructure. In our online activity, we rely on dozens of protocols every single day, without even thinking about it. However, there is one ubiquitous protocol that is hard not to think about explicitly from time to time: HTTP, the prefix of just about every URL that you type into your browser, the enabling protocol for the extensive universe of hypertext documents (HTML pages), and the links that glue them all together into what we know as the Web. But as you've known for a long time, the Web isn't just about hypertext; it includes various embedded technologies such as JavaScript, Flash, and emerging HTML5 assets such as audio and video streams. All of that rich interaction makes the term "hypertext" sound a little antiquated, doesn't it?

The notion of a cyberworld of documents, platforms, and applications that we can interact with via modern-day browsers (including ones on mobile or tablet devices) over HTTP is admittedly fuzzy, but it's probably pretty close to what most people think of when they hear the term "the Web." To a degree, the motivation behind the Web 2.0 thought process that emerged back in 2004 was to more precisely define the increasingly blurry notion of exactly what the Web was and what it was becoming. Along those lines, some folks think of the Web as it existed from its inception until the present era of highly interactive web applications and user collaboration as being *Web 1.0*, the current era of Rich Internet Applications (RIAs) and collaboration as the *Web 2.x* era, and the era of semantic karma that's yet to come as *Web 3.0* (see Table 10-1). At present, there's no real consensus about what Web 3.0 really means, but most discussions of the subject generally include the phrase "semantic web" and the notion of information being consumed and acted upon by machines in ways that are not yet possible at web scale. For example, it's still very difficult for machines to extract and make inferences about the facts contained in documents available online. Keyword searching and heuristics can certainly provide listings of very relevant search results, but human intelligence is still required to interpret and synthesize the information in the documents themselves. Whether Web 3.0 and the semantic web are really the same thing is open for debate; however, it's generally accepted that the term *semantic web* refers to a web that's much like the one we already know and love, but that has evolved to the point where machines can extract and *act on* the information contained in documents at a granular level.

2. *Inter-net* literally implies "mutual or cooperating networks."

Table 10-1. *Various manifestations/eras of the Web and their virtues*

Manifestation/era	Virtues
Internet	Application protocols such as SMTP, FTP, BitTorrent, HTTP, etc.
Web 1.0	Mostly static HTML pages and hyperlinks
Web 2.0	Platforms, collaboration, rich user experiences
Social web (Web 2.x ???)	People and their virtual and real-world social connections and activities
Web 3.0 (the semantic web)	Prolific amounts of machine-understandable content

Man Cannot Live on Facts Alone

The semantic web's fundamental construct for representing knowledge is called a *triple*, which is a highly intuitive and very natural way of expressing a fact. As an example, the sentence we've considered on many previous occasions—"Mr. Green killed Colonel Mustard in the study with the candlestick"—expressed as a triple might be something like *(Mr. Green, killed, Colonel Mustard)*, where the constituent pieces of that triple refer to the subject, predicate, and object of the sentence. The Resource Description Framework (RDF) is the semantic web's model for defining and enabling the exchange of triples. RDF is highly extensible in that while it provides a basic foundation for expressing knowledge, it can also be used to define specialized vocabularies called *ontologies* that provide precise semantics for modeling specific domains. More than a passing mention of specific semantic web technologies such as RDF (*http://www.w3.org/RDF/*), RDFa (*http://www.w3.org/TR/xhtml-rdfa-primer/*), RDF Schema (*http://www.w3.org/TR/rdf-schema/*), and OWL (*http://www.w3.org/TR/owl2-overview/*) would be well out of scope here at the eleventh hour, but we will work through a high-level example that attempts to explain some of the hype around the semantic web in general.

Open-World Versus Closed-World Assumptions

One interesting difference between the way inference works in logic programming languages such as Prolog[3] as opposed to in other technologies, such as the RDF stack, is whether they make *open-world* or *closed-world* assumptions about the universe. Logic programming languages such as Prolog and most traditional database systems assume a closed world, while RDF technology generally assumes an open world. In a closed world, everything that you haven't been explicitly told about the universe should be considered false, whereas in an open world, everything you don't know is arguably more appropriately handled as being undefined (another way of saying "unknown"). The distinction is that reasoners that assume an open world will *not* rule out

---

3. You're highly encouraged to check out a bona fide logic-based programming language like Prolog that's written in a paradigm designed specifically so that you can represent knowledge and deduce new information from existing facts. GNU Prolog (*http://www.gprolog.org/*) is a fine place to start.

interpretations that include facts that are not explicitly stated in a knowledge base, whereas reasoners that assume the closed world of the Prolog programming language or most database systems *will* rule out facts that are not explicitly stated. Furthermore, in a system that assumes a closed world merging contradictory knowledge would generally trigger an error, while a system assuming an open world may try to make new inferences that somehow reconcile the contradictory information. As you might imagine, open-world systems are quite flexible and can lead to some very interesting conundrums; the potential can become especially pronounced when disparate knowledge bases are merged.

Intuitively, you might think of it like this: systems predicated upon closed-world reasoning assume that the data they are given is complete, and they are typically non-monotonic in the sense that it is not the case that every previous fact (explicit or inferred) will still hold when new ones are added. In contrast, open-world systems make no such assumption about the completeness of their data and are monotonic. As you might imagine, there is substantial debate about the merits of making one assumption versus the other. As someone interested in the semantic web, you should at least be aware of the issue. As the matter specifically relates to RDF, official guidance from the W3C documentation states:[4]

> To facilitate operation at Internet scale, RDF is an open-world framework that allows anyone to make statements about any resource. In general, it is not assumed that complete information about any resource is available. RDF does not prevent anyone from making assertions that are nonsensical or inconsistent with other statements, or the world as people see it. Designers of applications that use RDF should be aware of this and may design their applications to tolerate incomplete or inconsistent sources of information.

You might also check out Peter Patel-Schneider and Ian Horrocks' "Position Paper: A Comparison of Two Modelling Paradigms in the Semantic Web" (*http://www2006.org/ programme/files/xhtml/4015/4015-patel-schneider/4015-patel-schneider-xhtml.html*) if you're interested in pursuing this topic further. Whether you decide to dive into this topic right now, keep in mind that the data that's available on the Web is incomplete, and that making a closed-world assumption (i.e., considering all unknown information emphatically false) will entail severe consequences sooner rather than later.

Inferencing About an Open World with FuXi

Foundational languages such as RDF Schema and OWL are designed so that precise vocabularies can be used to express facts such as the triple *(Mr. Green, killed, Colonel Mustard)* in a machine-readable way, and this is a necessary but not sufficient condition for the semantic web to be fully realized. Generally speaking, once you have a set of facts, the next step is to perform *inference* over the facts and draw conclusions that follow from the facts. The concept of formal inference dates back to at least ancient Greece with Aristotle's syllogisms, and the obvious connection to how machines can

4. See *http://www.w3.org/TR/rdf-concepts/*.

take advantage of it has not gone unnoticed by researchers interested in artificial intelligence for the past 50 or so years. The Java-based landscape that's filled with enterprise-level options such as Jena (*http://jena.sourceforge.net/*) and Sesame (*http://www.openrdf.org/*) certainly seems to be where most of the heavyweight action resides, but fortunately, we do have a couple of solid options to work with in Python.

One of the best Pythonic options capable of inference that you're likely to encounter is FuXi (*http://code.google.com/p/fuxi/*). FuXi is a powerful logic-reasoning system for the semantic web that uses a technique called forward chaining (*http://en.wikipedia.org/wiki/Forward_chaining*) to deduce new information from existing information by starting with a set of facts, deriving new facts from the known facts by applying a set of logical rules, and repeating this process until a particular conclusion can be proved or disproved or there are no more new facts to derive. The kind of forward chaining that FuXi delivers is said to be both *sound*, because any new facts that are produced are true, and *complete*, because any facts that are true can eventually be proven. A full-blown discussion of propositional and first-order logic could easily fill a book; if you're interested in digging deeper, the classic text *Artificial Intelligence: A Modern Approach* by Stuart Russell and Peter Norvig (Prentice Hall) is probably the most comprehensive resource.

To demonstrate the kinds of inferencing capabilities a system such as FuXi can provide, let's consider the famous example of Aristotle's syllogism[5] in which you are given a knowledge base that contains the facts "Socrates is a man" and "All men are mortal," which allows you to deduce that "Socrates is mortal." While this problem may seem too trivial, keep in mind that the same deterministic algorithms that produce the new fact that "Socrates is mortal" work the very same way when there are significantly more facts available—and those new facts may produce additional new facts, which produce additional new facts, and so on. For example, consider a slightly more complex knowledge base containing a few additional facts:

- Socrates is a man
- All men are mortal
- Only gods live on Mt Olympus
- All mortals drink whisky
- Chuck Norris lives on Mt Olympus

If presented with the given knowledge base and then posed the question, "Does Socrates drink whisky?", you would first have to deduce the fact that "Socrates is mortal" before you could deduce the follow-on fact that "Socrates drinks whisky." To illustrate how all of this would work in code, consider the same knowledge base now expressed in Notation3 (*http://www.w3.org/DesignIssues/Notation3*) (N3), as shown in Example 10-1. N3 is a simple yet powerful syntax that expresses facts and rules in RDF.

---

5. In modern parlance, a syllogism is more commonly called an "implication."

While there are many different formats for expressing RDF, many semantic web tools choose N3 because its readability and expressiveness make it accessible.

Example 10-1. A small knowledge base expressed with Notation3

```
#Assign a namespace for logic predicates
@prefix log: <http://www.w3.org/2000/10/swap/log#> .

#Assign a namespace for the vocabulary defined in this document
@prefix : <MiningTheSocialWeb#> .

#Socrates is a man
:Socrates a :Man.

@forAll :x .

#All men are mortal: Man(x) => Mortal(x)
{ :x a :Man } log:implies { :x a :Mortal } .

#Only gods live at Mt Olympus: Lives(x, MtOlympus) <=> God(x)
{ :x :lives :MtOlympus } log:implies { :x a :god } .
{ :x a :god } log:implies { :x :lives :MtOlympus } .

#All mortals drink whisky: Mortal(x) => Drinks(x, whisky)
{ :x a :Man } log:implies { :x :drinks :whisky } .

#Chuck Norris lives at Mt Olympus: Lives(ChuckNorris, MtOlympus)
:ChuckNorris :lives :MtOlympus .
```

Running FuXi with the `--ruleFacts` option tells it to parse the facts from the input source that you can specify with the `--rules` option and to accumulate additional facts from the source. You should see output similar to that shown in Example 10-2 if you run FuXi from the command line. Note that FuXi should appear in your path after you `easy_install fuxi`.

Example 10-2. Results of running FuXi from the command line on the knowledge base in Example 10-1

```
$ FuXi --rules=foo.n3 --ruleFacts

@prefix _7: <file:///Users/matthew/MiningTheSocialWeb#>.
@prefix rdf: <http://www.w3.org/1999/02/22-rdf-syntax-ns#>.

 _7:ChuckNorris a _7:god.

 _7:Socrates a _7:Mortal;
    _7:drinks _7:whisky.
```

The output of the program tells us a few things that weren't explicitly stated in the initial knowledge base: Chuck Norris is a god, Socrates is a mortal, and Socrates drinks whisky. Although deriving these facts may seem obvious to most human beings, it's quite another story for a machine to have derived them—and that's what makes things exciting.

It should be noted that the careless assertion of facts about Chuck Norris (even in the context of a sample knowledge base) could prove harmful to your health or to the life of your computer.[6] You have been duly warned.

If this simple example excites you, by all means, dig further into FuXi and the potential the semantic web holds. The semantic web is arguably much more advanced and complex than the social web, and investigating it is certainly a very worthy pursuit—especially if you're excited about the possibilities that inference brings to social data.

Hope

While the intentional omission of discussion of the semantic web throughout the bulk of this short book may have created the impression of an arbitrary and rigid divide between the social and semantic webs, the divide is actually quite blurry and constantly in flux. It is very likely the case that the undeniable proliferation of social data on the Web, combined with initiatives such as the microformats published by parties ranging from the Food Network to LinkedIn, Facebook's Open Graph protocol, and the creative efforts of data hackers such as yourself are greatly accelerating the realization of a semantic web that may not be all that different from the one that's been so overinflated with hype over the past 15 years. The proliferation of social data has the potential to be a great catalyst for the development of a semantic web that will enable agents to make nontrivial actions on our behalf. We're not there yet, but be hopeful! Or, to put it another way, at least consider the wise words of Epicurus, who perhaps said it best: "Don't spoil what you have by desiring what you don't have; but remember that what you now have was once among the things only hoped for."

6. See *http://www.chucknorrisfacts.com*.

Index

Symbols

3D graph visualization, interactive, 116
80-20 rule (Pareto principle), xiv, 300
@ (at symbol), beginning Twitter usernames, 11

A

access token (OAuth) for Facebook desktop app, 272–278
access token for Facebook application, 272
ActivePython, 1
address-book data, exporting LinkedIn connections as, 169
agglomerative clustering, 185
Ajax toolkits, 183
analytics, quality of (entity-centric analysis), 267–269
API calls, Twitter rate limits on, 11
Aristotle, syllogisms, 317
association metrics, 175, 230
authentication, 84
  (see also OAuth)
  Facebook desktop application, 274
authorization (see OAuth)
"The Automatic Creation of Literature Abstracts", 250

B

B-Trees, 60
BeautifulSoup, 23
Berners-Lee, Tim, xv
BigramAssociationMeasures class, 175
BigramAssocMeasures class, 226
bigrams, 224–231

collocations, contingency tables, and scoring functions, 228–231
computing for a sentence using NLTK, 225
computing, using NLTK in the interpreter, 175
using NLTK to compute collocations, 225
binomial distribution, 231
blogs, 239
  harvesting data from by parsing feeds, 245
  summarizing Tim O'Reilly Radar blog post (example), 252
  using NLTK's tools to parse blog data, 246
branching-factor calculations for graphs of varying depths, 29
breadth-first techniques
  brief analysis of, 29
  using breadth-first search to crawl XFN links, 26
browsers
  Chrome, Graph Your Inbox Extension, 81
  support for canvas element, 301

C

Cantor, Georg, 95
canvas element, support by browsers, 301
canviz tool, 18
cardinality of sets, 95
chi-square, 231
Chrome, Graph Your Inbox Extension, 81
chunking, 244
chunks, 242
circo tool, 15
cliques, detecting and analyzing in Twitter friendship data, 110–113

We'd like to hear your suggestions for improving our indexes. Send email to *index@oreilly.com*.

exploring one connection at a time, 282–286

Graph Your Inbox Chrome Extension, 81

GraphAPI class, methods, 282

graphs
creating graph describing retweet data, 12
creating graph of nodes and edges using
NetworkX, 3
interactive 3D graph visualization, 116
visualizing similarity with, 221

Graphviz
downloading and installing, 14
online documentation, 15
showing connectedness of #JustinBieber
and #TeaParty search results,
165
Twitter search results rendered in circular
layout, 15

greedy heuristic for clustering, 177

group_level argument, db.view function, 59

GVedit, 15

H

Hadoop, 237

hashtags
counting hashtag entities in tweets, 144
frequency of, in tweets containing
#JustinBieber or #TeaParty, 153

hCalendar microformat, 20

hCard microformat, 20

help function (NLTK modules), 205

hierarchical clustering, 185

HierarchicalClustering class,
setLinkageMethod method, 187

histogram showing popularity of each friend in
Facebook network, 298

homographs, 240

hRecipe microformat, 20
parsed results for a recipe, 37
parsing data for a recipe, 36

hResume microformat, 20

hReview microformat
distribution for recipe review data, 40
parsing data for recipe review, 38
sample results for recipe reviews, 39

HTML
pages and hyperlinks (Web 1.0), 314
sample geo markup, 31
semantic markup, 22

template displaying WP-Columbus tag
cloud, 161

HTTP, 314
errors in Twitter, 88
methods, acting upon URIs, 49

httplib module, 63

hypertext, 314

I

identity consolidation, 30

IDF (inverse document frequency), 209
(see also TF-IDF)
calculation of, 211

idf function, 215

IETF OAuth 2.0 protocol, 86

IMAP (Internet Message Access Protocol), 81
connecting to, using OAuth, 232
constructing an IMAP query, 233

imaplib, 233

ImportError, 3

indexing function, JavaScript-based, 66

inference
application to machine knowledge, 317
in logic-based programming languages and
RDF, 315

influence, measuring for Twitter users, 103–108
calculating Twitterer's most popular
followers, 105
crawling friends/followers connections,
104

Infochimps, Strong Links API, 114–116

information retrieval industry, 236

information retrieval theory (see IR theory)

intelligent clustering, 183

interactive 3D graph visualization, 116

interactive 3D tag clouds for tweet entities co-
occurring with #JustinBieber and
#TeaParty, 162

interpreter, Python (IPython), 18

intersection operations, 94
overlap between entities of #TeaParty and
#JustinBieber tweets, 156

IR (information retrieval) theory, 209, 215–216
finding similar documents using cosine
similarity, 219–221
introduction to TF-IDF, 209–215

inferencing about open world with FuXi, 317
installing development tools, 1
list comprehension, 7
map/reduce functions for CouchDB, 53
support for sets, 94
tutorial overview, 3
Python SDK for the Graph API, 282

Q

quicksort algorithm, 61
quopri module, 47
quoted-printable text, decoding, 47

R

radial tree layout, LinkedIn contacts clustered by job title, 187
rate-throttling limits (LinkedIn), 193
rational numbers, 95
raw frequency, 230
RDF (Resource Description Framework), 315
    knowledge base expressed with Notation3, 318
    open-world assumptions, 316
RDF Schema, 317
RDFa, 20
    metadata, insertion into web page, 278
    sample, for Open Graph protocol, 279
re module, 11
recall, 267
recipes and reviews in microformats, 35–40
Redis, 92
    exporting data to NetworkX, 108
    randomkey function, 103
    resolving screen names from user ID values, 114
    set operations, 94
    sinterstore function, 102
reduction functions, 52
regular expressions, using to find retweets, 11
rereduce, 59, 128
REST-based interface, CouchDB, 49
RESTful APIs
    mapping to twitter module, 5
    Twitter, 84
RESTful Web services, 49
results query (FQL), 286
retweeting, 10

retweets
    counting for a Twitterer, 138
    finding tweets most often retweeted, 142
    finding using regular expressions, 11
    graph describing who retweeted whom, 12
    most frequent entities appearing in, 140
    most frequent retweeters of #JustinBieber, 155
    most frequent retweeters of #TeaParty, 154
RGraphs, visualizing Facebook network, 290–295
Rich Internet Applications (RIAs), 314
rotating tag cloud, visualizing Facebook wall data as, 309–311
RT (retweet) token, 10
rubhub, 23

S

sample error, 267
scalable clustering, 181
scalable force directed placement (SFDP), 165
scoring functions, 229
screen names, resolving from user IDs, 93, 99
search API (Twitter), 5
search engines, 236
semantic markup, 22
semantic web, 313–319
    defined, 314
    inferencing about open world with FuXi, 317
    open-world versus closed-world assumptions, 316
    social web as catalyst for, 319
semantics, defined, 313
semi-standardized relational data, 169
sentence detection, 241
    in blogs, using NLTK, 245–249
sentence tokenizer, 248
set operations
    intersection of entities in #TeaParty and #JustinBieber tweets, 156
    Redis native functions for, 94
    sample, for Twitter friends and followers, 94
set theory, invention by Georg Cantor, 95
SFDP (scalable force directed placement), Graphviz, 165
similarity metrics

About the Author

Matthew A. Russell, vice president of engineering at Digital Reasoning Systems and principal at Zaffra, is a computer scientist who is passionate about data mining, open source, and web application technologies. He's also the author of *Dojo: The Definitive Guide* (O'Reilly). Connect with him on LinkedIn or follow *@ptwobrussell* on Twitter to keep up with all of his infrequent professional updates.

Colophon

The animal on the cover of *Mining the Social Web* is a groundhog (*Marmota monax*), also known as a woodchuck (a name derived from the Algonquin name *wuchak*). Groundhogs are famously associated with the US/Canadian holiday Groundhog Day, held every February 2nd. Folklore holds that if the groundhog emerges from its burrow that day and sees its shadow, winter will continue for six more weeks. Proponents say that the rodents forecast accurately 75 to 90 percent of the time. Many cities host famous groundhog weather prognosticators, including Punxsutawney Phil (of Punxsutawney, PA and the 1993 Bill Murray film).

This legend perhaps originates from the fact that the groundhog is one of the few species that enters true hibernation during the winter. Primarily herbivorous, groundhogs will fatten up in the summer on vegetation, berries, nuts, insects, and the crops in human gardens, causing many to consider them pests. They then dig a winter burrow, and remain there from October to March (although they may emerge earlier in temperate areas, or, presumably, if they will be the center of attention on their eponymous holiday).

The groundhog is the largest member of the squirrel family, around 16–26 inches long and weighing 4–9 pounds. They are equipped with curved, thick claws ideal for digging, and two coats of fur: a dense grey undercoat and a lighter colored topcoat of longer hairs, which provides protection against the elements.

Groundhogs range throughout most of Canada and northern regions of the United States, in places where open space and woodlands meet. They are capable of climbing trees and swimming, but are usually found on the ground, not far from the burrows they dig for sleeping, rearing their young, and protection from predators. These burrows typically have two to five entrances, and up to 46 feet of tunnels.

The cover image is from Wood's *Animate Creatures*. The cover font is Adobe ITC Garamond. The text font is Linotype Birka; the heading font is Adobe Myriad Condensed; and the code font is LucasFont's TheSansMonoCondensed.

CPSIA information can be obtained at www.ICGtesting.com
Printed in the USA
BVOW061536211112

306180BV00010B/18/P